Third Edition

THE NEW
LIBRARY KEY

Margaret G. Cook

THE H. W. WILSON COMPANY
New York - 1975

Library of Congress Cataloging in Publication Data

Cook, Margaret Gerry, 1903-
   The new library key.

   Includes index.
   1. Reference books. 2. Libraries. 3. Research. I. Title.
Z711.2.C75 1975   028.7   75-11754
ISBN 0-8242-0541-3

PREFACE

TO THE THIRD EDITION

THE NEW LIBRARY KEY is addressed to college students, especially freshmen, to teachers wishing to broaden their knowledge of recent publications in their subject fields, and to individual adults who have not had previous opportunities to become acquainted with the ever-growing services of libraries. Although advanced students in some subject fields have the aid of specialized bibliographic handbooks, such as Barzun and Graff's *The Modern Researcher*, Bell's *Reference Guide to English, American, and Canadian Literature*, or Lock's *Geography: A Reference Handbook*,[1] many upperclassmen, and even students beginning graduate work, find themselves at sea in a large library, unable to isolate the materials which will be helpful in fulfilling an assignment or selecting a good thesis topic. In addition to these perennial problems, the student or faculty member who has become accustomed to finding books classified according to the Dewey Decimal System in his former school or college is very likely to discover that the Library of Congress System of classification is now the basis of book arrangement. At the request of a number of college librarians, the author has included not only an explanation of how a library catalog works, but also a brief comparison of the two classification schemes.

Beginning library school students may find the KEY helpful in defining library terminology and clarifying library practices, and the trained but inexperienced librarian will find in it an up-to-date list of useful reference tools. This edition includes the latest editions or revisions of standard works, as well as new reference books, some of major importance, published since the 1963 edition of THE NEW LIBRARY KEY.

* * *

Instruction in the use of the library has not yet had the place it deserves in the college curriculum. Many of the writer's students in library school have said, "I could have gotten so much more out of college if I had known what I know now. Why didn't they tell us these things?" Yet today's college students have more opportunity to learn how to use their libraries effectively than did those of an earlier day.

---

[1] Fuller information on these and similar works may be found by consulting the index of this manual under the author or subject area.

Modern methods of teaching, with less reliance on the specific "required readings" and more on the "list of suggested titles," with more exploration over a wide range of opinion and information and less recitation from the textbook and lecture notes, have made it virtually impossible for a student to acquire a degree without also acquiring some experience in using his college library.

In the very large college or university it is frequently impossible to give entering students any formal instruction about their library. A tour of the building, showing the location and purposes of the various departments, can do no more than suggest the extent of the library's resources and emphasize the librarian's eagerness to help. Followed up by individual guidance for the interested student, this method will produce a number of unusually well-informed people, but many will fail to avail themselves of such help. The smaller college is often able to give such instruction in a series of lessons. But experience has shown that the student attaches little importance to instruction which carries no course credit, and pays it little heed.

College librarians and professors have found at least two solutions to the problem of motivation for "library lessons." One is, obviously, the required course, carrying credit of one or two semester hours, which meets weekly for a term and which is designed both to provide for the student a survey of the library's resources in general and to give him special help in the subjects which interest him most. The librarian is probably better equipped to teach such a course than the English teacher, for the librarian is better acquainted with the tools of all trades, and can relate them to one another and to the students' needs with more ease.[2]

An alternative to such a credit-bearing course is the unit included in the composition course, where the student, assigned the task of writing a paper based on so-called research, is introduced by the librarian to the tools related to his topic and directed in his use of them by teacher and librarian working together. In the writer's experience, this procedure is effective both in introducing the student to the materials and methods of research and in demonstrating to him how helpful librarians can be. If this unit is followed up informally in other classes and at all stages of the student's career by book talks related to the courses he is taking, he leaves college with the conviction that the library habit is a good one, though he may not have learned all the refinements which could enrich it for him still further.

It is the writer's hope that this manual may prove useful to teacher and librarian in either type of group instruction, and also to the indi-

---

[2] Cf. "Teaching Students to Use the Library: Whose Responsibility?" by Virginia Clark. *College and Research Libraries*, vol. 21, pp. 369-72+. Sept. 1960.

vidual library user. Since students and readers in general will come to this guide with varying amounts of experience in the use of books and libraries, it has seemed best to include both elementary material, though it may be familiar to many readers, and also details and information which will be of service to the individual already familiar with many library resources.

Some librarians and teachers have expressed the opinion that chapters on note-taking, organizing material for a "research paper," footnotes, and bibliographic form should be at the end of a manual such as this. On the basis of her own experience as a college librarian and as a teacher of prospective librarians, the author placed them early in the book, because she believes that the motivation to learn to use a library and reference books lies in an assignment to write a paper, and such an assignment usually comes early in the average student's college career. And, as Miss Clark has pointed out,[3] the student whose professors use the library is the one who learns to use it himself, becomes curious about the books available, and wants to become familiar with them. *This* motivation may come much later than the first "research paper," usually an assignment in freshman composition. It may be limited to the student's field of major interest, in which case he may use only the chapter devoted to that field.

It is the author's belief that it is a serious mistake to require a student (except, of course, one who is going to be a librarian) to learn about books in which he has no present interest, just because they are important books. They do not seem important to him, at the beginning of his college career, and such insistence may cause him to shun the library thenceforth, to his own disadvantage.

For these reasons, the chapters in THE NEW LIBRARY KEY are so arranged that the student may learn the things he needs to know about his college library, hence about any library, in the order in which he needs to learn them. He may also learn about reference books pertaining to the broad subject areas he studies in college, in chapters devoted to those subjects.

Acknowledgments

During her years as Assistant Librarian and Head Librarian at the New Jersey State Teachers College at Montclair, the author had ample opportunity to test her theories and methods on hundreds of college students, first as individuals with research questions, later as students in the required course in composition and as seniors being introduced

---

[3] *Ibid.*

to books and teaching aids for use during their six-week experience as practice teachers. The cooperation of her colleagues in the teaching faculty, especially the heads of the subject departments, in motivating and implementing the "library lessons" through their assignments was essential to the success of the program.

After the publication of the first edition of THE NEW LIBRARY KEY, the author was invited to spend two summer sessions at the School of Education of the University of British Columbia at Vancouver, teaching school librarians, teachers, and would-be school librarians about reference books and especially about training their students to use libraries. To the members of these classes and to the Library Staff of the University Library, especially the General Reference Department, which allowed both students and lecturer extraordinary privileges, the author is indebted, both for a chance to test her methods with an adult group and for an opportunity to become familiar with a number of reference books of Canadian or British origin, which have been the basis of an interest in Canadiana, as well as dictionaries and encyclopedias in languages other than those generally found in libraries of the United States.

The collections and staff of the Enoch Pratt Free Library and the patrons of the St. Paul Street Branch have also been contributors in ways too numerous to detail. A list of sources consulted will be found at the end of this book.

MARGARET G. COOK

Baltimore, Maryland
April 1975

CONTENTS

Preface to the Third Edition   3
Abbreviations and Bibliographic Terms   8

Chapter 1   Libraries and Readers   9
Chapter 2   The College Library   22
Chapter 3   The Book   29
Chapter 4   Library Catalogs   37
Chapter 5   Library Classification Systems   55
Chapter 6   Writing a Research Paper   64
Chapter 7   The First Places to Look for Information — Encyclopedias   76
Chapter 8   The First Places to Look for Information — Dictionaries   87
Chapter 9   Periodicals, Periodical Indexes, and General Indexes   106
Chapter 10   Printed Bibliographies and Booklists   120
Chapter 11   General Reference Books   128
Chapter 12   Special Reference Books — The Arts   142
Chapter 13   Special Reference Books — Geography, Archaeology, and History   153
Chapter 14   Special Reference Books — The Social Sciences   170
Chapter 15   Special Reference Books — Literature   180
Chapter 16   Special Reference Books — The Sciences   194
Chapter 17   Special Reference Books — Mythology, Religion, and Philosophy   207
Chapter 18   Non-Book Materials   219

Appendixes   230
Appendix A.   Research Handbooks and Bibliographic Manuals   230
Appendix B.   Detailed Bibliographies — Sources of Information for Librarians, Members of the Faculty, and Graduate Students   233
Appendix C.   Books and Articles About Reference Books   241

Index   247

ABBREVIATIONS AND BIBLIOGRAPHIC TERMS

The abbreviations and terms listed below appear so frequently on catalog cards and in bibliographies and footnotes that a student needs to become familiar with them. Abbreviations used in The H. W. Wilson Company publications are explained in each issue, and dictionaries also explain their symbols; these are not included here. Words in italics are the Latin terms from which some of these abbreviations are derived.

above, p —	previously mentioned on page —	ms. (plural mss.)	manuscript
abr.	abridged; abridgment	n.d.	no date of publication (in imprint)
anon.	anonymous		
below, p —	to be mentioned later, on page —	n.p.	no place of publication (in imprint)
bibl., bibliog.	bibliography	n.pub.	no publisher named (in imprint)
bul., bull.	bulletin		
c. 1920	copyright 1920 (on a catalog card, in the imprint)	n.s.	new series
		o.p.	out of print
c. 1920	*(circa)* about 1920 (on the author line of a catalog card or bibliographic entry)	op. cit.	*(opere citato)* in the work cited
		p.	page or pages
ca.	*(circa)* about	pam.	pamphlet
cf.	*(confer)* compare	*passim*	throughout; here and there (of terms, concepts, or the like that occur repeatedly throughout the work, chapter, or article cited)
cm.	centimeter		
comp.	compiled; compiler		
cop.	copy; copyright		
ed.	edition; edited; editor		
e.g.	*(exempli gratia)* for example	pl.	plate; plates
enl.	enlarged	pp.	pages
et seq., et sq.	*(et sequens)* and the following	pseud.	pseudonym (assumed name)
ff.	following	q.v.	*(quod vide)* which see
fl., flor.	*(floruit)* flourished		
front.	frontispiece (the illustration facing the title page)	rev.	revised; review
		seq.; sq.	*(sequens)* the following (page)
ibid.	*(ibidem)* in the same place	seqq.; sqq.	the following (pages)
		sup., supp., suppl.	supplement
id., idem	*(idem)* the same		
i.e.	*(id est)* that is	supra	*(supra)* above (previously mentioned)
illus.	illustrations; illustrated; illustrator		
imprint	on a catalog card or bibliographic entry, the place and date of publication and the publisher	t.p.	title page
		tr., trans.	translated; translator; transactions
		v.	*(vide)* see; also volume
infra	*(infra)* below (to be mentioned later)	viz.	*(videlicet)* to wit; namely; that is to say
loc. cit.	*(loco citato)* in the place cited	vol., v.	volume; volumes

Chapter 1

LIBRARIES AND READERS

IT IS POSSIBLE that there are many literate adults in the English-speaking world who have never entered a library of their own volition (not counting schoolchildren taken by teachers, or individual children sent either on an errand or as a form of discipline); there are many such adults even in cities which boast world-renowned public libraries. But almost everyone has seen and bought paperbacks at newsstands, supermarkets, and chain stores (including the international Woolworth's).

According to studies made in the 1960s, more than half the United States population over twenty-five years of age is "functionally illiterate." This is not, of course, true in most of the other "developed" nations, whose inhabitants read, and buy, more books than most Americans. Nevertheless, in 1970 UNESCO reported that a high proportion of the schoolchildren of the world are "victims of educational wastage." Three states in the United States have no state laws for compulsory school attendance, having repealed them in the mid 1950s.

The readers of this guide to library use are most certainly not only literate, but well acquainted with libraries, school or public, large or small. The city dweller, especially, becomes aware of libraries very early in life — during preschool story hours and classroom visits by children's librarians. Going to the school library (often nowadays called a "learning resource center") and to central or branch libraries for school assignments and fun reading, the city child may encounter more story hours, movies, puppet shows — whatever programs librarians can think of to encourage subsequent visits.

It is also true that there still are schools in the United States which have neither librarians nor libraries, and many communities where there is little or no library service of easy access, either because of location or because of limited hours of service. (As I write this, libraries throughout the United States are laying off staff, opening later, and closing earlier because of lack of funds.) But there are also people who make little use of the facilities which do exist, because they are unaware of the scope of service which they can call upon. Even college students, whose library is centrally located, with the collections and services planned especially to meet their needs, are often blind to their good fortune and thus fail to profit by it.

9

Large libraries are a little frightening to those not familiar with them. The entrance is broad and inviting but may lead to an imposing open area where the first things to meet the visitor's eye are ranges of cases containing the card catalog. (A few libraries have catalogs in book form.) The larger the library, the more complex the catalog. Fortunately, there is nearby a desk marked "Information," staffed by one or more librarians who are there expressly to direct the visitor, explain the library's arrangement, and answer questions.

Only small libraries are easy to browse in. Large ones are divided into sections or departments according to subject matter, hence the frequent use of display racks for new books or for books dealing with matters of current concern or of local interest. But beyond these displays are the various departments, one of the most important being the General Reference Department, where dictionaries in many languages, encyclopedias, and other multi-volume and multi-purpose works are kept, most of them restricted to use in the library.

The General Reference Department is not only a collection of reference books, but a collection, if you will, of reference librarians — people with knowledge of many subject fields and skills in using the books not only in their department but in the library as a whole. In fact, in a large library, they have access to information available almost anywhere in the world.

But there is much more in a library than the Reference Department, as anyone used to libraries knows. Therefore we shall consider first the kinds of books and other materials to be found in a library, then their arrangement and how to find them.

WHAT IS A LIBRARY?

Besides books (which gave libraries their name), there are in the collection many printed items which are not books and some things which are not printed at all. There are also many library materials which utterly defy attempts to classify them by subject. The following outline shows the main groups into which library materials fall.

1. The general collection of books which may be borrowed
    A. Fiction
    B. Nonfiction
2. Periodicals and newspapers
    A. Current issues
    B. Past issues in bound volumes or on microfilm reels, cassettes, microcards, or microfiches
3. Reference books
    A. Dictionaries and encyclopedias, general or by subject
    B. Bibliographies

      C. Periodical and other indexes

      D. Annuals and handbooks

      E. Biographical and historical dictionaries

      F. Atlases and gazetteers

4. Pamphlets and clippings

      A. Classified pamphlets (treated as books)

      B. Government publications (some of which may be treated as books, either Reference or Circulating)

      C. Vertical file material

          (1) Clippings from newspapers, etc.

          (2) Small pamphlets and government publications

5. Audio-visual materials

      A. Pictures and maps

      B. Slides, filmslides, and filmstrips

      C. Motion picture films

      D. Microcards, microfilms, and microfiches (outside of the periodical collection)

      E. Recordings: disc, tape, or cassette

      F. Globes, models, specimens

FICTION AND NONFICTION

For some reason it has become customary to divide books arbitrarily into fiction and nonfiction, fiction being defined loosely as narrative works of the imagination, written in prose. My dictionary excludes poetry and the drama from its definition of nonfiction, but for library classification experts, poetry and drama too fall into the general class of nonfiction, along with history, biography, scientific works, etc.

There are many works which seem to fall between the two categories — for example, works of humor and satire. Where do we place James Thurber, Leo Rosten, or Goodman Ace? In fiction we find novels so full of historical fact that they have footnotes and bibliographies; in nonfiction we find many so-called biographies so full of fancy that long conversations have been put into the mouths of historical personages who were unobserved and who kept no diaries. Among novels are psychological case studies penetrating enough to be assigned as required reading in courses in psychology. The writer of science fiction, often himself a scientist of note (for example, Isaac Asimov) may by extrapolation forecast discoveries which are yet to be made. On the other side, some recent nonfiction has presented highly controversial theories of economics or of scientific phenomena — especially the para-medical or pseudo-medical books currently popular which may lead the gullible reader to dangerous experiments.

In spite of all this, we continue to use the arbitrary division into fiction and nonfiction because it is convenient; it keeps together on the shelves of a library the works of the more prolific authors and spares us the necessity of reading every trivial love story to see if it has any subject value. Everyone understands that fiction is a story, no matter how much it may tell us about the ancient Greeks, as in the works of Mary Renault, or the early Britons, as in the novels of Bryher.

It is therefore agreed that the remainder of the circulating collection of the average library, usually the major part of the library's holdings, consists of nonfiction volumes, most of them about a single subject, broad or specific, a phase of a subject, or a group of related subjects.

NEWSPAPERS

Newspapers may be dealt with briefly, not because they are unimportant but because everyone knows what they are. They are usually daily publications, some morning, some evening, some (but not many) both. Many have large Sunday editions, with such supplements as a book review section, sections on the theater and other arts, innumerable advertisements (whose subsidies probably are the chief source of funds), and an editorial section which may attempt to give space to opposing opinions on important subjects. Newspapers acquire their information from at least two sources — Associated Press (AP) and United Press International (UPI) — plus their own correspondents on the local beat, in state capitals, in Washington, and wherever news is likely to "break." Aside from the New York *Times* and the *Wall Street Journal*, one of the most influential and reliable is *The Christian Science Monitor*, a frequently used reference tool and a source of some of the most valuable in-depth reporting on matters of international importance.

Many small towns have weekly or semiweekly papers, devoted almost entirely to local events, and large cities have weeklies published in self-contained areas of the city, perhaps in a language other than English, or for a clientele other than WASP. The most famous of these weeklies is *The Village Voice* (Greenwich Village, New York).

Some newspapers have been fully indexed and are available on microfilm for reference use. The indexes to the New York *Times* are universally valuable sources of information. They will be more fully discussed later.

PERIODICALS

The term *periodicals* is used in libraries, instead of *magazines*, because it tells more accurately what kind of publication is being described. The word *magazine* means a storehouse, or collection, often of munitions or military supplies, and hence by implication a group of more or less unrelated items. Such publications as the popular women's magazines, one of the supplements of our Sunday newspaper, and the digests are obviously correctly called magazines. The more general word *periodical* applies both to these and to other types of publications. A periodical is something which is published periodically, usually at stated intervals. These intervals may range from daily to annually, though the term is seldom applied to anything less frequent than semi-annually, nor more frequent than weekly.

Issues of a periodical may consist of groups of articles, stories, poems, or pictures brought together to attract a large number of readers with varied interests, or they may concern themselves with different aspects of a single subject. The special-interest periodicals include trade journals for the barber and the undertaker; professional journals for the physician, the teacher, the librarian, or the lawyer; "slicks" (lavishly illustrated magazines, printed on shiny paper) for the luxury trade, with landscaping, fashions, and house plans on a grand scale; and journals for hobbyists, either as a class or as specialists (in stamps, pets, antiques, etc.). The fifteenth (1973) edition of *Ulrich's International Periodicals Directory* lists more than 55,000 important periodicals in existence at the time it was compiled, and a new section is expected in 1975, with, as usual, a supplementary volume issued the following year. In a separate section, *Ulrich's* lists new periodicals (about 4,000) and those that have ceased publication during the preceding interval (about 1,700). (These events are commonly referred to as "births" and "deaths"; when periodicals combine, it is a "marriage.") To the average American, accustomed to seeing not more than fifty magazines displayed at a newsstand, these numbers may seem unbelievable; but most periodicals are distributed only by subscription, and hence are visible to the public only in libraries, while many seen on the newsstands would never be granted a place either in libraries or in the two lists mentioned above.

What is the reason for such multitudes of periodicals? What is their value? Many, of course, are worthless or even harmful. Campaigns against pornography, sensationalism, and the "comics" are going on all the time. But the great bulk of periodical material is indispensable to the student and the research worker. The periodical, especially the scholarly journal, is the medium in which scientific studies are reported and assessed, claims upheld and refuted. "Searching the literature" is the first step taken by any chemist, biologist, or social scientist before he embarks upon a research project, lest he undertake a problem already solved, or engage in fruitless experimentation already reported and described.

The periodicals in a library are therefore of inestimable value. Frequently their use is restricted in order to preserve them, since lost or damaged issues are sometimes impossible to replace. Few libraries allow bound volumes of periodicals to be taken from the building, and many keep microfilm copies which can be read only in reading machines. Sometimes duplicate issues of the popular magazines are provided for circulation so that one copy may be preserved in good condition for binding, but with the more costly journals such duplication is out of the question. The knowledge that students will be using these volumes for years may make all these restrictions easier to bear, annoying as they may seem at the moment of urgent need.

The great body of source material represented by the periodical files of a library would be very difficult to use if one had to leaf through volume after volume to find the desired information. The periodical indexes which make the process of searching quick and easy are discussed in Chapter 9. The most familiar of these is the *Readers' Guide to Periodical Literature*, usually referred to as the *Readers' Guide*.

The periodicals listed in *Ulrich's* total slightly less than a third of the serials included in the latest edition of the *Union List of Serials in Libraries of the United States and Canada* (New York, Wilson, 1965, 5 vols.) which lists 156,499 titles held by 956 libraries in North America.[1] The term *serials* takes in not only such items as are described above as *periodicals*, but any publications which have been issued at regular intervals and are usually numbered consecutively: publications of governments and international organizations (such as UNICEF) as well as of private societies, if they have information which appears to be of importance to scholars. Obviously, many serials are short-lived; their back issues may attain the status of rarities.

REFERENCE BOOKS

A reference book is simply a book to refer to, not one to be read all the way through. Because they contain many items of information, likely to be wanted by many different people, books in the Reference Room seldom circulate, that is, leave the library for home use, though libraries differ in their application of this principle. The outline on pages 10-11 lists the kinds of reference books most frequently found in libraries. These are discussed in later chapters, as are pamphlets and non-book materials.

---

[1] See Chapter 9 for full description.

ARRANGEMENT OF BOOKS

Earlier in this introductory chapter differentiation was made among the kinds of materials in a library, and the fact was noted that fiction is usually set aside and arranged according to author, taking for granted that this author arrangement is alphabetical. It was assumed that non-fiction would be arranged by some logical scheme that would make it easy for the borrower or searcher for information to find the books desired.

One can imagine many ways of arranging (or classifying) the books in a library. In our own personal collections we probably make use of several methods. For purposes of decoration we may choose a group for a certain shelf because the colors of the bindings accent the color scheme of the room. The row of cookbooks in the kitchen and the pile of *Popular Mechanics* in the basement workshop show our use of the subject classification method. The living room is apt to boast a table with the newest purchases; the attic shelters a heap of worn-out fairy tales and nursery rhymes. And those large flat volumes shoved under the desk are the atlas and the art album which are too big to stand on a shelf.

All of these classification schemes are useful in their own ways, and most of them have been used in libraries, but it is easy to see the disadvantages which some of them would possess. We may eliminate at once arrangement wholly by size or color, classifications indispensable in a shoe store or a button department, but largely irrelevant in a library. (Of course the library may provide special cabinets for oversize books which do not fit standard shelving.) And though libraries, too, relegate to storage many of their older books and display their newest ones in prominent places, arrangement of the whole collection in the order of purchase would be absurd.

Incongruous as it may seem, however, the seven hundred and forty books which formed the nucleus of the Library of Congress in 1801 were arranged according to these two systems: first by size (folios, quartos, octavos, and duodecimos), and secondly by accession numbers (that is, in the order in which they were received) — but remember that there were only seven hundred and forty books! By 1812 a subject arrangement of eighteen classes was adopted, which followed that used by Benjamin Franklin in his Library Company of Philadelphia in 1789. Franklin's scheme derived from that devised by Sir Francis Bacon (fl. 1600) and modified by d'Alembert (ca. 1716-1773), one of the French Encyclopedists.[2] There is still much similarity among these and sub-

---

[2] Cf. J. P. Immroth, *A Guide to Library of Congress Classification*, 2d ed. (Littleton, Colo., Libraries Unlimited, Inc., 1971), p. 11.

sequent rearrangements of the original Library of Congress and the present classification scheme of the Library of Congress (LC) and the system of Melvil Dewey (DC).

The reason for this historical digression is that most schools in the United States and Canada have used Dewey's classification system, as have most public and small college libraries. But large universities and colleges (especially those fairly recently established) and many large public libraries use the LC classification. Newly established smaller colleges are also using LC and their students are finding it difficult to make the transition. At the request of librarians who have used earlier editions of THE NEW LIBRARY KEY, Chapter 5 of this edition will attempt to clarify the differences and similarities of the two schemes.

LIBRARY RULES

A library, be it for school, college, insurance company, army camp, or general public, must have its sets of rules and regulations to govern its use. The more books it contains, and the more people it serves, the more rigid must its regulations be. Mention has already been made of the fact that reference books are almost never available for loan, because they cover so many subjects and are therefore apt to be needed by many people. It has also been pointed out that similar restrictions are often made on unbound periodicals. When they have been bound into annual or semiannual volumes still more restrictions are necessary, for three reasons: (1) since the cost of binding magazines is high — sometimes more than the subscription price — a bound volume costs more to replace; (2) the number of copies printed is limited by the number of subscribers; hence back issues are often difficult to secure and also cost more than they did originally; (3) the fact that a bound volume contains issues of several months or a full year makes it potentially useful to more people; it therefore takes on the character of a reference book. Nevertheless, some college libraries will lend bound periodicals and reference books for overnight use.

A second reason for rules is to assure equitable service to all the library's readers. This, it must be admitted, though desirable, is impossible. The people who habitually keep books until they are overdue, or "forget" to have them charged, are regular clients of every library. If any of the readers of this manual have been "overdue prone," it is to be hoped that they will reform at once.

Admission to the Stacks

Though restrictions on borrowing books have been discussed as examples of library rules, they are by no means the only restrictions encountered by library users. One of the great debates in professional library literature has been on closed versus open stacks. Some libraries allow the public to roam at will throughout the collection. Others have a selection of books in every subject field on open shelves in public departments, but keep the greater part of the collection in the stacks, which may occupy a central tower, or basement and sub-basement areas. This variation is usually caused by size of collection; a library of several hundred thousand volumes usually must keep the older and less used books in more compact storage. In college libraries with closed stacks, it is customary to give *stack permits* to members of the faculty, graduate students, and frequently to upperclassmen. The privilege of browsing in the stacks is sometimes more overwhelming than helpful, as the freshman looking for a life of Abraham Lincoln will discover when he finds more than a hundred of them.

Fines and Rental Charges

Most libraries have a system of fines for overdue books. The fines for adults are generally five cents a day; for children, one or two cents. In some large cities, libraries encourage very young children to acquire the habit of reading by issuing borrower's cards to them as soon as they are able to write (or print) their names. Occasionally the children fail to understand that they are expected to bring the books back, and, especially in underprivileged neighborhoods, an accumulated fine may well be beyond their ability to pay. Thus, in some library systems, no fines are charged on children's books, but the child is allowed only one book at a time. The theory behind this is that developing the habit of reading is more important to society than the cost of the books lost.

Some public and college libraries may have rental collections, either for best sellers at a small daily rate, or for costly textbooks at a nominal rate for a term or semester. However, so many textbooks are now available in paperback that students are apt to buy them at the college bookstore, or at a student-run exchange.

Circulation Procedures

The actual methods used at library circulation desks to record who has what and for how long vary widely. In the small school each child writes his name and homeroom number on the book card. In the very large library the borrower's card may be photographed or passed through a punch-card machine. A library user soon finds out how his library records its loans.

LIBRARY SERVICE TO ALL

Tax-supported public libraries are obligated to give free service to all residents of the taxing unit which supports them. With the system of revenue sharing now enjoyed, the geographical limits of a library's clientele may be statewide, especially when one library has been designated as the center from which books and other materials are distributed by truck or mail to other libraries in the state, or region, and they in turn circulate the items requested by their own borrowers.

For many years there has also been a service known as *inter-library loan* by which a borrower may secure books or microfilm copies from public, state or college libraries anywhere, for which he pays the expenses incurred; and "anywhere" may include, for example, the Library of the British Museum.

SUMMARY AND SUGGESTIONS

This first chapter has touched upon many aspects of libraries. The average library patron is often unaware of many facets of service which have been briefly mentioned here. More detail on a number of them is given in the chapters which follow. Meanwhile the suggestions noted below will give the library user a good introduction to any library:

Whether or not you have been a regular user of the library, explore a little. Look around. Discover the general plan of arrangement. If the library building is large, look for a diagram showing the location of the various departments. If none is posted, find an information desk, and ask for one. Figure 1 is a sample of the kind of information sheet which libraries often provide for their patrons.

Find the card catalog, the Reference Department, the encyclopedias, atlases, dictionaries. Go to the Registration Desk and get a borrower's card. If the assistant doesn't tell you about borrowing regulations, ask for them. Figure 2 shows some typical library regulations.

Find out about open or closed stacks, and the classification scheme. Take a little time to wander about, just looking. This may seem a waste of time, but it will save both time and effort later, when you want information in a hurry.

READY TO DO RESEARCH!

HERE IS A QUICK GUIDE

WHERE TO FIND IT

THE CARD CATALOG - Main floor. The catalog is divided into two sections:
      1. AUTHOR - TITLE catalog
      2. SUBJECT catalog
Call number of material is on upper left-hand corner of card

ARRANGEMENT OF BOOKS

BOOKS classified by Dewey Decimal System   (001-999) on 2nd floor
BOOKS classified by Library of Congress System (A - P Main floor
    (letter designations A-Z)   (Q - Z Second floor

Locations will vary as our building program progresses.

REFERENCE BOOKS - First four rows of stacks on the Main floor.
    Reference books have R or Ref. above the call number in the upper
left-hand corner of catalog cards, e.g.

       R   Ref.
      423 (Dewey)   PE   (Library of Congress)
                    1628

    ALL REFERENCE BOOKS are shelved on the Main floor.

ABSTRACTS - near center of Main floor.

U. S. GOVERNMENT DEPOSITORY COLLECTION and N.J. GOVERNMENT DEPOSITORY
COLLECTION Turn right just beyond entrance after passing through turnstiles.

RESERVE BOOKS - Lower floor - Reserve Rm. books are designated by a
    plastic cover on Author card in the catalog.

CURRICULUM MATERIALS - Curriculum Lab. - Second floor, front corner room.

PAMPHLET FILES - Second floor.

FICTION and BIOGRAPHY - Always consult the catalog for fiction and
    biography. Novels designated in the catalog by F or Fic are shelved
    on the Second floor after the 969's. Biographies designated B are
    shelved after the fiction. Other biographies are classified in
    their subject-related areas. Other fiction is classified as
    literature.

PERIODICALS

ALL PERIODICALS AND NEWSPAPERS are located on the Lower floor, west.
Periodical and newspaper indexes are on the Index Tables on the
Main floor. Consult these indexes for references to articles on specific
subjects and check the periodical holdings files on the index tables
or Reference desks or Periodical room. The files will indicate the
extent of our holdings in hard cover and on microfilm. Then proceed
to the Lower floor.

REMEMBER! FOR HELP, GUIDANCE, INFORMATION ASK A REFERENCE LIBRARIAN!

Figure 1: Sample Library Information Sheet

MONTCLAIR STATE COLLEGE LIBRARY

C I R C U L A T I O N   R E G U L A T I O N S

W E L C O M E TO YOUR LIBRARY.

HAVE YOU RECEIVED YOUR CARD? If not, inquire at the circulation desk.
READY TO BORROW LIBRARY MATERIALS? How? When? For how long?
****

CIRCULATING MATERIALS:

Circulating materials are presently located on the main and second
floors and usually have a card and pocket in the back of the book.

Loan period - Usually three weeks ---- but shorter at end of semester.
Wednesday is the due day each week (the exact date will be tagged on
the books or other materials you borrow.)
Renewals - One time only for members of our campus community. Please
bring material to Circulation Desk in person on or before the date due.
Please, no telephone renewals!
Library Card - Hold on to it! Present it when borrowing material.
Don't lend it to others. Remember you are responsible for all use
made of your card.
Fines - A nuisance to both of us, but necessary to keep books and
pamphlets available. Just return borrowed material in time and
avoid the 5¢ fine per day (no weekend fines, holidays are free too).
If you've really overdone it, and a bill is sent, a 25¢ service charge
is added to your borrower's account. The entire procedure can
easily be avoided!
****

LIMITED CIRCULATING MATERIALS.

The Reserve Room is located on the lower level, front. Books and
other material are placed on Reserve by your Professors as required
reading. Your Professor suggests a loan period which seems
equitable: Period loan (2 hours--read in library only); Overnight
loan; 3-day loan; and, one week loan.

ALL RESERVE Books must be BORROWED from the Reserve Room, and
RETURNED THERE. Additional information is available from the
RESERVE ROOM assistant in attendance. Please note the special
Fine schedule for Reserve overdue materials.
****

NON-CIRCULATING MATERIALS.

REFERENCE BOOKS, MICROFORMS (microfilm, microfiche), and
PERIODICALS do NOT Circulate.

CURRICULUM LABORATORY (2nd floor) materials do not circulate, unless
the librarian in charge of that collection gives permission.
****

LIBRARY HOURS (unless otherwise posted)

Monday - Friday	7:30 a.m. - 10:00 p.m.
Saturday	8:30 a.m. - 4:30 p.m.
Sunday	2:00 p.m. - 10:00 p.m.

DO YOU KNOW . . .

PHOTOCOPIERS ARE LOCATED ON ALL FLOORS. -------- 5¢ a copy
COIN AND BILL CHANGER IS ON MAIN FLOOR.
COIN OPERATED TYPEWRITERS, AND TYPING ROOM FOR PERSONAL TYPEWRITERS
   ARE ON LOWER LEVEL
PUBLIC TELEPHONES ARE AT NORTH END OF LOBBY

Figure 2A: Sample Library Regulations—Circulation

Circulation Desk

SPRAGUE LIBRARY FINE SCHEDULES for 1972-73:

Circulating books should be returned on or before the due date so
they can be reshelved and available to the many other borrowers on
the College campus. In addition, when books are returned ON TIME,
NO FINES are due.

FINES on OVERDUE BOOKS are 5 cents a day per book (not including
Saturdays, Sundays, and Holidays). This amounts to 25 cents a week,
a sum which mounts quickly when you have a large number of books
overdue. Fines are collected at the Circulation Desk when they have
mounted to the first 25 cents or more.

There's no charge for mailing an overdue notice (but by the time it is
mailed you will already owe a fine so it is far better not to wait for a
notice before returning books). However, if we ALSO send you a Fine
notice in the mail, there's an additional 25-cent service charge. Hence,
normally, we will simply add the fine to your account.

Be sure to clear your account with us before the end of the semester.
At that time outstanding obligation lists are compiled and grades or
transcripts are withheld based on these listings.
OVERDUE BOOKS:
     We assess a borrower the original Cost of a book plus a $2.00
processing fee for a lost book or any books never returned to the library.

RESERVE ROOM FINE SCHEDULE

Period and/or overnight loans   25 cents fine for the first overdue
                                       hour, plus 10 cents each additional
                                       hour up to 75 cents per day.

Three-day and/or One-week loans   25 cent fine per day for overdue book.

Harry A. Sprague Library
Montclair State College
1 9 7 2 - 7 3

Circulating Book Fines - - 5 cents per day per book (excluding Saturdays,
                              Sundays and Holidays.)

Note: Faculty book loans are to the end of a Current Semester.
       Renewals are requested.

Figure 2B: Sample Library Regulations—Fines and Rental Charges

Chapter 2

THE COLLEGE LIBRARY

THE FOLLOWING DESCRIPTION of a librarian's approach to a newcomer in a library may appear Utopian to people who have suffered from a sense of being invisible when they have entered a strange library and stood hesitantly, or roamed aimlessly, wondering how to find "something to read" or a specific piece of information. Newcomers in a library deserve considerate attention from the library staff members — the kind of interested and friendly attention which will make them feel at home, free to ask questions and to receive assistance and advice; the kind of attention which will make them "Friends of the Library" as voters, taxpayers, or alumni.

When a student enters college as a freshman, it is quite likely that one of the activities of Freshman Week will be a guided tour of the college library. This includes the introduction of those members of the library staff who are available to help him[1] to find his way around. The graduate student or new faculty member may lack this organized introduction or may be given a special tour of his own, but he already has the advantage of knowing, more definitely than the freshman, what he wants, and, to some extent, what he may expect to get from the library.

Anyone entering our Utopian library for the first time and looking about uncertainly for a place to begin will be approached by a librarian with an offer to help. This librarian may be a Reference Librarian, a Readers' Assistant or Readers' Adviser, or, in a small library, "just" the Librarian. The title makes no difference. This is a person who can help the reader, not only by explaining the classification scheme or the catalog, but by leading him to whatever resources the library can muster for his needs.

---

[1] This chapter, and others to follow, will be discussing problems of individual students. In recent years there has been considerable emphasis upon equality of the sexes, and much awkward phraseology, such as "chairperson" (instead of "Madam Chairman," a phrase which is itself as sexually equipoised as one could hope for). If one were writing for a British readership, one might use the pronoun "one" when referring to the individual student of either sex, but one would find such a proliferation of "one"s rather ludicrous. Therefore readers will find in these pages, as in previous editions of this book, the use of "he" and "him" according to longstanding American usage.

THE DEPARTMENTS OF A COLLEGE LIBRARY
Reader Service Departments

The small library in a very small college may be confined to a few large rooms which provide all the library service available, combining the functions of reference department, study area, and general reading room. Larger colleges and universities, like large public libraries, find it necessary to divide their collections and separate their services. The first public divisions to be set apart in a college library are likely to be the Reserve Book Room and the Reference Department.

The Reserve Book Room provides shelf space for multiple copies of books set aside at the request of faculty members as required or recommended reading. This is usually a large room, with plenty of tables and chairs, and is a convenient place to study. A rule of comparative silence should obtain. The student who prefers to study elsewhere may discover that there are provisions for taking out these books for one or two hours, or overnight, although some libraries make it a policy to keep all reserve books within the Reserve Book Room.

The Reference Department, which may have begun operations at one end of the general reading room, is the next to be set apart. Here the student will find all the reference books discussed in later chapters: encyclopedias, dictionaries, atlases, indexes, bibliographies, yearbooks — and one or more professional librarians to direct him in their use and help him become familiar enough with them to rely on himself. This self-reliance should be developed early in a student's college life. When he first enters a library he naturally must be shown where things are, and when he first encounters a new type of reference book it is only reasonable that he should expect to be shown how to use it, but one of the functions of education is to learn how to find out things for oneself, and in fact to learn to prefer to do so. Later chapters explain in some detail the use of dictionaries and encyclopedias, indexes, and catalogs. With these as examples, the student can quickly explore an unfamiliar volume and discover how to make it work.

Another department which the college library frequently establishes is the Periodicals Department. Here are found both current issues and bound volumes of the journals subscribed to, plus the various indexes which make them readily useful. This department may also house microfilm or microcard copies of bulky sets, or long runs of newspapers such as the New York *Times*, together with reading machines which enlarge the microcopies to readable size.

In Chapter 1 mention was made of special displays of new books, and of a department frequently designated as the Popular Library, containing fiction and a selection of readable, and perhaps new, books chosen from many subject areas.

Similarly, the college library is apt to have a Browsing Room, intended for leisure reading and furnished with rugs, some comfortable chairs, and reading lamps. The books may be attractive editions of the classics, the thousand or so "best books," and a selection of modern titles which a well-rounded education should include. Pens and notebooks are usually taboo here; it is a quiet retreat, not a study hall. The Browsing Room may also be used on occasion for poetry readings, talks by visiting authors, and radio or chamber music concerts.

Other rooms may be set aside in the large college library for special subject collections. These may be large reading rooms similar to the Reserve Book Room, or seminar rooms for the use of faculty and advanced students exclusively. A university with many schools will have departmental libraries scattered over the campus, all under the jurisdiction of the university librarian, but providing special collections for their own students. The same sort of subdivision is found in the public libraries of large cities, where the materials for study and research are divided into subject departments. In public libraries the first subject departments to be separated from the general collections are likely to be Art, Music, Technology, and Business. A number of libraries have established Business branches in locations convenient for businessmen (the Business Library of Newark, New Jersey, will soon celebrate its seventieth anniversary).

For the advanced student these special departmental libraries in separate schools are a convenience, but for the new student, with a general curriculum to follow during his first year or two they pose problems. Hence the larger universities set up general libraries for undergraduates, duplicating in part the more or less elementary material required in curricula for the first two years of college, together with duplicates of the major reference sets: dictionaries, encyclopedias, atlases, and so forth, and the periodical indexes and other types of indexes and bibliographies, which will be discussed at length in the later chapters of this book. Harvard was one of the first universities to provide a library for undergraduates; it occupies a huge building on several levels and has spacious rooms for students to work in quiet, well-lighted surroundings.

Administrative and Processing Departments

All the divisions heretofore mentioned are concerned with direct service to the reader to provide him with books and other reading matter. There are several other phases of library administration essential to this relationship between books and readers, but less direct and more concerned with making and keeping records.

One of the newcomer's first activities in a library is registering for a library card. Perhaps that Freshman Week visit to the college library ended with standing in line to pick up a card already prepared from lists furnished by the Registrar's office. There is something very encouraging to the new student about having a library card all ready for him; as little children say when they have learned to print their names, they have "joined" the library. In a college where this practice is routine, the percentage of students who use the library and the number of books circulated per student far exceed the norm.

In colleges where this is not the practice, the student should find out how to become a cardholder. Usually a matriculation card will suffice, and it may entitle the student to a card at the local public library also. As for the circulation procedures, the student may: write his number on a book card, have his card photographed with the book card and a dated "date due" card, sign his name — any of these or possibly other methods may be in use.

The Circulation Desk, where books are charged out and received, and the Registration Desk are frequently manned by clerical assistants. In public libraries these are usually full-time employees; in college and university libraries they are usually students who work on a part-time basis, perhaps for the prevailing minimum wage, perhaps for a scholarship. Because these clerical assistants are not professional librarians, the questions they can answer, other than those having to do with their duties, are largely directional: Where is a certain department? Can someone explain what this means? If there is a librarian near, the inquirer will be referred to him. And if the library is a small one in which registration, circulation, reserve book information, and reference service are all handled from one desk, there is sure to be a professional librarian within reach. But it is generally wiser to assume that in most libraries the person who receives returned books is not the one who can produce a diagram of a frog's nervous system, or can disentangle a request for a long poem by some one named Ford and locate a play by Tennessee Williams.

One of the more tedious tasks of the Circulation Department staff is sending overdue notices. It is particularly important in a college library that books be returned as soon as possible, for although demand based on class assignments is temporary, it is heavy while it lasts. The person receiving an overdue notice may not consider it a "service," but as a potential user of some other book that is overdue he will realize that it is an essential one.

Two of the most important divisions of a library are those concerned with getting books and making them ready for use. The functions of the Acquisition or Order Department, especially for a college or university library, require very special knowledge and abilities plus the cooperation of members of the faculty and the subject specialists on the library staff. The latter will include among their duties checking certain periodicals whose contents include notices of forthcoming books, reprints, and new editions, and reviews of new titles and revised editions. This information will be checked against the library's holdings and the record of books already ordered. Frequently important titles or new editions will be ordered without consultation with members of the faculty.

Meanwhile, there are always some professors who find books reviewed in journals which apply to their individual interests and the courses which they teach, or are planning. These reviews may not have come to the notice of the librarian specialist. There is a special rapport between the departmental librarian and the teachers in that department, however, and Professor A's dearest wish is often anticipated by Librarian B.

If a university library is trying to fill out a collection of old or rare books which are considered essential to postgraduate or faculty research, regular examination of the catalogs of secondhand and remainder dealers is part of the Order Librarian's routine. Purchases may be made from British and European bookstores, and some university librarians make periodic trips abroad to get the best editions or copies available.

The Cataloging and Preparation Department, where new books are classified and then prepared for use, is also of major importance and frequently employs more people than any other. Here we find other specialists on the staff: people who read several languages and/or are especially well informed in such areas as art, music, the branches of science, and technologies. These specialists must assign to each book its place in the scheme of classification, verify the author's name, and specify which, or how many, subject entries, as well as such "added entries" as joint authors (two or more people who share the responsibility for a book's contents), editors, and translators. (See Chapter 4 for explanation and expansion of this theme.) Even histories, biographies, and books on psychology and other social sciences need to be handled by a cataloger who knows a good deal about their subject matter if they are to be properly treated.

After a book has been classified and cataloged, it goes through the hands of typists who provide it with pocket and book card. It then goes on to a series of people who paste in pockets, mark or label the spine of the book with the "call number," and send it by stack assistant or page to the proper department. There it will be examined by the members of the departmental staff who may or may not have had a hand in its acquisition and shelved in open shelves or stacks, ready for use. As in the circulation department, much of this routine "manual labor" is performed by full- or part-time nonprofessional staff; college libraries employ many students for these ancillary jobs.

THE LIBRARY'S PLACE IN THE COLLEGE

Throughout this manual it can be seen that what is true of books and other library materials in a college library is just as true in other types of libraries. But the college library bears a special responsibility to its college, its faculty, and its students. It is planned for their use, and its activities are geared to the exigencies of the academic year and the academic day.

Whereas public libraries may be open from nine to nine, and closed on Sunday, the college library may be open from seven in the morning to ten at night, and provide somewhat curtailed service even on Sundays and holidays. When a book is in great demand, the public library will buy a few extra copies which will be rented for a nominal fee per day, but the college library will buy ten to twenty more copies, put them "on reserve," and lend them for periods of one or two hours, or overnight.[2] At the other extreme, it may waive the two- or four-week rule and lend a book for a whole semester. (This last is less likely to occur if the book may be purchased in a paperback.) Rush orders will be sent for more copies of a book when a class is unexpectedly large, or, as was mentioned above, great pains will be taken to find either for purchase or through interlibrary loan, a rare volume for a professor who needs it.

In the college library, single issues of periodicals will be kept for use throughout the college year, even though one or two volumes may have been completed, and not sent to be bound until slack time (in August, for example, if the summer session is ended, rather than in December or January when the volume may be complete but the demand is still great). Many libraries have only the most important titles bound and subscribe to microform editions for reference use and reduction of storage space requirements.

In other words, the library is not just a department of a college; it is a part of every department. It is no exaggeration to say that the student who fails to use the library's resources in any subject is not getting his money's worth out of that subject.

SUMMARY

The long hours when the college library is open and the provision of many copies of books in demand are the most obvious ways in which the college library helps the student. But the books and services pro-

_____
[2] Probably the most extreme restriction was observed in a college library where books on reserve were available for only fifteen minutes at a time.

vided to the teaching staff are indirectly services to the students as well. Professors and instructors are urged, exhorted, and prodded to recommend books for purchase. Portions of the library budget are designated for each department of instruction. Special allotments are made to establish collections for new courses and new graduate departments. Members of the library staff make themselves familiar with the needs of the various departments, suggest materials they could use, give book talks to classes, and share responsibility for certain aspects of graduate research (for example, they may direct the candidate for a graduate degree to possible sources, or oversee his bibliography and footnotes). These services are not always apparent to the undergraduate (except the book talks), but their contributions to the teaching functions of the faculty are recognized as essential, and the American Association of University Professors recognizes qualified professional librarians as having faculty status and admits them to membership.

There was a time when the librarian's chief function was custodial. He *kept* the books. In many medieval libraries the books, hand-lettered on parchment in enormous tomes, were chained fast to the lecterns where they might be read. There were never very many books, according to modern standards, and the librarian knew the contents of them all. He had to give little thought to cataloging, and none at all to circulation procedures, and he probably devoted most of his time to making copies for other libraries.

Libraries still have custodians, but they are concerned with the maintenance of the buildings rather than guardianship of the books. The modern librarian takes more pride in the books that are in use than those on the shelves. And the librarian in a college has as his chief concern the contributions which the library, its books and its staff, make to the chief objective of the college, the diffusion of knowledge.

Chapter 3

THE BOOK

To MAKE the fullest use of a book, the reader should know the importance of all its parts. The contents of this chapter refer especially to books of fact, or *nonfiction*, for a novel seldom appears with explanatory matter in addition to the text, unless it uses foreign terminology or is published as a school edition with explanatory notes. But in a work written to give information all the parts which have been added to the body of the text add to its usefulness or enjoyment. A book of travel or history needs maps to show where the events took place, the biographer may include genealogical charts, and a traveler who uses foreign words should add a glossary to explain them just as a scientist does when he introduces terminology likely to be unfamiliar to the reader.

There are special requirements to meet special needs, but almost all works of nonfiction have in common parts which are so familiar to the reader that he is apt to take them for granted and ignore them. By doing so he may fail to get full value from the book. In order to profit from what follows, the reader is advised to take in his hands a book, preferably a new one, fresh from the bookseller, for this scrutiny should begin with the outside cover.

DUST JACKET

Most new books, with the exception of many textbooks and other volumes designed for use rather than appreciation, are originally covered with a brightly colored and illustrated *dust wrapper* or *jacket*, designed both to protect the book until it is sold and to sell it to the people who will appreciate it. (Sometimes, of course, the jacket illustration has so little to do with the book's tone and content that it is bought by the wrong person, or rejected by one who would enjoy it.) This jacket will probably have either on the back or on one of the flaps a picture of the author and some mention of his previous work, or some details of his life. The front flap usually has a "blurb" which describes the contents in terms intended to attract the reader. One should not accept the blurb too freely, beyond its hint of contents, for it is a selling device and may compare the author to Einstein, Machiavelli, and Thomas Wolfe in one burst of purple prose. Elsewhere on the jacket may be excerpts from reviews of the book, or of the author's previous works. These too may be misleading, for a sentence out of context may not fairly represent the intention of the entire review. Once in a while a jacket may open out to show a large map or a chart or diagram. The person owning this book will keep its jacket on it. In a library it may be removed and filed for ready reference, or trimmed off and inserted in a pocket attached to the back cover. Nowadays, of course, many libraries keep the jackets on the books, with transparent plastic covers, which add both to their attractiveness and their longevity.

BINDING

Now we come to the book itself. The binding, usually of cloth pasted on heavy cardboard, is in three parts: the front and back covers, and the spine. The spine is the portion visible when the book stands upright on a shelf between other books, and usually bears the title, author's or authors' surnames, and the publisher's name in short form, as *Harper* for Harper & Row, or *Oxford* for The Oxford University Press. It is on the spine that libraries place the numbers and letters of the book's call number so that it can be kept in its proper place among books like it. If you fail to find a book of fiction in its proper place by author, it may be because the library's "pages" have shelved it under the publisher's name, sometimes more prominently displayed than the author's, when there is no call number to guide them.

ENDPAPERS

The first things we see on opening a book, from either front or back, are the endpapers. These are of heavy paper, usually single large sheets extending the full width of the open book, designed to hold the book firmly in its binding; they are usually white, or sometimes a plain color, and frequently decorated with a design in keeping with the subject matter of the book. Sometimes the endpapers bear maps or charts or illustrations not repeated in the book. If they are intended to add to the reader's enjoyment they defeat their purpose in library books, for the library's marks of ownership, pockets, etc., cover parts of these illustrations, and rebinding when the book becomes worn destroys them completely.

PRELIMINARY PAGES

At this point it is necessary to introduce two printers' terms frequently used by bibliographers in describing books: *verso* and *recto*. All right-hand pages are *rectos*, and are odd-numbered. All left-hand pages are *versos*, even-numbered. Obviously these come from the Latin, as does so much of the bibliographer's terminology. Verso replaces with one word the frequently encountered expression "over the page" or "overleaf." The title page is almost always a recto, and so are the first pages of table of contents, preface, introduction, and index, as well as the first page of Chapter 1.

Next after the endpaper comes the flyleaf, which is usually blank, but if the volume is one of a series the series title may appear on it. The next recto is the half title, bearing only the brief title of the book. A list of the author's works frequently appears on the verso of the half title, i.e., facing the title page. If there is a frontispiece (a full-page illustration, perhaps a portrait of the author or of a person prominent in the book), it is a verso facing the title page. Flyleaf and half title are inserted mainly to protect the title page.

Title Page

The title page bears a great deal of important information about the book, and to the discerning reader it also gives hints of the publisher's good taste. This page will have a pleasing appearance if the lines of type are well spaced, in balanced arrangement, and if the typefaces themselves are harmonious. It was once considered artistic to decorate title pages with arabesques, medallions, and fancy borders; simplicity is now preferred.

A typical title page presents in large type, somewhat above the center of the page, the full official title of the book. This may be much longer than the title as it appears on the spine or front cover (the *binder's title* or *cover title*) or on the half title page. Frequently the official title includes an explanatory subtitle and a statement of edition or revision. Next we have the author or authors, their names as they wish them to appear (in full, initials only, or pseudonyms) with or without academic degrees, titles, present or previous positions which indicate their authority. The names of others who have contributed to the book, such as editors, illustrators, or compilers, are given next. At the bottom of the page we find the publisher's name in its official form, with one or more cities in which the firm has offices and, usually, a date. This may be the year in which this copy was printed or the year in which the book was copyrighted or recopyrighted. To be absolutely sure that a book is up to date, one must always turn to the copyright page.

Copyright Page

The verso of the title page contains copyright dates and names the copyright owner. Books published after September 15, 1955, bear the symbol ©, which protects the copyright holders in all countries which adhere to the Universal Copyright Convention. A book frequently revised will have a copyright date for each revision. Additional printings may be listed here, but the latest copyright date shown is the year the book was first printed in its present form.

Preface

If a book has a preface it will follow the title page. It may be called Foreword or Acknowledgments. It is here that the author tells his reasons for writing the book, acknowledges the help and encouragement given him by others, and refers to libraries or private collections which he has used. Prefaces are usually brief and matter-of-fact. Notable exceptions to both these rules are the prefaces to the plays of George Bernard Shaw, in which he set forth all his theories on the drama, history, social problems, or whatever subject his plays presented. In one edition, his preface to the 110 pages of *Saint Joan* covers 55 pages; *The Doctor's Dilemma*, 116 pages long, has a 92-page preface; and *The Shewing Up of Blanco Posnet* is 43 pages long and its preface almost exactly doubles it, at 85 pages! But whether short or long, the preface should not be ignored if the reader really wants to know what the book is all about.

Table of Contents; List of Illustrations

These two lists are sometimes sufficient indication of the book's contents to tell the reader whether or not it has what he wants. The table of contents is an outline showing the divisions of the subject matter into chapters, and because the pages are usually given in nonfiction, it shows the relative importance which the author gives to the parts, according to the amount of space he devotes to each. One should not reject a book as a possible source of specific information — because the subject is not named in a chapter heading — without first checking the index. But if the reader wishes detailed treatment of a subject, the table of contents will show how much detail he may expect. As for the list of illustrations, it may list only full-page plates, and smaller pictures in the text may be referred to only in the index. A lack of illustrations may be a serious fault in one book, as in a book of travel or biography, but may be unimportant in another.

All the preliminary pages mentioned so far, if numbered at all, are usually marked with small Roman numerals (i, iii, v, vi, x, cli, and so forth). The half title and title pages are never numbered, but are usually counted as i and iii.

INTRODUCTION

From this point on, pages are numbered with Arabic numerals, but again, page 1 is seldom marked. It is the first page of the introduction, if there is one. When a book has a section specifically named Introduction it has been planned to introduce the subject matter of the book to the reader. It may have been written by the author of the book, or by someone else: perhaps a friend or colleague who has urged him to write it, or who vouches for his authority; perhaps the editor of a series in which this book is a part, or an editor who has prepared this work for publication or republication.

BODY OR TEXT

All the numbered chapters of a book, with pages numbered by Arabic numerals, form the body or text.

NOTES

In order to clarify statements or cite books or articles quoted or referred to, authors frequently make explanatory or bibliographic notes, numbered consecutively within each chapter and linked to the body of text by similar numbers. Many books have these footnotes, placed beneath the text, in smaller type. Notes may also be found grouped together at the ends of chapters, or all together at the end of the book, before the first appendix. If notes are infrequent, they may be indicated by such symbols as * (asterisk) or † (dagger).

APPENDIXES

Many books have several additional parts at the end of the main text. The first of these may be appendixes (or appendices) containing texts of documents or other source materials referred to in the book, and other useful matter, left out of the main text in order not to interrupt the continuity of thought, or because they are mentioned in various parts of the text and are more accessible at the end. A textbook on United States Government is almost certain to have appendixes giving the text of the Constitution and its amendments, titles and duties of members of the President's cabinet, and similar information.

BIBLIOGRAPHY

This term has been mentioned in preceding chapters. It is, in this context, a *list of sources*. In a book which is the result of extensive research, these sources may include not only published materials like other books and magazine articles but also laws and statutes, newspaper reports, and unpublished letters and diaries, manuscripts, official papers such as deeds, wills, town clerks' records, parish lists of baptisms and marriages. While it is customary for all such materials to be included in one long list at the end of a book, they may also be found grouped at the end of each chapter, or referred to in footnotes. The reader should look for notes and bibliography before he settles down to read, lest he fail to find the references which will make things clearer and more interesting.

GLOSSARY

An alphabetical list of technical or foreign words used in the text is often added at the end of a book to avoid inserting footnotes or explanatory parentheses in the text as the words first appear. Some writers like to use foreign words, in the belief that there is no English word to express the exact shade of meaning, or that they give a flavor to the narrative. Unfortunately, these are not always the writers who add glossaries to the text, nor those who use or spell foreign words correctly.

INDEX

The index to a book or set of books is a list, alphabetically arranged, of all the topics, people, and places mentioned in the text. Each item is followed by the number of the page or pages on which the subject is mentioned, or by the volume and pages if there are two or more volumes. The quality of the index contributes to or detracts from the value of the book. No important reference should be omitted, but some indexers overdo, and include the most casual mention of a name, though the paragraph cited may contribute no information on it.

It is not always easy to tell which references under a subject will be the most useful. Sometimes the more important passages are indicated in blacker type, or by an asterisk. If not, it is best to look up first those covering more than one page.

Cross References in Indexes

The reader of a book and its author sometimes use different names for the same thing. The reader wishing to find forms for his personal correspondence looks in a book of etiquette, and finds "Correspondence, *see* Letters," meaning that under the word Letters he will find page references to the sections on correspondence. This is called a *cross reference*, or a *"see" reference*. Another kind is a *"see also" reference*, in which some pages are given for the subject looked under, and then the reader is referred to one or more topics for related material; for example, "Weather, pp. 4-5, 21; *see also* Climate." Some indexers, rather than make cross references, use both entries. For example, an index to this book could have one entry for the term Cross References, another for "See" References, and a third for "See Also" References, all giving the same page number. Or the index might use Cross References as the preferred entry, because that is used as the heading of the section, and say, " 'See' and 'See Also' References, *see* Cross References." Some indexers make no cross references, and it is up to the reader to exert his ingenuity and comb his vocabulary for synonyms in order to find the subjects used.

Subdivisions of a Subject in Indexes

A good index will not only give all pages on which pertinent mention of a subject may be found, but also indicate subdivisions of that subject. These subdivisions may be given in the order in which they appear in the text, alphabetically, or chronologically, as in the case of a person's life, or a series of historical events, or battles in a war. These subdivisions may be printed in a paragraph, as:

> BEARS, 12, 21, 35-40, 96; black, 35, 39, 40; black cinnamon, 40; black Labrador, 35; brown, 35, 36

or indented in a column, as:

> BEARS, 12, 21, 35-40, 96
>> black, 35, 39, 40
>>> cinnamon, 40
>>> Labrador, 35
>> brown, 35, 36

Kinds of Indexes

In addition to the index of subjects mentioned in a book, there may be several other kinds. A collection of poetry, for example, usually has: (1) an alphabetical list of authors whose works have been included; (2) an alphabetical list of titles of poems; and (3) an index of first lines. Each index has its own title at the head of its first page, and, since all are listed in the table of contents, it is not difficult to find the right one.

The reader, in using most alphabetical lists in libraries, from the card catalog on, will find that the alphabetical position of a title is determined not always by the first word, but by the first word not an article, no matter what language is being used. Thus *The Dynasts* files under D, *Die Zauberflöte* under Z, *L'Abbé Constantin* under A. But in an index of first lines of poetry, these articles are part of the metrical scheme, and the reader will find many entries under *A*, *An*, or *The*.

CONCORDANCE

There is another very special type of index called a *concordance*, which shows *in context* each use of all important words in a book. For example, a book of quotations will have not an index of first lines or titles, but a concordance in which every quotation is listed under every important or memorable word in it, because people looking for quotations may remember them only vaguely, or may desire quotations using a certain word. For example, the first line of the witches' incantation in *Macbeth* — "Double, double toil and trouble" — appears in the concordance of Bartlett's *Familiar Quotations* (fourteenth edition, 1968) in three places, under *double*, *toil*, and *trouble*.

Concordances to the works of Shakespeare, and a few other great writers, have been published as separate volumes, and there are a number of concordances to the Bible (see pages 216-217). Some editions of the Bible contain a brief concordance, but a complete one obviously must be several times the size of the work indexed, and requires a separate volume.

THE WHOLE BOOK: MAKE-UP OR FORMAT

While the reader has been examining his book to discover all the parts which make it a useful tool, he has probably also found himself judging its appearance, and deciding that for some reason, not quite clear to him, perhaps, he likes or dislikes it. Mention has already been made of the jacket design and the make-up of the title page as indications of the publisher's taste. The texture of the cloth used for the binding, the color contrasts between lettering and cloth, and the size and style of lettering on the cover and spine may add to these impressions.

We are easily influenced by the size of type used in the body of a book, usually preferring one neither large and widely spaced nor small and crowded. Even small type looks larger when there is plenty of space between the lines. This well-spaced line is said to be "leaded," because when type used to be set by hand a strip of lead was placed between the lines of type to keep them apart. The margins also affect one's impression of a page. There should be enough room around the printed portion so that it seems firmly in place. Print which comes too close to the outer edges seems to be slipping off the page, and if it comes too close to the inner edge it is hard to see. Libraries sometimes reject an edition on the basis of this narrow inner margin, for it makes rebinding impossible.

Readers of *Alice in Wonderland* will remember that Alice didn't care for the book her sister was reading because it had no conversation in it. While we cannot expect to find conversation in every book we read, we are more or less consciously repelled by a spread of pages with no paragraph indentions and no breaks in a solid mass of text. Both the eye and the mind need places to pause. This is especially true of a book of poetry. The small volumes of verse, perhaps not more than fifty pages, in which a poet's work first appears, are usually more attractive than his *Collected Works*. Most of this attractiveness comes from the large spaces around and between the lines, which give the reader room to savor the imagery and listen to the sound. Some of it comes also from the softer, richer, matte-finish paper used for small books of verse. The collected works, or the collections of poetry made for textbooks, too often are printed in fine print, in double columns, on thin shiny paper. This may be necessary in order to get a great deal into one volume, but if the reader thinks he has an aversion to poetry, let him try reading it in small doses from well-made books.

Chapter 4

LIBRARY CATALOGS

IN THE FIRST chapter, the catalog of a library was mentioned briefly, and in Chapter 2 some space was assigned to the department of a college library where books and other materials are cataloged. This chapter will be devoted to a description and an explanation of the functions and possible forms of library catalogs, which are probably most frequently encountered as cards in drawers or "trays," but may be a series of volumes or rolls of microfilm. There will be an account of the various ways in which the entries may be arranged, the types of entries, and, most important of all, the amazing amount of information about a book (or series or set of books) which may be derived from a single catalog entry.

ARRANGEMENT OF CATALOGS

Just as a well-organized book of nonfiction will have a detailed index, a well-organized library will have a detailed catalog, containing one or more entries for each book, interfiled in alphabetical order. Most libraries have catalogs on cards, some have them in books, and a few libraries (the Library of Congress for instance) have catalogs in both forms.

It is customary for these catalogs, whether on cards or in books, to be what are known as *dictionary catalogs*. The words listed in a dictionary are not grouped by part of speech into separate sections for nouns, verbs, adjectives, adverbs, conjunctions, and the like. Rather, all words are given in alphabetical order (though if a single word is used as more than one part of speech, its definition will be divided accordingly — the word *out* in an unabridged dictionary is an imposing example).

Similarly, in a dictionary catalog, entries for author, subject, title, editor, compiler, and sometimes publisher will be interfiled with entries for other books, in alphabetical order. There are logical filing rules which govern the separation of these kinds of entries: people before places; a person as author before the same person as subject; two or more people with the same last name filed alphabetically by their forenames. An examination of any card catalog or of any encyclopedia will give clear examples of this.

A catalog with subject, author, title, and other types of entries inter-filed is often difficult for the average library user to understand. Two methods are customarily used to distinguish the subject entries. One is to type them in RED CAPITALS, or at least in red; the other is to use BLACK CAPITAL LETTERS for all subject entries. This makes it easier to distinguish, for instance, between a copy of the poems written by Henry VIII, King of England, and a biography of that same HENRY VIII, KING OF ENGLAND.

Either of these methods makes it possible to remove the subject cards from the dictionary card file and make a separate *subject catalog*, so that the searcher for material *about* a person, place, or other entity (such as a college, museum, or business firm) will not find subject material interfiled with entries for the same person or organization as author or publisher. There are, of course, innumerable subject entries: Students, Civil rights, Peace, Politics, Ecology, Sewage, Roads, Set theory, Vector analysis, Chemistry, Architecture, Electronic digital computers, Tomatoes, and so forth and so on. The tactic of making a separate subject catalog is used in many college libraries and is comparable to the separate sections of *Books in Print*, *Forthcoming Books*, and other reference tools, which will be discussed in Chapter 10 under the heading Current Bibliographies.

A few large libraries in America, and many in Europe, do not have alphabetical catalogs, but arrange entries in large subject groups with subdivisions, according to their own classification scheme. These *classed catalogs* are not easy to use, requiring extensive knowledge of the subject being studied. The graduate student engaged in advanced research may have occasion to use such catalogs, but can of course receive expert assistance from the staffs of the libraries concerned.

PRINTED CATALOGS IN BOOK FORM

As noted above, some libraries print their catalogs in book form instead of on cards. Among the most famous printed catalogs are those of the British Museum in London and the Bibliothèque Nationale in Paris. These libraries are comparable to the Library of Congress in being official depositories for all books published in their respective countries, as well as collectors of scholarly works from all over the world. In recent years the Library of Congress has also published its catalog in book form, the entries being reduced photographic reproductions of the printed cards. These are published in two series, one of author entries, the other of subjects. Many college and public libraries subscribe to these series, as well as to the catalogs of the British Museum, Bibliothèque Nationale, and others.

Some public libraries with large branch systems have, in recent years, adopted the catalog in book form, basing the individual entries upon those of the Library of Congress, with periodic supplements and cumulations to update the record of holdings. But, as new titles are added daily to the library collection, these supplements must be further updated by short card files to fill the gap.

The only local book catalog with which I am familiar, as a branch librarian in the system, is that of the Enoch Pratt Free Library of Baltimore, Maryland. Not only does this library have more than twenty-five branches, but it is also the designated center for extension service to the public libraries throughout the state. As this state-wide service expanded, it became obvious that the classification scheme then in use should be converted to the Library of Congress Classification system. (This system will be discussed in Chapter 5 and compared with the Dewey Decimal system, which it resembles.) It was obvious that if such a change were to be made, it should begin with the newly published books being added, and a change to a catalog in book form could begin with these new books. (This is, of course, a greatly simplified explanation of a very complex new enterprise.)

The advantage of a book catalog is that it can be issued in as many copies as are apt to be subscribed for, supplying not only each department of the Central Library and each branch, but all the colleges, universities, and public libraries which are likely to use the loan and reference services of the main library.

FORM AND CONTENT OF CATALOG ENTRIES

Since the catalog card, or a photographic reproduction of it, is the basis for most of the above-mentioned book catalogs, the remainder of this chapter will show various types of catalog entries on cards and point out in detail the information about a book which they convey.

Author Cards

In Chapter 3, we described in detail the parts of a book, discussing their significance to the reader. Each of those parts has its place on the catalog card, which carries a full description of the book. The *author card* is the basic card from which all the others are made; it is often called the *main card*, the *unit card*, or the *official entry*. The author card may be the only one in the catalog to represent a book. If, for example, a poet has compiled his own *Collected Works*, with no editorial assistance from anyone, the only card would be that under his name, for the title is not distinctive, no one else had anything to do with the job, and no subject card is needed. If, on the other hand, the collected works of a poet were compiled and edited by another, there would be a second card, or *added entry*, filed under the name of the compiler and editor. The following samples illustrate the differences (Figures 3, 4, and 5).

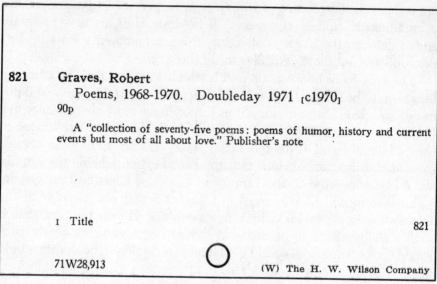

Figure 3: Author Card

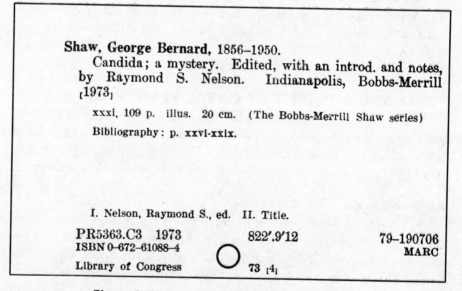

Figure 4: Author Card, Work Edited by Another

The reader will see that the only difference between Figure 4 and Figure 5 is that the name of the editor has been repeated above the name of the author, indented to a place above the first word of the title; this card will of course be filed under the editor's name, since the added entry line is now the first line on the card. All cards for a book, except the author card, begin at the second indention, with the author's name standing out at "primary indention" between the added entries

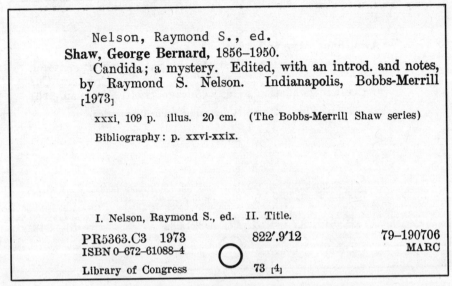

Figure 5: Editor Card for Book Listed in Figure 4

above and the title below. This convention of the primary indention is useful to the reader, because he can tell from it who is considered responsible for the book. In the next two samples, the work of many people has been brought together. The work of May Hill Arbuthnot (Figure 6) consisted of collecting poems and arranging them; the book has no editorial matter. In the second sample (Figure 7) the designation of editor is clearly indicated by the language used on the title page: "selected and edited by Veronica S. Hutchinson."

Other personal added entries may be for translator or illustrator.

Sometimes a book is prepared by a person or group of people as a part of their duties as employees of a government department, an institution, or an association. Then the author of the book is not officially the person or persons who wrote it, but the organization to which they are responsible. In such cases, the author, or main entry in the catalog is the name of the organization, as in Figures 8, 9, and 10.

Some standard works of literature, written many years ago, usually by unknown authors, or told and retold through the centuries, are printed over and over again, in many languages, in many editions. These editions are all entered under a common name, as if it were the author. Among these are the great religious books, such as the Bible, Zend-Avesta, or Koran, and folklore like the Kalevala, Nibelungenlied, Beowulf, or Mother Goose. (See Figures 11 and 12.)

The reader will note that the sample catalog cards shown in Figures 1 through 12 are printed cards. The first card and the final four were printed by The H. W. Wilson Company, which issued these cards

Arbuthnot, May Hill, 1884–   *comp.*
    Time for poetry; illustrated by Salcia Bahnc. A teach-
er's anthology to accompany The new basic readers, Curriculum foundation series. Chicago, Scott, Foresman ₍1951₎
    438 p. illus. 22 cm. (Curriculum foundation series)

    1. English poetry (Collections) 2. Children's poetry.   ɪ. Gray,
William Scott, 1885–   ed. The new basic readers. ɪɪ. Title.

    PN6101.A7   821.082   51—2431

    Library of Congress   ◯   ₍53q²10₎

Figure 6: Compiler as Main Entry

Hutchinson, Veronica Somerville, *ed.*
    Candle-light stories, selected and edited by Veronica S.
Hutchinson, with drawings by Lois Lenski. New York, Min-
ton, Balch & co., 1928.
    7 p. l., 3–146 p. incl. illus., plates. col. front., col. plates. 26ᵐ.

    ɪ. Title.

    PZ8.H97Ca   28–21502 rev

    Library of Congress   ◯   ₍r47u3₎

Figure 7: Editor as Main Entry

from 1938 until 1975; the remainder are Library of Congress cards.
In general appearance they are very much alike, and to the average
library user the difference would be insignificant. On the Library of
Congress card everything is derived from the book itself, and everything which can be said about the book is there, including variations
of paging, and the height of the book in centimeters. If the Library of

United States. Congress. House. Committee on Ways and Means.
  Summary of the major provisions of Public law 93–406 : the Employee retirement income security act of 1974 / Committee on Ways and Means, U. S. House of Representatives. — Washington : U. S. Govt. Print. Off., 1974.

  vi, 17 p. ; 24 cm.

  At head of title: 93d Congress, 2d session. Committee print.
  $0.40

  1. Pension trusts—United States.   I. Title.

KF3512.A25   1974   344′.73′01252   74–602580
                                                                    MARC

Library of Congress   O   75

Figure 8: United States Government Department as Author

912   **Hammond (C.S.) and Company, inc.**
          Hammond's Ambassador world atlas.

          First published 1954. Frequently reprinted with revisions of the statistics, maps and political data
          "A world atlas and gazetteer of topical and regional maps. Geographical, demographic and political features are shown. Descriptive gazetteer entries and street maps of the world's larger cities ₍and a glossary₎ are included." Publishers' weekly
          Folio volume

1 Atlases   ɪ Title   912

59W5,016   O   (W)   The H. W. Wilson Company

Figure 9: Publisher as Author

Congress has a book with a misspelled word on the title page, the misspelling is reproduced on the catalog cards, with (!) inserted after the error.

Wilson cards are usually slightly less detailed, but have descriptive notes for the information of the reader. And where the Library of Congress shows us that *Candle-light Stories* is a quarto by giving its height

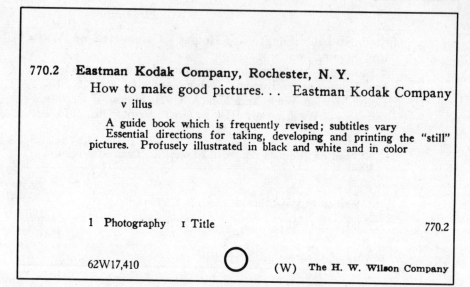

Figure 10: Manufacturer as Author

as 26cm, Wilson indicates the size of *Hammond's Ambassador World Atlas* with "Folio volume." Wilson cards printed since July 1, 1960, show authors' names as given on the title page and omit birth and death dates. Many libraries are now following this simplified and time-saving procedure, but library catalogs for many years to come will continue to have some cards which give these dates, along with a growing number which do not.

Many libraries use both these sources for printed cards: Library of Congress for scholarly works, government publications, books in foreign languages; and Wilson cards for books of general interest and children's books. Many publishers and dealers who specialize in service to libraries now supply a set of cards with each book, to which the library cataloger need add only the classification (call number) and check to see that the subject headings used conform with the library's practice. If no cards are available from any source the book will be cataloged in the library, and copy may be supplied to the Library of Congress for its use if requested. (See Figure 14.)

Some public libraries make all their own cards because they are needed for branch and departmental libraries and can be duplicated inexpensively. College and university library catalogs contain many Library of Congress cards, because they have complete bibliographic detail and supply reliable information as to author's name, edition, and so forth for the kinds of books which colleges buy. For this reason, detailed discussion of the items to be found on Library of Congress (LC)

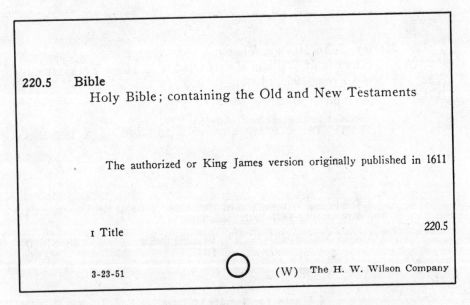

220.5   Bible
         Holy Bible; containing the Old and New Testaments

         The authorized or King James version originally published in 1611

         I Title   220.5

         3-23-51   O   (W) The H. W. Wilson Company

Figure 11: Anonymous Classic Entered Under Common Name

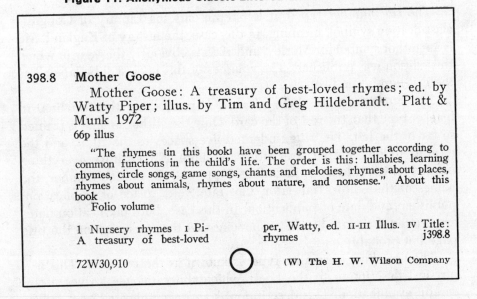

398.8   Mother Goose
         Mother Goose: A treasury of best-loved rhymes; ed. by
         Watty Piper; illus. by Tim and Greg Hildebrandt. Platt &
         Munk 1972
         66p illus

         "The rhymes [in this book] have been grouped together according to
         common functions in the child's life. The order is this: lullabies, learning
         rhymes, circle songs, game songs, chants and melodies, rhymes about places,
         rhymes about animals, rhymes about nature, and nonsense." About this
         book
         Folio volume

         1 Nursery rhymes I Pi-   per, Watty, ed. II-III Illus. IV Title:
         A treasury of best-loved   rhymes   j398.8

         72W30,910   O   (W) The H. W. Wilson Company

Figure 12: Anonymous Classic Entered Under Common Name

cards will not only make it easier for the student to use the catalog, but
will also point out the amount of information about a book which can
be obtained even before one decides to examine the book itself. A careful study of the rather simple catalog entry illustrated in Figure 13 will
tell the student everything he needs to know about this work, except
whether he will find it interesting.

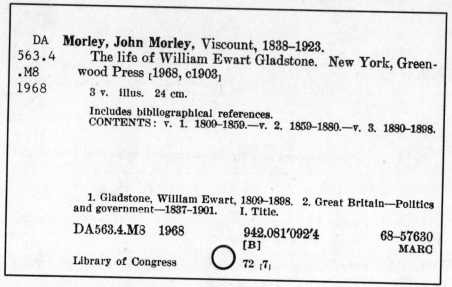

DA   **Morley, John Morley,** Viscount, 1838–1923.
563.4   The life of William Ewart Gladstone. New York, Green-
.M8   wood Press ₍1968, c1903₎
1968   3 v. illus. 24 cm.

         Includes bibliographical references.
         CONTENTS: v. 1. 1809–1859.—v. 2. 1859–1880.—v. 3. 1880–1898.

         1. Gladstone, William Ewart, 1809–1898. 2. Great Britain—Politics
      and government—1837–1901.   I. Title.

      DA563.4.M8   1968   942.081'092'4   68–57630
                                         [B]   MARC
         Library of Congress   72 ₍7₎

Figure 13: Sample LC Card

The *call number* typed at left represents the Library of Congress classification symbol, meaning, in this case, the history of England. M8 is an author symbol for Morley, and 1968 is obviously the year in which this edition was published. The volumes of this book will be labeled as the call number indicates.

The *author's name,* John Morley, is printed on the top line, in blacker type than the rest of the card. Only the author's name is printed so far to the left. The *title,* indented five spaces to the right, and the *imprint* follow. Author, full title, and imprint constitute everything printed on the title page, including, if present, the edition number; the names of the editor, translator, illustrator, etc.; place of publication; publisher; and date of publication. In this case, both publication dates are printed in square brackets, showing that they were not on the title page but probably on its verso.

The next line, in smaller type, is known as the *collation.* This is a physical description to the book, which the cataloger arrives at by careful examination. This description is an uncomplicated one — three volumes, illustrated (perhaps with portraits), about ten inches in height.

There are two descriptive notes. One may assume, as no one is given credit for them, that the bibliographical references were supplied by Morley. The CONTENTS note will suggest that the reader wishing to know about Gladstone's career as Prime Minister will be most interested in Volumes 2 and 3.

At the bottom of the card are the suggested added entries (other cards) which could be used in cataloging this book. As there is nothing distinctive about the title, the cataloger would cross off the item, a signal to the typist not to make a title card. The first two subject entries, indicated by Arabic numerals, would be typed on cards identical with the main entry, in CAPITAL LETTERS, at the title indention, above the author line. That is, the reader would also find cards for this book filed under both GLADSTONE and GREAT BRITAIN. In fact, if he had looked under GLADSTONE he would have found other books about him — the advantage of subject entries, or of a separate subject catalog.

The lines below are: at the left, the LC number which has been typed at the top of the card; at the center, two possible Dewey classifications — a decimal which could be curtailed at either of the slant marks, or B for Biography, for libraries which prefer to keep all biographies together. The number at the far right is used to order copies of the cards for this book from the Library of Congress.

Figures 14 and 15 represent publications of governmental agencies. In Figure 14 it will be seen that Mr. Waagé was solely responsible for writing the report, but the series note (in curved parentheses) indicates that this is a bulletin of a Maryland government department, and the final lines, below the LC class number show that the copy was provided by the Enoch Pratt Free Library, although the card was printed by the Library of Congress. The contents note shows that this would be valuable to field geologists; thus, four subject cards (entries) are suggested (Arabic numbers indicate subject entries). The small Roman numeral I for a title entry might also be useful, and in a Maryland library a series entry is suggested.

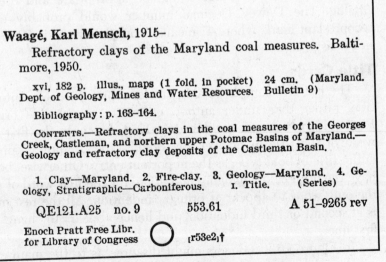

Figure 14: Government Bulletin With Single Author

Pennsylvania.   Bureau   of   Industrial   Development.   Industry Section.
    Statistics for electric utilities.
    [Harrisburg] Dept. of Commerce.
         v. 28 cm. (Pennsylvania public utility census series)
    "Release no. U-1."

       1. Electric utilities—Pennsylvania—Statistics.   I. Pennsylvania.
    Dept. of Commerce.   II. Series.

HD9685.U6P46   338.4'7'3636209748   72–622879
Library of Congress   ◯   72 [2]

Figure 15: Serial Publication by Government Agency

Figure 15 is a card for a serial publication of the Pennsylvania Department of Commerce, which is its publisher. The collation here shows that there will be numerous volumes; the space before the small v. is for insertion in pencil of the number of items in this series added to the library, while the note "Release no. U-1" shows that this is the first of the series on Utilities. In the LC classification, HD is the letter symbol for Economic history; 9685 is the number for Special industries and trades; U6 is the symbol for Utilities, and P46 stands for Pennsylvania. All the indicated headings would be appropriate and useful in the catalog. The Dewey Decimal number would probably end at the second slant mark, where 47 means Pennsylvania, as in 974.7 — History of Pennsylvania.

Title Cards

The last two sample catalog entries represent books entered under title, rather than under author, editor, or responsible organization. Figure 16, which was produced in 1954, has only the first important word of the title in blacker, or "bold," type. Figure 17 presents the entire title in bold type, as the important entry. Otherwise, both entries have the form called *hanging indention*, for the first word of the title is the only word to appear at primary indention. All the rest of the card is at second or third indention, and hence appears to "hang" from the first line.

In Figure 16, catalogers might disagree as to the main entry. The work might, with equal justice, have been entered under BOLLINGEN FOUNDATION, which sponsored the expedition, or under RAMBOVA, N,

The **Tomb** of Ramesses VI. ₍New York₎ Pantheon Books
₍1954₎

    2 v. illus. (part col.) 32 cm. (Bollingen series, 40. Egyptian religious texts and representations, v. 1)

    "This study is based on the work of an expedition sponsored by the Bollingen Foundation ... October, 1949, to June, 1951."

    CONTENTS.—pt. 1. Texts, translated with introduction by A. Piankoff; edited by N. Rambova.—pt. 2. Plates, recorded by N. Rambova; photographed by L. F. Husson.

    1. Rameses VI, King of Egypt. 2. Egypt—Religion. 3. Egyptian literature. (Series: Bollingen series, 40. Series: Egyptian religious texts and representations, v. 1)

PJ1551.E3 vol. 1   299.31   54—5646

Library of Congress   ○   ₍55k7₎

Figure 16: Title Entry

How can presidential nominating conventions be improved? Highlights of The convention problem, issues in reform of presidential nominating procedures by Judith H. Parris. Washington, Brookings Institution ₍1972₎

    9 p. 23 cm. (Brookings research report 127)

    Cover title.

    1. Political conventions. 2. Nominations for office—United States. 3. Presidents—United States—Election. I. Parris, Judith H. The convention problem. II. Series.

H62.B714 no. 127   329′.0221′0973   72-190647
₍JK2255₎   MARC

Library of Congress   ○   72

Figure 17: Title Entry

who seems to have been largely responsible for the preparation of the two volumes, instead of under the title. Perhaps the most interesting thing here is the difference in emphasis shown by the two classifiers. The Library of Congress class, PJ1551, indicates Egyptian language and literature, whereas the Dewey number means non-Christian religions. Note also that the first suggested subject entry is the more commonly used spelling of Rameses, not the spelling used in the book title.

It can be seen from the samples illustrated that it is possible for the reader to learn much about a book without seeing anything but the catalog card, because it is so fully described. One can make other deductions from the card. The title of the book often suggests its possible usefulness to the individual reader. Under the subject heading GENETICS one may find two such titles as *Theory of Genetics* and *The New You and Heredity*. The first title suggests that this is a scholarly work, intended perhaps for a college textbook. The second shows that the book is directed to the general reader, not the specialist. The student will doubtless choose to read the second if he is looking for a popular introduction to the subject. He will also learn from the catalog card that *The New You and Heredity* is a revised edition of an earlier *You and Heredity*, showing that the first edition had a good sale, and that the author has revised it and brought it up to date.

Subject Cards

It has already been said more than once that almost every book in the library is represented in the catalog by an author card. Title cards are less frequent, but it is likely that most works of nonfiction will be represented by at least one subject card. It is also likely that the student searching for material for a paper, or any person hunting for information, will make more use of the subject cards than of any others in the catalog. The arrangement of these cards, with their many kinds of subdivisions, is confusing if one does not understand the principles which underlie the filing rules.

One of the most complicated subjects in most American libraries is U.S.—HISTORY. This is typical of the histories of all countries, in that there are three types of subdivisions, by time, by literary form, and by descriptive adjective. Examples of these three are: U.S.—HISTORY—COLONIAL PERIOD, U.S.—HISTORY—ESSAYS, and U.S.—HISTORY, MILITARY. Further complications ensue when we have form subdivisions of period divisions, e.g., U.S.—HISTORY—CIVIL WAR—FICTION, and period subdivisions of descriptive divisions, e.g., U.S.—HISTORY, MILITARY—CIVIL WAR.

The reader will note that the adjectives are separated from the subhead HISTORY by a comma, because they limit the term to a type of history, e.g., military, while the period of time covered is not limited at all. On the other hand, the period subdivisions give definite limits to the length of time covered, and the form subdivisions specify the method of treatment. These are separated by dashes.

Thus we may have

U.S.—HISTORY

U.S.—HISTORY, MILITARY

> U.S.—HISTORY, MILITARY—CIVIL WAR
> U.S.—HISTORY, MILITARY—CIVIL WAR—ESSAYS
> U.S.—HISTORY—REVOLUTION
> U.S.—HISTORY—CIVIL WAR
> U.S.—HISTORY—CIVIL WAR—ESSAYS

According to this method of filing, all cards which refer to the history of the United States in all aspects, from the beginning to the present, precede cards referring to the military aspect of history. Finally, entries for general history of certain periods of history appear in chronological order. This arrangement is logical, but it is admittedly complicated.

Many subjects have both substantive and adjectival divisions. According to the logical method suggested above, we would have the following arrangement of cards on EDUCATION:

> EDUCATION
> EDUCATION—BIBLIOGRAPHY
> EDUCATION—HISTORY
> EDUCATION, COMPARATIVE
> EDUCATION, SECONDARY
> EDUCATION OF ADULTS

These could also be arranged alphabetically, as follows:

> EDUCATION
> EDUCATION—BIBLIOGRAPHY
> EDUCATION, COMPARATIVE
> EDUCATION—HISTORY
> EDUCATION OF ADULTS
> EDUCATION, SECONDARY

When we add to the above list the titles of books, such as *Education of Moderns,* or *The Education of Henry Adams,* the filing of a dictionary catalog becomes even more confusing.

It is exactly for this reason that many libraries, especially in colleges, have made the separate *subject catalogs* already referred to in this chapter. However, if it is necessary to use a *dictionary catalog,* the following comments on library filing will prove useful. In Chapters 7 and 8, on encyclopedias and dictionaries, some variations possible in alphabetical arrangement will be discussed. But in an encyclopedia, all the entries are subjects, though they may be persons, places, ideas, or theories. In a library catalog, especially a dictionary catalog, there are also authors, editors, titles, and other types of entries. Three rules generally followed are especially useful.

1. When the same word is used for a person, a place, and the title
of a book, that is the order in which they are filed; e.g.:

WASHINGTON, GEORGE

WASHINGTON, D.C.

Washington merry-go-round

2. When the library has books *by* an author, and also books *about*
him, the author entries precede the subject entries, e.g.:

Shakespeare, William
  Twelfth night

  SHAKESPEARE, WILLIAM
Chute, Marchette
Shakespeare of London

3. When *De, Van,* or *Von* are parts of English names, as William
De Morgan or John Van Buskirk, entries for these people are filed in D
or V. But in French, German, or other foreign names, where the *de,
van,* or *von* is not capitalized, the word after the particle is the entry
word, e.g.:

Beethoven, Ludwig van

Lafayette, Marie Joseph Paul Yves Roch Gilbert du Motier,
  Marquis de

Spanish names present special problems, as a Spaniard often adds
his mother's maiden name or the name of a place connected with his
family after his patronymic, and sometimes even third and fourth
names may be added, e.g.:

Cervantes Saavedra, Miguel de

Benavente y Martínez, Jacinto

Valera y Alcalá Galiano, Juan

CROSS REFERENCES IN A CATALOG

The catalog has cross references just as the index to a book has.
Most of them are from one subject to other allied subjects. These are
very useful to the reader, for they suggest aspects of his subject which
he might not have thought of. Catalogers try to foresee subjects which
readers might think of in order to make enough references from them
to the subject headings actually used. For example, we generally speak
of studying American History, but that phrase cannot be used as a
subject heading in a catalog, because logically it would have to include
the histories of all countries on both American continents. Therefore a
reference is made as illustrated in Figure 18. On the other hand,
AMERICA—DISCOVERY AND EXPLORATION is a valid heading. When

America was discovered, the United States did not exist, and the discoverers roamed over the coastal areas of both continents.

Another principle to be remembered is that one should look first for the more specific heading, only referring to broader subjects if nothing is found in the narrower field. If a book on monkeys is wanted, the heading ZOOLOGY will be useless. This principle is discussed in the suggestions on asking a librarian for assistance (see page 76). The student looking for SCIENCE when he wants a picture of a magnetic field is wasting his time.

Author References

When an author has used one or more pseudonyms, or when a woman is known equally well by her maiden name and her name after marriage, entries are filed in the catalog referring from the name not used by the library to the one under which the works have been entered. If Mark Twain's books have been listed in the catalog under CLEMENS, the cross-reference shown in Figure 19 will appear in the catalog.

Some authors use several pseudonyms, or write under their real names as well, using a different name for each type of book, or, if writers of detective stories, for books starring different fictional detec-

```
AMERICAN HISTORY    see

    U.S. - HISTORY
```

Figure 18: Cross Reference in Catalog

```
       Twain, Mark, pseud.    see

    Clemens, Samuel Langhorne
```

Figure 19: Author Reference for Pseudonym

tives. Some libraries make no attempt to enter all these books under the authors' real names, but may make references from each name to all the others, indicating that "books by this author may also be found in this catalog under. . . ."

Title References

Two types of title references may commonly be found in catalogs. The individual plays of Shakespeare have been published in dozens of editions. An author entry for each is listed in the catalog, but it is a common practice to make a single *title reference*, as in Figure 20.

Similar entries may be made for works of other authors which have been published in many editions, and for plays which appear frequently in collections.

The second type of title reference has to do with the kind of title used as a main entry, mentioned earlier, such as Mother Goose. If the library has an edition of this in French, there will be a reference back to the English title, as shown in Figure 21.

```
        Romeo and Juliet (play)
    Shakespeare, William, 1564-1616


        For editions in this library, see cards
    under
        Shakespeare, William, 1564-1616
           Romeo and Juliet
```

Figure 20: Title Reference for Multiple Editions

```
        Ma mère l'oye

        For editions in this library, see entries
    under
        Mother Goose
```

Figure 21: Title Reference from a Foreign Language

Chapter 5

LIBRARY CLASSIFICATION SYSTEMS

IN CHAPTER 1, where the relationship between libraries and readers was introduced, a brief summary of the possible arrangements of books was presented, with a promise to devote a chapter to the two systems of subject classification of books most frequently used in libraries in the United States and other countries: namely, the Dewey Decimal Classification (DC) and the Library of Congress Classification (LC).

The obvious difference between the two systems is that one is based on ten major numerical divisions, from zero to nine; the other, on twenty-one divisions, identified by letters of the alphabet. Both systems are derived from logical philosophical premises, and both lend themselves to expansion and, basically, to comparison with one another.

Some analogy to this situation may be found in the use of various systems of measurement, and the problems of conversion from one to another. Systems of currency vary from the decimal coinage of the United States, Canada, and most European and Asian countries to the complications of the old British system of £/s/d, before the British Isles, while keeping the old names of "pounds," "shillings," and "pence," decimalized their values early in the 1970s, to the consternation of many natives.

Similarly, we had shared with Britain measures of weight, volume, and dimension for solid commodities, liquids, raw food products, drugs, and land. Now we are following Britain by converting these measures to the metric system of centimeters, meters, liters, grams, kilograms, etc., not only for scientific purposes (we are all familiar with the kilowatt hour, the gram and cc in our prescription drugs) but for other measures as well. The U.S. Army veteran is well aware of the number of kilometers he can travel on a liter of "petrol," instead of miles to the gallon of "gas," and school systems all over the country are preparing their teachers for the coming change to the metric system.

In spite of our growing familiarity with the metric system, we are now faced more and more often with the necessity of accepting a non-decimal system of book classification. This necessity is caused by one factor — the proliferation of human knowledge. While the DC has been used in libraries large and small since 1876, and while it is still used in school libraries and in many large public and college libraries, the LC system has been adopted by university libraries and large city libraries in recent years because its use of the alphabet allows more than twice as many main subject divisions.

Assuming that most high school graduates will have become used to "Dewey," the DC, and that a large number of college libraries and public libraries as well will be changing over to LC, and considering that many colleges and universities, old and new, have been using LC for years, the two systems will be briefly compared. The outlines below give the main classes of each system. Each will be discussed further, so that the reader who has grown accustomed to DC may understand some of the characteristics of LC and, if necessary, make an easy adjustment from one to the other.

Dewey Decimal Classification: First Summary[1]		Library of Congress Classification
000	Generalities	A	General works: Polygraphy
100	Philosophy & related disciplines	B	Philosophy and Religion
		C	History: Auxiliary Sciences
200	Religion	D	History: General and Old World
300	The social sciences	E-F	History: America
400	Language	G	Geography, Anthropology, Folklore, etc.
500	Pure sciences	H	Social Sciences
600	Technology (Applied sciences)	J	Political Science
		K	Law
700	The arts	L	Education
800	Literature (Belles-lettres)	M	Music
900	General geography & history	N	Fine Arts
		P	Philology and Literature
		Q	Science
		R	Medicine
		S	Agriculture, etc.
		T	Technology
		U	Military Science
		V	Naval Science
		Z	Bibliography and Library Science

[1] Reprinted from abridged edition 10 (1971) of *Dewey Decimal Classification*, by permission of Forest Press Division, Lake Placid Club Education Foundation, owner of copyright.

THE DC SYSTEM

The Dewey Decimal Classification system, invented by Melvil Dewey and introduced to librarians in 1876, divides its ten main classes into ten more, as shown in Figure 22, the Second Summary. Each of these one hundred subclasses is further divided into ten subdivisions. Here a decimal point may be introduced, and innumerable subdivisions created by adding digits to the right of the decimal point.

Except for the 000s (zero-hundreds), which comprise general bibliographies and catalogs, material on librarianship, rare books and manuscripts, and museum management, and such generalia as encyclopedias, general periodicals, and newspapers (many of which fall into the category of reference books), the nine subject groups in the Dewey system have been said to treat subjects in the order in which people probably began to think about them. The 100s, Philosophy and Related Disciplines, deal with man's attempt to understand his experiences. In the current eighteenth edition a place has been made for parapsychology and occultism as well as other new theories of philosophy and psychology. Many things outside himself cannot be explained, so man developed beliefs in invisible forces which brought about the phenomena of nature. The 210 class thus deals with "natural" religion (primitive beliefs, or the more sophisticated religions of the Nordic or Hellenic cultures), 220 is devoted to the Bible, and 230-280 to various phases and activities of Christianity, while other religions and comparative religion are treated in 290. In the 300s we come to man's relations with others, and his attempts to train children to take their place in society. In the 400s we find the sounds and written symbols he made to communicate with his fellows. The 500s record his study of the laws of nature, the phenomena about him which he has ceased to attribute to supernatural causes; and the 600s describe his ways of making use of this knowledge for his own comfort and convenience (or destruction). Art and literature, the 700s and 800s, deal with self-expression and the record of man's interpretation of his experience. The 900s record all the past history of mankind, the discoveries about the surface of the earth and its history before he came to live upon it, as well as the lives of individuals who have contributed to some phase of development of all that has gone before.

The Dewey Decimal Classification has a system of mnemonic devices which makes it possible not only to remember hundreds of number combinations and their meanings, but also to devise new subdivisions almost ad infinitum. The most frequently used of these devices are the "country-language" divisions. For example, in the number 942, 900 means history, 940 European history, 942 English history. Similarly, 943 is German history, 944 French. By taking these same place numbers and adding them to the number for geography, 910, we have 914.2, geography of England; 914.3, of Germany; 914.4, of France. The numbers for the literatures of England, Germany, and France are 820, 830, and 840 respectively, and grammars and dictionaries of these languages are found in 420, 430, and 440.

Naturally, while these details are important to the librarian, all the reader needs to know is that this method exists, if the library he is using is classified by DC. Most libraries display near the entrance an outline of the classification system, or a chart of subject departments, so that the patron may enter with some idea of where he wishes to go.

000	**Generalities**	500	**Pure sciences**
010	Bibliographies & catalogs	510	Mathematics
020	Library & information sciences	520	Astronomy & allied sciences
030	General encyclopedic works	530	Physics
040		540	Chemistry & allied sciences
050	General serial publications	550	Sciences of earth & other worlds
060	General organizations & museums	560	Paleontology
070	Journalism, publishing, newspapers	570	Life sciences
080	General collections	580	Botanical sciences
090	Manuscripts & book rarities	590	Zoological sciences
100	**Philosophy & related disciplines**	**600**	**Technology (Applied sciences)**
110	Metaphysics	610	Medical sciences
120	Knowledge, cause, purpose, man	620	Engineering & allied operations
130	Popular & parapsychology, occultism	630	Agriculture & related
140	Specific philosophical viewpoints	640	Home economics
150	Psychology	650	Managerial services
160	Logic	660	Chemical & related technologies
170	Ethics (Moral philosophy)	670	Manufactures
180	Ancient, medieval, Oriental	680	Miscellaneous manufactures
190	Modern Western philosophy	690	Buildings
200	**Religion**	**700**	**The arts**
210	Natural religion	710	Civic & landscape art
220	Bible	720	Architecture
230	Christian doctrinal theology	730	Plastic arts Sculpture
240	Christian moral & devotional	740	Drawing, decorative & minor arts
250	Local church & religious orders	750	Painting & paintings
260	Social & ecclesiastical theology	760	Graphic arts Prints
270	History & geography of church	770	Photography & photographs
280	Christian denominations & sects	780	Music
290	Other religions & comparative	790	Recreational & performing arts
300	**The social sciences**	**800**	**Literature (Belles-lettres)**
310	Statistics	810	American literature in English
320	Political science	820	English & Anglo-Saxon literatures
330	Economics	830	Literatures of Germanic languages
340	Law	840	French, Provençal, Catalan
350	Public administration	850	Italian, Romanian, Rhaeto-Romanic
360	Social pathology & services	860	Spanish & Portuguese literatures
370	Education	870	Italic languages literatures Latin
380	Commerce	880	Hellenic languages literatures
390	Customs & folklore	890	Literatures of other languages
400	**Language**	**900**	**General geography & history**
410	Linguistics	910	General geography Travel
420	English & Anglo-Saxon languages	920	Biography, genealogy, insignia
430	Germanic languages German	930	General history of ancient world
440	French, Provençal, Catalan	940	General history of Europe
450	Italian, Romanian, Rhaeto-Romanic	950	General history of Asia
460	Spanish & Portuguese languages	960	General history of Africa
470	Italic languages Latin	970	General history of North America
480	Helenic Classical Greek	980	General history of South America
490	Other languages	990	General history of other areas

Reprinted from abridged edition 10 (1971) of *Dewey Decimal Classification*, by permission of Forest Press Division, Lake Placid Club Education Foundation, owner of copyright.

Figure 22: Dewey Decimal Classification
Second Summary—The 100 Divisions

THE LC SYSTEM

The Library of Congress Classification system was developed beginning in 1898, after extensive exploration of a number of schemes, specifically for the National Library. Parts of it have never been expanded (e.g., K — Law, the only further development of which has been KF for laws of the United States). Other parts have been revised several times to keep pace with the growth of knowledge. By 1916 a number of other libraries had adopted LC, including some large university libraries. This fact was mentioned with surprise by the Librarian of Congress in his annual report for that year.

Class Z (Bibliography and Library Science) was the first section to be developed, in 1898, as it was felt that it would be the basis for the arrangement of the rest of the collection. Whether or not this turned out to be true for the average public or university library, class Z devotes Z4-Z8 to the History of books, Z116-Z550 to the Book industries, Z551-Z8999 to Book prices, Booksellers catalogs, and to Bibliographies, subdivided by National, Subject, and Personal. The only parts that seem to us rather amusing are the numbers from Z43 to Z100, which include Penmanship, Typewriting, and Shorthand, which somehow seem rather out of place, until we realize that many catalog cards were handwritten, well into the twentieth century, especially for languages not using the Roman alphabet.

Getting acquainted with a new system of arranging books in libraries is not unlike learning a new language. Perhaps it is better to forget the old one, for the time being at least — the new one will soon seem as logical and easy to understand as the old.

The LC system uses letters of the alphabet as class headings. Two classes of the Library of Congress system have already been mentioned: K and Z. There are a possible 19 letters remaining, omitting I because it might be confused with 1, and O because it might be confused with either zero or Q. W, X, and Y are reserved for further expansion (in fact a full expansion of W has been devised for medical libraries), and X is often used above the class letter to indicate Reference Books, which usually do not circulate. Y could also be confused with V, and so will be reserved as long as possible.

So, in LC we have 21 main classes, in place of the ten in DC. To each of these 21 it would be possible to add 21 subdivisions, by adding a second letter, making a possible 441 subclasses. To date, however, there are only 200 subclasses. There are three letters, E, F, and Z, which have no letter subclasses, and only ten which have ten or more. In no class or subclass may more than four numerals be added to a letter or a combination of two letters, as in Z8999, for Personal bibliographies, or TH9599 for Fire extinction. Furthermore, LC numbers are placed on the books and on the catalog cards (as shown on Figures 13 to 17 in Chapter 4) in such a way that they are not too broad for the space allowed on the catalog card, nor for the label or lettering on the spine of the book. There are some exceptions to this rule, when a book's subject is a very narrow one, but the average reader is unlikely to encounter a five-digit class number except in the Library of Congress itself.

COMPARISON

The DC, as Dewey's system is usually called, has recently been revised (1970-1972) and the current eighteenth edition is more extensive and more complicated than ever. The third and largest volume, the *Relative Index*, reflects additional revision since the first volumes were sent to the printer and hence does not always agree with them. Library cards published in 1972 reflect the enormous expansion of DC numbers, and only the largest university libraries would be likely to follow them to the last number to the right of the decimal point. For example, in adapting the card shown in Figure 23, the University of Colorado Library might (if it is classified according to DC) use the Dewey number as given, provided that statistics on Denver's water supply would be valuable to a student or faculty member working on the problems, ecological or otherwise environmental, of the city of Denver. However, the last nine digits could be eliminated, as the number for Denver is 978883. It must be remembered, also, that the D3A24 of the LC number would also be a part of the call number under Dewey. On the other hand, any technical school of a university or junior college or a tech-

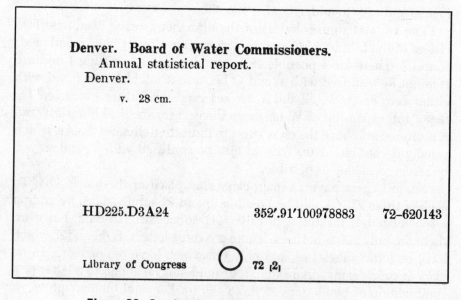

Figure 23: Catalog Card With LC and DC Numbers

nical institute studying the problems of water supply for any city could use this series of statistical reports, and find it more easily if filed by the comparatively simple label

HD225
D3
A24

the LC classification symbol.

As neither the purpose of THE NEW LIBRARY KEY nor its scope permits, or in fact requires, a full discussion of the differences and similarities between the Dewey and Library of Congress classification schemes (this is a matter for advanced students in Library Schools), we shall have to make do with more simplified methods. A table of the two hundred subclasses of LC would cover twice the space given to the hundred items in Second Summary of DC, which appears on page 58.

Professor Howard F. McGaw of Western Washington State College at Bellingham has developed an outline making some mnemonic associations between Dewey and LC classes. It was published in the December 1972 *Wilson Library Bulletin,* with "a few editorial touches." With his permission, I have condensed his original outline and added some qualifying phrases. The results are shown in Figure 24.

Note that, in the older DC system, relatively more space is allotted to philosophy and religion, traditional subjects, whereas in the LC both these subjects are brought together in one class, B, and more space is given to the applied and social sciences, and to history. The two systems also differ in their treatment of geography and anthropology. In LC, these subjects are grouped together in one class, G (for geography), between history (C-F) and the social sciences (H-L). In DC, however, geography is considered a part of history (910) and anthropology is treated separately as a life science and as a social science. Bibliography is another anomaly — DC puts it first (010) with other reference tools, while LC puts it last (Z — the bibliography comes at the end of the book).

ARRANGEMENT OF BOOKS ON THE SHELVES

If one has in mind the way in which the class numbers have been developed, it is not difficult to understand the shelf order of books classified according to the DC. All numbers have three digits to the left of the decimal point. Books are arranged in strict numerical order.

It should always be remembered that this is a decimal system. For example, the numbers given below are some of the subdivisions of 973 (United States History) in their proper order:

973.1	973.31
973.11	973.318
973.15	973.52448
973.2	973.6

000	A	*General material* comes first. Includes encyclopedias, newspapers, periodicals, and yearbooks.
100	B(BA-BJ)	*Philosophy* next: it's a Basic discipline (we still use Ph.D., even when the degree-holder's specialty is not Philosophy).
		BF *Psychology.* A Branch of Philosophy, in both systems. (150)
200	B(BL-BX)	*Religion* shares with Philosophy the earliest theories of the meaning of life. B for Beatitudes.
300	H,J,K,L	*Social sciences.* Very broad under Dewey, but divided into several more narrow fields in LC.
		H *Generalia, Sociology,* and *Economics*
		J *Political science.* J is a crooked letter; some politicians are crooked. (320 and 350)
		K *Law.* Ever hear of a kangaroo court? (340)
		L *Education.* Learning (370)
400	P(PA-PM)	*Language,* one half of Literature (which is 800 in the Dewey system). P for Philology.
500	Q	*Pure science.* Query or Quest.
600	R,S,T,U,V	*Applied sciences,* next to the pure sciences on which they are based.
		R *Medicine.* Rx for a physician's prescription. (610)
		S *Agriculture.* S for Seed. (630)
		T *Technology.* (600)
		U *Military science.* "Uncle Sam wants YOU!"
		V *Naval science.* Includes shipbuilding — V for Vessel.
700	M,N	*Arts.* "The Seven Lively Arts."
		M Music. (780)
		N FiNe Arts. (the other 700s)
800	P(PN-PZ)	*Literature* is doubly effective language (400 in the Dewey system).
		P for Prose and Poetry. (See also 400, P for Philology.)
		PR (820) English literature came first, but
		PS (810) American literature takes precedence in the DC.
900	C,D,E,F	*History.* Think of 900, at the end of the Dewey system, as "to the end of time"; C through F as the "Chronicle of Father Time."
910		G *Geography.*

Figure 24: Mnemonic Guide to LC and DC Systems

In very small libraries, the classification number (on the left of the decimal) is all that is lettered on the books, so the alphabetical arrangement by author requires that one read the authors' names. Sometimes the publisher has not printed the author's name on the spine of a book; then the library must do so. Somewhat larger collections provide for alphabetical arrangement by adding merely the first letter of the author's name below the classification number. Thus books in American history by both Chapman and Cheney would be marked

973

C

For larger collections, where there might be thirty or forty books in 973 by people whose names begin with C, a more accurate system is used, and what is known as a Cutter number is placed below the class number to form a complete call number. The Cutter number is taken from an ingenious table invented by C. A. Cutter (another pioneer in library science), in which figures are arranged after each initial letter so that the names come alphabetically. For example, Chapman is represented by C37 and Cheney by C42. If more than one book by Chapman is classified in the same number, either a third digit or a small letter is added. With the combination of Dewey class numbers and Cutter numbers, the following row of call numbers represents a small shelf of books on American history. Three are by Chapman.

973	973	973	973	973	973	973.1	973.2
B22	C37	C375	C375a	C38	D16	A14	A12

We have said that fiction is arranged on the shelves alphabetically according to the authors' last names. This may leave us with large numbers of books by a single author, or by several authors with the same last name, to be placed in order. The next step is to place the books alphabetically by title. Thus *Gold,* by Stewart Edward White, *The Once and Future King,* by T. H. White, and *The Unwilling Vestal,* by Edward Lucas White, would stand in the order given. If a library wishes to differentiate among these three Whites, it must assign Cutter numbers to fiction as well as to non-fiction, for observation will show that the author's first names or initials almost never appear on the binding of a book.

One other variation appears in the arrangement of books. Obviously it is the person written about who is important in biography, not the author. But many libraries use merely the letter B as the class number for lives of individuals. Hence, in order to keep together all lives of Lincoln, for instance, we give the Cutter number for Lincoln first, following it by another Cutter number for the author of the work, e.g.,

B
L7S22

for Carl Sandburg's *Abraham Lincoln.*

In the LC system, books are arranged first according to the class letter, alphabetically, and then in strict numerical order by the number following the class letter. For example, these LC numbers are in the proper order:

P90
P101
PA 3160
PE 101
PR 911
PR 2989

Cutter numbers are always added to LC designations, as they are to DC numbers.

Chapter 6

WRITING
A RESEARCH PAPER

MOST READERS OF THE NEW LIBRARY KEY are college students, graduate
or undergraduate, and, if they have needed some help in understanding
the unfamiliar Library of Congress classification system as compared
to the familiar Dewey Decimal system, we may assume that they are
already library users. We may also assume that they are not unfamiliar
with dictionaries and encyclopedias. Hence it seems reasonable to di-
gress at this point from discussion of the materials to be found in libraries
and devote the next few pages to the methods and forms of research
necessary to prepare a report, whether oral or written; for much of the
serious and systematic use of college libraries is directed toward that
end.

Whether the report being prepared is a short source theme, a term
paper, or a doctoral dissertation, a systematic and logical method of
search, with accurate techniques of recording it, is essential if the student is to avoid wasting time, effort, and patience. The greater part
of this book is concerned with *finding* information in libraries; this
chapter is concerned with *using* it.

THE PRELIMINARY SEARCH

As soon as a report has been assigned, or a subject tentatively chosen,
the student begins to hunt for materials which will help him. The freshman who has been told to report orally on molybdenum will begin with
the index of his textbook, and if that fails him will go to a dictionary to
find out what molybdenum is, then to encyclopedias, and from there to
numerous sources suggested by what he has already found and by the
librarian whose help he has enlisted. But at the very beginning he has
already three kinds of sources: textbook, dictionary, encyclopedia —
and possibly other books listed in the latter. All of these, including the
books listed in the encyclopedia, should be noted fully, at once, so that
the student will not have to waste time later looking them up again.

The record of search for molybdenum begins with the textbook
and/or the dictionary, then goes on to encyclopedias, other books, pamphlets, magazine articles. But what is the best form for this record to
take? First, it should give *full bibliographic detail*. This phrase means
that the books and parts of books or articles should be described so

64

exactly that anyone could find the same information without difficulty. For such a description we must have the author and title of the book or article, its publisher and date of publication, and edition, if possible, and the exact page or pages on which the information was found. We have all been annoyed by the author who says, "Was it not Thoreau who said . . . ?" or, "Smith's discussion of this topic states . . . ." As likely as not, it was not Thoreau, but Emerson, or Elbert Hubbard, and probably he was misquoted. As for Smith, there are a good many people named Smith, more than one of whom may have written on this subject. Such vagueness may be permissible in informal writing, though not desirable, but a student has no license to employ it.

One further suggestion. Every source should be noted on a separate card. Three inches by five inches is a handy size which can be carried in the pocket or handbag. Odd slips of paper, margins of class notes, the other side of a shopping list are not recommended. Neither is it wise to use large sheets of paper, noting a dozen or more sources as found. They will have to be transferred to cards eventually so that they can be arranged alphabetically for constant checking, rearranged in the order in which they will be used in preparing the report, then rearranged again for listing in the bibliography. This is the first step in saving time.

The search for materal for a brief oral report will not be long, but it will include several encyclopedia references, a book or two discovered by searching the indexes of books on inorganic chemistry or metallurgy, as well as books suggested in the encyclopedias. The librarian will find some pamphlets on new uses of molybdenum, and the encyclopedia yearbooks yield some interesting discoveries also, which suggest that there will be articles in scientific journals. The freshman may not go so far, but a graduate student assigned the same topic will go much further. Nevertheless he will begin at the very beginning with the definition of the term, just as the freshman does.

No matter how extensive the search, the forms used to record it are substantially the same. These always include four items:

1. The author or authors of the book or article, when given or available.

   Examination of encyclopedias will show the student that if the author's name does not follow an article, a symbol representing his name refers the reader to a list of authors either at the beginning of the volume or in the first volume of the set. Some articles are prepared by editors, but their names are also available in Volume I.

2. The title of the book or article.

   Again, in an encyclopedia, the title of the article is of course the heading under which it is listed.

3. Facts of publication.
   a. For a book: the place of publication, name of publisher, latest copyright date.[1]
   b. For an encyclopedia article: the title of the set; edition, if named; place of publication; name of publisher; and date.
   c. For an article in a periodical: the title and date of the issue — month and day (if given) as well as year.[2]

4. The volume and pages where the information was found.

As the student examines each book or article, he finds more books or articles mentioned and records those which seem to be potentially useful, each on a separate card. Some of these, on examination, may yield still more references. But a warning must be given here: The bibliography in each book naturally lists only books already published when it was being written. These in turn refer to still older books. For a historical study the older books may be very useful. For a topic of current interest, or for scientific and technical subjects, such references may be not only useless but often downright misleading. The student should hunt for more recent information, by means of periodical indexes, current bibliographies, and pamphlets, as already suggested. The chapters on reference books may suggest some sources, but again, the help of one's teachers and librarians should be sought.

The order of items and punctuation on the sample bibliographic card (see Figure 25) follows library cataloging practice for a book with many authors. For the average book, the catalog entry may be followed. It is logical, in a form universally understood, and is considered satisfactory for bibliographies by many teachers. Some colleges and universities have developed their own approved forms, made available to students in style manuals. One of the most exacting and complete, and probably the most widely used, is the *Manual of Style* of the University of Chicago Press, which requires all its publications, including doctoral dissertations, to conform to its rules. A number of handbooks based upon it have been written for the guidance of beginners in research. A brief list of these can be found in Appendix A.

TAKING NOTES

Collecting material for a research paper or report cannot be done one step at a time. While the student will make some of the cards for his working bibliography without seeing the books cited (items found in bibliographies in other books, articles listed in periodical indexes,

---

[1] See discussion of copyright page in Chapter 3, p. 31.
[2] For an alternative form of working bibliography card for a magazine article, see suggestions under Using Indexes in Chapter 9, p. 108-14.

McGraw-Hill Encyclopedia of Science
  and Technology
N.Y., McGraw-Hill, 1971.   vol. 8, p. 666

Everyday Uses of Molybdenum, by
J. I. Briggs. 1966.

Figure 25: Sample Bibliographic Card

books listed in card catalogs but not examined at once), he will examine other books as found, and take notes on their contents at once, to avoid wasting time getting the book again. The definitions of molybdenum are excellent examples. As soon as they are found, they should be copied verbatim, for they include the symbol, atomic number, atomic weight, and specific gravity of this substance. The dictionary and encyclopedia may give different details, and other sources will yield longer passages, which the student will not feel called upon to copy, but to treat in one of the ways to be discussed shortly. Notes on the contents of material likely to contribute to his report should be made on larger cards than those used for the working bibliography. Four inches by six inches is a good size, for it is not too large to carry in a small notebook and not too small to hold rather extensive notes. The upper left-hand corner should be used for a tentative subject heading, in pencil. The upper right should give briefly the author and title of the book or article. More is not necessary, for the full bibliographic detail is on the bibliography card. The rest of the card may be devoted to notes. If a book contributes to several phases of the subject, several cards should be used for the notes. This is not wasteful, but a saving of time and energy. (See Figure 26 on page 68, below.)

The method to be used in taking notes depends both on the use to be made of them and on the way in which the original material was written. It has already been suggested that dictionary definitions should be copied verbatim. There will be other bits of information where the

Molybdenum - description   Mc-Graw-Hill Encyc.
                                          vol. 8, p. 662-3

Symbol Mo   Density   10.22 g/cm³
Color   silvery gray   Melts at 2610° C
Atomic no. 42   Boils at 5560°C
Atomic wt. 95.95   Vaporizes at
Group VI-B   117.4 kcal/mol

Molybdenum - uses   McGraw-Hill Encyc.
                           vol. 8 p. 663-4
85% of the Mo produced today is used
for iron-base alloys (steel, cast
iron, & some super alloys).
Improves strength & corrosion
resistance; contributes to weldability

Figure 26: Sample Note Cards

original words of the source carry authority and should be used. There
will be times when the author has said something so much better than
anyone else can say it that his own words should be used. But most of
the notes taken in preparation for papers and reports should be in
shorter and more condensed form. However, whether the author's
words are quoted or paraphrased, full credit for the use of his ideas

and knowledge must be given in footnotes. This matter is discussed more fully on page 70.

Good notes are based upon careful and thoughtful reading. This does not necessarily mean that the material must be read slowly, or even word for word. A quick examination of factual writing will show that the author has used one or more of several techniques. One is the method of the news story: the most important information is in the first paragraph, and the rest of the article expands, giving more details. This method is also frequently used in encyclopedias, especially those intended for children, where the basic facts are given first, in simple language, and the more difficult material, in increasingly technical or specific terminology, follows. It is necessary to read only as far as one's interests or needs require.

Another method, one which has made generations of high school seniors miserable, is the one used by Edmund Burke in his well-known "Speech on Conciliation With the Colonies," a method by which every sentence and every paragraph is a part of a complicated argument which can be reduced to a complicated outline. This method is suited to argumentation rather than to simple exposition, but it can be found in scientific works where a theory is being propounded or analyzed.

A third is the method used in most expository writing: each paragraph develops a single idea, and this idea is usually to be found in either the first or the last sentence of the paragraph. Students will recognize this as the "topic sentence" mentioned in textbooks of English composition. This type of paragraph structure is the one most frequently encountered in factual matter. The reader soon learns to observe whether an author habitually begins his paragraphs with his important idea, or ends with it. If the author is attempting to instruct, as in this manual, the first is apt to be the topic sentence. If he wishes to stimulate or amuse, he is more apt to lead up to his flash of wit or startling idea by devious ways and save the punch line for the end.

A card on which the student has taken down the main idea of each paragraph will be sufficient to remind him of the full contents of an article or chapter, so that he will know whether or not he will need to go back to it for more details. Normally, if his grasp of the subject is good enough, this preliminary note taking will be all that is necessary.

Much of this advice on taking notes from printed matter may be applied to lecture notes as well. A carefully prepared lecture frequently begins with the major points to be covered, in much the same way that a news item does. The alert student soon finds that a single page of notes will give him as good an idea of the contents of a lecture as ten pages on which another student has tried, and failed, to take down every word.

SUMMARY OF THE FIRST STEPS

The preparations for writing a research paper begin with two steps: (1) collecting source material and taking down a bibliographic description of each source; (2) examining the source material and taking notes on its contents. The preliminary search is not selective; one notes every item found which seems to bear on the subject, and examines it. If this examination shows that the item has no value for the paper, the 3" × 5" card should be placed in a temporary Reject File to remind the student that it has already been examined and found wanting. In an extensive search, one may find the same book listed in several bibliographies, and each must be checked against the working bibliography to avoid duplication.

Notes of the contents of acceptable material are made on 4" × 6" cards, giving tentative subject headings in pencil at the upper left, and brief author and title at the upper right. The cards are filed alphabetically under these subjects for future use. When all the material has been read and all notes taken, these subject cards can be rearranged according to the outline of the paper, and there remains only the task of writing, incorporating the information and quotations according to plan. This is not, of course, to be dismissed as an easy task, but if the preliminary work is well organized, it is far easier than it would be otherwise.

FOOTNOTES AND BIBLIOGRAPHY

At the beginning of this chapter the student was advised to record accurately the author, title, publisher, date, and edition of books examined and the pages on which information was found. There are two reasons why this record is necessary. The first is practical: One frequently finds it necessary to go back to at least a few of his sources for more information, more details, or a comparison of two or more items which seem to conflict or to contradict each other. Exact references make this process quick and easy.

But even more important is the necessity of giving credit to one's source of information. The student will have observed that almost every book or magazine article carries a statement showing the date and ownership of copyright. This term means exactly what it says: The right to copy the contents belongs to the copyright holder. This may be the author or his heirs, the publisher, or the institution by which the author is employed. Infringement of copyright by publishing copies of a book, article, or poem without permission is punishable by law. Infringement by using portions of another's work without referring to the source may result in a very awkward situation, if not actually in a lawsuit.

The necessity of giving credit for one's sources of information is both a matter of ethics and a matter of common sense, whether or not one has any claim to being an authority on the subject of his study. Textbooks are full of footnotes and bibliographic references to sources of bits of information, theories, and opinions. The historian, biographer, explorer, inventor, or scientific investigator bases his research on the work of many forerunners, and by giving them credit for their contributions to his knowledge establishes his own reputation for reliability and scholarship. The college student similarly builds up his own reputation in the eyes of his teachers by painstaking accuracy and meticulous honesty. It is better to have too many footnotes than not enough.

But some judgment should be displayed in making unverified statements which may be assumed to be common knowledge or which may be verified by observation. The descriptive comments on various encyclopedias and dictionaries given in Chapters 7 and 8 are based on frequent use of these works, and may be checked by the interested reader. The principles for forming footnotes and bibliographic entries which follow are the common property of anyone who reads and observes. Similarly, items of information which have been taught us all in school, and may be checked in every encyclopedia or dictionary require no footnote. The sum of two and two, the date of the bombing of Pearl Harbor, or the names of the planets in our solar system are equally bits of universal knowledge.

The author who leans over backward to give his authorities and to clarify his statements has been cleverly parodied by Frank Sullivan in "A Garland of Ibids for Van Wyck Brooks" which appeared in the *New Yorker*, April 19, 1941 (vol. 17, p. 15), as a review of Brooks's *New England: Indian Summer*. This piece was reprinted in *A Subtreasury of American Humor*[3] and in later collections.

Bibliographic Forms

There are a number of excellent manuals which give examples of forms to be used in compiling bibliographies, most of them based on the style manual of the University of Chicago Press (see Appendix A). Much can be learned about the forms of footnotes and bibliographic entries by studying examples of each in textbooks and treatises. Moreover, many college departments have established their own prescribed style for students to follow in research papers. But as a brief introduction to the subject a few basic principles and forms will be presented here, for the beginner.

---

[3] E. B. White and K. S. A. White, eds. *A Subtreasury of American Humor*. New York, Coward-McCann, 1941. p. 263-266.

Earlier in the chapter the student was advised to note certain items descriptive of the books or articles he found useful for his research paper. These were:

1. Author's full name.
2. Full title of the book or article, including subtitle and statement of edition.
3. Facts of publication, i.e., place of publication, name of publisher and date (copyright date of edition used).
4. Number of volumes or pages.

In a bibliography, these items are given in the above order, with the author's name reversed, so that books can more easily be arranged alphabetically by last names. According to the conventions of the University of Chicago Press, the place of publication is separated by a colon from the name of the publisher, but many publishers use a comma there, conforming with practice in library catalogs. The comma is used in the examples given in this manual. The following imaginary items show:

1. A book.

Smith, John Henry. *A History of Rome.* New York, Coliseum Press, 1973. 2 vols.

2. A magazine article by the same author.

Smith, John Henry. "The Romans Do." *Roman Quarterly,* vol. 27, p. 93-129. Spring, 1967.

It should be noted that in a typewritten manuscript titles of books and periodicals are underlined, while titles of articles or chapters are placed in quotation marks.

Footnotes

If a footnote refers to a book as a whole, it will give exactly the same information as the bibliographic entry, except that the author's name will appear in direct order, as:

John Henry Smith. *A History of Rome.* New York, Coliseum Press, 1973. 2 vols.

When the footnote refers to specific pages in the book, and it is fully described in the bibliography, the footnote may omit facts of publication, and give merely:

John Henry Smith. *A History of Rome.* vol. 1, p. 24.

There are several conventional methods of shortening footnotes when the same book or article is mentioned frequently. Let us suppose that for a paper on the Romans the student has used these two imaginary sources by Smith, and one each by Jones and Richardson. A group of footnotes, perhaps all on one page, perhaps on several pages, might appear as follows:

[1] J. H. Smith. *A History of Rome.* vol. 2, p. 67-69.
[2] *Ibid.*
[3] James Jones. *Roman Ruins.* p. 24.
[4] J. H. Smith. *op. cit.* vol. 1, p. 393.
[5] James Jones. *loc. cit.*
[6] Robert Richardson. *When in Rome.* chap. 2 *passim.*
[7] J. H. Smith. "The Romans Do." *Roman Quarterly*, vol. 27, p. 97. Spring, 1967.
[8] *Ibid.* p. 99.

Assuming that all these references are fully described in the bibliography, each has been given in the shortest possible form here. Note 7, a periodical reference, cannot be abbreviated when it first appears as a footnote.

It will be observed that the term *ibid.* has been used in notes 2 and 8. This is an abbreviation for the Latin word *ibidem* meaning "in the same place." But it has different meanings, nevertheless, in these two notes. In note 2 *ibid.* refers to vol. 2, p. 67-69 of Smith's *A History of Rome.* In note 8 it refers to Smith's article in the *Roman Quarterly.* *Ibid.* always refers to the title last mentioned, though several pages may have elapsed between the two footnotes. (The writer once leafed back through more than 30 pages to find the book referred to by an *ibid.* But this is carrying things too far. If a number of pages intervene, it is more courteous to the reader to repeat the reference.)

In note 4 we used the abbreviation *op. cit.* This means *opere citato,* or "in the work mentioned," and the footnote refers in this case to a page in Smith's book. This abbreviation cannot be used again for Smith after his second title has been cited, for the reader would not know which of his works was meant.

Note 5 uses the abbreviation *loc. cit.* for *loco citato,* or "in the place mentioned." It refers the reader to the same page by Jones which was mentioned before. *Ibid.* after Jones's name would have meant the same thing, but *ibid.* alone could not be used here, because another reference to Smith had intervened.

In note 6 the term *passim* has been used. This means "here and there" or "throughout," and signifies that the whole of Chapter 2 is the basis for the information used. Other abbreviations referring to a long section are *ff,* for "following," or *sqq., et sqq., seqq., et seqq.,* also meaning "following." Any of these may be used after a page number to indicate a passage covering several pages. (See Abbreviations and Bibliographic Terms, page 8.)

The List of Sources

The basic forms for bibliographic entries describing books and periodicals are given on page 72. These may be modified in many ways to cover special cases. For example, the form used for books may be used for pamphlets, while an article in an encyclopedia may be described in the same way as a magazine article. For other variations the student should consult his instructor or a librarian for a list of style manuals. One of the briefest and clearest presentations of bibliographic form is to be found in "Appendix B: Documentary Forms" of Williams and Stevenson's *Research Manual.*[4] Others are listed in Appendix A of the present work, pages 230-33.

When the paper is written, and the Bibliography or List of Sources is to be compiled, several decisions must be made.

A. Should a bibliography be appended, or will the footnotes be sufficient?

B. How many of the items in the working bibliography should be included?

C. How should the items be arranged?

Let us consider these in order.

A. Should a bibliography be appended?

If the student has used very few sources, and has made full reference to all of them in footnotes, he may dispense with a final listing of sources, with the approval of his instructor. But if he has used sources to which he has not referred directly, but which have been part of his background of information, a List of Sources should appear, listing uncited sources along with those mentioned in footnotes. (See category 2 under B, below.) Most college teachers require source lists so that students may acquire the habit of making them.

B. How many items in the working bibliography should be included in the final list?

This decision rests on the purpose of the list. The working bibliography probably included items in three categories: (1) the sources which were most pertinent to the subject under consideration and which were cited in footnotes; (2) works which have general bearing on the subject, were read or examined by the student, but not specifically cited in the paper, though they contributed to his background information and would prove useful to other researchers in the field; (3) works which seemed to be likely sources of information, but on examination

---

[4] C. B. Williams and A. H. Stevenson. *Research Manual for College Studies and Papers,* 3d ed. rev. by C. B. Williams. New York, Harper & Row, 1963.

proved to be irrelevant or even erroneous. All items in category 1 belong in the final bibliography. Items in category 2 may be omitted from the bibliography if the student is instructed to mention only the works actually cited in footnotes; but if they have contributed substantially to his paper, he will wish to mention them either in a separate list or in his preface. Category 3 would be omitted from an elementary treatment, but the advanced student, research worker, historian, etc., would be apt to make a separate annotated list, indicating their inadequacy for his study or suggesting where they might prove useful.

C. How should the bibliography items be arranged?

Assuming that the list of sources included books, articles in periodicals and encyclopedias, and pamphlets, the decision as to arrangement rests largely on the length of the list. Ten or a dozen items may be listed alphabetically by author (or title, in the case of anonymous articles), with books and articles interfiled. As the list becomes longer, and as the number of periodical articles increases, it seems more reasonable to separate the items by form.[5] This is particularly true when the sources include newspaper articles, manuscripts, diaries, or letters, documents and records, such as are mentioned under Bibliography in Chapter 3, The Book.

SUMMARY

Footnotes and a bibliography are necessary in any paper based on facts and opinions not entirely derived from the writer's experience. They give authority to the writer, and also indicate possible sources of any errors. Both courtesy and honesty require them. Consistency of form makes them more accurate and easier to use.

---

[5] See last paragraph in the section Using Indexes (Chapter 9, p. 113-14) for further comment on arrangement of magazine articles.

Chapter 7

The First Places to Look for Information
ENCYCLOPEDIAS

THE REFERENCE DEPARTMENT and the Reference Librarian were mentioned more than once in the first two chapters, as they will be in chapters to come. The student will visit the one and consult the other many times during his college career and thereafter. But one of the purposes of this book is to make him partially independent, able to begin his search for information intelligently and ask for help intelligently also.

When asking questions, the most important thing to remember is: Be specific. The person who says "Where are your science books?" is apt to be asked "Did you have anything special in mind?" Some people appear to think of books as vast general compendiums in which all phases of a subject are treated. They try to place the bit of knowledge desired in the broadest area to which it may belong. By a series of questions, the librarian may eventually discover that the person who asked for science wanted to know how the tree toad sings, or the one who asked for planets wanted myths about Jupiter and Venus.

A second rule: Be accurate. An assignment imperfectly heard and incorrectly spelled may prove such a mystery that only psychic powers (or long experience) can decipher it, or such a boner that it becomes a legend. The student who asked for a play by Aristotle called *The Three Unities* and the one who wanted *The Importance of Lady Windermere's Fan Being Earnest* are cases in point.

Third: Help yourself. It is not reasonable for a college student to exepct the librarians to find book listings in the catalog, write down the call numbers, get the books, look in their indexes, turn to the proper pages — or to look up a word in a dictionary or an entry in an encyclopedia. Granted that not all encyclopedias are easy to use, or that one may have trouble finding the right subject entry, one should still make the effort. No librarian will refuse to help, but there is great satisfaction in helping oneself.

As the student progresses and learns more about how a library works, he will find himself more self-reliant and better able to find things without help. A good way to begin is to become acquainted with the most useful general reference books, the dictionaries and encyclopedias. To many people, the terms *encyclopedia* and *reference book* are synonymous. A few would add *dictionary* and *atlas*, and, for many, these would suffice. For the student, they serve merely as the first steps on the path of knowledge. But, because of their broad coverage, encyclopedias and dictionaries are the first sources of information to be explored. Two other characteristics add to their importance: brevity and alphabetical arrangement.

At this point some definition of terms is needed. What is a dictionary? By derivation, it is a place for words. According to present-day practice, this "place" may vary from pocket size to twelve large volumes. It may be confined to one-word definitions (synonyms) or give the history of each word from its first appearance to the present. It may, of course, give equivalent words in two or more languages. It may have such special features as pronunciation and examples of usage, or be confined to terms in a small area of knowledge, as chemistry, medicine, aviation, dialect, or slang. In recent years there have also been published some good dictionaries of abbreviations, acronyms (words made out of the initial letters of the words in a name of an organization, as *UNESCO, WAC, SEATO*), clichés (terms to be avoided!), rhymes, and usage. Some of these will be mentioned in Chapter 8.

One characteristic which may be assumed of all dictionaries is that the arrangement will be alphabetical. From this convention has arisen another meaning for the word *dictionary*: that is, an alphabetically arranged collection of brief items of information in a special area, e.g., biography, history, art, dates, etc. These are discussed in the chapters devoted to these areas of knowledge.

What is an encyclopedia? By derivation, a complete circle of learning; in practice, a compendium of knowledge, in all fields of learning, again usually alphabetical in arrangement, comparatively brief in treatment. There is some similarity in these definitions, and some confusion in the use of these two terms. The use of *dictionary* as mentioned above, in a single field of knowledge, makes it almost synonymous with *cyclopedia*, a word generally used in titles of works limited to a single field, e.g., *New Century Cyclopedia of Names*. (Note, however, that *encyclopedia* and *cyclopedia* are synonymous.)

Let us, for the present, confine our use of *dictionary* to mean a book about words. It is concerned primarily with words as operatives in speaking and writing, that is, as verbs, adjectives, names of things, abstract or concrete. It gives as much information as possible about these words: how they are spelled and pronounced, ways in which they are used, how they were derived from words of other languages, or from words formerly used in our language. All the so-called parts of speech in a language are listed in a dictionary.

An encyclopedia is concerned only with nouns or substantive phrases. Some are abstract nouns like philosophy, ethics, music. More are con-

crete, like names of insects, animals, musical instruments. Many more
are proper names, i.e., people and places, or events and ideas connected
with them, like Taft-Hartley Act, Monroe Doctrine, Elizabethan Era,
Franco-Prussian War.

But there is a type of dictionary, very common in English (and
existing in other languages as well), which is encyclopedic in scope.
That is, it includes not only the operative words of the language and
the ordinary abstract and concrete nouns, but also the proper nouns
most often used — places: cities, countries, rivers, lakes; people: presidents, sopranos, writers, scientists; and events: wars, battles, treaties.
It is important to remember, then, that encyclopedic information is
frequently found in a dictionary, but linguistic information about individual words will not be found in an encyclopedia.

After this brief introduction to these two major forms of books of
general information, we shall give our attention to encyclopedias first
and proceed to dictionaries later, because general encyclopedias are
comparatively few in number, even when one includes those published
outside the United States and in languages other than English.

USING ENCYCLOPEDIAS

Encyclopedias present more problems than one might suppose from
their alphabetical arrangement. Simplicity is not guaranteed by the
alphabet. Naturally, in English, all words beginning with M precede
words beginning with N, but what about such names as Macadam,
MacAdam, and McAdam? Or New England and Newark; or Panama
and Pan American Union?

If we examine a telephone directory, which is the alphabetical listing most frequently used by the greatest number of people, we see that
words beginning with Mac are filed together whether the letter following the c is a capital or lower case. That is, MacAdam, John would precede Macadam, Peter. But the telephone book places the Mc's later,
with see also references back and forth. Library usage, however, files
Mc as if it were spelled Mac, for the simple reason that they sound the
same, and one often cannot remember which way the name to be found
is spelled. (One often finds lists in which other names are interfiled
according to sound, as Abbot — Abbott, Green — Greene, Curtis —
Curtiss.) Encyclopedias are apt to follow library usage with respect to
the Mac's.

But in the case of New England and Newark, there are two schools
of thought. Most library catalogs will place New England first, arguing
that New is a complete word, and all phrases beginning with New precede words or phrases in which New is only the first syllable of the first
word. The Encyclopedia Americana follows this reasoning.

A simple way to remember this method is to think of it as "short before long," or, if you consider the space between words as "nothing," it is "nothing before something."

Other encyclopedias disregard the space between *New* and *England* and place the single word *Newark* before the compound *New England*.

SAMPLES OF FILING ORDER IN TWO ENCYCLOPEDIAS

Encyclopedia Americana	*Collier's Encyclopedia*
New England	Newark
New Guinea	New England
New Jersey	Newfoundland
New Mexico	New Guinea
New Zealand	New Jersey
Newark	Newman, John Henry
Newfoundland	Newmarket
Newman, John Henry	New Mexico
Newmarket	New Zealand

The same problem affects the filing of *Panama,* which precedes *Pan American Union* in some encyclopedias and follows it in others. It is not necessary to remember which method any particular encyclopedia follows — this author has never found it possible to do so — but one should be aware of the fact that both methods are used, and let it become automatic to observe which is characteristic of the volume he is using at the moment. Failure to do so may mean failure to find an article several pages farther along.

LENGTH OF ARTICLES

The other major difficulty in using an encyclopedia arises from the editorial policy as to length of articles. Some sets are characterized by long monographic articles which survey broad subject areas from many angles, notably those on individual countries in the *Encyclopaedia Britannica.* Here, for example, Napoleon's reign is included in a long article on the history of France, with a page and a half under the subhead The First Empire. In addition there is a long article in the N volume, under Napoleon I. But on consulting the index volume we find under Napoleon I about seventy-five references, ending with: "*see also* Napoleonic Campaigns, French Revolutionary Wars." Thus we see that all aspects of his career can be discovered only through the entries in the index.

Encyclopedias, if well edited, are not only fully indexed, but also give references in the text to other articles where additional material may be found. These references usually come at the end of the articles, though some are indicated throughout the text by *q.v.*, which stands for the Latin expression *quod vide* (which see). Still more value is given to an article if it is followed by a brief bibliography, listing books or articles where the reader may find more extensive treatment of the subject. Such bibliographies are found in many articles in the major sets, and in the *Columbia Encyclopedia. Collier's* has placed all its bibliographies in the last volume, along with the Index.

WHAT NOT TO EXPECT OF AN ENCYCLOPEDIA

It has already been pointed out (see page 77) that an encyclopedia is concerned only with discussion of nouns and substantive phrases. But there are limitations too on the number and types of articles. The sets intended primarily for children and young people attempt to give facts, briefly and simply, about things children are interested in, or things their school assignments require them to learn. Thus they will treat with some detail the early Spanish explorers in the Americas, but will mention only briefly the Spanish Civil War in the twentieth century. Articles on astronomy will pay more attention to descriptions of our sun and moon than to the mathematical means and extrapolation by which the existence and position of a new planet have been calculated.

Editorial boards have special interests or theories about what an encyclopedia is for. *Collier's*, for instance, tries to fill the needs of the average American, not the specialist or the scholar. Hence it has excellent articles on popular subjects such as sports. The *Americana* has a reputation for excellence in science. The *Britannica* leans towards the humanities and history, especially in the editions up to and including the eleventh, published in 1911. Hence a library, even a small one, tries to have several different sets, and keeps the old *Britannica* for its fine scholarly articles on philosophy, history, Greek art, etc., but uses the very latest edition for information on physics, anthropology, or ecology.

This brings us to the encyclopedia's greatest limitation. It can never be completely up to date. It can seldom have information on events or discoveries of the year preceding its publication. The process of getting out a completely new edition requires several years, during which new material supersedes old almost before it can be written. For purposes of comparison, let us consider the process by which any book is produced — say a historical novel. The author may well spend five years or more collecting material and writing his book. The manuscript then goes through the hands of one or more readers, thence to an editor, probably back to the author for cutting, revision, or some rewriting. Then it is set up in type; galley proofs are run off, read for errors, corrected; second galley proofs are read; then page proofs. After final printing, the book is folded, sewed, cut, bound, fitted with a dust jacket, delivered to jobbers and booksellers, and eventually reaches the individuals and libraries that purchase it. Along with these mechanical operations are the activities connected with advertising and selling it. The entire production process after the final revision of the manuscript may well require a full year.

Publishing an encyclopedia is complicated far beyond the wildest nightmares of the fiction editor. The decisions as to policies such as those mentioned above are made by a board of editors. While no doubt more sound than if one man were responsible, the process of reaching agreement is lengthened in direct ratio to the number of people involved. The subjects to be covered are next divided among the editors, who must decide what articles are to be written, and by whom. Perhaps the man best qualified to write an article is not available, so another must be found and followed up until the article is in the editor's hands. Finding the best people to write the articles and getting them written is probably the most difficult of the encyclopedist's tasks. Getting the articles in order, choosing and inserting illustrations, securing permission to publish statistical tables and photographs, decisions as to quality of paper and color of binding, number and size of volumes — all the time adding new information and removing that which it replaces and having the index made — all of this not only requires patience and virtual omniscience, but also takes a great deal of time.

The publishers have developed two methods of dealing with this problem of time. One is the system of publishing yearbooks to supplement the set, sometimes available to purchasers at a special price for eight or ten years. These yearbooks give briefly the important events and discoveries of the previous year. The other is the principle of continuous revision, by which new material is collected to be included in later editions. Several publishers issue a new edition each year, but only a small proportion of the articles has been revised in each edition. According to a former editor of the *Encyclopaedia Britannica*, only about 20 percent of the articles are subject to revision as frequently as every ten years. This revision may mean simply inserting the figures from the latest census, adding a death date to an article on a prominent person, or actually rewriting an article completely if new facts require it. Some editors try to fit revised articles into the same space occupied by the portion they replace, so that only one or two pages need be set up in type anew. Others, finding that the importance of a subject has grown, will insert extra pages in order to give it full treatment, numbering them, for example, 253a, 253b, etc. Sometimes an entirely new article, on a subject not previously covered, will be inserted on paper of equal quality but of a contrasting color, to call attention to the fact that this is information on a subject not previously included. The presence of "a, b, c, d" pages and pages of different colors will be evidence of recent revision, but their absence does not imply that no revision has taken place.

This explanation of the methods of revision shows that while no encyclopedia is ever completely up to date, neither is one which follows these procedures ever completely obsolete. The student who sees in the reference department of his library one new encyclopedia and several other sets somewhat more worn will know that the library is following a policy of spaced purchases in order to provide the most recent material available within budgetary limits.

But it can be seen that while encyclopedias are useful and important reference tools, they cannot be expected to give us all the facts we need. Other sources of information must be consulted. On the other hand, these limitations should not cause us to ignore them entirely. Children often go to a library and say that "Teacher said not to use the encyclopedia" and some college professors say it, too. But there are times when the encyclopedia gives the best information available in that library, or the best available in English, or the best at the reader's level of reading and comprehension.

Finally, both dictionary and encyclopedia should be consulted for definition of terms. Sometimes one will be curious about a thing without knowing enough about it to know what field of learning it belongs to. A dictionary will probably define it briefly, though perhaps, to us, incomprehensibly, because we are not acquainted with the field of knowledge to which it belongs. But the dictionary will tell what that field is, and we can go from there to an encyclopedia for further explanation. If our curiosity is not yet satisfied, we know now from the fuller treatment given in the encyclopedia what kind of book will give still more information, and from the bibliography, we have a number of references to specific books.

ENCYCLOPEDIAS IN ENGLISH
One-Volume Works

There is only one reasonably useful one-volume encyclopedia[1]:

Columbia Encyclopedia. 3d ed. rev. and enl. William Bridgewater and Seymour Kurtz, eds. New York, Columbia University Press, © 1963. illus., maps. Later printings include 4-year supplements (e.g., 1963-67).

> Originally published without illustrations, many of which were issued as a supplement to the 1950 edition in 1956. This large volume is especially useful for identification of people and places possibly omitted from larger works in recent editions.

---

[1] A number of the compilers of lists of encyclopedias — see Appendix C — also mention the *Lincoln Library* as a useful home reference tool. It is not included here, because, while it claims to have material not available elsewhere and to be "frequently reprinted with revisions," it also has much material not updated since its first publication in 1924.

Multi-Volume Sets

Those listed here fall into two classes, differentiated partly by cost, partly by the users for whom they are intended. Many other sets are available, some of which have some measure of reliability, while others are merely reprints of articles from older works no longer under copyright, with some updating of statistics. There are many ways by which an individual who plans to invest in an encyclopedia may get advice. Many sources of information are listed in Appendix C, Books and Articles About Reference Books. Librarians are able to provide up-to-date reviews and commentary from their professional periodicals, and the various consumers' guides have also evaluated reference books. The college student will be likely to consult most frequently the major encyclopedias listed below.

Chambers's Encyclopaedia. 4th rev. ed. M. D. Law and M. Vibert Dixon, managing eds. Oxford, Chambers's Library Service; Elmsford, N.Y., Pergamon Press, 1966-67. 15 vols. illus., maps, index.

The only major encyclopedia published in England since 1929, when the *Encyclopaedia Britannica* became a United States product. As one reviewer said, it is "a sober and sturdy work" in contrast to the "flashier and brasher merchandise" of some American publishers. It is very popular in Canada among university students, and deservedly so.

Collier's Encyclopedia. New York, Crowell-Collier Educ. Corp., 1971.

The first edition was issued a few volumes at a time between 1949 and 1951. The 1971 edition, examined recently, has a section on the Initial Teaching Alphabet under "Alphabet," while material on the New Math may be found under "Mathematics, New," as well as under "Curriculum: The New Mathematics," with a *see* reference from "New Mathematics." You can't miss it!

Encyclopedia Americana. New York, Grolier Educational Corporation, Americana Division. 30 vols. First published in 1829 by the Americana Corporation. Since 1936, this set has been under continuous revision. Annual supplement; new edition issued annually since 1923.

The *Americana* places great emphasis on the sciences and technology. It, too, has information on the New Mathematics, but not under "Mathematics." It is to be found in Volume 20, following "New Market, Battle of," on pp. 183 I,J,K,L. (See earlier comment on "a,b,c,d" pages.)

Encyclopaedia Britannica. Chicago, Encyclopaedia Britannica, 1929- . Annual supplements.

The history of the *Britannica* is told in great detail and with both enthusiasm and humor by Kogan in his book *The Great EB* (see Appendix C).

The annual supplements, called *Britannica Book of the Year,* are published early in the year following the year covered. Presumably they contribute to the continuous revision of the encyclopedia described below.

The publishers announced that the 1961 edition was the most extensively revised since 1934, when the principle of continuous revision was introduced.

According to this statement, the practice had been to make revisions involving from 3 to 6 million words a year, out of a total of about 40 million. Approximately 7.5 million words were changed in 1960 and 8.5 million in 1961. The *Britannica* of course adds new names to its list of contributors, but claims to have retained in this edition its "long admired *Britannica* classics," e.g., Macaulay on Bunyan and Goldsmith, Freud on psychoanalysis, and G. B. Shaw on socialism. Some, at least, of these are not unmixed blessings, and they have, in addition, been drastically abridged.

A new edition of the *Britannica* was published in 1974. Nicknamed "Britannica 3," it is radically different in form and content from earlier editions. It consists of a one-volume *Propaedia* or outline and guide to the set, a ten-volume *Micropaedia* composed of short factual entries, and a nineteen-volume *Macropaedia* containing essays which treat various subjects in depth. At the time of this writing, the set had not been reviewed by enough qualified people in the public press to justify recommendation.

The student may expect to find recent editions of all these publications in both college and public libraries. Many college and university libraries in the United States and most such libraries in Canada will have other encyclopedias of British publication as well.

The next three sets are directed more specifically toward family use.

Britannica Junior. Chicago, Encyclopaedia Britannica, 1934- . Continuous revision as defined earlier. New edition issued annually.

Compton's Encyclopedia and Fact-Index. Chicago, Compton, 1922- . no. of volumes varies by edition. Beginning in 1960, Compton's also has a yearbook covering events of the previous year.

This encyclopedia was purchased in 1961 by *Encyclopaedia Britannica*, with the understanding that *Compton's* would continue to have its own organization. A feature of the earlier *Compton's* was the Fact-Index at the end of each volume, which not only gave information on topics not covered in the longer articles in the volume, but also sent the reader to other volumes for related material. For example, under "Columbus, Christopher," the reader would be sent to other volumes for articles about Queen Isabella, explorers, and the discovery of America. This special feature made the set as a whole accessible to more people at one time, and was reintroduced in 1974.

World Book Encyclopedia. 1917- . Chicago, Field Enterprises (present publisher). 1972 edition in 22 vols., the last a combined Research Guide and Index. Annual supplements and continuous revision.

Intended for children and young people but useful to adults as well. Distinguished by excellent color illustrations, including transparencies, maps, charts, and diagrams. Many public libraries use the World Book for adults with reading comprehension difficulties, because of its superior color illustrations and maps.

The fact that these and other encyclopedias are competing for both home and school markets has forced them all into rigorous programs and improvement (or change) in both content and format.

FOREIGN LANGUAGE ENCYCLOPEDIAS

For the student who can read a language other than English, even feebly, there is often much useful information in one of the great foreign encyclopedias, especially those in Italian or Spanish, which are noted for their fine color plates. The encyclopedic publications, in French, of the Librairie Larousse are especially valuable on matters pertaining to French culture. There are new editions of the German encyclopedias which appear to be reliable and free of the Nazi influence which marred them earlier. The great Russian encyclopedia frequently sent out new pages to be inserted in place of those carrying information on people or theories no longer approved by the high Soviet. (In 1955 there was comment in various newspapers on a memo received by subscribers requesting that certain pages on Lavrenti Beria be removed and new material inserted. Needless to say, the American libraries which receive these pages insert them without removing the old! How long ago it seems that George Orwell warned us against the "unthink" of 1984!) A new Russian encyclopedia began publication in 1970 and is listed on page 86.

None of the foreign encyclopedias in French, German, Italian, or Spanish is difficult to use for biographical information, if one learns the abbreviations which mean "born," "died," "son" or "daughter," etc. These abbreviations are easily found in any polyglot dictionary, including the foreign-language section of the *Random House Dictionary*, which will be discussed in the following chapter.

French

Many of the older and larger universities have the first great *Encyclopédie* edited by Denis Diderot.[2] Modern French encyclopedias include the following works.

Encyclopédie Française. . . . Paris, Comité de l'Encyclopédie Française, 1935-1966. 20 looseleaf vols. illus., index.

This encyclopedia is classified, not alphabetical, and contains many fine illustrations, especially line drawings.

Grand Larousse Encyclopédique. Paris, Larousse, 1960-1972. 21 vols. illus., maps.

Actually a ten-volume encyclopedia, issued between 1960 and 1964, plus a ten-volume supplement, containing new material and updating information in the earlier set. Volume 21, the index, was issued in 1972. Like the *Larousse du XXᵉ Siècle*, which it supplants, the *Grand Larousse* is both dictionary and encyclopedia. The articles are short, illustrations in black-and-white and color are numerous, and there are many maps.

---

[2] A reprint of a portion of this, with English text, is noted in Chapter 16, Science and Technology. See Index.

La Grande Encyclopédie. Paris, Larousse, 1972-   . To be in 20 vols., plus index. An earlier encyclopedia with the above title was published by Lamirault in Paris, between 1886 and 1902, 31 vols.

German

Brockhaus Enzyklopaedie. 17th ed. Wiesbaden, Brockhaus, 1966- To be in 20 vols. illus.

The 16th edition, which bore the title *Der Grosse Brockhaus* (12 vols.), was published between 1952 and 1957. (Even earlier editions, published as *Brockhaus' Konversations-Lexikon*, have reference value.)

Meyers Enzyklopaedisches Lexikon. 9th newly revised ed. Mannheim, Bibliographisches Institut, 1971-   . To be in 25 vols.

The previous edition, published in Leipzig, was never completed. It was strongly influenced by Nazi ideology, and another similar work (1961-67) reflected the East German point of view. The 9th edition (1971-   ) named above shows the influence of the West German government.

Other Languages

Bol'shaia Sovetskaia Entsiklopediia, 3d ed. General editor, A. M. Prokhorov. Moscow, Izd. Sovetskaia Entsiklopediia, 1970-   . To be complete in 30 volumes. Will probably have one or two index volumes.

This naturally places emphasis on communist and socialist ideology. Articles are signed, bibliographic references dated. Well illustrated with graphs, charts, drawings, photographs, maps and plates.[3]

Under an agreement with the Moscow publisher, an English edition, entitled *The Great Soviet Encyclopedia* (3d ed., 1970), is now being published by the Macmillan Company of New York. Volume 1 appeared in December 1973. The announced plan is for Volumes 2-5 to be published in 1975, and the others thereafter at the rate of five a year through 1979. The agreement permits translation without the supervision of the publisher of the original set, with a comparable obligation on the part of Macmillan to retain the Soviet viewpoint, ideology, and dogma.

Enciclopedia Italiana di Scienze, Lettere ed Arti. Rome, Istit. della Encic. Ital., 1929-1961. 40 vols., incl. 3 supplements and index. illus.

Both this and the Spanish encyclopedia listed below are especially strong in world biography. Authorities agree that the *Enciclopedia Italiana* far surpasses any other in quality and number of illustrations.

Enciclopedia Universal Ilustrada Europeo-Americana. Barcelona & Madrid, Espasa-Calpe, 1905-1933, 80 vols. in 81. illus. Biennial supplements are still being published.

This great Spanish encyclopedia is usually referred to as "Espasa" (the publisher) for obvious reasons. As the title suggests, it is very useful for Latin America.

---

[3] I am indebted to a review in *College & Research Libraries*, January 1971, as I do not read Russian.

Chapter 8

The First Places to Look for Information
DICTIONARIES

THE STUDENT WISHING to know which dictionary to buy, and which of those he finds in a library will provide the information to suit a specific purpose, may find in the following pages "more than he wanted to know" at first; then, becoming more involved with the use of words and the need to express accurately what is to be said or written, he may begin to share this writer's enthusiasm for all the kinds of dictionaries. The second edition of THE NEW LIBRARY KEY devoted ten pages to dictionaries. In the ten years since that edition was published, most of the good ones have been revised or enlarged, and categories in which there were three or four titles now may have ten.

Years of work with a wide variety of students have shown me that not everyone is careful to say what he means. Furthermore, it is obvious that a speaker does not necessarily mean what he has said: e.g., if you say a book "isn't too interesting," you mean that you did not find it interesting at all. And certainly anyone listening to a radio or television interview becomes aware that "you know?" means "I don't know how to express my feelings about this."

At the beginning of Chapter 7 there is a section explaining the difference between encyclopedias and dictionaries, emphasizing the fact that some of the larger and more general dictionaries are "encyclopedic in scope." Dictionaries listed in the first two groups which follow are "encyclopedic" — they include facts about people and places, and often have many kinds of useful information in illustrations, appendixes, tables of weights and measures, and lists of foreign words and phrases. One even includes two-way glossaries between English and four other languages. (See further discussion on pages 91-93, under Characteristics of a Dictionary.)

UNABRIDGED DICTIONARIES (ENCYCLOPEDIC)

The word *unabridged* has at least two meanings. When it is used, for instance, to describe a paperback reprint of a popular novel, it means that the reprint is complete, no sections have been left out, the book appears with every word that was in the original edition. But when it is used of dictionaries, it means that most of the words in use by fluent speakers, readers, and writers of the language have been included. Some dictionaries, as the comments below will bring out, include many scientific and technical terms, some include colloquialisms, slang, and solecisms; others may give these less space, but include obsolete, obsolescent, and/or regional usages, e.g., Scottish, Australian, New England, or western United States. Only the etymological dictionaries (see pages 94-95) attempt to include words no longer in current use, unless they appear in literary works still more or less familiar to students, even though they are not a part of everyday speech. An unabridged dictionary contains from 250,000 to 600,000 words, depending upon the limitations suggested above. Emphasis is given here to the dictionaries published in the United States, though British publications will also be listed in the sections following. There are now in use four American unabridged encyclopedic dictionaries, and one British, which is used widely in Canada. They are listed here in alphabetical order.

Chambers's Twentieth Century Dictionary. William Geddie, ed. London, Chambers, 1965-
> Published by the house responsible for *Chambers's Encyclopedia*, and valuable for British usage, pronunciation, and terminology. Also published in the United States.

Funk & Wagnalls New Standard Dictionary of the English Language. I. K. Funk, Calvin Thomas, and F. H. Vizetelly, eds. New York, Funk & Wagnalls, 1963.
> Based on the Funk & Wagnalls *Standard Dictionary* . . . , originally published in 1893, and frequently updated by inclusion of new words and new information, e.g., census figures, names of new nations or well-known people.
> All Funk & Wagnalls dictionaries give all entries (words) in a single alphabet, including people and places. They are especially strong on synonyms, and use both the familiar keys to pronunciation and a "revised scientific alphabet" based on the international phonetic alphabet. Meanings are given with the common and current usages first and older meanings and uses later. The etymology is given at the end of the entry. There are many fully cited quotations clarifying usage, some from current literature.

Random House Dictionary of the English Language; the unabridged edition. Jess Stein, ed. in chief. New York, Random House, 1966. illus.
> A vocabulary of more than 260,000 entries, with numerous supplements, including signs and symbols; directories of colleges and universities, both U.S. and foreign, arranged by country; concise two-way dictionaries of French, Spanish, Italian and German; basic manual of style; proofreading symbols, forms of address; U.S. Constitution; Charter of the U.N.; gazetteer and color atlas; tables of weights and measures; and five non-Roman alphabets on the back endpapers. The vocabulary includes geographical and biographical names and places strong emphasis on scientific and technical terms, including medical terminology. Pronunciation is clearly shown.

Webster's New International Dictionary of the English Language. 2d ed. William Allan Neilson, ed. in chief. Springfield, Mass., Merriam, 1934. New words sections, 1939, 1945, 1959, 1961.

The most obvious differences between this second edition of *Webster's* and the *Funk & Wagnalls* lie in *Webster's* separate biographical and geographical lists and divided pages on which dialectal, colloquial, obsolete, and obsolescent words are listed and briefly defined in a special section across the bottom of some pages. This "basement storage" was particularly useful to the student of literature (and the maker of crossword puzzles). The order of definition in this *Webster's* is usually chronological, with the etymology given first, then the earlier meanings, and the more common meanings toward the end of the entry. Total number of words, including the biographical and geographical lists: about 600,000.

Webster's Third New International Dictionary of the English Language. Philip Babcock Gove, ed. in chief. Springfield, Mass., Merriam, 1961.

This edition was in preparation for fifteen years. It is entirely different from its predecessor, and most libraries will probably keep the older work on their shelves as well as the new. Its emphasis is upon current usage, and it is permissive as to locutions which have been frowned upon by teachers, editors, and many of the older generation whose training was more authoritarian. Aside from the more relaxed attitude toward current usage, the third edition has discarded the biographical section and the gazetteer, because these matters are more fully treated in two of Merriam's other publications — *Webster's Biographical Dictionary* (see page 137) and *Webster's Geographical Dictionary* (see page 156). No proper names are included except when they are part of a word or phrase in common usage. Reviews of this dictionary have appeared in the leading reviewing media. A very detailed adverse review in the *New Yorker*[1] expresses opinions held by many, especially those for whom a dictionary is a guide to good usage. On the other hand, reviews in the *Christian Science Monitor, Harper's Magazine,* and the London *Times Literary Supplement* were favorable. *The Atlantic Monthly* gave representation to both points of view in this remarkably informative controversy; Wilson Follett condemned the new edition roundly in the January 1962 issue ("Sabotage in Springfield; Webster's Third Edition," vol. 209, p. 73-77) and Bergen Evans defended its contents and underlying principles with equal vigor in the May 1962 issue ("But What's a Dictionary For?" vol. 209, p. 57-62). The new edition is set in very small type, to accommodate added entries and quotations, and is therefore less readable than its predecessor.

DESK OR ABRIDGED DICTIONARIES (ENCYCLOPEDIC)

The American College Dictionary. Clarence L. Barnhart, ed. in chief. New York, Random House, 1947-1962. Frequently revised in the interim. Replaced by *Random House Dictionary of the English Language, College Edition.* (See below.)

The *American College Dictionary* is still useful. It is notable for legible, though comparatively small, type; definitions using fairly common words to

---

[1] Dwight Macdonald. "The String Untuned." *New Yorker,* vol. 38, p. 130-134ff. March 10, 1962.

define difficult terms; an especially intelligible method of signifying pronunciation and word histories; and special attention to differentiation of synonyms. Tables of words beginning with such prefixes as *non-*, *re-*, and *un-* are useful (these are to be found in other Random House dictionaries also). Obsolete, obsolescent, and colloquial words, French and Latin words in common use, proper names, some slang, and many regionalisms are included. Most entries are short. About 132,000 words in about 1,450 pages.

The American Heritage Dictionary of the English Language. William Morris, ed. New York, American Heritage Publishing Co.; Boston, Houghton, Mifflin, 1969. illus.

Like the Random House dictionaries, this is a reaction to *Webster's Third New International.* Usages are closer to "an educated North American standard."[2] A salient feature is the use of marginal illustrations, whose relationship to the text is not always evident.

The Barnhart Dictionary of New English Since 1963. Clarence L. Barnhart, Sol Steinmetz, and Robin K. Barnhart, eds. New York, Harper; Bronxville, N.Y., Barnhart; Toronto, Fitzhenry & Whiteside, 1973.

". . . a lexical index of the new words of the last decade, a record of the most recent terms required and created by our scientific investigations, our technical and cultural activities, and our social and personal lives. Each entry has one or more quotations of a length sufficient to help convey the meaning and flavor of the term; and pronunciations, etymologies, and usage notes are added in many cases to assist the understanding of a word and its use. . . . 1963 . . . marks the termination of the record of new English, except for sporadic examples, in most general dictionaries now available to the general public. The new words and phrases were collected from . . . United States, British and Canadian sources . . . from 1963 to 1972. The 5,000 or so new entries and meanings have been selected from over one million quotations. . . . Each quotation has a full bibliographical reference." — *Preface.*

The pronunciation system is adapted from that of the IPA (International Phonetic Association), thus differentiating, for example, the British and American sounds of *o* in *hot.* The paper is a pleasant off-white, thin but opaque, but the type, while clear, is small (much of the smallest size being *italic* as well). Many readers will need to use some type of magnifying equipment to read the illustrative quotations. Nevertheless, the book is addictive, leading the reader on from page to page, as a good encyclopedia does.

Random House Dictionary of the English Language, College Edition. Laurence Urdang, ed. in chief. New York, Random House, 1968.

With a vocabulary of more than 155,000 entries, including geographical and biographical names, selected from the 260,000 in the unabridged edition. Pronunciation is clearly shown, definitions are lucid, meanings most frequently needed are given first, illustrative phrases are provided by the editorial staff, not taken from current "literature" as in *Webster's Third,* and scientific and technical terminology is well represented. A number of the features of the parent volume are included, but not the four foreign-language dictionaries, of course.

---

[2] See long and detailed reviews in *Library Journal,* Dec. 15, 1969, and other library periodicals about that date.

Shorter Oxford English Dictionary on Historical Principles. 3d ed. Oxford, Clarendon Press; New York, Oxford University Press, 1944 with addenda 1955 and corrections 1962. 2 vols.

Includes words in regular literary and colloquial use. Reduced from the monumental *New English Dictionary . . .* (see below, page 95) partly by using abbreviations and omitting quotations. An excellent medium-sized dictionary for use by students and the general reader of works written and published in the British Commonwealth. This should be as useful to the American reader as the dictionaries published in the United States are to Canadians, Australians, and other English-speaking peoples who are puzzled by American usage and spelling.

Webster's New Collegiate Dictionary. 8th in the series. Henry Bosley Woolf, ed. in chief. Springfield, Mass., Merriam, 1973.

About 152,000 entries. Definitions are clear and concise, and meanings are given in historical order, with sample phrases to illustrate usage. Geographic and biographical names are listed separately. The *New Collegiate* is perhaps the most permissive of abridged dictionaries and has been criticized, as was *Webster's Third,* for its laissez-faire approach to usage. This revision contains 22,000 new words and meanings, including some which are not listed elsewhere, along with a few "in" terms which may be "out" in subsequent editions.

Webster's New World Dictionary of the American Language, Second College Edition. David B. Guralnik, ed. in chief. Cleveland, World, 1970. Frequently reprinted with minor revisions.

About 155,000 entries. The different meanings of a word are given in historical order, and Americanisms are indicated by a star. Biographical and geographic names are included in the main alphabet, an arrangement some readers prefer. Through its descriptive labels, this dictionary offers more guidance on usage than recent Merriam-Webster dictionaries.

All the dictionaries listed here should be familiar to the college student, because they can be used for different purposes. If possible, one's personal library should contain more than one — the comments given above, plus careful examination of several should make it possible for the student to make his choice, depending on such preferences as size of type, order of definitions, examples of use, differentiation of synonyms, levels of language, etymological or encyclopedic emphasis, etc.

CHARACTERISTICS OF A DICTIONARY

Some of the most interesting things about dictionaries are in the part nobody reads, the Introduction. We expect our dictionaries to settle disputes about the *correct* meaning or pronunciation of a word, though the editors take great pains to tell us in the introduction that the dictionary is a record of usage, as shown in the printed word and in cultivated speech. No lexicographer today pretends to be an arbiter of correctness, though the great Samuel Johnson arrogated that function to himself.

Annoyance at the omission of a new technical term would be dispelled if we understood the process of choosing the words to be included, and the length of time it takes to compile each edition. The great unabridged dictionaries of English usually contain somewhat over 400,000 words, though there are at least a million, if we were to count all obsolete, technical, cant, and slang words. The most famous example of a dictionary which has never been up to date is the *Dictionnaire de l'Académie Française*, whose editors are so fearful that a word may be vulgar, slang, or even colloquial, that many words have passed into and out of use without ever appearing on its pages. The American lexicographer is probably the most hospitable to colloquial and slang terms. As for pronunciation, here too American dictionaries record usage in the United States, based largely on what is known as Standard American, the speech of the greatest number of reasonably well-educated inhabitants of the United States. The speech patterns of the New England and southern states are also recorded as correct though they may differ substantially from this standard.[3]

All the dictionaries listed above contain full directions for use and explanations of all abbreviations and symbols and of the order of items in each article. The reader is urged to examine these for himself in whatever dictionary comes to hand. There are, however, a few differences which should be noted in using the major unabridged American dictionaries. One often hears reference to "the first meaning" of a word. In *Webster's New International Dictionary*, second edition, the meanings are given in historical order, and so the desired current usage of a word may be one of the last meanings defined in the article. In *Funk & Wagnalls New Standard Dictionary*, on the other hand, the meaning given first is the one in most common use currently. Webster gives etymology at the beginning of each article, Funk & Wagnalls gives it at the end. Both quote from printed sources to show how words have been used in sentences, but Webster is more apt to quote from English literary works of the eighteenth and nineteenth centuries, while Funk & Wagnalls frequently refers to American newspapers and magazines as well, and always gives the exact page reference where the quotation may be found. Probably the greatest fault, common to both, is a tendency to confuse the reader by defining a word with other words even more unfamiliar. The reader is advised to compare the definitions of *rib* in several dictionaries for baffling and amusing examples.

---

[3] Anyone wishing to pursue further this matter of "What does the dictionary say?" is referred to Chapters 11 and 12 of *The Development of Modern English*, 2d ed., by Stuart Robertson and F. G. Cassidy. New York, Prentice-Hall, 1954. p. 327-418.

The reader should be advised, at this point, that most of the comments made above about the second edition of *Webster's New International Dictionary* do not apply to the 1961 third edition. Most of the quotations from early literary figures are out, and such authorities as Gypsy Rose Lee, Norman Mailer, and J. D. Salinger are in. The only word printed with a capital initial letter is *God*, though words usually capitalized have that fact indicated. This tremendous work of painstaking lexicographers will certainly be useful to those whose knowledge of colloquial English is sketchy (as, for instance, Europeans, Asians, or Africans confronted with the sports section of a daily paper, or a comic book), but, as Dwight Macdonald points out in the *New Yorker* article referred to above, words which have long been differentiated are here made synonymous: e.g., *nauseous, nauseated; disinterested, uninterested; imply, infer; not too, not very.*

DICTIONARIES OF SYNONYMS AND ANTONYMS (NOT ENCYCLOPEDIC)

All the dictionaries in this group have the same purpose: to suggest words of similar meaning in order to vary, clarify, or adorn one's speech or writing. The Crowell edition of Roget's *Thesaurus* is compiled on the same principles as its predecessors, but is more simply organized; it no longer lists synonyms and antonyms in parallel columns, but only synonyms. No attempt is made to differentiate between synonyms, since fullness rather than definition is the object of a thesaurus; it is meant to be a "treasure house of words." However, the other books in this group might be called "sorting rooms of words." They explain, in paragraph form, with examples, the similarities and analogies between so-called synonyms, emphasizing the fact that few are truly exactly the same in meaning.

Fernald, James Champlin. *Funk & Wagnalls Standard Handbook of Synonyms, Antonyms, and Prepositions.* rev. ed. New York, Funk & Wagnalls, 1947.

> This is now out of print, but is still available in libraries. It remains especially useful because of its emphasis on changes in meaning brought about by the use of prepositions, e.g., do up, do in, come about, etc., which make English so difficult for those learning it as a second language.

Hayakawa, S. I., and others. *Funk & Wagnalls Modern Guide to Synonyms and Related Words.* New York, Funk & Wagnalls, 1968.

> Over 6,000 synonyms and related words, well differentiated. Concise definitions and illustrative sentences elucidate the nuances of the synonyms. However, this book does not explain changes in meaning caused by prepositions, as the *Standard Handbook* . . . described above does.

March, Francis Andrew and March, Francis Andrew, Jr. *March's Thesaurus-Dictionary*. Norman Cousins, ed. New supplement by R. A. Goodwin giving words and phrases which have become current since 1900. New York, Doubleday (Hanover House), 1958.

Words are in dictionary order, with cross references to the words under which full differentiations of meaning are given. Reprinted in 1968 under the title *March's Thesaurus and Dictionary of the English Language*.

The New Roget's Thesaurus of the English Language in Dictionary Form. Revised and greatly enlarged ed. Norman Lewis, ed. Based on Mawson's alphabetical arrangement. Garden City, N.Y., Garden City Books, 1961.

Roget's International Thesaurus. 3d ed. New York, Crowell, 1962.

This edition is especially useful for idiomatic usage, giving illustrative phrases.

Roget's *Thesaurus* will be found in every library, in one edition or another. The original work was arranged by subject classes, and the present Crowell edition uses a modified version of that arrangement; the *New Roget's Thesaurus* is in dictionary form, however. The alphabetized edition, together with Hayakawa, March, or *Webster's New Dictionary of Synonyms*, listed below, will be most useful to the student. (Roget has a reputation as the *sine qua non* of synonyms, just as *Robert's Rules of Order* is required for conducting a meeting, although there are many much simpler books on parliamentary procedure for the beginner.)

Webster's New Dictionary of Synonyms; a Dictionary of Discriminated Synonyms and Antonyms and Analogous and Contrasted Words. 2d ed. Springfield, Mass., Merriam, 1968.

A new edition of *Webster's Dictionary of Synonyms* (1942, minor revisions, 1951). It looks like a Webster dictionary, as the new biographical and geographic dictionaries do, and the reader feels comfortable with it. It has been updated and the terminology is modern, whereas March and Roget still reflect their nineteenth century origins.

ETYMOLOGICAL DICTIONARIES (NOT ENCYCLOPEDIC)

Americanisms: A Dictionary of Selected Americanisms on Historical Principles. Mitford M. Mathews, ed. Chicago, University of Chicago Press, 1966.

A selection of approximately 1,000 entries from *A Dictionary of Americanisms* . . . (below). This abridgment may be in small libraries which do not need the larger work. Available also in paperback for student purchase.

Dictionary of American English on Historical Principles. Sir W. A. Craigie and James R. Hulbert, eds. Chicago, University of Chicago Press, 1936-1944. 4 vols. New ed. in preparation, 1962.

A *Dictionary of Americanisms on Historical Principles.* Mitford M. Mathews, ed. Chicago, University of Chicago Press, 1951. 2 vols. 1 vol. edition issued in 1956.

Klein, Ernest. *A Comprehensive Etymological Dictionary of the English Language, Dealing With the Origin of Words and Their Sense Development, thus Illustrating the History of Civilization and Culture.* Amsterdam, Elsevier, 1966-1967. 2 vols.

> Nearly 50,000 entries, including etymologies of family and mythological names.

A *New English Dictionary on Historical Principles.* Sir James A. H. Murray and others, eds. Oxford, Clarendon Press, 1888-1933. 10 vols. and supplements. A revised supplement, edited by R. W. Burchfield, covers new material ranging from 1884 to 1977. Volume 1, *A to G,* was published in 1972; Volume 2, *H to P,* will appear in 1975; and Volume 3, *Q to Z,* in 1977.

> The *New English Dictionary* . . . is frequently referred to as the *N. E. D.* or the *O. E. D.* (for *Oxford English Dictionary,* the title of later editions). It was begun in the middle of the nineteenth century and compiled by examining every written work available in English from 1150. Doctor Johnson's definition of a lexicographer as "a harmless drudge" did not apply to the dedicated men (and more recently, women) who participated in this task. The massive work, published over a forty-five-year period, has spawned a number of smaller dictionaries selected from it, including:

> *Oxford Dictionary of English Etymology.* C. T. Onions, ed. Oxford, Clarendon Press, 1966.

> *The Shorter Oxford Dictionary on Historical Principles.* 3d ed. Revised and edited by C. T. Onions. Oxford, Clarendon Press, 1962. 2 vols.

> The *Shorter O.E.D.* includes a selection of all features of the original, about two thirds of the words, and many quotations. For the average student, this is often sufficient.

> A compact edition of the *Oxford English Dictionary* . . . was published by Oxford University Press in 1971. It contains the entire set, photographically reduced, with a special magnifying device to read it with!

Partridge, Eric. *Origins: A Short Etymological Dictionary of Modern English.* 4th ed. London, Routledge, 1966.

DICTIONARIES OF USAGE

There are always questions about the use of words which are not answered in conventional dictionaries, and of course the smaller the dictionary, the fewer questions it answers. Even the multi-volume *New English Dictionary* is not sufficiently up-to-date to include the new words coined daily in this highly inventive age, nor does it attempt to fathom the mysteries of usage in the United States. Later chapters will include dictionaries of technical and scientific terms, but recent years have seen the publication of several types of dictionaries to tell us which are the right ways to use words which are perhaps somewhat alike in sound or in meaning (e.g., *as, since, because; compose, comprise; militate, mitigate;* and those old problems, *shall* or *will, who* or *whom, I* or *me,* and the recent use of *like* in what to the purist are most unlikely places).

Bernstein, Theodore M. *Miss Thistlebottom's Hobgoblins; the Careful Writer's Guide to the Taboos, Bugbears and Outmoded Rules of English Usage.* New York, Farrar, Straus and Giroux, 1971.

    The author was a copy editor and later assistant managing editor of the New York *Times.* He deplores the overly pedantic and sometimes ridiculous rules set by teachers, grammarians, etc., such as "never use a preposition to end a sentence with," a rule Winston Churchill said "up with which I will not put." Also included are Ambrose Bierce's *Write It Right,* William Cullen Bryant's *Index Expurgatorius,* and James Gordon Bennett, Jr.'s "Don't List" for reporters on the New York *Herald.*

Bryant, Margaret M. *Current American Usage.* New York, Funk & Wagnalls, 1962.

    This is a compilation based on work done cooperatively by members of the National Council of Teachers of English to study and record controversial word usage in the United States. It aims to point out how Americans *do,* not *should,* speak and write. Regional differences are noted.

Copperud, Roy H. *American Usage: The Consensus.* 1st series. New York, Van Nostrand-Reinhold, 1970.

    Compares seven current usage dictionaries as well as "the leading conventional dictionaries" on disputed points in usage, e.g., punctuation, sentence structure, and subject-verb agreement.

Evans, Bergen and Evans, Cornelia. *Dictionary of Contemporary American Usage.* New York, Random House, 1957.

    Dr. Evans ran several popular television programs. This book, on which his sister collaborated, has been the center of much controversy, for Dr. Evans supports contemporary usage against established "correctness"; e.g., *It's me,* and the already mentioned uses of *like.* Dr. Evans' 1961 book *Comfortable Words* (Random House) expands his theory on modern usage, with examples discussed at some length.

Follett, Wilson. *Modern American Usage.* Edited and completed by Jacques Barzun in collaboration with Carlos Baker and others. New York, Hill and Wang, 1966.

    Troublesome words and phrases, in dictionary arrangement; at times amusing as well as useful. Punctuation and *shall, will* (*should, would*) in an appendix.

Fowler, Henry W. *Dictionary of Modern English Usage.* 2d ed. Revised by Sir Ernest Gowers. Oxford, Clarendon Press; New York, Oxford University Press, 1965.

    This edition includes new comparisons between British and American usage.

Lexicographical Centre for Canadian English, University of Victoria. *A Dictionary of Canadianisms on Historical Principles.* Walter S. Avis, ed. in chief. Toronto, Gage, 1967.

A record of words and expressions either native to Canada or used or pronounced differently in Canada, than, for instance, in the United States. Those who listen to the Canadian radio broadcasts may find it enlightening.

Nicholson, Margaret. *Dictionary of American-English Usage*. London and New York, Oxford University Press, 1957.

This is partly an attempt to explain American usage to British readers. It is to a great extent based on *A Dictionary of Modern English Usage*, by Henry W. Fowler (Oxford University Press, 1937).

Orkin, Mark M. *Speaking Canadian English: An Informal Account of the English Language in Canada*. Don Mills, Ontario, General Publishing Co., 1970.

Even more enlightening than the *Dictionary of Canadianisms* . . . prepared at the Lexicographical Centre for Canadian English, listed above. Orkin, a lawyer by profession, has also written *Speaking Canadian French* (Don Mills, Ontario, General Publishing Co., 1967).

Partridge, Eric. *Usage and Abusage; a Guide to Good English*. 6th ed., rev. and enl. London, Hamish Hamilton, 1965.

This is, of course, British usage again. Mr. Partridge has also compiled a dictionary of slang, with a strong flavor of the British Commonwealth, which is listed in the following section.

Urdang, Laurance, ed. *The New York Times Everyday Reader's Dictionary of Misunderstood, Misused, Mispronounced Words*. New York, Quadrangle, 1972.

The author was managing editor of the *Random House Dictionary* (unabridged). No doubt he encountered these 20,000 words in his reading; and his book is as much fun to read and as worth using as Fowler's.

Vizetelly, F. H. and De Bekker, L. J. *A Desk Book of Idioms and Idiomatic Phrases in English Speech and Literature*. Reprint of the 1923 edition. Detroit, Gale, 1970.

The value of this old book to today's reader is to point out that idioms are not confined to foreign languages, as he may have thought.

DICTIONARIES OF SLANG

American slang is treated historically in H. L. Mencken's *The American Language* (4th ed. corrected, enlarged, and rewritten, New York, Knopf, 1936; supplements 1 and 2, 1945-48); for early British slang, a reprint of J. C. Hotton's *Slang Dictionary* (1887) issued by the Totowa, N.J., firm of Rowman and Littlefield in 1972 might be useful to readers of Dickens, and perhaps to those who enjoy the Regency novels of Georgette Heyer. The rhyming cant of the London streets will be found in Partridge, listed below.

Berrey, L. V. and Van den Bark, Melvin. *American Thesaurus of Slang*. 2d ed. New York, Crowell, 1953.

More than 100,000 terms under 940 headings. Still in print, but probably now more "historical" than current.

Partridge, Eric. *Slang Today and Yesterday*. 4th ed. rev. London, Routledge; New York, Barnes & Noble, 1970.

> According to the author's postscript to this edition, it has "many 'modernizations', few corrections."

Wentworth, Harold and Flexner, S. B. *Dictionary of American Slang*. New York, Crowell, 1967.

> The 1960 edition, like the *Dictionary of American English* (p. 94) and the *O.E.D.*, was "on historical principles." It contained about 20,000 definitions. This edition includes a supplement of more than 1,000 new words. It should be especially useful to the historical novelist who wishes to avoid linguistic anachronisms.

DICTIONARIES OF FOREIGN WORDS IN COMMON ENGLISH USAGE

Bliss, Alan Joseph. *A Dictionary of Foreign Words and Phrases in Current English*. New York, Dutton, 1966.

> Not based on the work of others, this has more than 5,000 entries, clearly defined, giving the phrase in the original language and the century when it was first used in English. When an illustrative quotation is given, specific reference to the source is made.

Carroll, David. *The Dictionary of Foreign Terms in the English Language*. New York, Hawthorn, 1973.

> Especially useful for treatment of Latin phrases and abbreviations, but also provides French, German, and current non-European terms.

Guinagh, Kevin. *Dictionary of Foreign Phrases and Abbreviations*. 2d ed. New York, Wilson, 1972.

> This edition contains 750 new entries, adding twenty percent to the content of the 1965 edition. Latin and French predominate in the foreign language expressions, proverbs, axioms, etc. Foreign abbreviations also appear in the single alphabetical list. These abbreviations should be helpful in using the foreign language encyclopedias referred to in Chapter 7.

Walton, Mary and others. *'Isms*. 2d ed. Sheffield, Eng., Sheffield City Libraries, 1968.

> For words ending in *-ism, -ology, -phobia*, etc. The words are listed under subject, and also alphabetically, so he who fears cats should have no trouble in finding *ailurophobia*. (Most such words seem to have Greek or Latin roots.)

Leo Rosten's *The Joys of Yiddish* (New York, McGraw-Hill, 1968) might be useful to non-Jews.

DICTIONARIES OF PRONUNCIATION

British Broadcasting Corporation. *BBC Pronouncing Dictionary of British Names, With an Appendix of Channel Island Names*. Edited and transcribed by G. M. Miller. New York, Oxford University Press, 1971.

> According to the editor, "the BBC has gathered together the fruits of more than forty years of research into the pronunciation of proper names in the

United Kingdom." Included are both personal and place names. Pronunciation is indicated both by the international phonetic alphabet and by respelling.

Franklyn, Julian. *Which Witch? Being a Grouping of Phonetically Compatible Words.* Boston, Houghton Mifflin, 1966.

Words whose spelling and/or pronunciation are similar are listed together, with differences in meaning clarified.

Noory, Samuel. *Dictionary of Pronunciation.* 2d ed. New York, A. S. Barnes, 1972.

The author is of Turkish origin, and his early education in a number of schools required him to learn to spell in Turkish, Arabic, Syriac, French, and English. He is thus well aware of problems of speakers whose native language is not English.

In this context, cf. also Urdang's *New York Times Everyday Reader's Dictionary of . . . Mispronounced Words*, cited on page 97.

RHYMING DICTIONARIES

Another useful compilation is a rhyming dictionary, which perhaps a poetic genius may not need, but in which an ordinary man or woman wanting to write a jingle or a limerick to accompany a gift or a box-top, or a writer of lyrics for popular songs can find not only help but indeed inspiration, for it will bring to his attention words he may never have met before.

Holofcener, Lawrence, comp. and ed. *Practical Dictionary of Rhymes; Based on New Principles for Songwriters and Other Versifiers.* New York, Crown, 1960.

The compiler is a successful writer of popular songs, and his lists of rhymes suggest many amusing possibilities.

Johnson, Burges, ed. *New Rhyming Dictionary and Poet's Handbook.* rev. ed. New York, Harper, 1957.

Includes information on verse forms and rhyme schemes.

Stillman, Frances. *The Poet's Manual and Rhyming Dictionary;* based on *The Improved Rhyming Dictionary* by Jane Shaw Whitfield. New York, Crowell, 1965.

About the first quarter of the book gives a clear explanation of verse forms. The rhyming dictionary is divided by vowel sounds, arranged in paragraphs according to the number of syllables. Similar to Johnson (above).

Wood, Clement. *Wood's Unabridged Rhyming Dictionary.* Introduction by Ted Robinson. Cleveland, World, 1943.

The most extensive of these works.

DICTIONARIES OF ABBREVIATIONS, ACRONYMS, AND INITIALISMS

Once upon a time there were just *abbreviations*, formed by using enough letters in a common word to be intelligible, while deleting enough to save space; e.g., *ft.* for *foot* or *feet, yd.* or *yds.* for *yard* or *yards*, and in fact *abbrev.* for *abbreviation.* The next step was the initialisms, such as A.K.C. for American Kennel Club, A.M.A. for American Medical Association (and equally for the American Manufacturers Association), U.A.W. for United Auto Workers, and the much earlier I.W.W. for Industrial Workers of the World (who had the reputation of being on strike rather often, and were hence sometimes referred to as I Won't Work). Of late, the use of the period after each initial has gone out of fashion, and most initialisms are printed without punctuation — AMA, UAW, and, for College Entrance Examination Board, CEEB, for example.

Acronyms are akin to initialisms; they are initials which form words. Frequently the word comes first— in the field of Ecology, for instance, GOO preceded the phrase Get Oil Out. The Women's Lib movement has produced the name NOW for National Organization for Women, and a rather repellent OWL, for Older Women's Liberation. The library profession has recently become addicted to acronyms, the latest to come to notice being SLICE, which translated is the Southwestern Library Interstate Cooperative Endeavor. The reader is invited to make a pun on that!

For a long while there were no dictionaries of these "short forms"; sets of letters were rarely differentiated by "field," and abbreviations used in special fields, as in the sciences, business, economics, law, and especially warfare, came in and out of use with astonishing rapidity. Writers familiar with these short forms used them with no explanation, leaving the uninitiated in a state of frustration. Many Americans have read British novels about the First World War in which every heroine was a V.A.D. From the context one could finally discern that she did some sort of nursing of the wounded (usually finding her long lost brother, husband, or lover under the bandages), but even the knowledge that the letters meant Volunteer Aid Detachment would have done little to dispel the mystery.

Crowley, Ellen T. and Thomas, Robert C., eds. *Acronyms and Initialisms Dictionary.* 3d ed. Detroit, Gale, 1970.

> More than 80,000 entries. Supplements published annually. The publisher's announcement cites new acronyms for space activities and equipment, pollution control groups and methods, drugs, technical processes and materials, agencies, movements, breakthroughs, and popular expressions. The supplements are each titled *New Acronyms and Initialisms.*

Crowley, Ellen T. *Reverse Acronyms and Initialisms Dictionary.* Detroit, Gale, 1972.

> A companion to the above, but giving the name abbreviated, *followed* by the acronym. An index by meaning, so to speak.

De Sola, Ralph. *Abbreviations Dictionary*. International ed. New York, Meredith, 1967.
> More than 50,000 entries.

Kleiner, Richard, comp. *Index of Initials and Acronyms*. New York, Auerbach, 1971.
> Lists 7,000 terms; "not intended to be all-encompassing." Based on the compiler's experience as a newspaper editor.

Pugh, Eric. *A Dictionary of Acronyms and Abbreviations*. 2d rev. ed. Hamden, Conn., Archon, 1970.
> A mere 10,000 entries, more or less, but contains some not in De Sola. Emphasis is on Management, Technology, and Information Science.

Rybicki, Stephen. *Abbreviations: A Reverse Guide to Standard and Generally Accepted Abbreviated Forms*. Ann Arbor, Mich., Pierian Press, 1971.
> The words and phrases abbreviated are given alphabetically, with an alphabetical index by abbreviation. Probably the most useful for the average user.

FOREIGN LANGUAGE DICTIONARIES

The student of foreign languages must become acquainted with the best dictionaries of the language of his choice. The beginner (and the professional translator) will need the works in which English equivalents are given for the foreign words, and vice versa. (*Equivalent* is used here with the same limitations that *synonym* implies.) The more advanced student will also need a dictionary comparable to *Webster's* or *Funk & Wagnalls,* that is entirely in the foreign language. Any college library and many public libraries will have a selection of the best of both types.

In the earlier editions of THE NEW LIBRARY KEY, no foreign language dictionaries were listed, with the exception of the *Duden Pictorial Encyclopedia* (New York, Ungar, 1958), now in five volumes, in which a full-page illustration, with each item numbered, is followed by the names of the numbered items in English, French, German, Italian, and Spanish. For each language an alphabetical index is provided, which includes adjectival and verb forms which appear in the original listings. When it was available in one volume, and comparatively inexpensive, I used to recommend it to students about to embark upon their six-week stint of "practice teaching" as a way for the teacher of science to attract a student who liked French, for instance, to science because so many scientific terms come from French. Conversely, the student whose interest was in science could be persuaded to study a foreign language by a reversal of emphasis. This technique is still perfectly valid, if the high school library can afford the dictionary.

During the later 1960s and in the early 1970s so many new or newly revised foreign language dictionaries, mostly bilingual with English, have been published that it now seems wise to include a selection of the best, for the guidance of both student and librarian. In accordance with the Library of Congress Classification system, the classical languages will be treated first (there is only one new title in Greek, and one now beginning to be published in Latin).

Greek

Liddell, H. G. and Scott, Robert, comps. *A Greek-English Lexicon*. 9th
    ed., with supplement, 1968. Supplement edited by E. A. Barber
    and others. New York, Oxford University Press, 1843-1968. 2 vols.
    Liddell and Scott's *Greek-English Lexicon* had reached its 9th edition in
    1940. In 1953, the supplement was planned, to make use of new information
    derived from the publication of many inscriptions and papyri. Dr. Barber
    and his assistants have not only listed new words that have emerged, but
    have also corrected errors of dating, translation, orthography, etc., in the 9th
    edition, and have added new bibliographical information, including scholarly
    publications and periodicals. With the supplement, this is actually the 10th
    edition, an indispensible and unique source for years to come.

Latin

Oxford Latin Dictionary. New York, Oxford University Press; Oxford,
    Clarendon Press, 1968-
    Being issued in fascicles (sections). The 1968 announcement forecast eight
    fascicles, of which the first three had been published by 1973. Until this
    work has been completed, there is still Lewis and Short's *Harper's Latin Dic-
    tionary* (first published in 1907 and reprinted in 1955 by the Clarendon
    Press), though it does not include entries for the principal suffixes used in
    word formation, to be found in *O.L.D.*

French

Larousse & Co., Inc., has a New York as well as a Paris address. It
remains the most prolific source of both dictionaries and encyclopedias
in French.

Dictionnaire du Français Contemporain. Jean Dubois and others, eds.
    New York and Paris, Larousse, 1972.
    Most nuances of the contemporary language explained and shown in con-
    crete examples.

Grand Larousse de la Langue Française. Louis Guilbert, René Lagane,
    Georges Niobey, eds. Paris, Larousse, 1972-   . To be in 6 vols.
    "Encompasses all possible (!) information and up-to-date knowledge on
    vocabulary, grammar, and linguistics" (publisher's announcement).

Larousse Modern French-English, English-French Dictionary. Mar-
    guerite-Marie Dubois, ed. Paris, Larousse, 1972.
    The editor is a professor at the Sorbonne.

Nouveau Petit Larousse, 1971. Paris, Larousse, 1970.

>An illustrated encyclopedia-dictionary, in French only.

Among bilingual dictionaries, the following works are also outstanding.

Mansion, J. E. *Harrap's New Standard French and English Dictionary.* Revised and edited by R. P. L. Ledésert and Margaret Ledésert. London, Harrap; New York, Scribner, 1973-   . To be in 4 vols.

>The basic format and method of Mansion's original 1934 work (listed below) have been retained, but with new entries and modernized definitions. Outdated terms and definitions have been deleted, without eliminating words important in reading the older literature. This edition includes new technical terms and introduces regionalisms of Belgium, Switzerland, and Canada. The abbreviations supplement has been revised, and colloquialisms have been updated. The French-English volumes were published in 1973; the English-French volumes are scheduled for 1978.

Mansion, J. E. *Harrap's Shorter French and English Dictionary.* rev. and enl. ed. London, Harrap; Boston, Heath, 1967.

>Includes French Canadianisms and Americanisms, e.g., *sweater* listed as a French word.

Mansion, J. E. *Harrap's Standard French and English Dictionary.* London, Harrap; New York, Scribner, 1970. 2 vols.

>First published in 1934, revised in 1940; the 1970 issue includes supplements added in 1962.

There are also two bilingual dictionaries of slang.

Leitner, M. J. and Lanen, J. R. *Dictionary of French and American Slang.* New York, Crown, 1966.

>Indicates part of speech, gender, and level of meaning (colloquial, vernacular, argot, obscene, or vulgar).

>"Bright-eyed and bushy-tailed" turned up in this dictionary, in the English-French section.

Marks, Joseph. *The New French-English Dictionary of Slang and Colloquialisms.* Revised and completed by G. A. Marks and A. J. Farmer. New York, Dutton, 1971.

>French slang translated into British English. (An Americanized edition would be useful, but this volume does include a table of British slang.)

German

Das Grosse Deutsche Wörterbuch. Gerhard Wahrig, ed., Gütersloh, Bertelsmann; New York, Adler's Foreign Books, Inc., 1966.

>Advertised as "the German equivalent to Webster's *Collegiate*." All German, as Larousse is all French.

Jones, Trevor. *Harrap's Standard German and English Dictionary.* Boston, Heath; London, Harrap, 1963-   . To be in 2 vols.

>Volume 1 (German-English) gives part of speech, pronunciation according to the I.P.A. system, and the English equivalent (with American English given only when British English is unsatisfactory). A team of lexicographers has been working on this since 1950. As of 1973, however, there has been no announcement of the English-German volume.

Langenscheidt's New Muret-Sanders Encyclopedic Dictionary of English and German. Otto Springer, ed. Berlin, Langenscheidt, 1962-1974. 4 vols.

> Distributed in the United States by Optimum Book Marketing (New York). The first two volumes are an English-German dictionary, while the last two are German-English. The set covers literary and colloquial usage, and includes both British and American English.

Italian

Cambridge Italian Dictionary. Barbara Reynolds, ed. London, Cambridge University Press, 1962-   . 2 vols. announced.

> Volume 1 (Italian-English) was issued in 1962 and is exhaustive and informative. Volume 2 (English-Italian) is still in preparation.

Dictionary of the Italian and English Languages. Vladimiro Macchi, ed. Florence and Rome, Sansoni Editore; London, Harrap, 1970-   . To be in 4 vols.

> Also referred to as *Sansoni.*

> Part 1, Italian-English, is to be in two volumes, with 100,000 head-words. Volume 1 (A-L) has been completed. No announcement of projected publication dates for Volume 2 (M-Z) or for Part II, English-Italian, has been made.

> Examination of Part I, Volume 1 shows it to be as nearly complete linguistically as one may hope for. Colloquial Italian is ably rendered in colloquial English. For example, *collare nella lotta,* which means literally *collar in a fight or struggle,* is translated as *half nelson.*

Follett/Zanichelli Italian Dictionary: English-Italian/Italian-English. Compiled by Giuseppe Ragazzini and others. Chicago, Follett, 1968.

> Desk format; fullest and most usable in this size. Includes illustrative phrases, idioms, etc. The Italian is standard Tuscan; the English includes both British and North American (U.S. and Canadian) usage. Irregular verbs in English and Italian are listed in Appendixes.

Spanish

Collins Spanish-English/English-Spanish Dictionary. Colin Smith and others, comps. New York, Collins, 1972.

> Not only close to current idiom, but easy to use in format. Not in "dictionary-ese." Includes proper names and their derivatives.

The New World Spanish-English and English-Spanish Dictionary. Salvatore Ramondino, ed. Introduction by Mario Pei. New York, World, 1968. paperback ed., 1971.

> Emphasizes usage in the Western hemisphere and includes words and phrases used in Spanish-speaking sections of the United States.

Simon and Schuster's International Dictionary: English/Spanish, Spanish/English. Tana de Gámez, ed. New York, Simon & Schuster, 1973.

> While inferior in format to some other Spanish-English dictionaries, this

book includes many terms in current use, such as *sonar, black light,* and *snap judgment.*

Vox Modern College Spanish and English Dictionary. Edited by the staff of Biblograf, S.A. 1960 ed., newly rev. in 1970. New York, Scribner, 1970.

According to the publisher's announcement, this dictionary "emphasizes the normal language of contemporary society." Also published in "concise" and "compact" versions, each having approximately 30,000 fewer entries than the preceding.

Polyglot and International

Bergman, Peter M. *Concise Dictionary of 26 Languages in Simultaneous Translations.* New York, New American Library, 1968.

Includes Swahili and Esperanto.

If any reader becomes a cataloger in a university library, this will be indispensable. Also for the far-flung diplomatic corps and the members of the press or media who accompany them.

Dreyfuss, Henry. *Symbol Sourcebook.* New York, McGraw-Hill, 1972.

More than 6,000 symbols arranged by subject: travel, astronomy, geography, mathematics, weather, sports; also symbols used by hobos, doctors, printers, astrologers, electricians. In the back of the book the symbols are classified by shape, and there is a section on color symbolism.

Chapter 9

PERIODICALS, PERIODICAL INDEXES, AND GENERAL INDEXES

IN THE FIRST chapter the term *periodical* was defined, and considerable attention given to the scope and usefulness of a periodical collection. The importance of periodicals as sources of information cannot be overemphasized. A reliable editor takes great pains to secure articles by people who are experts in their fields, or by professional free-lance writers who can work up a subject into an interesting and accurate account. The fact that an issue of a periodical is small as compared to a book makes it possible for it to be almost completely up to date. Only the daily newspaper is more so. Although sometimes a monthly magazine will have made a poor guess as to how some political issue will be decided, and occasionally even a weekly goes to press one day too soon to be aware of a sudden change in public policy, they can easily correct their mistake in the next issue if need be, and the average reader bears no grudge against them for human fallibility. The specialized journals are more cautious, and wait until a topic can be treated authoritatively before printing articles on it.

BASIC PERIODICAL INDEXES: HISTORY AND ARRANGEMENT

Poole's Index to Periodical Literature, 1802-81. rev. ed. Boston, Houghton, 1891. Supplement, Jan. 1882-Jan. 1, 1907.

The problem of finding articles on any subject among the multitude of periodicals was once very difficult. In 1847 William Frederick Poole was a student at Yale. In the course of his studies he found it necessary to use many periodicals, and, becoming annoyed at the need to look through the indexes of so many volumes to find what he wanted, he made a subject index, in longhand, and allowed his fellow students to use it. In 1848 this index of 154 pages was printed and purchased by some libraries, but the need for a magazine subject index for current material was not then so clearly recognized as it is today. It was not until 1876, at the first meeting of the American Library Association, that a group of fifty librarians made arrangements to work on such an index with Poole as editor. The collaborators donated their services, and the American Express Company carried the bundles of magazines and index slips free of charge. In 1882 the first large volume, indexing 232 magazines from 1802 to 1881, was published, and between 1882 and 1906 five supplements were issued. *Poole's Index* is still in use, and has become far more valuable because of the publication of the *Cumulative Author Index for Poole's Index to Periodical Literature, 1802-1906* (Ann Arbor, Mich., Pierian Press, 1971).

As noted above, Poole's was a subject index, and entries appeared under the names of writers only when writers were treated as subjects. In fact, when today's reader searches current indexes of any sort, he is usually looking for material about a subject, or a person as subject. If he comes upon an author whose name is familiar under the subject he is seeking, he may look up that author to find what else he has written which may be pertinent to his search.

But after a time, authors become more important. In the nineteenth century, the period covered by *Poole's Index*, authors now known to be important were writing voluminously, not only books but short stories and articles — frequently critical or appreciative articles about one another, and often under pseudonyms. As the new author index is computer-produced, the reader must not be turned off by entries under both Boz and Dickens, Clemens and Twain, or Titmarsh as well as Thackeray. (The preface states that "problems of verification" remain.)

In the meantime, *Poole's Index* has been supplemented by the *Nineteenth Century Readers' Guide* (New York, Wilson, 1944) which indexes by author, subject, and illustrator fifty-one periodicals published in the 1890s. Fourteen of the periodicals have been indexed beyond 1899 in order to provide complete indexing for those which later were included in other Wilson indexes.

Readers' Guide to Periodical Literature. New York, Wilson, 1905-   .

Various other magazine indexes have been published briefly, and the *Annual Magazine Subject Index*, begun in 1907 by the F. W. Faxon Company, continued to be published until 1949, indexing a number of periodicals not covered elsewhere.

But the index which no library can live without, the *Readers' Guide to Periodical Literature*, began in 1900 and was soon able to take the place of *Poole's Index*, relieving the librarians who contributed to Poole's work of their self-imposed task.

The *Readers' Guide* is published by The H. W. Wilson Company according to the method of continuous cumulation. On the twenty-fifth of every month except July and August a small index is published covering all issues of the indexed periodicals which appeared during the last two weeks of the previous month (approximately 160 periodicals are now indexed). At the end of the month these entries are inter-filed with new material to make a larger monthly issue. Issues are then cumulated quarterly, and, after the end of the year, a cloth-bound an-nual cumulation is published. Since 1968, there have been no cumulated volumes covering more than one year. Cumulation is made possible by the fact that every line is a separate block, or slug, of type. After use in a single issue, the slugs are stored and then interfiled with new type for the next cumulated number. All issues except the small mid-monthly have green covers, whether paper or cloth.

Next to the encyclopedias, the *Readers' Guide to Periodical Litera-ture* and similar indexes are probably the most useful reference tools in a library. The importance of periodicals as sources of information has already been pointed out — their up-to-dateness and the vast variety of information which they present in brief and (usually) readable form. With an index to this material ready for use within two weeks of publi-cation date, it is possible to find statements from several points of view on controversial issues, comment on recent scientific discoveries, texts of important speeches and documents. Yet this detailed indexing is easy to use and simple to interpret.

Semi-monthly issues and cumulations of the *Readers' Guide* contain (1) a list of the periodicals indexed, listed according to the abbrevia-tions used for them, and (2) a list of abbreviations used in the entries. (See Figures 27 and 28.)

Readers' Guide entries differ from catalog entries in several re-spects: (1) while there are many author entries, the listings by subject are by far the most important, for this index is used much more fre-quently to find information about a subject or person than to find an article or story by a person; (2) the arrangement of entries under sub-ject is alphabetical by title rather than by author, for the reason that much magazine material is unsigned; (3) because the entries are all articles by or about a person or about a subject, and almost always a part of a single issue of the magazine indexed, volume and page refer-ences are given; (4) subject subdivisions are indicated by centered headings in bold type consisting of the subdivision alone, instead of the entire heading as given on catalog entries. Typical *Readers' Guide* entries are shown in Figure 29.

Occasionally an entire issue of a periodical consists of one book-length article. Such periodicals are not apt to be in *Readers' Guide*, however, but in the more specialized indexes listed on pages 115-18.

USING INDEXES

In using any periodical index (or any of the indexes and bibliogra-phies listed in this chapter, or elsewhere in this book) it is wise to stop and think about which index to use, what volume to begin with, as well as what heading to look under. If the subject is of comparatively current interest, such as the ubiquitous and apparently insoluble traffic problem, the industrial use of atomic energy, some other phase of ecology, a hot political issue, or a prominent personality, one should begin with the most recent issue of an index and work backward in time, until either nothing more is found under the heading, or a date has been reached before which nothing *could* be found — e.g., before the advent of superhighways, before ecology became a household word, or before the prominent personality became prominent.

One usually has some time limit on the information desired, but a topic such as the reasons for using mice or rats in experiments concerning human health, or the development and decline of the novel in America, might take one back as far as periodical indexes and bibliographies go. Other topics have definite limits, run their course through a number of years, and never appear again in periodical literature, though they may turn up again in books or dissertations. Discredited scientific or economic theories, local politicians, Public Enemy No. 1 of an earlier day, run a brief course through the public prints, and disappear into oblivion. For such topics an encyclopedia article will give inclusive dates, and one's search of periodical indexes can be limited.

In taking notes from periodical indexes the student needs to modify the form of his 4″ × 6″ working bibliography cards. Instead of author and title of article on the top line, the name, date, volume, and page number of the magazine are more useful, with author and title following, and a note in the lower left telling the index and heading by which it was found (e.g., *RG* for *Readers' Guide*). Then all cards for one periodical may be arranged chronologically and examined (one should begin with the latest and work backward) before another series is searched for. This technique is especially important in large libraries with closed stacks, or with periodicals stored on film, microfiche, or microcard, where call slips must be presented at a service desk and only a limited number of items may be delivered to or used by a reader at one time. As each article is read (we are referring to newspapers or periodicals now) notes can be taken if it proves useful; if it does not, the card can be placed in the "reject file," along with notes on books which do not contribute to one's study. Two sample working bibliography cards are shown in Figures 30 and 31.

The reader will, of course, note that the subjects mentioned under "Using Indexes" are all to be found on the sample page from the *Readers' Guide* included later in this chapter, and that the asterisk in the second sample "working bibliography card" (Figure 31) does *not* indicate that the magazine *America* is available in Braille or "talking book" for the blind, as it does not appear beside the name of the magazine, in the list of periodicals indexed.

Aging–Aging
Am Artist–American Artist
Am City–American City
Am Educ–American Education
Am For–American Forests
*Am Heritage–American Heritage
Am Hist R–American Historical Review
Am Hist Illus–American History Illustrated
Am Home–American Home
Am Imago–American Imago
Am Lib–American Libraries
Am Rec G–American Record Guide
Am Scholar–American Scholar
Am West–American West
America–America
Américas–Américas
Ann Am Acad–Annals of the American
   Academy of Political and Social Science
Antiques–Antiques
Archit Forum–Architectural Forum
Archit Rec–Architectural Record
Art in Am–Art in America
Art N–Art News
*Atlantic–Atlantic
Audubon–Audubon
Aviation W–Aviation Week & Space
   Technology
*Bet Hom & Gard–Better Homes and
   Gardens
BioScience–BioScience
Bull Atom Sci–Bulletin of the Atomic
   Scientists
Bus W–Business Week
Camp Mag–Camping Magazine
Car & Dr–Car and Driver
Ceram Mo–Ceramics Monthly
*Changing T–Changing Times
Chemistry–Chemistry
Chr Cent–Christian Century
Chr Today–Christianity Today
Clearing H–Clearing House
Commentary–Commentary
Commonweal–Commonweal
Cong Digest–Congressional Digest
Conservationist–Conservationist (Albany)
*Consumer Rep–Consumer Reports
*Consumer Res Mag–Consumers' Research
   Magazine
Craft Horiz–Craft Horizons
Current–Current
Cur Hist–Current History
Dance Mag–Dance Magazine
Dept State Bull–Department of State
   Bulletin
Design–Design
Dun's–Dun's
*Ebony–Ebony
Educ Digest–Education Digest
Engl J–English Journal
Environment–Environment
Esquire–Esquire

*Farm J–Farm Journal (Central edition)
Field & S–Field & Stream
Film Q–Film Quarterly
Flying–Flying
Focus–Focus
*For Affairs–Foreign Affairs
Forbes–Forbes
*Fortune–Fortune
*Good H–Good Housekeeping
Harp Baz–Harper's Bazaar
*Harper–Harper's Magazine
Harvard Bus R–Harvard Business Review
*Hi Fi–High Fidelity and Musical
   America
Hobbies–Hobbies
*Holiday–Holiday
*Horizon–Horizon
Horn Bk–Horn Book Magazine
Horticulture–Horticulture
Hot Rod–Hot Rod
House & Gard–House & Garden
   incorporating Living for Young
   Homemakers
House B–House Beautiful
Intellect–Intellect
Int Wildlife–International Wildlife
*Ladies Home J–Ladies' Home Journal
Lib J–Library Journal includes School
   Library Journal
Liv Wildn–Living Wilderness
MH–MH
McCall's–McCall's
Mademoiselle–Mademoiselle
Mech Illus–Mechanix Illustrated
Mo Labor R–Monthly Labor Review
Mod Phot–Modern Photography
Motor B & S–Motor Boating & Sailing
Motor T–Motor Trend
Ms–Ms.
*Mus Q–Musical Quarterly
NY Times Mag–New York Times
   Magazine
*Nat Geog–National Geographic Magazine
Nat Parks & Con Mag–National Parks &
   Conservation Magazine
*Nat R–National Review
Nat Wildlife–National Wildlife
Nation–Nation
Nations Bus–Nation's Business
*Natur Hist–Natural History
Negro Hist Bull–Negro History Bulletin
New Cath World–New Catholic World
New Repub–New Republic
New Yorker–New Yorker
*Newsweek–Newsweek
Oceans–Oceans
Opera N–Opera News
Org Gard & Farm–Organic Gardening
   and Farming
Outdoor Life–Outdoor Life
PTA Mag–PTA Magazine

Figure 27: Periodicals Indexed in *Readers' Guide*

Parents Mag–Parents' Magazine & Better
    Family Living
Parks & Rec–Parks & Recreation
Phys Today–Physics Today
Plays–Plays
Poetry–Poetry
Pop Electr–Popular Electronics
*Pop Mech–Popular Mechanics
Pop Phot–Popular Photography
Pop Sci–Popular Science
Progressive–Progressive
Psychol Today–Psychology Today
Pub W–Publishers' Weekly

Radio-Electr–Radio-Electronics
Ramparts–Ramparts
*Read Digest–Reader's Digest
Redbook–Redbook
*Ret Liv–Retirement Living

Sat Eve Post–Saturday Evening Post
*Sat R World–Saturday Review World
Sch Arts–School Arts
School Teach Jr/Sr High–Scholastic
    Teacher Junior/Senior High Teacher's
    Edition

*Sci Am–Scientific American
Sci Digest–Science Digest
Sci N–Science News

Science–Science
Sea Front–Sea Frontiers
*Seventeen–Seventeen
Sky & Tel–Sky and Telescope
Smithsonian–Smithsonian
Society–Society
Space World–Space World
*Sports Illus–Sports Illustrated
Sr Schol–Senior Scholastic (Teacher
    edition)
Suc Farm–Successful Farming (Midwest
    edition)
Sunset–Sunset (Central edition)
Time–Time
Todays Educ–Today's Education
*Todays Health–Today's Health
Travel–Travel
UN Mo Chron–UN Monthly Chronicle
UNESCO Courier–UNESCO Courier
*U S News–U.S. News & World Report
Vital Speeches–Vital Speeches of the Day
Vogue–Vogue
Weatherwise–Weatherwise
Wilson Lib Bull–Wilson Library Bulletin
*Writer–Writer
Writers Digest–Writer's Digest
Yachting–Yachting
Yale R–Yale Review

*Available for blind and other physically handicapped readers on talking books, in braille, or on magnetic tape. For information, address Division for the Blind and Physically Handicapped, Library of Congress, Washington, D.C. 20542.

Figure 27 (continued)

*	following name entry, a printer's device	cont	continued	por	portrait
		corp	corporation	pseud	pseudonym
		D	December	pt	part
+	continued on later pages of same issue	dept	department	pub	published, publisher, publishing
		ed	edited, edition, editor		
abp	archbishop	F	February	q	quarterly
abr	abridged	Hon	Honorable	rev	revised
Ag	August	il	illustrated, illustration, illustrator	S	September
Ap	April			sec	section
arch	architect			semi-m	semimonthly
assn	association	inc	incorporated	soc	society
Aut	Autumn	introd	introduction, introductory	Spr	Spring
av	avenue			sq	square
bart	baronet	Ja	January	sr	senior
bibliog	bibliography	Je	June	st	street
bibliog f	bibliographical footnotes	Jl	July	Sum	Summer
		jr	junior	sup	supplement
bi-m	bimonthly	jt auth	joint author	supt	superintendent
bi-w	biweekly	ltd	limited	tr	translated, translation, translator
bldg	building	m	monthly		
bp	bishop	Mr	March		
co	company	My	May	v	volume
comp	compiled, compiler	N	November	w	weekly
		no	number	Wint	Winter
cond	condensed	O	October	yr	year

Figure 28: Abbreviations Used in *Readers' Guide* entries

ENVIRONMENTAL health
Effects of pollution on health; proceedings of the sixth Berkeley symposium on mathematical statistics and probability, ed. by L. M. LeCam and others. Review
Environment 14:40-2 O '72. S. Norvick

ENVIRONMENTAL movement
Confrontation; when environmentalism confronts economics. il Forbes 110:32-3+ N 15 '72
Conservation: environmetal action line. M. Frome. Field & S 77:80+ D '72
Doomsday syndrome, by J. Maddox. Review Sci N 102:371 D 9 '72. K. Frazier
Environmental challenge to men and institutions; address, September 1972. M. Strong. Nat Parks & Con Mag 46:22-5 N '72
Tips for reducing pollution in your daily living. F. Graham, jr. il Todays Health 50:42-5 N '72

FICTION
Why they aren't writing the great American novel anymore; comparison of 19th century novels with 20th century journalism; with appendices. T. Wolfe. il Esquire 78:152-+ D '72
See also
French fiction
Jews in literature
        Authorship
Elusive plot. D. Eden. Writer 85:9-10+ D '72
        Bibliography
Fiction (cont) W. B. Hill. America 126:549-50; 127:420+ My 20, N 18 '72
        Technique
Your secret writing weapons. P. Gunn. Writer 85:26-7 D '72

GAGE, Joan
(ed) See Graham, R. Mrs Billy Graham: teaching children to believe in God
(ed) See Hope, B. Bob Hope answers his Vietnam critics and tells how he tried to free our prisoners of war

GOODMAN, Paul
Paul Goodman; address, October 22, 1972. G. Dennison. Nation 215:504-6+ N 20 '72 *

GOODMAN, Walter, ca 1873
Courting Cachita; story; excerpt from The pearl of the Antilles, ed. by K. C. Tessendorf. il Américas 24:32-6 O '72

GORDON, Barbara (Wickelgren)
Superior colliculus of the brain; with biographical sketch. il Sci Am 227:10, 72-82 bibliog (p 128) D '72

HACKETT, Walter
Christmas carol; dramatization of story by C. Dickens; reprint from December 1967 issue. Plays 32:81-90 D '72

HECHT, Ben, and MacArthur, Charles
Front page. Criticism
        America 127:470-1 D 2 '72 *

HIGHWAY 1, U.S.A.; opera. See Still, W. G.

HIJACKING. See Robberies and assaults

HOPE, Bob
Bob Hope answers his Vietnam critics and tells how he tried to free our prisoners of war; interview, ed. by J. Gage. por Ladies Home J 89:68+ D '72

IRVIN, Robert W.
Exciting options for your '73 car. il Mech Illus 68:82-4 S '72
What's really new in the 1973 cars. il Mech Illus 68:79-85+ O '72

IRVING, Clifford, family
Clifford Irving's children: innocent victims of the hoax that failed. C. Breslin. por Redbook 140:89+ N '72

IRVING, Jules
Curtain at Lincoln Center. J. Kroll. il Newsweek 80:89 N 20 '72 *

JOHNSON, James P. and Churchill, F. O.
Black and bibliographical. Wilson Lib Bull 47:248-50, 374-7 N-D '72

JOHNSON, Lady Bird. See Johnson, C. A. T.

JOHNSON, Mendal
Everything you always wanted to know about sailplans. il Motor B & S 130:48-9+ N '72

JOHNSON, Ted. See Johnson, G. T.

JOHNSON, William
Striking it rich at Snowbird. il Sports Illus 37:65-6+ N 20 '72

KISSINGER, Henry Alfred
Dr Kissinger discusses status of negotiations toward Viet-Nam peace; transcript of news conference, October 30, 1972. Dept State Bull 67:549-58 N 13 '72
Kissinger; interview, ed. by O. Fallaci. New Repub 167:17-22 D 16 '72
Vietnam maxims; excerpt from January 1969 issue of Foreign affairs, ed. by W. F. Buckley, jr. Nat R 24-1318 N 24 '72
        about
Clouds over Paris; with report by H. Hubbard. il pors Newsweek 80:26-7 D 4 '72 *
Facts hard and soft. S. Alsop. Newsweek 80:112 D 18 '72 *
Henry Kissinger: the go between. il por Sr Schol 101:20 N 27 '72 *
Kicking sand. J. Osborne. New Repub 167:9-10 D 16 '72 *
Kissinger: the uses of power, by D. Landau. Review
        America 127:499 D 9 '72. B. H. Smith *
Mastermind as mouthpiece. B. Collier. Sat R 55:8-9 N 18 '72 *
Peace by inauguration day? il por Newsweek 80:23-4 N 27 '72 *
Peace talks: putting the heat on Thieu. il por Newsweek 80:41 D 11 '72 *
Peace talks: the last word? il por Newsweek 80:20-1 D 18 '72 *.
This is my battle station. il pors Life 73:36-42 D 1 '72 *

LABOR grievances. See Grievance procedures

LANIER, Doris, and Lightsey, Ralph
Verbal SAT scores and high school averages as predictors. bibliog Intellect 101:127-8 N '72

LEESON, Jeanne Tellier
Third graders in stitches. il Sch Arts 72:8 D '72

LESSER, Murray L.
Sail area for cruising boats. Motor B & S 130:49+ N '72

MACARTHUR, Charles. See Hecht, B jt. auth.

MAGIC flute; opera. See Mozart, J. C. W. A.

MAGIC mountain (amusement park) See Amusement parks

MICE
Chromosome mapping in the mouse. D. A. Miller and O. J. Miller. bibliog il Science 178:949-55 D 1 '72
Genetic mapping of a murine leukemia virus-inducing locus of AKR mice. W. P. Rowe and others. bibliog il Science 178:860-2 N 24 '72
Hemoglobin beta chain structural variation in mice: evolutionary and functional implications. J. G. Gilman. bibliog il Science 178:873-4 N 24 '72
Mice for research; Jackson laboratory. il Chemistry 45:20-1 D '72

MOON
Origin and evolution of the earth-moon system. Sky & Tel 44:368 D '72

        Exploration
        Equipment
Apollo ending as science hits its stride. il Aviation W 97:53-4+ D 4 '72

        Surface
Landing site could add to data on forces that shaped lunar terrain. W. H. Gregory. il Aviation W 97:42-6 D 4 '72

Figure 29: Sample Entries From *Readers' Guide*

Forbes, Nov. 15, 1972, vol. 110, p. 32-3+ illus.
Confrontation; when environmentalism
confronts economics.

R.G. Environmental movement

Figure 30: Sample Working Bibliography Card

America, Dec. 9, 1972, vol. 127, p. 499
Kissinger: the uses of power, by
D. Landau. Review [by B. H. Smith]*

R.G. Kissinger, Henry Alfred — (about)

Figure 31: Sample Working Bibliography Card

Transferring the items in one's working bibliography to the final List of Sources placed at the end of the research paper was discussed in Chapter 6. Two possible methods of arrangement were suggested there, namely (1) interfiling books and magazine articles in one alphabetical list, by author (if known), provided that there are not more than a dozen entries, or (2) making one list of books and another of periodical material. A modification of the second method, in a long bibliography, with many articles taken from each of a number of magazine issues, is to enter the items alphabetically by name of periodical, then chronologically in order of publication. This simplifies matters for future students who may wish to examine the same material, and, more important, for the professor under whose direction the paper was written.

GENERAL INDEXES

Some periodical indexes include references to books and pamphlets as well as to magazine articles. Two items mentioned briefly in Chapter 1 are listed here, with supplementary publications; in addition a number of indexes which are more or less general in scope are mentioned in this section. Indexes limited to special subject fields or referring only to nonbook materials are discussed later in this chapter and in subsequent chapters devoted to particular subjects.

As any student knows, often a book published many years ago provides information not to be found in recent publications. The fact that many of the indexes listed here and elsewhere were not compiled recently sometimes makes them more valuable than current books by authors so up-to-date that nothing said before 1965 has any value, as far as they are concerned.

The indexes listed here are both up-to-date and retrospective.

Ash, Lee and Lorenz, Denis, eds. *Subject Collections. A Guide to Special Book Collections in Libraries.* 4th ed. New York, Bowker, 1973.

> This supplements the three titles by Downs, listed below. It tells which libraries emphasize or maintain special collections (including books, indexes, catalogs, pictorial material). Arranged in geographical order under each subject or other category. Tremendously valuable to the research worker.

Bruncken, Herbert. *Subject Index to Poetry: A Guide for Adult Readers.* Chicago, American Library Association, 1940.

> Poems are listed here by subject, so that one may find verses to illustrate or emphasize a point. Especially useful to public speakers and toastmasters. (Books of quotations arranged by subject are useful in the same way. See list in Chapter 11, under Books of Quotations.)

Downs, Robert Bingham. *American Library Resources; a Bibliographical guide.* Chicago, American Library Association, 1951. *Supplement, 1950-1961,* 1962.

> A classified list of bibliographies of American library holdings.

——*Resources of New York City Libraries; a Survey of Facilities for Research.* Chicago, American Library Association, 1942.

——*Resources of Southern Libraries; a Survey of Facilities for Research.* Chicago, American Library Association, 1938.

> The latter two books describe in detail the special collections in the libraries indexed and have minute indexes by subject. They are invaluable to the doctoral candidate wishing to visit the best collections in his chosen field of study.

Eagle, Selwyn, ed. *Library Resources in London and South East England*. London, The Library Association: Reference, Special and Information Section, 1969.

An alphabetical listing of the research resources of 1,123 libraries in the area. Two indexes: one "topographical" (not much help if you don't know much about English postal districts), the other by subject. Similar listings have been published for seven other areas of the British Isles, and others are in preparation.

Essay and General Literature Index. New York, Wilson, 1900-

Indexes collections of essays and miscellaneous articles in many areas of knowledge, but particularly in the humanities and social sciences, published between 1900 and the present. This makes available thousands of articles in hundreds of miscellaneous works and collections of essays. Many critical articles are included, and there is also some biographical material. Authors, subjects, and some titles are listed in dictionary arrangement, with copious cross references. A list of books indexed appears in each volume, and an advance list is sent to subscribers each month, so that they may purchase the books if desired.

Now published semiannually, with an annual and a permanent five-year cumulation. The first large cumulated volume, 1900-1933, was published in 1934 and followed by a series of seven- and five-year cumulations. In 1972, *Essay and General Literature Index: Works Indexed 1900-1969* was published. This seventy-year list cites all the nearly 10,000 titles analyzed in the seven previous permanent cumulations.

Book Review Digest, described in Chapter 10 under Book Reviewing Media, may also be used as a subject index to recent literature. The cumulated indexes in every fifth volume form a subject and title index to books of general interest published during each five-year period. For a selective list of fiction, see the *Fiction Catalog*, described in the same chapter.

Lewenski, R. C., comp. *Subject Collections in European Libraries*. New York, Bowker, 1965.

This belongs to the same category as the preceding titles. A more detailed and up-to-date treatment of European libraries is needed, to include some of the countries to which there has been little access until recently.

Other important indexes are listed below.

SPECIALIZED INDEXES

Abridged Readers' Guide to Periodical Literature. New York, Wilson, 1935-   .

Monthly during the school year; cumulated annually. The *Abridged Readers' Guide* indexes 44 periodicals chosen by librarians of elementary schools, small high schools, and very small public libraries. The magazines included are useful for teachers, and the probable interests of children are considered in the selection. It is a good tool for teaching students to use a periodical index and thus has value to students who intend to teach. However, with the present trend towards cooperation among libraries within regions or small states, whereby the small library may secure microfilm copies, photocopies, or noncurrent issues of periodicals from its regional center, more small libraries are likely to use the full-size *Readers' Guide*, as the branches of large city libraries are apt to do. Students in schools using either the *Abridged Readers' Guide* or the larger edition still have the use of public library collections of magazines.

Agricultural Index. New York, Wilson, 1917-1964.

Monthly, cumulative subject index to about 115 periodicals and many books, bulletins, pamphlets and reports. Superseded in September 1964 by *Biological & Agricultural Index (q.v.).*

Applied Science & Technology Index. New York, Wilson, 1958- .

One of the two successors to the *Industrial Arts Index (q.v.).* Monthly except July, cumulated quarterly and annually. Subject index to 225 periodicals in aeronautics, automation, chemistry, construction, electricity and its uses, engineering, geology, industrial arts, physics, space technology, transportation, and related subjects.

Art Index. New York, Wilson, 1929- .

An author and subject index to approximately 152 periodicals and museum bulletins, both domestic and foreign, selected by the subscribers to the *Index*. Locates reproductions of individual works of art and references to book reviews. Quarterly, cumulated annually.

Bibliographic Index. New York, Wilson, 1937- .

Bibliographies in English and other languages, indexed by subject. Includes those published separately as books or pamphlets, and as parts of books, pamphlets, or articles. Also, about 2,200 periodicals are examined for bibliographic lists containing fifty or more citations. This index will be particularly helpful to the student writing a term paper, for, by consulting a bibliography on his subject, he may save himself much unnecessary checking. Issued April, August, and December (annual cumulation). Before 1969, cumulations covered three or five years.

Biography Index. New York, Wilson, 1946- .

Quarterly, cumulative subject index, by name and by profession or occupation, to biographical material in approximately 2,200 magazines indexed in the other Wilson indexes; individual and collective biographies; incidental biographical material in nonbiographical books; obituaries of national and international interest from the New York *Times*. Bound annual and three-year cumulations.

Biological & Agricultural Index. New York, Wilson, 1964- .

Successor to *Agricultural Index (q.v.).* Monthly except August, cumulated annually. Subject index to 189 periodicals published in the United States, Canada, and the British Commonwealth.

Business Periodicals Index. New York, Wilson, 1958- .

The other successor to the *Industrial Arts Index (q.v.).* Monthly except August. Cumulative subject index to about 150 periodicals in accounting, advertising, banking and finance, insurance, labor and management, marketing, public administration, taxation, and specific businesses, industries, and trades.

Catholic Periodical and Literature Index. Haverford, Pa., Catholic Library Association, 1930- .

A bimonthly index, cumulated every two years. Indexes only Catholic magazines, not Catholic material found in other magazines. However, the *Catholic Digest*, indexed here, carries articles from secular magazines. Includes books for the layman.

Education Index. New York, Wilson, 1929-   .

Monthly, except July and August, with cumulations similar in schedule to *Readers' Guide.* Subject index to approximately 230 periodicals and other publications, e.g., yearbooks, proceedings, and monographs, as well as publications of the United States Office of Education. No multi-annual cumulations since 1963.

Engineering Index. New York, Engineering Index, Inc., 1884-   .

Originally a card index to current material, issued weekly, and cumulated into monthly and annual volumes. Has had various publishers. More than 1,000 technical journals and other publications are listed by subject. Abstracts of the articles are given, and an author index is provided. Also available on microfilm.

Facts on File. New York, Facts on File, Inc., Oct. 30, 1940-   .

A small weekly news digest in looseleaf form, culled from a number of metropolitan dailies, with a cumulative index. The index is cumulated at five-year intervals, as well. Like the *New York Times Index,* it can be used as a guide to news items in any current source. Its annual publication, formerly called *Facts on File Yearbook,* was from 1960 to 1963 called *News Year.* Since 1965 Facts on File, Inc. has also published an annual *News Dictionary,* edited by Lester A. Sobel — a dictionary arrangement of news items under name, place, and subject.

Humanities Index. New York, Wilson, 1974-   .

Quarterly, with annual cumulations. Indexes articles from about 260 periodicals according to author and subject. Book reviews are listed in a separate section.

Index to Legal Periodicals. New York, Wilson, 1952-   .

A cumulative author and subject index to more than 350 publications. Primarily an index to periodicals, it includes yearbooks, annual reports of institutes, and annual reviews of work in a given field. In three parts: Subject and author index, Table of cases, Book review index. Case notes at the end of each subject. Monthly except September, annual and three-year cumulations. The publisher is advised on editorial and indexing policy by a special committee of the American Association of Law Libraries.

Industrial Arts Index. New York, Wilson, 1913-1957.

Subject index to more than 200 periodicals, some published outside the United States. Superseded in January 1958 by *Applied Science & Technology Index* and *Business Periodicals Index (qq.v.).*

International Index; a Quarterly Guide to Periodical Literature in the Social Sciences and Humanities. New York, Wilson, 1907-1965.

Until 1921 this was published as *Readers' Guide Supplement.* Quarterly, with annual and two-year cumulations. Index to about 170 periodicals. Superseded in June 1965 by *Social Sciences & Humanities Index (q.v.).*

New York Times Index. New York, New York Times, 1913-   .

Frequency of publication has varied. Now published semimonthly, with annual cumulations. Though page references are to the New York *Times,* this, like *Facts on File (q.v.)* serves as an index to events and can be used as an index to other newspapers and magazines. The *Times* is available on microfiche for use in many libraries.

Public Affairs Information Service Bulletin. New York, Public Affairs
Information Service, 1915-   .
>   Weekly, with annual and five-year cumulations. Indexes books, periodicals,
>   pamphlets, and government publications on governmental activities and
>   public affairs in the broadest sense, including adult education and libraries.

Social Sciences & Humanities Index. New York, Wilson, 1965-1973.
>   Quarterly, with annual cumulations. Successor to *International Index (q.v.).*
>   An author and subject index to more than 200 periodicals in the fields of
>   anthropology, archaeology, history and classical studies, economics, sociol-
>   ogy, political science, language, literature and the theater, philosophy, reli-
>   gion and theology. This was superseded in 1974 by two separate indexes,
>   one on the social sciences and one on the humanities, to allow greater in-
>   dexing coverage in both fields.

Social Sciences Index. New York, Wilson, 1974-   .
>   Quarterly, with annual cumulations. Articles from more than 260 periodi-
>   cals are indexed by author and by subject. In a separate section of the index,
>   book reviews in the social sciences are listed alphabetically, by the authors of
>   the books.

DIRECTORIES OF PERIODICALS

Very brief mention was made in Chapter 1 of some of the most important and comprehensive directories or catalogs of serial publications.
A fuller list of the most useful follows.

Ayer Directory of Newspapers, Magazines and Trade Publications.
Philadelphia, N. W. Ayer & Son, 1880-
>   An annual directory of newspapers and magazines published in America.
>   Arranged geographically for those wishing to know what is published in any
>   city, with an alphabetical index to tell where a specific paper or magazine is
>   published. Frequency, price, editors, and political affiliation are among the
>   details given. Lists about 22,000 items.

Ulrich's International Periodicals Directory. 15th ed., 1973-1974. New
York, Bowker, 1973.
>   Lists more than 55,000 periodicals published throughout the world, and
>   gives more attention to publications in Latin America, Japan, and India than
>   earlier editions. This directory also lists abstracting and indexing services
>   such as the major subject matter of this chapter, and new titles which began
>   publication within the last two years. The 16th edition will appear in 1975.
>   This is revised at two-year intervals.

Irregular Serials and Annuals, an International Directory. E. I. Koltay,
ed. New York, Bowker, 1970. 2d ed. 1972.
>   This also is expected to be reissued and updated biennially. It lists more
>   than 18,000 publications issued irregularly or not more than once a year. It
>   covers U.S. and foreign serials, arranged by subject, with title and subject
>   indexes (i.e., a serial which treats more than one subject will be listed in the
>   major category and also indexed under minor subjects). It has a combined
>   index, including the concurrent edition of *Ulrich's,* and will continue to be
>   revised at the same two year intervals.

The Union List of Serials in Libraries of the United States & Canada.
3d ed. Edna Brown Titus, ed. New York, Wilson, 1965. 5 vols.
> This gives the location in libraries of serial publications available in North America. It naturally includes many titles no longer published and is especially valuable to scholars for that reason.

New Serial Titles, published quarterly by the Library of Congress, a union list of serials commencing publication after 1949, acts as a supplement to the above. The quarterly issues are cumulated into larger issues at intervals.

Chapter 10

PRINTED BIBLIOGRAPHIES AND BOOKLISTS

THE TWO TERMS, *bibliographies* and *booklists*, resemble the lists of books which they represent. A booklist — usually brief and informal — suggests a group of books chosen to introduce a subject, or to introduce the reader to the pleasures of reading a certain type of book. Public libraries frequently issue lists of ten or a dozen books, suggestions for people who "want a good book." The term *bibliography* means booklist, too, but usually refers to a more systematic and more inclusive selection. It may also be used to describe a complete listing of everything known to have been published on a subject, or of everything known to have been written by an author.

On page 13 we referred to searching the literature before embarking upon a scientific investigation. This search includes examination of bibliographies as well as periodical indexes and library catalogs. Every branch of knowledge has its special bibliographies, some compiled so long ago as to be classics, some published annually by associations or government departments by and for specialists in their fields. Most of these are listed in *Bibliographic Index*, described in Chapter 9, or in Theodore Besterman's *World Bibliography of Bibliographies* . . . (4th ed., Lausanne, Societas Bibliographica, 1965-1966, 5 vols.). Sometimes the catalog of a great library is the major bibliography in the field. This is true of the National Library of Medicine, formerly the United States Army Medical Library, whose printed catalog is the most important list of medical literature in the world.

A subject specialist must become acquainted with the bibliographies in his field, but a list of them would be out of place in this handbook for the general reader. There are, however, a number of current bibliographic publications which he should know. Most of these will be found in every college library, and in most public libraries.

CUMULATIVE BOOK INDEX

The most inclusive continuous general bibliography is the *Cumulative Book Index*, usually called *CBI*. This is a publication of The H. W. Wilson Company, and, like *Poole's Index*, grew out of a personal need. When Halsey W. Wilson was an undergraduate at the University of Minnesota, he earned his expenses by operating a book store for his fellow students. Like all booksellers, he received catalogs of their publications from many publishers, and searched them all diligently for the books desired by his customers. But unlike other booksellers, he had the creative imagination to see that a publication incorporating all these separate catalogs into one and listing every book by its subject and title as well as its author would be of great value to librarians, publishers, and booksellers alike. The first issue of the *Cumulative Book Index* was published in February 1898, a pamphlet of sixteen pages. During the first months of publication it became obvious that monthly cumulation was impossible, and a program of periodic cumulations interspersed with issues for a single month was launched, a program which is substantially the method used today. Since 1928, *CBI* has been a world list of books published in English, not just a list of those published in the United States.

Entries in the *Cumulative Book Index* vary in completeness. Just as in a library catalog, the entry under the author's name is the main entry, thus the most complete. It contains the author's full name, with dates of birth and death, complete title as it appears on the title page, size, exact pagination and other collation (illustrations, maps, etc.), and full imprint and price. If the book has been published by two or more publishers in different countries (e.g., United States, England, and Canada) the individual publishers and prices are all noted. Finally, the number by which Library of Congress cards may be ordered is given.

Subject entries omit collation and LC card number, while title entries give only brief title, abbreviated author, publisher, and price. If a second author has collaborated in preparation of a book, the entry under his name is a mere *see* reference to the first author. Examples of various types of entries may be seen in Figure 32.

UNITED STATES CATALOG

Useful as the *Cumulative Book Index* was as a list of current publications, it did not fully supply the information needed by booksellers and libraries. Since 1873 the R. R. Bowker Company had been issuing the *Publishers' Trade List Annual*, a compilation of publishers' catalogs which is discussed below. An index by author and title of all the books in print was needed, and this Mr. Wilson prepared to supply. The first *United States Catalog*, published in the fall of 1899, consisted of two volumes, one an author list, the other an index by title. Three later editions, published in 1902, 1912, and 1928, were dictionary catalogs similar in format to *CBI*. Since World War II, however, books have gone in and out of print so fast that only an annual catalog could attempt to be up to date, and no further editions of the *United States Catalog* are planned.

Lynn, Bruce G.
  The Grenadines; undiscovered islands of the
    Caribbean [photographed by the author]
    Q pa $5.95 '68 Dukane press, inc, 2901 Simms
    st, Hollywood, Fla. 33020
    LC 68-59420
Lynn, Margaret, pseud. See Battye, G. S.
Lynn, Robert Athan, 1930-
  Basic economic principles. 2d ed 375p $14.50 '70
    McGraw
    LC 70-92698
  Marketing principles and market action. 290p
    il 86s '69 McGraw
    SBN 07-039255-2
Lynton, Ernest Albert
  Superconductivity. 3d ed 219p il 30s '69 Me-
    thuen
    SBN 416-11790-2   LC 73-404530
Lyon, Jean Currens. See Carpenter, A. jt auth.
Lyons, Gene Martin, 1924-
  The uneasy partnership; social science and
    the federal gov. in the 20th century. 394p
    $8.50 '69 Russell Sage
    LC 72-93761
The lyric poetry of Charles D'Orleans. Fox J. H.
  $7 Oxford
Lysegard, Anna
  Introduction to COBOL. 152p 30.75kr '69 Stu-
    dentlitteratur
    LC 75-438389
Lyser, Alice Irene
  (comp) See California. University. Library.
    Spain and Spanish America in the libraries
    of the University of California
Lysergic acid diethylamide
  Stafford, P. G. and Golightly, B. H. L.S.D. in
    action. 35s '69 Sidgwick
Lytton, Hugh
  (ed) See Guidance and counselling in British
    schools

M. G. automobile
  Ball, K. MG Midget TA-TF 1936-1955 auto-
    book. 2d ed rev 40s '69 Autopress
Ma Bell's millions. Phillips, J. P. $3.95 Vantage
Maas, Jeremy
  Victorian painters. F 257p il col il $22.50 '69
    Putnam
    LC 69-12341
McAlister, John T. 1936-, and Mus, Paul
  The Vietnamese and their revolution: written
    under the auspices of the Center of int.
    studies, Princeton university. 173p $5.95 '70
    Harper
    LC 74-103920
MacAlpin, Rory
  The choice. 157p 16s '69 Hale, R.
    SBN 7091-0944-X
Macao
                        History
  Boxer, C. R. Fidalgos in the Far East 1550-
    1770. See main entry

Figure 32: Sample Entries in *Cumulative Book Index*

PUBLISHERS' TRADE LIST ANNUAL
AND *BOOKS IN PRINT*

It has been pointed out that books go in and out of print too rapidly
to make a new *United States Catalog* worthwhile. Yet here is a work
called *Books in Print*, an annual which does, in fact, list most items
in print. The coverage of the two works and the completeness of indexing account for the apparent paradox. The *United States Catalog* is a
dictionary catalog. Every book is listed by author, title, and subject,
and many are listed under joint author, editor, and additional subjects
as well. Many of these entries give enough detail so that the book can
be ordered from any one of them. Also, many of the works listed are

publications of learned societies and other organizations which may issue only one publication a year. The correspondence necessary to discover the status of such publications would be voluminous.

The other work is of a different nature. The *Publishers' Trade List Annual* is a collection of the catalogs of the major American publishers, arranged alphabetically by the names of the publishers. Since 1873 this has been compiled annually, bound, and sold by the R. R. Bowker Company. The 1974 edition is in six immense volumes.

The word *trade* in this title is significant. A *trade list*, in the book business, is a list of books generally offered for sale by book dealers, and *trade books* are those designed to interest the general reading public. This eliminates many publications of university presses, textbook publishers, firms whose output is limited to a narrow field, and the various associations and other one-book publishers mentioned above. It is true that more and more university presses are issuing trade books, and a number of them are included in *PTLA*. If one knows the publisher of a book, it is a simple process to look it up in that publisher's catalog in *PTLA* and find out whether it was in print at the beginning of the year. Until 1948, it was necessary to know the publisher, because there was no index to this work; one's first step was to look in *CBI* to find the publisher, then in *PTLA* to find the book.

Since 1948 an index to *PTLA* has been issued, called *Books in Print*. This gives one-line entries under author, title, and series, stating publisher and price. For further details one turns to the publisher's catalog in the appropriate *PTLA* volume. It should be remembered that *Books in Print* does not eliminate the need to use *CBI*, for few publishers' catalogs state edition or original date of publication of their works, and a book may be still in print though actually in need of revision. In 1957 Bowker began issuing an annual *Subject Index to Books in Print* (now called the *Subject Guide to Books in Print*). Sometimes one book may appear under several different subjects, and biographical or historical fiction is often listed, but for the most complete and up-to-date information it is still necessary to consult *CBI*, partly for books published outside the United States, or by the smaller publishers, and of course especially for fiction, poetry, and essays on miscellaneous subjects, which cannot be assigned subject headings. In addition, publishers often list in their catalogs books to be published during the year, giving the probable month of issue or merely stating "in preparation." *CBI* must be searched for these, also, as a book may be listed as "in preparation" for several successive years.

In any country where large numbers of books come off the press every day, booksellers and librarians need current lists to fill the gaps between issues of works like the monthly issues of *CBI*. The R. R.

Bowker Co. has stepped into the breach again, this time with *Forth-coming Books*, and its companion *Subject Guide to Forthcoming Books*. These are both published bimonthly, but each covers the current month and four to come; i.e., each bimonthly issue overlaps, updates, and expands the previous one. To quote the verso of the front cover of a recent issue: "All categories of books are included: adult trade books, technical and scientific books, juveniles, el-hi and college texts, paper-backs, imports, revised editions and reprints." *Forthcoming Books* has separate alphabetical listings of authors and titles. The entries in the *Subject Guide* are alphabetical by title under the subject listings, and frequently appear under more than one subject listing.

For up-to-date information on books newly published, Bowker's *Publishers Weekly*, with its "Weekly Record" section, has been widely used by bookdealers and librarians. Originally a small magazine de-signed to give information on publishers, authors, and trends in the book trade, it has always contained a few good critical reviews of books likely to be in demand. The "Weekly Record" section lists books, paper-backs, and pamphlets of more than 49 pages issued during the preced-ing week. Beginning in September 1974, the "Weekly Record" became a separate publication, with the same title, available by subscription. Book reviews in *Publishers Weekly* and the *Weekly Record* will be listed and/or excerpted in some of the indexes of book reviews de-scribed later in this chapter. In England, among the listings of current British books is the *British National Bibliography*, published since 1950 by the Council of the British National Bibliography in London. This is "a subject list of new British books, based upon books deposited at the Copyright Office of the British Museum," issued weekly, and cumulated quarterly and annually. It is classified by the Dewey Decimal system, with full author, title, and subject index.

The publication of *Books in Print* has created a "genre" which has expanded to encircle the globe, or at least the highly literate sections of it. No matter what foreign publisher may produce a "Books in Print" for his countrymen, it is very likely to be distributed in the United States by Bowker. The following are now available — if not from Bowker, the national publisher will be mentioned.

Australian Books in Print. Melbourne, D. W. Thorpe (available in U.S. from Bowker).

British Books in Print. London, Whitaker (available in U.S. from Bow-ker). 2 vols.

> The British equivalent of *Publishers Weekly* is *The Bookseller*, which serves as the basis for this list. *BBIP* has a long history, dating back to *The Reference Catalogue of Current Literature*, first produced by Joseph Whitaker, the founder of *Whitaker's Almanack* (q.v.).

Canadian Books in Print (Catalogue des Livres Canadiens en Librairie).
Toronto, University of Toronto Press, annual, publ. in late fall.
Also available at the press' headquarters in Buffalo, N.Y.

German Books in Print (Verzeichnis Lieferbarer Bücher). 1st ed. 1971/
72. 2 vols. Distributed, except in Europe, by Bowker.

Libros en Venta. New York, Bowker, 1964.

> The Spanish equivalent of *Books in Print.* Recent supplements listing
> books published since 1967 have been issued by Bowker irregularly, as
> follows: *L. en V.,* 1967/68, pub. 1969; 1969/70, pub. 1972; 1971, pub.
> April 1973.
>
> This doubtless presents problems to the compilers, as it includes (as do
> the French and German equivalents) books published in the Spanish lan-
> guage anywhere in the world.

Repertoire des Livres Disponibles. Paris, France, Expansion; New York,
Bowker, 1971-   . 2 vols. Annual revision.

> The best French equivalent to *Books in Print.*

BOOK SELECTION AIDS

The H. W. Wilson Company is responsible for five selected bibliographies of books designed for the general reader. These are frequently referred to as the Standard Catalog series. All volumes in this
series list books under author, title, and subject, and give descriptive
annotations. They also have subject analytics referring to chapters in
books, and author and title analytics for plays in collections and, in
several of the catalogs, for short stories in collections.

The titles in this series are intended as guides to the purchase of
books for schools and small libraries, whose opportunities to use the
larger "Books in Print" type of guide may be limited by budget, or
perhaps by a shortage of staff time or a paucity of good bookstores
nearby. New editions of the books in the Standard Catalog series are
published at five-year intervals, with annual supplements between editions. The latest edition of each is indicated below.

Children's Catalog. 12th ed. 1971.

Fiction Catalog. 8th ed. 1970.

Junior High School Library Catalog. 3d ed. 1975.

Senior High School Library Catalog. 10th ed. 1972. (A Catholic-school
supplement is also available with this.)

Public Library Catalog (formerly *Standard Catalog for Public Libraries*). 6th ed. 1973.

College libraries may find both the *Fiction Catalog* and the *Public
Library Catalog* useful in selecting books for general reading for both
faculty and students. Teachers' colleges and teacher-training schools
within universities will find the other three titles in this series useful

for courses in children's literature and the reading interests of "young adults."

Another bibliography found in teachers' colleges is *El-Hi Textbooks in Print* (New York, Bowker), which includes not only the latest editions of textbooks but also "pedagogical" books. It is published annually in March, in time for ordering textbooks for the next school year, and was formerly called *Textbooks in Print*, and, before 1956, the *American Educational Catalog*.

BOOK REVIEWING MEDIA

Anyone who enjoys reading resents time spent on silly and poorly written books, as the restaurant customer resents being served tasteless or poorly cooked food. We can get advice about restaurants from travel guides and our friends, and we can get information about books from various sources, including the "Best Seller" lists, but unfortunately, the Best Seller is very seldom the best book.

When the second edition of THE NEW LIBRARY KEY was published, there were three American weekly book-review magazines. Now only the *New York Times Book Review*, which is included in the Sunday *Times*, remains. Other newspapers and weekly magazines have a few reviews. But for advice on a good book to read in your spare time, we are back to the advice in the first two chapters of this book: Ask a librarian.

Of course there are plenty of sources of book reviews: The scientific and scholarly journals naturally give books in their fields considerable attention, and there are a number of sources of good critical comment which are used by librarians; those with the broadest coverage are *Choice*, the *Kirkus Reviews*, and the *Library Journal*, none of which hesitates to make unfavorable comments or bluntly say "not for purchase."

In addition, four publications are important not only for reviews of current books, but for retrospective criticism.

Book Review Digest. New York, Wilson, 1905-   . Monthly except February and July; bound annual cumulations.

> Lists and gives excerpts from reviews appearing in current magazines for books of general interest. Entries are alphabetical by authors of books reviewed. Title and subject index in each issue and in annual cumulations. Since 1921, there has been a five-year cumulated index in every fifth volume (1921, 1926, 1931, etc.); since 1971, the five-year index has been published as a separate volume. One very useful feature of the index is the subject indexing of fiction.

Book Review Index. Detroit, Gale Research Co., 1965-

> Index to all reviews in more than 200 periodicals. Gives author's name, title of book, reviewing publication, date and page of review. The *Index*

ceased publication in 1968, but, presumably because of demand from subscribers, has been collecting material for 1969 to date. Clothbound annuals for 1969-1972 were published in the summer of 1973. Beginning with 1973 the *Index* is issued bimonthly, and every second issue cumulates with the one preceding it, ending with annual cumulations from 1973 on.

Books Abroad. Norman, Okla., University of Oklahoma Press, 1927- . Quarterly.

Intended to give American readers a survey of publications from the rest of the world. More than 200 book reviews in each issue —each notice is short, but the choice is limited to literary and liberal arts titles and belles lettres in some sixty languages. Each issue has a number of survey articles, and at least one critical essay on an author or a genre. The reviews are in English, by scholars and subject specialists.

Eichelberger, Clayton L., and others, comps. *A Guide to Critical Reviews of United States Fiction, 1870-1910.* Metuchen, N.J., Scarecrow Press, 1971. Supplement, 1974.

A list of book reviews from thirty American and English periodicals, including the New Orleans *Daily Picayune* and *Godey's Lady's Book* and other regional and seldom-indexed sources. Anonymous works for which no authors could be established are listed by title in an appendix. Should be a useful supplement to the early volumes of the *Book Review Digest*.

Chapter 11

GENERAL
REFERENCE BOOKS

THE GENERAL REFERENCE books included in this chapter contain bits and pieces of information. Some of these books are limited in scope to one field of knowledge, such as the dates of events, or folklore and customs of other times, or the "right way" to do something: set a banquet table, conduct a meeting, or write a letter to a bishop or a congressman. Some will be limited to the events of one year or one country.

Most of these books, and others like them, will be in libraries, usually in the Reference Department or in the reference area of a subject department. They contain very diverse collections of facts, so we call some of them *fact finders*. They were compiled to answer the questions which arise out of one's reading and conversation. Those published some years ago answer questions based on the literature of an earlier day, identify characters in books, and explain allusions to mythology and history. The young American whose knowledge of literature is limited to the required readings he has worked his way through is often bewildered by the mention of people and historical events important in their day but now remote and obscure. Some effort to learn their significance adds to one's general background as well as to one's enjoyment of the book in hand.

The section which follows is a sort of ollapodrida, a miscellany of works which could fit anywhere; in the Library of Congress classification system, most of these books would fall in AC.

Barnhart, Clarence L. and Halsey, William D., eds. *New Century Cyclopedia of Names.* New York, Appleton, 1954. 3 vols.

> Identifies places, people, literary works, characters in books and mythology, biblical references. A revised and enlarged edition of the earlier *Century Cyclopedia of Names* (1911).

Benét, William Rose, ed. *The Reader's Encyclopedia.* 2d ed. New York, Crowell, 1965.

> Benét based his 1948 edition on Crowell's *Reader's Handbook* and referred in his preface to the works by Brewer mentioned below. The 1965 edition, prepared by a staff of editors, adds much new material, including a number of illustrations and chronological lists of rulers of England and France, presidents of the United States, and popes. It explains references

128

to history and mythology encountered in literature and has new biographical information on writers from Homer to Ionesco and Ginsberg. *Brewer's Dictionary of Phrase and Fable (q.v.)* is similar to the new Benét but with more emphasis on English literature, while Brewer's *The Reader's Handbook of Famous Names in Fiction . . . (q.v.)* may be useful for older material.

Unfortunately, when new material is added to a reference book, something old may be left out, perhaps something to which the reader wishes to refer. So librarians and book-lovers keep the old edition beside the new. This is true of many of the following:

Brewer, E. C., comp. *Brewer's Dictionary of Phrase and Fable*. Centenary ed. Revised by Ivor H. Evans. New York, Harper, 1970.

> In spite of excisions, this is a valuable book, to which 205 pages have been added. It has a five-page biographical memoir by Brewer's grandson and a two-page list of the works he wrote or edited.

Brewer, E. C., comp. *The Reader's Handbook of Famous Names in Fiction, Allusions, References, Proverbs, Plots, Stories and Poems*. Philadelphia, Lippincott, 1899. Reissued in 2 vols. by Gale Research Co. (Detroit), 1966.

> A facsimile reprint. A 1935 edition, also published by Lippincott, is o.p. but available in libraries.

Butler, Audrey, comp. *Everyman's Dictionary of Dates*. 6th ed. London, Dent; New York, Dutton, 1971.

> Useful for dates concerning national anthems, the war in Cambodia, discoveries of new drugs, etc. British editorship and emphasis.

Carr, H. Gresham, ed. *Flags of the World*. rev. ed. New York, Warne, 1961.

> New edition "as up to date as possible, in these days of frequent changes in the political world," according to the publisher's announcement. Thirty-six plates in color, showing more than three hundred flags.

Chambers, Robert. *The Book of Days, a Miscellany of Popular Antiquities in Connection With the Calendar*. Edinburgh, Chambers, 1891. 2 vols. (The 1st edition published 1862-64 is out of print, but an 1886 edition has been reissued in one volume by Gale Research Co., Detroit, 1967.)

> Arranged according to the calendar, with an article for each month, and for each day. Emphasis is on British history and folklore, saints, festivals, etc., but there are some excellent sections on festivals and folklore of Continental Europe. Excellent index. Contains much half-legendary, half-historical material hard to find elsewhere.

Douglas, G. W. *The American Book of Days*. 2d ed. Revised and enlarged by Helen Douglas Compton. New York, Wilson, 1948.

> Suggested by Chambers's work, but restricted to American information. Includes birthdays of well-known people, local festivals. Invaluable to teachers trying to find ideas for assembly programs. A 3d edition is in preparation.

Edwards, Eliezer. *Words, Facts, and Phrases: A Dictionary of Serious, Quaint, & Out-of-the-Way Matters.* Philadelphia, Lippincott, 1881. Reissued by Gale Research Co. (Detroit), 1968.

    The same type of compendium as those by Brewer and Walsh (*q.v.*). It has been out of print for many years and is the more interesting for that reason. Those interested in Black Studies will be fascinated by the entry under "Africans."

Eggenberger, David. *Flags of the U. S. A.* New York, Crowell, 1960.

    Many color illustrations. Includes the fifty-star flag and begins with Columbus.

Funk & Wagnalls Standard Dictionary of Folklore, Mythology and Legend. Maria Leach, ed. New York, Funk & Wagnalls, 1949-50. 2 vols. Revised ed. in 1 vol., 1972.

    The newest cyclopedia of folklore. Especially good on ritual, dances, folk music, etc., of American Indians and other aboriginal races.

Ickis, Marguerite. *The Book of Festivals and Holidays the World Over.* Illustrated by Richard E. Howard. New York, Dodd, Mead, 1970.

    Up to date (1970) not only on Europe and the Americas, but also on customs of Africa and the Middle and Far East. Supplements her earlier *Book of Festival Holidays* (1964). Arranged by the calendar; useful for travelers and for program planning. See also Douglas's *American Book of Days* (above) and Spicer's two titles below.

Kane, Joseph Nathan. *Famous First Facts.* 3d ed. New York, Wilson, 1964.

    A greatly enlarged revision of the original work. Alphabetical listing of "firsts" in the United States, with a chronological index by year, a geographical index, and plenty of cross references. Indexed also by day of the month and by personal name; therefore can be used as a source of anniversaries to be celebrated.

—— and Alexander, G. L. *Nicknames and Sobriquets of U.S. Cities and States.* 2d ed. Metuchen, N. J., Scarecrow Press, 1970.

    Not so inclusive as Shankle (*q.v.*) nor so scholarly, as sources are not given. Local publicity offices are probably responsible for many of the nicknames. The text is arranged alphabetically by state, subdivided by city, and followed by an alphabetical nickname index.

The Negro Almanac. 2d ed. Harry A. Ploski and Ernest Kaiser, eds. New York, Bellwether, 1971.

    A well-indexed compilation, including a chronology, historical documents, and famous Negro personalities (this may help to update *Who's Who in Colored America*, issued by the Burckel Co. in 1950). The 1967 edition of the *Almanac* is still useful for older material omitted from the revision. Other references on Negroes in the United States will be found under U.S. History in a later chapter.

Post, Emily. *Etiquette.* 10th ed. New York, Funk & Wagnalls, 1960.

    This last edition of a standard work incorporates much new material suggested by the letters Emily Post received and answered in her syndicated newspaper articles. She had relaxed her earlier rigid standards for approved behavior, in accordance with present-day customs. Frequently revised by Elizabeth Post.

Robert, Henry M. *Robert's Rules of Order Newly Revised.* 7th ed. Glenview, Ill., Scott Foresman, 1970.

> Actually only the second complete revision of this manual of parliamentary procedure (that is, how to run a meeting). Completely rewritten in simpler and clearer terms and organized with first things first by Sarah C. Robert with the help of H. M. Robert III and others.

Shankle, George E. *American Nicknames: Their Origin and Significance.* 2d ed. New York, Wilson, 1955.

> Includes people, places, and baseball teams. Too bad it has not been revised, but who could keep up with sports and their nomenclature, except sportswriters themselves?

Sharp, Harold S., comp. *Handbook of Pseudonyms and Personal Nicknames.* Metuchen, N.J., Scarecrow, 1972. 2 vols.

> "Nicknames, stage names, noms de plume, sobriquets of criminals and saints, statesmen and politicians, East and West. Thoroughly cross-referenced" (publisher's announcement).

Spicer, Dorothy Gladys. *Festivals of Western Europe.* New York, Wilson, 1958.

> "Descriptions of some of the major traditional festivals of . . . Belgium, Denmark, France, Germany, Italy, Luxembourg, The Netherlands, Norway, Portugal, Spain, Sweden, and Switzerland," according to the publisher's announcement. Companion volume to the following.

——*Yearbook of English Festivals.* New York, Wilson, 1954, o.p.

> A very readable book, giving, by days, descriptions of local celebrations and customs in the cities, towns, and villages of England. Indexed by customs, by counties, and by regions. Supplements Chambers's *Book of Days* by describing festivals which the modern traveler may be able to see for himself.

United States. Bureau of the Census. *Historical Statistics of the United States, Colonial Times to 1957.* Washington, Government Printing Office, 1960. Supplement (to 1962) with revisions, 1965.

> Data on many aspects of American life, from pre-Revolutionary times. The annual *Statistical Abstract* (see page 140) will supply the latest information.

Vanderbilt, Amy. *Amy Vanderbilt's Etiquette.* New York, Doubleday, 1972.

> Amy Vanderbilt's book is in demand. She conducts newspaper and magazine Q & A columns and lends herself to commercials on TV. There are also specialized books of etiquette, for teenagers, brides, and so forth, and of late the women's magazines, notably *McCall's*, have published advice to the uncertain.

Walsh, W. S. *Curiosities of Popular Customs, and of Rites, Ceremonies, Observances and Miscellaneous Antiquities.* Philadelphia, Lippincott, 1935.

> Good to explain allusions in older works, now left out of more recent compilations.

——*Handy Book of Curious Information.* Philadelphia, Lippincott, 1913. Reissued by Gale Research Co. (Detroit), 1968.

> Sea serpents, early eclipses, and other semilegendary matters.

BOOKS OF QUOTATIONS

Books of quotations are used for one of two reasons. If one is preparing a speech or an article or a sermon, he may want to find well-phrased statements or bits of verse which apply to his topic, and he will use one of the quotation books arranged by subject, just as the toastmaster uses a classified collection of funny stories. On the other hand, if he wishes to identify a verse or phrase, see who said it and when, he will attack the books of quotations through their exhaustive indexes, as detailed as the concordances described above (pages 35-36). Libraries buy many books of quotations, because each compiler bases his collection on his own interests and his own background of reading. Some authors, like Shakespeare and Bacon, Emerson and Mark Twain, will be generously represented in most collections, but even for them the choice of quotations will vary widely. With two exceptions, the books listed below give entries in English only. The Cohens' *Penguin Dictionary* and the *Oxford Dictionary of Quotations* give quotations in various languages, including Greek and Latin.

The reader will note that books of quotations and of proverbs are interfiled here, one obvious reason being that there are only four books of proverbs. Another equally practical reason is that some quotations or portions of them are so familiar, or perhaps sententious, that one thinks of them as proverbs, and some proverbs (really unattributable quotations) are so similar to wise lines by famous writers that one expects them to be quotations.

Adams, A. K., comp. *The Home Book of Humorous Quotations*. New York, Dodd, Mead, 1969.

> Adams's compilation, arranged by subject, includes about 9,000 items under 500 headings, with a concordance and index to authors.
>
> This is obviously intended to be a companion volume to B. E. Stevenson's *Home Book of Quotations, Classical and Modern* and his other Home Books listed below.

Bartlett, John. *Familiar Quotations: A Collection of Passages, Phrases and Proverbs Traced to Their Sources in Ancient and Modern Literature*. 14th ed. edited by E. M. Beck. Boston, Little, Brown, 1968.

> Arranged chronologically by author, with the usual key-word concordance. In this edition, some of the earlier authors have been dropped, and writers and men in public life who have enriched our vocabulary since 1955 (the year of the 13th edition) have been added. Among "new" authors quoted are not only Confucius, but also many others who wrote in such foreign languages as Japanese, Sanskrit, and Russian. There are quotations from political figures, scientists, and the classics as well.

Cohen, J. M. and Cohen, M. J., eds. *The Penguin Dictionary of Quotations*. Baltimore, Penguin Books, 1960.

> Includes quotations in French, Italian, German, and Latin (followed by English versions). Quotations from Greek, Russian, and Spanish are given only in English translation. This book is arranged alphabetically by author

(with a large section under Anonymous) and has a full concordance, occupying approximately one third of the book. An excellent item for student purchase.

Evans, Bergen, comp. *Dictionary of Quotations.* New York, Delacorte, 1968.

Arranged alphabetically by topic and indexed by author and key word. There are also two essays: "On Looking It Up" and "How to Use This Book." Witty commentaries after many entries make this a particularly good book for browsing. It differs from books that serve primarily to provide exact wording of quotations and identification by author and title.

Hoyt, J. K., comp. *New Cyclopedia of Practical Quotations.* rev. ed. compiled by K. L. Roberts. New York, Funk & Wagnalls, 1948.

One of the largest of these works. Arranged by subject, but with index of authors and detailed concordance.

Oxford Dictionary of English Proverbs. 3d ed. edited by William G. Smith, revised by F. P. Wilson. London and New York, Oxford University Press, 1970.

The original preface to this *Dictionary of Proverbs* states quite categorically that if the reader searching for a proverb doesn't know its first word, he does not know the proverb, giving as an example "Curses, like chickens, come home to roost." The author of this manual has heard any number of references to chickens coming home to roost, including a number of undesirable character traits, exaggerated statements, etc., but *never* curses. The preface also said that there would be cross references from other words "if necessary." Apparently "chickens" were not considered necessary, until the 1970 edition, in which cross references abound, including "chickens." Therefore the 3d edition can be unequivocally recommended to the American reader as well as to those who know about curses.

Oxford Dictionary of Quotations. 2d ed. London and New York, Oxford University Press, 1953.

Arrangement is alphabetical by author. Includes languages other than English. Greek passages are given in the Greek alphabet, with English translation. Concordance.

Stevenson, Burton Egbert, comp. *Home Book of Quotations, Classical and Modern.* 9th ed. New York, Dodd, Mead, 1959.

Contains more than 50,000 extracts, arranged by subject, with author index and concordance. The reader will find no quotations from the works of Shakespeare or from the Bible here, as there are two titles in the Home Book series devoted to these sources.

——*Home Book of Proverbs, Maxims and Familiar Phrases.* New York, Macmillan, 1948.

Tripp, Rhoda Thomas, comp. *The International Thesaurus of Quotations.* New York, Crowell, 1970.

A "marriage" (as one reviewer put it) of thesaurus and dictionary of proverbs and quotations. Under 1,067 numbered concepts like Respect, Sorrow, Timidity, and topics like Mailmen, Photography, and Sex are about 16,000 relevant quotations or proverbs from classic to everyday sources. Indexed by author and source as well as by category. Probably few will find "familiar" quotations, but many will find provocative or amusing ones. Useful for masters of ceremonies and introducers of speakers.

Whiting, Bartlett Jere and Whiting, Helen W., comps. *Proverbs, Sentences, and Proverbial Phrases: From English Writings Mainly Before 1500*. Cambridge, Mass., Harvard University Press (Belknap), 1968.

> Suggested by George Lyman Kittredge in 1923 — and completed after forty-five years of reading everything of a literary nature extant in Old and Middle English. Arranged alphabetically by subject, with the quotations for each subject in chronological order; cross references, and two indexes.

Before we leave the books of quotations and other more or less literary types of fact finders, the reader should be reminded that reference books which fall into other subject areas will be found later, in the subject-oriented chapters; for example, books of quotations from Shakespeare alone will be in the chapter on Literature (although of course Shakespeare occupies a large part of most compilations), and books of Bible quotations and other reference books dealing with religion should be sought under Religion.

BIOGRAPHICAL DICTIONARIES

While encyclopedias and dictionaries give biographical data on hundreds of people, living and dead, these are a mere sampling of the thousands whose lives may be interesting or significant. The collections listed here are a few of the more important general biographical dictionaries published in England and the United States, as well as a few general reference works valuable for their biographical information, though not strictly biographical dictionaries. The larger libraries have many more of these, plus several important ones printed in French or German, and many limited to people in a single profession or important in a single field of endeavor. Some of the latter are listed with other books, by subject, in later chapters.

Appleton's Cyclopaedia of American Biography. James Grant Wilson and John Fiske, eds. New York, Appleton, 1887-1900. 7 vols. Reprinted in 1968 by Gale Research Co. (Detroit).

> Older colleges and universities may have the original edition of this valuable work, though perhaps in dilapidated condition. It contains biographies varying in length from a paragraph to several pages on people who died between 1789 and 1901. Portraits, in the form of steel engravings, of many lesser-known Americans accompany the text. The first six volumes form the original set, Volume 7 being a supplement. The main set is indexed in Volume 6; Volume 7 has its own index. The index entries are for subjects and for the names of people mentioned in passing, who are not accorded articles of their own.

Chambers's Biographical Dictionary. rev. ed. J. O. Thorne, ed. Edinburgh and London, Chambers, 1968; New York, St. Martin's, 1970.

Fully revised and rewritten. Outdated entries have been reviewed and updated, making room for contemporary figures. Biographees are indexed by subject categories, and bibliographic entries are frequent. More than 15,000 people included, famous and obscure.

Current Biography. New York, Wilson, 1940- . Monthly except August; cumulated annually in a single alphabet under the title *Current Biography Yearbook.*

Fairly long articles, many with portraits, on people who may have become prominent only recently. Excellent as a source of information on radio, television, and motion picture personalities, as well as statesmen, scientists, artists, and others in the news.

Brief obituary notices, each with a reference to the New York *Times* obituary, are given. Cumulated indexes for 1940-1950, 1951-1960, and 1961-1970 are included in the yearbooks for 1950, 1960, and 1970 respectively, and there is a separately printed hardbound *Current Biography Cumulated Index 1940-1970.*

Dictionary of American Biography. New York, Scribner; London, Milford, 1928-1937. 20 vols., index, and 3 supplements. Supplement 3 (to Dec. 31, 1945) was published in 1973 and contains an index to all supplements.

Limited to people no longer living who have lived in the United States and have made some contribution to American life. More than 14,000 entries to date. This set is the American equivalent of the *Dictionary of National Biography*, described below. The articles are prepared by well-known scholars, and each is followed by a bibliography. It is to be hoped that eighteen years or more will not always be allowed to elapse between the closing date of a supplement and its publication.

Dictionary of Canadian Biography. George W. Brown, ed. Toronto, University of Toronto Press, 1966- .

Like the *Dictionary of American Biography* above and the *Dictionary of National Biography* (British) which follows, this set will include no living biographees. Unlike them, each volume includes only people who died within a specified time span. Volumes published to date are: Volume 1, people who died before 1701, published in 1966; Volume 2, 1701-1740, published 1969; and Volume 10, 1871-1880, published 1972. (Obviously, the period to be covered in each volume has been predetermined by the general editor.) The contributors include scholars from Europe and the United States as well as Canada.

Dictionary of National Biography. Leslie Stephen and Sidney Lee, eds. Originally published by the London firm of Smith, Elder, 1885-1901, in 63 vols. Reprinted in 1938 by Oxford University Press in 21 vols. with Supplement 1. Supplements 2 through 7, published between 1912 and 1971, cover the years 1901-1960. Supplement 7 contains an index to all supplements.

Biographies of inhabitants of the British Isles and the colonies, dominions, etc. Excludes people living at the time of publication of each volume. Supetc. Excludes people living at the time of publication of each volume. Contains more than 31,000 biographies. Some articles are practically book length in themselves, notably that on Queen Victoria.

The International Who's Who. London, Europa Publications and Allen
& Unwin, 1935-   . Annual.

   Annual biographical dictionary, with highly condensed information on living
   people of international importance in governments, literature, the arts, and
   the sciences. Similar in content to the publications of the Marquis company
   (*Who's Who in America*, etc.) and A. & C. Black (*Who's Who*, etc.), which
   see below. Since 1971 this has also been available from Gale Research Co.
   (Detroit) and the British Book Centre (New York). Published every September.

International Year Book and Statesman's Who's Who. London, Burke's
Peerage, 1953-   . Annual.

   Considered by some librarians to be superior to the *Statesman's Year-Book*
   (see page 140) for information on the nations of the world, with the added
   advantage of the who's who section, which keeps the student up to date on
   government officials, though nothing but the daily newspaper can give us the
   last word in this area.

Ireland, Norma Olin, comp. *Index to Women of the World; from Ancient to Modern Times.* Westwood, Mass., F. W. Faxon, 1970.

   Includes references to about 13,000 women "arranged alphabetically by
   letter, with date and identification (nationality and occupation) given for
   each. . . . All periods of history have been included as the author felt that
   the inclusion of Bible women, saints, etc. would increase the book's usefulness" (publisher's announcement). Includes all women in *Current Biography*,
   1940-1968; *New Yorker's* "Profiles," 1925-1968; and *Time's* cover stories,
   1924-1968. Women authors and librarians are featured also.

James, Edward T. and James, Janet W., eds. *Notable American Women,
1607-1950; a Biographical Dictionary.* Cambridge, Mass., Harvard
(Belknap), 1971. 3 vols.

   The publisher's announcement indicates "1,359 famous and infamous
   American Women all in one place." Articles prepared by more than 700
   contributors over a fifteen-year period. Comparable in quality to the *Dictionary of American Biography*, mentioned above. Appendix groups individuals by occupation. Mr. James is an editor of *D.A.B.*, and the work was
   sponsored by Radcliffe College.

*New York Times Biographical Edition: A Compilation of Current Bio-
graphical Information of General Interest.* New York, Times,
1970-   .

   A weekly looseleaf service, including biographical reprints from the *Times*,
   varying in length from brief obituaries to feature articles from the *New
   York Times Magazine* (Sunday). Two looseleaf binders are provided, and
   weekly indexes, which are cumulated monthly, quarterly, and annually.

New York Times Obituaries Index: 1858-1968. New York, Times, 1970.

   One large (1,136 p.) volume, computer-compiled from the *New York
   Times Index*. Entries consist of the individual's name, pseudonym or nick-
   name where appropriate, and a reference to the year, date, section, page, and
   column of the original *Times* obit. Frequently refers to follow-up stories on
   funeral or will. The references are to the microfilm edition of the *Times*.

   There is also an obituaries index to the London *Times* (1900-1971),
"an international sourcebook to over 120,000 well-known people."

United States. Congress. *Biographical Directory of the American Congress, 1774-1961.* Washington, Government Printing Office, 1961.

> Includes tables listing the Presidents and their wives, members of the Supreme Court, cabinet officers, etc. Supplemented by current issues of *Official Congressional Directory.*

United States. Congress. *Official Congressional Directory.* Washington, Government Printing Office, 1809- .

> A new edition is issued for each session. Includes autobiographical sketches of each senator and member of the House of Representatives, varying in length according to each one's preference.

Webster's Biographical Dictionary. William Allan Neilson, ed. in chief. Springfield, Mass., Merriam, 1971.

> Brief sketches, including pronunciation of names. More than 40,000 individuals included, about one third of them living.
> First published in 1943; minor revisions in later editions.

Wer Ist Wer? das Deutsche Who's Who. Publisher varies. 1948- . Quadrennial. Title varies.

> Lists some prominent people not in *Who's Who in Germany.* The 1974 edition was published by Societäts Verlag (Frankfurt am Main).

Who's Who. London, Black, 1949- . Annual.

> Brief information about living British subjects, including residents of the dominions, and some citizens of the United States and other countries. Since 1962, the American publisher has been St. Martin's Press.

Who Was Who. London, Black; New York, Macmillan, 1920- .

> Published at intervals, these volumes bring together all biographies of people whose names have been removed from *Who's Who,* because of death, since 1897. Currently decennial.

Who's Who in America. Chicago, Marquis, 1899- . Biennial.

> Does for the United States what *Who's Who* does for Great Britain. The 1972-1973 edition, published in June 1972, was the first to be issued in two volumes, with 15,000 new names among its 80,000 entries. No doubt succeeding editions will be as large or larger.[1]
> The Marquis company has also published Who's Who volumes for major areas of the United States, in which people of local importance are listed, some of whom may "make it" to the national volume.

Who's Who of American Women; a Biographical Dictionary of Notable Living American Women, 1958/59- . Chicago, Marquis, 1958- . Biennial.

> Editorial policy is to include "women outstanding as women, without regard to their achievements or positions in relation to men." Exactly what this means is not clear to this reader, but women active in civic, club, and religious activities, literature, the professions, and the arts are to be found in these volumes. It has proved to be especially useful in giving short biographical sketches of Negro women, not easy to find since *Who's Who in Colored America* (Burckel, 1950) has gone so long unrevised.

---

[1] See Appendix C for descriptive note on Cedric A. Larson's *Who,* a book about the Marquis company and its Who's Who publications.

Who Was Who in America: Historical Volume, 1607-1896. rev. ed. Chicago, Marquis, 1967; *Who Was Who in America, 1897-1968.* Chicago, Marquis, 1942-1968. 4 vols. of which Volume 4 includes an index to all four.

One may assume that additional volumes will be published at intervals. As for the *Historical Volume*, practically anyone of importance is doubtless covered in greater detail in the *Dictionary of American Biography* and its supplements.

ALMANACS AND YEARBOOKS

These terms refer to a large group of publications: annual supplements to encyclopedias or to the biographical dictionaries described in the middle section of this chapter; compendia of useful information about the world, like *The Statesman's Year-Book*, described in this section; reports of government departments — national, state, or local; reports of scientific and educational organizations; and such annual publications as stamp catalogs, automobile or motorcycle repair manuals, and official rule books for popular sports. Even travel guides, to faraway places or nearby resort areas, are likely to be revised annually.

It would be impossible and unnecessary for anyone to attempt to become acquainted with all publications of this type. Even the specialist only tries to know those in his particular field. And some yearbooks or annuals will be found with the reference books for specific subjects, as will the biographical dictionaries about artists, musicians, scientists, and writers.

Those listed in this section are so broad and diversified in their coverage that it is difficult to assign them to a special subject group. They include statistical information, recent history, economic and political facts, and data about climate, agriculture, and industry. Some refer specifically to the United States, Canada, or Britain, but most are of broad geographic scope.

Annual Register of World Events; a Review of the Year. New York, St.
    Martin's; London, Longman's, 1890-   . First published in 1761,
    covering events of 1758. Presently edited by Sir Ivison Macadam.

A running summary of the events of the preceding year, first in the United Kingdom, then in the British Commonweath and in other parts of the world, followed by chapters on the year's activities in religion, science, etc. This is presented with that combination of thoroughness, impartiality, and humor which we have learned to expect of even the most serious of British writers.

Canadian Almanac and Directory, 1847-   . Toronto, Copp Clark Co.,
    1847-   . Since 1965, also published in the U.S. by the Pitman
    Publishing Co. (New York).

A large, detailed volume, rather expensive for an almanac. In some ways similar to the *Official Associated Press Almanac (q.v.)* but more logically arranged and much more inclusive. (The Canadian Bureau of Statistics at

Ottawa publishes the smaller paperbound *Canada*, a yearbook full of interesting information for Canadians and travelers alike.)

The Council on Foreign Relations issues a number of valuable yearbooks, presently published in New York by Simon & Schuster.

Documents on American Foreign Relations, 1938/1939-   . Presently edited by William P. Lineberry and Elaine P. Adams.

    The 1970 volume, issued in 1972, was, at the time of its publication, the only collection of current United States foreign policy documents available to the general public.

Political Handbook and Atlas of the World, 1927-   . Presently edited by R. P. Stebbins and Alba Amoia.

    The 1970 edition has been completely redesigned and updated. It was supplemented in 1971 by a new annual, *The World This Year*, under the same editors.

The United States in World Affairs, 1947-   . Presently edited by William P. Lineberry.

Europa Publications in London is the source of a number of very valuable yearbooks, which have changed name and format a number of times. Before the Second World War this publisher launched two looseleaf encyclopedias: *Europa: The Encyclopaedia of Europe* (a guide to European organizations with information on individual countries); and *Orbis: Encyclopaedia of Extra-European Countries.*

In 1948, the firm initiated an annual, *The Middle East*, giving geographical, historical, economic, political, and industrial information, and including a who's who of the region. This series was enlarged to include North Africa in 1955.

The *Europa Yearbook* was launched in 1959 and expanded in 1960 to two volumes, Volume 1 covering Europe, and Volume 2 covering Africa, the Americas, Asia, and Australasia. To expand the coverage of Volume 2, Europa has begun new annuals: *The Far East and Australasia* appeared in 1969, and the first issue of *Africa South of the Sahara* was published in 1972. It may be noted that Gale Research Co. of Detroit is now handling Europa publications on this side of the Atlantic.

Her Majesty's Stationery Office of Great Britain, like the United States Government Printing Office, is the publisher of many documents, including yearbooks. Among them are the following works:

Great Britain. Central Statistical Office. *Annual Abstract of Statistics*, 1854-   . Available in New York from the British Information Service.

    Similar to our *Statistical Abstract*, listed below.

Great Britain. Central Office of Information. *Britain: An Official Handbook*, 1948/1949-   .

    Each section of this has an extensive bibliography.

Other worthwhile almanacs include the following volumes:

Information Please Almanac. New York, Simon & Schuster, 1947-   .

    First edited by John Kieran, the "Information Please" expert with the most diversified knowledge. Since edited by Dan Golenpaul, producer of the original "Information Please" radio program. A readable collection of miscellaneous information, similar to the *World Almanac*, but containing many items not in the latter, and less confusing in arrangement. Each issue has a special introductory article on a topic of current importance.

Official Associated Press Almanac, 1973-   . New York, Almanac Publishing Co., 1972-   .

    From 1969 until 1972, published as the *New York Times Encyclopedic Almanac*. This book is informative, reliable, and interesting to read, even if one is not trying to find a particular fact. Of course, that is true of most almanacs, including the old-fashioned *Farmer's Almanac*, which tells which phase of the moon is most favorable for planting corn, and so forth.

The South American Handbook, 1924-   . Chicago, Rand McNally; London, Trade and Travel Publications, 1924-   .

    Facts on travel, business, history, weather, government, etc. Maps, statistics, good index.

Statesman's Year-Book. London, Macmillan, 1864-   . Now distributed in the U.S. by St. Martin's Press (New York).

    Information on the governments of the world. One section is on Great Britain and her commonwealth, another on the United States, then one on other countries of the world. Officials named, statistics given, and bibliographies and reference books on each country listed.

United Nations. *Statistical Yearbook*, 1948-   . Formerly published by Columbia University Press; now published by the United Nations (New York).

    World statistics, similar to the information on the United States given in the *Statistical Abstract of the United States*.

United Nations. *Yearbook of the United Nations.* New York, Columbia University Press, 1946/1947-   .

    Published at the end of each year, giving a detailed account of the work and achievements of the UN and its specialized agencies.

United States. Bureau of the Census. *Statistical Abstract of the United States.* Washington, Government Printing Office, 1879-   .

    A collection of statistical data on many aspects of American life. Most of the material is collected by various departments of the United States Government, but much is also from private agencies. Tables frequently give comparative figures for fifty years by decade, sometimes by smaller intervals. Earlier statistics are given in *Historical Statistics of the United States, Colonial Times to 1957*, described earlier in this chapter (see page 131).

World Almanac and Book of Facts, 1868-   . New York, Newspaper Enterprise Associates, Inc.

    A collection of all kinds of useful and curious information, in rather hit-or-miss arrangement, with a detailed index. Includes many types of statistics on sports, economics, etc., as well as almanac information as to sunrise and

sunset, tides, phases of the moon, etc. From 1931 through 1966, issued by
the New York *World-Telegram & Sun*; newspapers in other cities also publish similar annuals, with emphasis on matters of local interest.

The Year Book and Guide to East Africa, 1950-   . London, Hale;
Chicago, Rand McNally.

The Year Book and Guide to Southern Africa, 1901-   . London,
Hale; Chicago, Rand McNally.

Both these yearbooks, edited by A. Gordon-Brown, are revised annually.
Each includes an atlas and folding map, cultural and historical information,
data on agriculture, industries, and native peoples, and plans of the principal
towns.

Chapter 12

Special Reference Books
THE ARTS

THE NEXT SIX CHAPTERS deal with reference books in subject groups, in much the same way that they have been handled in previous editions; most titles will be followed by descriptive and/or critical comments. Depending on the number of books considered, there may be groups within groups. In many subject areas, Dictionaries and Encyclopedias and Biographical Dictionaries will be standard subdivisions. An attempt has been made to limit these lists to the books or sets of books which will be most useful to students and to their instructors and professors. Books necessary only to specialists will be few, and here and there the reader will find books included not so much for their reference value as for their readability.

THE PERFORMING ARTS—MUSIC

A comparison of this edition of THE NEW LIBRARY KEY with the second edition will demonstrate that a good reference book does not go out of date when it treats adequately a field in which there has been little change or, dealing with a changing field, is periodically revised, but that completely new compilations of facts are made necessary by new knowledge and differing points of view. Since 1963, six titles in this section have been dropped as obsolete; nineteen have been revised, or supplements to them have been published; and about twenty new titles have been added to the list. This is indicative of what the reader may expect to find in subsequent chapters, and he will encounter a similar rate of change in college library collections.

Dictionaries and Encyclopedias

Everyman's Dictionary of Music. 5th rev. and enl. ed. Eric Blom, comp. Revised by Sir Jack Westrup and others. New York, St. Martin's, 1972.

> Eric Blom is the editor of Grove's more extensive work, listed below. *Everyman's* is primarily intended for home or school purchase, but is useful for quick identification of composers and their works, explanations of music terms, and descriptions of instruments.

Grove's Dictionary of Music and Musicians. 5th ed. Eric Blom, ed. New

142

York, St. Martin's, 1955. 10 vols. including supplement. Supplement, edited by Denis Stevens, 1961.

Originally compiled by Sir George Grove, this dictionary covers every phase of music and music history from 1450 up to the present, with special attention to England and America. Composers' works are arranged by type rather than chronologically, a boon to the student of such prolific composers as Mozart.

Harper's Dictionary of Music. Christine Ammer, ed. New York, Harper & Row, 1972.

A comparatively small work for amateurs and laymen. Biographical material is brief. Features include clear drawings of instruments, pronunciation of entry words, tables of "Romantic Composers," "Symphonic Poems," etc., and discussions of serial music and rock. Christine Ammer is editor in chief of the later volumes of the *New Oxford History of Music* (*q.v.*).

Harvard Dictionary of Music. 2d ed. Willi Apel, ed. Cambridge, Mass., Harvard University Press (Belknap), 1969.

First published in 1944 and frequently listed in bibliographies as *Willi Apel's Harvard Dictionary of Music* (or, occasionally, as *Willi Appel's*, in lists not carefully proofread). This dictionary contains no biographies; otherwise, it is very useful.

International Cyclopedia of Music and Musicians. 9th ed. New York, Dodd, Mead, 1964.

Originally edited by Oscar Thompson. The first edition (1938) was particularly good on music schools and black contributions to music, especially on the place in choral music of the choirs of such colleges as Hampton Institute. For some years the *Cyclopedia* was revised under the editorship of Nicolas Slonimsky, and the 9th edition announced the editorship of Robert Sabin. Despite an overemphasis on musicians and movements of the forties and fifties, this is still one of the best one-volume reference works as well as the largest (more than twice the size of the *Oxford Companion to Music*, below).

Scholes, Percy A. *The Oxford Companion to Music.* 10th rev. and reset ed. John Owen Ward, ed. London and New York, Oxford University Press, 1970.

No index or bibliographies, but this dictionary/encyclopedia is one of the best and certainly the most readable of these general compendia of musical facts. Previous edition published in 1955.

Biographical Dictionaries

The books listed in this section offer reliable biographical information but are less scholarly in approach than the dictionaries, encyclopedias, and histories of music listed above.

Baker, Theodore. *Biographical Dictionary of Musicians.* 5th ed. Completely revised by Nicolas Slonimsky. New York, Schirmer, 1958. Supplement, 1971.

Compact biographies of composers and performers.

Ewen, David. *Composers of Tomorrow's Music: A Non-Technical Introduction to the Musical Avant-garde Movement.* New York, Dodd, Mead, 1971.

Biocritical essays on nine composers including Ives, Webern, Boulez, and Xenakis. Photographs and references to other sources included in the text.

——. *Composers Since 1900.* New York, Wilson, 1969.

Biographical sketches of 220 composers, with small portraits and selective lists of compositions. Much of the material is based on personal interviews or correspondence. Replaces three earlier volumes: *Composers of Today, American Composers Today,* and *European Composers Today.*

——. *Great Composers, 1300-1900.* New York, Wilson, 1966.

Nearly 200 composers of the past – biographical, critical, and personal information; 152 portraits, chronological and nationality listings.

——. *Popular American Composers from Revolutionary Times to the Present.* New York, Wilson, 1962. *First Supplement,* 1972.

Similar in content to the above. The supplement updates the biographies of composers in the 1962 volume who are still productive and adds 31 new biographies, including writers of rock and country-and-western music, musical comedies, motion picture scores, and commercial popular songs.

——. *The World of Twentieth Century Music.* Englewood Cliffs, N.J., Prentice-Hall, 1968.

A replacement for Ewen's *Complete Book of 20th Century Music* (1952). Not a scholarly work, but a useful supplement to his other books on modern composers.

Histories of Music

The New Oxford History of Music. J. A. Westrup and others, gen. eds. London and New York, Oxford University Press, 1954-   . To be in 11 vols.

This set has been gradually replacing the *Oxford History of Music* (2d ed., 1931-1938). Ten volumes have been published, each edited by a prominent scholar and devoted to a particular period. Each volume contains its own index and bibliography, and the final volume will include a combined index to the entire set, chronological tables, and bibliographies.

Pincherle, Marc. *Illustrated History of Music.* rev. ed. Georges Bernier and Rosamond Bernier, eds. Translated by Rollo Myers. London, Macmillan, 1962.

This was published in French in 1959 by Gallimard in the series *Collection de l'Œil. L'Œil* is an art magazine of which the Berniers are editors. Probably a more accurate title would be "History of Music, illustrated by Georges and Rosamond Bernier." The book is particularly useful for its pictures of early instruments. There are 40 color plates and more than 200 black-and-white illustrations. The revised edition has added an index.

Slonimsky, Nicolas. *Music Since 1900.* 4th ed. New York, Scribners, 1971.

A descriptive chronology up to the middle of 1969. A large "Letters and Documents" section includes letters from composers and such memorabilia as the "Resolution of the Fire and Police Research of Los Angeles on Subversive Perils of American Folk Music" and a letter from Ralph Nader on noise pollution produced by rock bands. The 3d edition, published in 1949, was about half the size of this one.

Miscellaneous

Ewen, David, comp. *Encyclopedia of Concert Music*. New York, Hill & Wang, 1959.

——. *The New Encyclopedia of the Opera*. New York, Hill & Wang, 1971.

These two companion encyclopedias are in dictionary arrangement, with information about all phases of music — orchestras and individual performers, opera plots and characters, stage directors, critics, musicologists, etc. — and with cross references from a composer's biography to his compositions. The second book is based on Ewen's *Encyclopedia of the Opera* (1955) but largely rewritten.

Feather, Leonard G. *Encyclopedia of Jazz*. rev. and enl. ed. New York, Horizon, 1960.

Biographical sketches of more than 2,000 musicians; bibliography and discography. A companion volume, *Encyclopedia of Jazz in the Sixties* (1966), updates the material and introduces new musicians.

Fuld, James J. *The Book of World-Famous Music: Classical, Popular and Folk*. rev. and enl. ed. New York, Crown, 1971.

A guide to all the important compositions, composers, operas, ballets, librettists, and lyricists. The first line of music for each of 1,000 compositions is given in the original key. There is a list of famous compositions for which no known copy exists, and information on copyright laws in various countries.

Haggin, B. H. *New Listener's Companion and Record Guide*. 3d ed. New York, Horizon, 1971. Also available in paperback.

A guide to recorded music, performers, composers, critics, and criticism. Conveniently arranged, readable, and useful, although the index seems unnecessarily complicated. A good book for the collector.

Lawless, Ray M. *Folksingers and Folksongs in America: A Handbook of Biography, Bibliography, and Discography*. rev. ed. New York, Duell, 1965.

McSpadden, J. W. *Operas and Musical Comedies*. enl. ed. New York, Crowell, 1954.

Includes about 370 plots. Unlike Green's book, listed below, this is worldwide in coverage. It may be supplemented by reference to *Opera News*, published weekly during the opera season, for information, also international in scope, on opera productions.

Mattfeld, Julius. *Variety Music Cavalcade, 1620-1969: A Chronology of Vocal and Instrumental Music Popular in the United States*. 3d ed. Englewood Cliffs, N. J., Prentice-Hall, 1970.

A two-page introduction by Abel Green, editor of *Variety*.

Metropolitan Opera Annals: A Chronicle of Artists and Performances.
William H. Seltsam, comp. Introduction by Edward Johnson. 2d
printing, with Index to Composers and List of Errata. New York,
Wilson, 1949. Supplements covering the seasons 1947/48 through
1965/66 issued in 2 vols., 1957 and 1968.

> The second supplement has a foreword by Francis Robinson and covers
> the last seasons at "The Old Met." A special feature is the complete list of
> artists' debuts from 1883 to 1966.

Sears, Minnie Earl. *Song Index.* New York, Wilson, 1926. Supplement,
1934. o.p.

> Although out of print, these volumes can be found in many libraries. They
> index collections of songs under author, composer, title, and first line. Often
> useful in finding verses not included in the indexes to poetry (see *Granger* in
> index, for example). The two volumes list 19,000 songs, many of which sound
> familiar as verse but have never been included in collections or anthologies
> of poetry.

THE PERFORMING ARTS—THEATER

The books in this section deal with the history of the theater, past
and present, and with "theater arts," such as stagecraft and design.
Material on the drama as literature will be found in Chapter 15.

Cheney, Sheldon W. *The Theater: Three Thousand Years of Drama,
Acting and Stagecraft.* rev. and reset illustrated ed. New York,
McKay, 1972.

> Originally published in 1929. This is the third major revision with about
> sixty added illustrations. Includes two new chapters discussing the changes
> in the theater between 1930 and 1970, an enlarged bibliography, and an im-
> proved index.

Freedley, George and Reeves, J. A. *A History of Theatre.* rev. ed.
Supplementary section by George Freedley. New York, Crown,
1955.

> An illustrated history of the development of the drama from its beginnings
> in Egypt to modern America, giving an account of every form, type, and
> artistic movement. Famous actors and playwrights are considered, as well as
> the development of theater buildings, costume, make-up, and scenery.

Geisinger, Marion. *Plays, Players, & Playwrights: An Illustrated History of the Theatre.* New York, Hart, 1971.

> A chronological history in what might be termed encyclopedic form —
> from the Greek and Roman theater to the twentieth century American musi-
> cal. Special articles on the Russian theater and the *commedia dell'arte.* Brief
> entries on stage designers and theater design.

Green, Stanley. *The World of Musical Comedy.* New York, Ziff-Davis,
1960.

> From Victor Herbert through the 1959/60 season. The main body of the
> work consists of biographical sketches of composers and lyricists, with ap-
> pendixes giving opening dates, lengths of runs, casts, etc., mainly in the

United States. This may easily be supplemented by reference to *Facts on File* and thence to the *New York Times Index* for reviews.

National Directory for the Performing Arts and Civic Centers. Dallas, Handel, 1974-   . Annual.

According to *Choice* (February 1974), "This important new directory reflects the growing vitality of the performing arts throughout the U.S. It provides, for the first time, abundant information on the numerous established amateur and professional organizations in dance, vocal and instrumental music and theatre." Revised and updated annually.

Rigdon, Walter, ed. *The Biographical Encyclopaedia and Who's Who of the American Theatre.* New York, Heineman, 1966.

A British publication for the theater enthusiast. Contains more than 3,000 biographical sketches of living persons in the American theater as well as a list of some 9,000 figures of international or historical importance. Includes New York productions since 1900, playbills nationwide, and histories of theater buildings, awards, and repertory companies.

Who's Who in the Theatre. 15th rev. ed. London, Pitman, 1972.

Another British publication increasing its coverage of American theatrical figures. Also contains playbills. It is considerably less expensive than Rigdon's book, but not, however, so all-encompassing.

Costume

Bradshaw, Angela. *World Costumes.* New York, Macmillan, 1961.

A reissue of an earlier work (1952), lavishly illustrated.

Crawford, M. D. C. *One World of Fashion.* 3d ed. Revised and edited by Beatrice Zelin and J. E. Watkins. New York, Fairchild, 1967.

Consists of drawings from *Women's Wear Daily* which depict the fashions and decor of all periods and places. Like all the books in this section, *One World of Fashion* is useful in costuming period plays.

Davenport, Millia. *The Book of Costume.* New York, Crown, 1948. Originally in two volumes; later issued in a one-volume edition.

A history of dress, illustrated by pictures of sculpture, armor, manuscript illumination, etc., as well as pictures of actual costumes of later days. A history of society as reflected in costume.

Hill, Margot H. and Bucknell, Peter A. *The Evolution of Fashion: Pattern and Cut from 1066 to 1930.* London, Batsford; New York, Reinhold, 1968.

Similar to Crawford (above) in format and size, with drawings on the right and notes on the left. A guide to making historical costumes of the British middle class.

Payne, Blanche. *History of Costume.* New York, Harper & Row, 1965.

Ancient Egypt (2700 B.C.) to the twentieth century. Illustrations taken from drawings, paintings, sculpture, and photographs.

Wilcox, Ruth Turner. *The Dictionary of Costume.* New York, Scribner, 1969.

Worldwide costume of the past and present. Has more text in relation to illustrations than Crawford or Hill (above).

Dance

Brinson, Peter and Crisp, Clement. *The International Book of Ballet.* New York, Stein & Day, 1971.

Martin, John. *Introduction to the Dance.* New York, Norton, 1939.
> Reprinted at intervals; paperback edition available from Dance Horizons (Brooklyn, N.Y.).

Sorell, Walter. *The Dance Through the Ages.* New York, Grosset, 1967.
> A history of the dance from primitive times up to jazz and rock. Includes ritual dancing, folklore, and dance in the theater. Magnificent full-page illustrations, some in color. A special feature is a Table of Cultural Chronology, from 1400 to 1950, in parallel columns with headings:

Dance	Music & Opera	Theater	Fine arts	Literature & Philosophy	Science	Politics

Terry, Walter. *The Dance in America.* New York, Harper & Row, 1971.

Motion Pictures and Television

Focal Encyclopedia of Film and Television Techniques. Raymond Spottiswoode, gen. ed. New York, Hastings, 1969.

Halliwell, Leslie. *The Filmgoer's Companion.* 3d ed., rev. and enl. with an introduction by Alfred Hitchcock. New York, Hill & Wang, 1970.
> An encyclopedia dictionary for the general reader. Particularly useful for information about actors — who played the butler, etc.

International Encyclopedia of Film. Roger Manvell, gen. ed. New York, Crown, 1972.
> Treats the cinema mainly as an art, but also as an industry. Articles on actors, directors, producers, techniques, general topics, and the national cinemas of different countries. Over 1,000 illustrations.

New York Times Film Reviews, 1913-1968. New York, New York Times and Arno Press, 1970.
> About 16,000 reviews, starting with silent pictures. The arrangement is chronological and the films are indexed by titles, persons, and corporations. For reviews of films after 1968, consult the *New York Times Index* and *Readers' Guide.*

THE PICTORIAL AND PLASTIC ARTS

The proverb *ars longa, vita brevis* means that man's life is too short to learn all there is to know. But sometimes *ars longa* seems to apply to the arts themselves — and to the books about them. The second edition of THE NEW LIBRARY KEY listed seventeen books on the visual arts; all of them are still valuable, but over thirty new titles have been added to the list. Therefore the reference books will be classified as to form or content, rather than simply listed alphabetically.

The pictorial and plastic arts include painting, sculpture, graphics, photography, ceramics, stained glass, and tapestry. Most of the reference books listed here deal with several of these fields, if not with all; specialized volumes devoted entirely to one field can often be found in the circulating collection. In the LC system, books on photography are classified under Technology (TR). Other art books are classified under N.

Dictionaries and Encyclopedias

Encyclopedia of World Art. New York, McGraw-Hill, 1959-1968. 15 vols.

> The arrangement is alphabetical, with signed articles, many including extensive bibliographies. Approximately one half of each volume is composed of plates, both color and black-and-white. A major contribution to art history.

Haggar, Reginald G. *A Dictionary of Art Terms.* London, Daily Express (Oldbourne); New York, Hawthorn, 1962.

> Includes a glossary of French, German, and Italian terms.

McGraw-Hill Dictionary of Art. Bernard S. Myers and Shirley D. Myers, eds. New York, McGraw-Hill, 1969. 5 vols.

> Not a work to rival the publisher's fifteen-volume encyclopedia, above, but perhaps properly termed an encyclopedic dictionary. Contains 2,300 illustrations, of which about 400 are in color, and 200 drawings. Includes definitions, biographies, museums, styles, periods, and bibliographies. The entries vary in length from less than twenty-five words to major survey articles covering several pages.

O'Dwyer, John and Le Mage, Raymond. *Glossary of Art Terms.* New York, Philosophical Library, 1950.

> A dictionary giving technical terminology for the tools of the artist, as well as the language of art history and criticism.

Oxford Companion to Art. Harold Osborne, ed. Oxford, Clarendon Press, 1970.

> More than 3,000 brief articles by art historians and specialists; similar in coverage to the *McGraw-Hill Dictionary . . .* , above. Alphabetical arrangement and cross references expedite its use, and there is a bibliography of more than 3,000 English and foreign titles. Harold Osborne is editor of the *British Journal of Aesthetics.*

Phaidon Dictionary of Twentieth-Century Art. New York, Praeger, 1973.

> From Matisse and Picasso to Andy Warhol, neoimpressionism to op art. Includes bibliographies and 66 illustrations.

Praeger Encyclopedia of Art. New York, Praeger, 1971. 5 vols.

> According to the *Library Journal* reviewer, this bears comparison with the *McGraw-Hill Dictionary of Art,* published two years earlier. It has more contributors who are not from the United States or Britain, being an enlarged and partly rewritten version of the French three-volume *Dictionnaire Universel de l'Art et des Artistes* (Hazan, 1967). A library having the McGraw-Hill, Oxford, Phaidon, and Praeger compendiums, plus the McGraw-Hill *Encyclopedia* (which is based on an Italian work), should be able to supply a vast range of points of view.

Savage, George and Newman, Harold. *An Illustrated Dictionary of Ceramics.* New York, Van Nostrand, 1974.

> Defines some 3,000 terms, concentrating on historical and aesthetic information. Illustrated.

Biographical Dictionaries

Canaday, John E. *Lives of the Painters.* New York, Norton, 1969. 4 vols.

> Begins with the Italian Renaissance. A chronological survey of European and American painters, concluding with Cézanne. The first three volumes contain 450 biographies, with a little criticism thrown in. The fourth consists of 352 plates, half of them in full color, and a comprehensive index.

Champlin, John Denison and Perkins, Charles C. *Cyclopedia of Painters and Paintings.* New York, Scribner, 1886-1887. 4 vols. Reprinted by Kennikat Press (Port Washington, N.Y., 1969).

> Dictionary arrangement, with articles about individual paintings and biographical articles about artists. Gives locations of museums and collections housing the original works at the time of compilation (some of this material is out of date, but may be of historical interest). Black-and-white illustrations.

Cummings, Paul. *Dictionary of Contemporary American Artists.* 2d ed. New York, St. Martin's, 1971.

> A great deal of factual information on 787 artists, with many small black-and-white reproductions of their more recent work. The first edition was published in 1966.

Fielding, Mantle. *Dictionary of American Painters, Sculptors and Engravers.* Philadelphia, 1926. Enl. ed. published by Modern Books and Crafts (Greens Farms, Conn. 1974).

> This book and Cummings's (above) supplement the New-York Historical Society's dictionary (below).

Great Photographers. By the editors of Time-Life Books. New York, Time-Life, 1971. Distributed by Morgan & Morgan.

> Sixty-eight photographers, from the mid-1800s to the 1960s, are treated here. Illustrated.

Mallett, Daniel Trowbridge. *Mallett's Index of Artists: International-Biographical; Including Painters, Sculptors, Illustrators, Engravers and Etchers of the Past and Present.* New York, Bowker, 1935. Supplement, 1940. 2 vols. Reprinted by Peter Smith under the title *Index for Artists: International and Biographical* (New York, 1948).

> An enormous amount of information given very briefly by means of abbreviations and symbols. Contains occasional inaccuracies but very useful as a starting-point in research.

New-York Historical Society. *Dictionary of Artists in America, 1564-1860,* by G. C. Groce and D. H. Wallace. New Haven, Conn., Yale University Press, 1957.

Who's Who in American Arts. New York, publisher varies, 1935-   .

> Originally issued by the American Federation of Arts. Frequency and publisher varied until Bowker began in 1953 to issue this directory every

three years. The 11th edition was published in 1973. Entries are arranged alphabetically and indexed geographically, and Canadian artists are included. A new feature in 1973 is a Professional Classification Index.

Histories of Art

Gombrich, E. H. *The Story of Art*. 11th ed. New York, Phaidon, 1966. Distributed by Oxford University Press.

　　Probably the most readable short history of art, profusely illustrated.

Newhall, Beaumont. *The History of Photography from 1839 to the Present Day*. rev. and enl. ed. New York, Museum of Modern Art, 1964. Distributed by Doubleday.

　　The germ of this book was a catalog published for one of the Museum's special exhibitions. The book is widely accepted as the standard history of the art and is beautifully illustrated in black-and-white and color. Museum catalogs of all sorts may be found in the library's pamphlet collection and should be consulted for information on individual photographers who may have exhibited their work.

Reinach, Salomon. *Apollo: An Illustrated Manual of the History of Art Throughout the Ages*. rev. and enl. ed. New York, Scribner, 1935.

　　Small one-volume encyclopedia of art, with many small illustrations. Often useful for information on artists now considered minor.

Taylor, Francis Henry. *Fifty Centuries of Art*. New York, Harper, 1960.

　　This well-illustrated history goes back to the cave drawings of prehistoric man in Europe, covers the art and architecture of early Central and South America, and comes up to the present day.

Museums

American Association of Museums. *The Official Museum Directory, United States and Canada*. 3d ed. New York, Crowell-Collier Educational Corporation, 1970.

　　Lists 6,700 museums and their contents, facilities, and publications. The museums are indexed alphabetically, by name and location, and categorically, by the nature of their collections (obviously, not all are art museums). There is also an index of key personnel.

　　This book was formerly entitled *Museums Directory of the United States and Canada*. The first edition was published in 1961 by the A.A.M. and the Smithsonian Institution.

American Art Directory, 1898-　　. Sponsored by the American Federation of Arts. New York, Bowker, 1952-　　. Triennial since 1952.

　　Guide to (at present) more than 2,000 American and Canadian museums, art societies, art schools, art departments, etc. The directory also contains an overseas section and a comprehensive index.

Bilzer, Bert and others, eds. *Paintings of the World's Great Galleries: The Histories and Treasures of the 30 Most Famous Galleries in the World*. Translated by Peter Gorge. New York, Praeger, 1961.

　　Includes much biographical and descriptive material, in alphabetical order. Fine color reproductions.

Christensen, Erwin O. *A Guide to Art Museums in the United States.* New York, Dodd, Mead, 1968.

> Describes 88 museums in 59 cities — history, viewing hours, outstanding holdings (chiefly paintings) — and includes about 500 small black-and-white reproductions.

Museums of the World: A Directory of 17,000 Museums in 148 Countries, Including a Subject Index. Eleanor Braun, comp. New York, Bowker, 1973.

> In addition to art museums, lists scientific, technological, historical, memorial, and archeological collections. Arranged alphabetically under five continental divisions, by countries and cities. The museums are indexed by location and type, and there is also an index of personnel. Large public libraries, museums, and universities with important art departments will be most likely to have this directory.

Indexes

Art Index, 1929-   . New York, Wilson, 1929-   .

> This quarterly index to more than 150 periodicals and museum bulletins is discussed in Chapter 9.

Monro, Isabel S. and Monro, Kate M. *Index to Reproductions of American Paintings.* New York, Wilson, 1948. Supplement, 1964.

——. *Index to Reproductions of European Paintings.* New York, Wilson, 1956.

> These three volumes index reproductions in about 1,500 books and 300 exhibition catalogs. Locations of the originals are given when known. Indexes of this type make it fairly easy to locate a copy of a painting when you know its artist, title, and/or subject. The problem of identifying a picture seen but untitled calls for the help of experts.

ARCHITECTURE

Briggs, Martin S. *Everyman's Concise Encyclopedia of Architecture.* New York, Dutton, 1959.

> Like all publications in Everyman's Reference Library, this is small, concise, and informative. Illustrations are in black and white.

Fletcher, Sir Banister F. *A History of Architecture on the Comparative Method.* 17th ed. Revised by R. A. Cordingley. London, Athlone Press; New York, Scribner, 1961.

> The first edition of this work was published in 1896. It has especially fine detailed illustrations, including floor plans and reconstructions, as well as photographs, some of buildings destroyed in war. Bibliographic and historical notes add to its usefulness.

Jordan, R. F. *The World of Great Architecture: From the Greeks to the Nineteenth Century.* New York, Viking, 1961.

> Notes to the plates by Dr. Bodo Cichy.

Chapter 13

Special Reference Books
GEOGRAPHY, ARCHAEOLOGY, AND HISTORY

ONE CANNOT STUDY history without maps; therefore geography and history must be paired. And here the Dewey and Library of Congress systems of classification cause us little trouble. With the DC we have all the 900s to cover; with LC we have C, D, E, F, and part of G. History may also involve archaeology, at least when ancient cultures are studied; therefore, archaeology will be included in this chapter, although it is sometimes classified as a social science. Chapter 14 will deal with the other social sciences, which LC places in H, J, K, and L and which Dewey distributes among the 300s, 600s, and 900s.

GEOGRAPHY
Atlases

At this point further definition of terms is necessary. Most people are familiar with the idea of an atlas, though perhaps not with the great variations which may occur in the actual books. Reference to a dictionary tells us that an atlas is either (1) a bound collection of maps, or (2) a collection of pictures illustrating any subject. (This latter definition applies particularly to a type of publication called an atlas of human anatomy, with detailed illustrations of all parts of the human body — one of the basic books in the training of physicians.)

The two definitions taken together come near to describing the major atlases published nowadays, for they are likely to include many pictures, as well as tables and diagrams. The reader will do well to examine atlases carefully to be sure that they provide the kinds of maps desired.

The atlases listed here present the world as it is today. Some of them have long articles describing each political division, statistical tables, special maps showing climate, rainfall, vegetation, mineral resources, etc. And any good atlas has an alphabetical index of place names, indicating the location of each place on a map. Historical atlases and pictorial histories will be listed later in this chapter, in the historical section.

Hammond, Inc. (formerly C. S. Hammond) of Maplewood, N.J., not only prepares maps for other publishers, as in the Britannica atlas listed below, but also publishes its own atlases of various sizes and prices. The deluxe two-volume *Hallmark* edition includes historical and Biblical maps and an "ecology unit"; the large single-volume *Medallion* is only four pages shorter, while the *Ambassador* omits the historical and Biblical maps and some of the ecology features. The *Ambassador*, like the others, has several types of maps for each country and state, uses various projections, includes altitude maps, statistical information, and has an index of 100,000 entries. It gives the zip code number for each postal unit which has one and includes postal zone maps for a number of large cities. For France, in addition to a map of the present-day *départements*, there is a special map showing the original provinces. For Switzerland, a map in deep colors shows which languages predominate in various areas. Each country's flag is reproduced in good color.

These three large atlases (as well as four smaller ones) were issued in 1971 and contain the 1970 census figures for the United States. Census figures for other countries are acknowledged and dated in the introductory matter.

Other valuable atlases include the following:

Encyclopaedia Britannica World Atlas. Chicago, Encyclopaedia Britannica. First edition, 1949. Revised at intervals.

> Maps by Hammond. Includes much statistical information. The maps in this appear, reduced in size, in the index volume of the *Encyclopaedia Britannica*, in editions before 1974.

Der Grosse Bertelsmann Weltatlas. Gütersloh, Bertelsmann, 1961.

> A small new German atlas, with unusually good gazetteer information, especially for Europe.

National Geographic Atlas of the World. rev. 3d ed. Washington, D.C., National Geographic Society, 1970.

> Readers of *National Geographic Magazine* are aware of the large folded maps that are often enclosed in current issues of the magazine, and of their value. Librarians usually extract these maps upon receipt and place them in Map Files or in Vertical File folders. Maps issued after the date of the latest edition of the *Atlas* should be remembered as possible supplementary material.

Stieler, Adolf. *Stieler's Atlas of Modern Geography*. 10th ed. Gotha, Justus Perthes, 1934-1938. 2 vols.

> While now wholly out of date as to national boundary lines, this still has great value for the infinite detail of its place location. During World War II sets of this atlas were borrowed from libraries "for the duration" by United States Air Force installations to aid them in pin-point bombing.

The *Times*, London, in collaboration with John Bartholomew & Sons, Ltd., Edinburgh. *The Times Atlas of the World: Comprehensive Edition*. 2d rev. ed. Boston, Houghton, 1971.

> Nearly 400 color maps; index-gazetteer with nearly 200,000 place names. Both this and the Hammond *Medallion* cited above give heights, depths, and distances in feet and meters. More than forty languages used in the glossary.

Local place names given in Anglicized versions only if the original spellings are unfamiliar. Based on five-volume edition of 1955-1960.

United States Geological Survey. *The National Atlas of the United States of America.* Washington, 1970.

The result of nearly twenty years of planning. Data from eighty-four federal agencies and some primary sources. Two sets of maps are included: "General Reference Maps" and "Special Subject Maps." This too gives zip codes.

Gazetteers

The gazetteer is a list of place names, with some information about each place. The list is alphabetical, and the information includes more or less exact location of the place, indicating whether it is a town or a county, a river, lake, or mountain, and giving some historical or descriptive matter. Articles in gazetteers vary in length from one line to several paragraphs. The briefer entries are to be found when the gazetteer doubles as index to an atlas, so that location can be indicated on a specific map, or when it is a section of a dictionary, as in the second edition of *Webster's.*

The Columbia Lippincott Gazetteer of the World. L. E. Seltzer, ed. New York, Columbia University Press, 1962 (reprint of 1952 edition, with 32-page supplement).

Lists about 130,000 names, with more than 30,000 cross references. Gives a great deal of information about important places, as well as brief identification of many very small ones.

The *Times*, London. *Index Gazetteer of the World.* London, Times, 1965.

Gives a much smaller amount of information about many more places than the *Columbia Lippincott Gazetteer.* Includes 345,000 places, 198,000 of which are in the *Times Atlas of the World (q.v.).*

Dictionaries

Geography is a field which has relatively few types of specialized reference books. Except for the research manual, of which Wright and Platt's *Aids to Geographical Research*, now out of print, was an outstanding example, the geographical dictionary is often the last recourse, barring actual exploration.

Moore, W. G. *A Dictionary of Geography.* 4th ed. New York, Praeger, 1967.

This will be discussed in the chapter on Science, because its scope is more closely related to scientific aspects of geography.

Stamp, Sir Lawrence Dudley, ed. *Dictionary of Geography.* New York, Wiley, 1966.

Defines geographical terms and gives concise biographies of prominent geographers and brief accounts of countries and many cities. Includes references to other books.

Webster's New Geographical Dictionary. Springfield, Mass., Merriam, 1972.

This is similar to a gazetteer but includes Biblical and historical place names as well as modern ones. Like *Webster's Biographical Dictionary* (q.v., Chapter 11), it is intended to provide in a separate volume material omitted from the controversial third edition of *Webster's New International Dictionary.*

ARCHAEOLOGY

Bray, Warwick and Trump, David. *The American Heritage Guide to Archaeology.* New York, American Heritage, 1970; paperback ed., Penguin.

Written by two British archaeologists. The emphasis is on the prehistoric, and coverage is worldwide. Roman and Anglo-Saxon Britain are well covered. The treatment is mature but very brief — only nine lines on the Dead Sea Scrolls. The drawings by Judith Newcomer are useful.

The Cambridge Ancient History. 3d ed. London, Cambridge University Press, 1970-   . Volume 1, Part 1, *Prolegomena and Prehistory.* I. E. S. Edwards and others, eds.

This volume presents the results of important archaeological discoveries. Detailed references to the sources of information in the text are given in footnotes. Tables at the end of this volume (and the fascicles being issued for succeeding volumes) represent the consensus of "three of the world's foremost chronologists," according to Professor Lazenby of the University of Notre Dame.

Cottrell, Leonard, ed. *The Concise Encyclopedia of Archaeology.* 2d ed. London, Hutchinson; New York, Hawthorn, 1971.

The general opinion of archaeologists seems to be that Cottrell is a popularizer. This book has, however, some long articles (including one on the Dead Sea Scrolls) by experts. The first edition was published in 1960.

Larousse Encyclopedia of Archaeology. Gilbert Charles-Picard, gen. ed. Paris, Larousse. English edition published by Putnam, New York, 1972.

Articles tell how archaeologists work, and embrace studies in Western Asia, the Nile valley, and Central, North, and South America. Six hundred "monochrome" illustrations, forty color plates.

Willey, Gordon R. *An Introduction to American Archaeology.* Volume 1, North and Middle America. Volume 2, South America. Englewood Cliffs, N.J., Prentice-Hall, 1966-1971.

Enthusiastically reviewed in *Scientific American.*

HISTORY

History is a term subject to widely different interpretations. Historiographers (students of the history of historical writing) have noted that historians have expanded their interests from military and political history to include economic and social trends and progress and the contributions of science and the arts, philosophy, and religion to the course of events. The student is advised, therefore, to explore books in all these fields when in search of historical information. The general encyclopedias, biographical dictionaries, and fact finders already listed contribute much, and books on the arts, literature, and science should be consulted also. The lists given below contain only reference works of the most general type. For histories of specific periods or regions, the student must consult catalogs and bibliographies.

World History—Ancient, Medieval, and Modern

Historical Atlases and Pictorial Works

Campbell, Gordon and Evans, I. O. *The Book of Flags*. 6th ed. London, Oxford University Press, 1969.

> Flags of all countries, including the new African states, are depicted here in color and black-and-white, along with miscellaneous flags of various types. About half the book is devoted to the British Commonwealth. For more color illustrations and for special standards, recent atlases and pamphlet files should be consulted.

Darby, H. C. and Fullard, Harold. *The New Cambridge Modern History*. Volume 14: *The Atlas*. London, Cambridge University Press, 1971.

> Designed to accompany the *History*, but a fine atlas in its own right. Maps grouped by areas and then chronologically. Indexed by subject. May be found shelved with the set of the *N.C.M.H.*

Gilbert, Martin. *Recent History Atlas: 1870 to the Present Day*. Cartography by J. R. Flower. New York, Macmillan. 1969.

> Begins where Shepherd's *Historical Atlas* (*q.v.*). leaves off. Ends with late-sixties action in Vietnam. Nine other atlases covering various areas or time periods are planned. To date four have been published: *British History Atlas; American History Atlas; Jewish History Atlas; First World War Atlas* (cartographer, Arthur Banks). This latest is chronological except for special sections on air and sea warfare.

Gohm, Douglas. *Antique Maps of Europe, the Americas, West Indies, Australasia, Africa, the Orient*. London, Octopus Books, 1972.

> Begins with brief biographies of the mapmakers, from Sebastian Munster (1489-1552) to Thomas Monk (1784-1851). Magnificent maps, a number in color; examples of fine cartography up to the mid-nineteenth century.

Heyden, A. A. M. van der and Scullard, H. H., eds. *Atlas of the Classical World*. New York and London, Nelson, 1950.

> Printed by Elsevier of Holland (distinguished for excellent color reproduction). Includes 73 maps in six colors and 475 illustrations, many of which are aerial photographs of the landmarks of pagan antiquity.

Historical Atlas of the World. Oddvar Bjørklund and others, eds. London and Edinburgh, Chambers; New York, British Book Centre, 1971.

> The most recent historical atlas to date, covering the world from 3000 B.C. to the 1960s.

Kiepert, Heinrich. *Atlas Antiquus.* Chicago, Rand McNally, 1900.

> Contains reproductions of twelve early maps showing the world as it was known to Ptolemy, Julius Caesar, etc.

The March of Civilization in Maps and Pictures: A Graphic Reference Book Covering Man's Development and Conquests from 4000 B.C. to the Present Day. Maplewood, N.J., Hammond, 1955.

> Besides historical maps this includes a section called "The Races of Mankind" with "racial portraiture" by Malvina Hoffman and text by Henry Field and W. D. Hambly. The "racial portraiture" consists of photographs of the sculptures made by Hoffman for the Field Museum in Chicago, at Dr. Field's request.

Meer, Frederic van der. *Atlas of Western Civilization.* English version by T. A. Birrell. 2d rev. ed. Princeton, N.J., Van Nostrand, 1960.

> A combination history, atlas, and art gallery. Reproductions of masterpieces in many of the famous collections of Europe, photographs of European cathedrals, castles, etc.

Muir's Historical Atlas: Ancient, Medieval and Modern. R. F. Treharne and Harold Fullard, eds. New York, Barnes & Noble, 1963.

> Divided into two sections which are also published separately: the *Atlas of Ancient and Classical History* (2d ed., 1956) and the *Historical Atlas: Medieval and Modern* (9th ed., 1962).

Palmer, R. R. and others, eds. *Historical Atlas of the World.* Chicago, Rand McNally, 1961.

> Includes political changes to the end of 1960. Available in paperback.

Shepherd, William R. *Historical Atlas.* 9th ed. New York, Barnes & Noble, 1964.

> The best and most inclusive historical atlas.

Chronologies

De Ford, Miriam A., comp. *Who Was When? A Dictionary of Contemporaries.* 2d ed. New York, Wilson, 1950.

> A series of chronological tables listing in parallel columns people who contributed to the development of political and military history, art, literature, philosophy, etc. Has an alphabetical index giving birth and death dates. A new edition updating material to 1974 is in preparation.

Keller, Helen Rex, comp. *Dictionary of Dates.* New York, Macmillan, 1934. 2 vols. Volume 1, *The Old World;* Volume 2, *The New World.*

> The events of history chronologically arranged under name of country.

Mirkin, Stanford M. *What Happened When.* New York, Washburn, 1966.

> Emphasis on the nineteenth and twentieth centuries. In a sense, this supplements Chambers's *Book of Days* and Steinberg's *Historical Tables (qq.v.).*

Mitchell, Adelheid. *Historical Charts of the Humanities.* New York, Prentice-Hall, 1939. o.p.

> This is a more graphic presentation of the same sort of information as is found in *Who Was When?* Each person is represented by a horizontal line extending from his birth to his death. At the top of each page are dates

marking off intervals, so that the reader may see at a glance exactly who was living at a certain date, in a number of fields. In the first pages, covering ancient history, there is a page to a century. For modern times, the intervals are shorter. A similar work by Steinberg (listed below), originally published in England, may be found in many college libraries.

Steinberg, Sigfrid H. *Historical Tables, 58 B.C.–A.D. 1965.* 8th ed. London, Macmillan; New York, St. Martin's, 1966, o.p. 1973.

Viorst, Milton. *The Great Documents of Western Civilization.* Philadelphia, Chilton, 1965.

> The introduction to this book deals with ancient history. The fifteen chapters cover Western civilization from the rise of Christianity to World War II and the nuclear age.

Dictionaries, Encyclopedias, and Handbooks

Avery, Catherine B. and others, eds. *The New Century Italian Renaissance Encyclopedia.* New York, Appleton, 1972.

> More than 4,000 alphabetically arranged headings; more than 100 illustrations. Art, religion, politics, biographies of heroes and heroines, philosophers and explorers. Basically a general handbook.

Devambez, Pierre, and others, eds. *The Praeger Encyclopedia of Ancient Greek Civilization.* New York, Praeger, 1967. French original edition, 1966.

> For the general reader. Treats briefly 750 topics dealing with all phases of ancient Greek civilization, each entry initialled by the French scholar who wrote it. Four hundred handsome illustrations and readable style.

Dupuy, R. Ernest and Dupuy, T. N. *The Encyclopedia of Military History from 3500 B.C. to the Present.* London, Macdonald; New York, Harper, 1970.

Eggenberger, David. *Dictionary of Battles.* New York, Crowell, 1967.

> Important battles from ancient times to about 1965. Also entries for wars, with the names and dates of major battles; and for countries, with chronological list of wars and battles. Cross references to variant names of battles. About 100 small maps and a bibliography.

Fines, John. *Who's Who in the Middle Ages.* London and New York, Holt, 1970.

> Information on about 100 persons who lived between the end of the Roman Empire and the fifteenth century. The selection is British-oriented and interesting. Biographies are longer than those in *Who's Who in the Ancient World.* There is a lack of good brief biographical matter for this period, and the style is readable.

Harbottle, Thomas B. *The Dictionary of Battles.* Revised and updated by George Bruce. New York, Stein & Day, 1971.

> Supersedes the reprint issued by Gale in 1966 of the original 1905 publication. Bruce has added cross references; brief statements of tactics and outcome are also included as well as sketches showing placement and number of troops, ships, or aircraft. Spans all of recorded history (to about 1970) with emphasis on the western world. Bibliography and index. Recommended for military students and "old soldiers."

Langer, William L., comp. and ed. *An Encyclopedia of World History.* 5th ed. Boston, Houghton, Mifflin, 1972.

> Covers world events from prehistory to January 1, 1971. The editor and contributors are well known in their fields. The prehistory section uses and describes new methods of dating artifacts, etc. The chronology has expanded sections on Africa and the Middle East since 1945. New maps, cross references, and improved genealogical tables. In addition to datable events like wars and treaties, there is new material on art, literature, science, and technology. An index of nearly 200 pages is included in the approximately 1,600-page volume.

Larned, Josephus Nelson. *New Larned History for Ready Reference, Reading, and Research.* rev. and enl. ed. Donald E. Smith, ed. in chief. Springfield, Mass., Nichols, 1922-24. 12 vols. o.p.

> An alphabetical collection of excerpts from historical writings, laws, and documents, with chronological arrangement under countries. Many cross references and an excellent index. Many famous Supreme Court cases are noted. Maps and illustrations. Unfortunately out of print, but most libraries have it, probably in very delicate condition, as the paper is fragile. One of the reprint publishers should be encouraged to reproduce or, better still, update it.

Larousse Encyclopedia of Ancient and Medieval History. Marcel Dunan, gen. ed. New York, Harper, 1963.

The London Times History of Our Times. Marcus Cunliffe, ed. New York, Norton, 1971.

> A survey of the last twenty-five years, by British and American writers. More than 1,000 illustrations, maps, and charts.

Milestones of History: 100 Decisive Events in the History of Mankind. S. G. F. Brandon and others, eds. New York, Norton, 1971.

> Contributors include Christopher Hibbert and Hugh Thomas, some of whose works will be listed later in this manual. Book consists of 100 essays which "cover the development of civilization, from ancient Egypt to the Apollo 11 moon landing" (publisher's announcement). There are 2,000 illustrations, 500 in color.

The New Century Classical Handbook. Catherine B. Avery, ed. New York, Appleton, 1962.

> In spite of the suggestion in the title that there had been an earlier Century classical handbook, there is no evidence in the preface, or in the catalog of the Library of Congress, that this is not an entirely new work. This 1,162-page volume has more than six thousand entries, some very short, some several pages long. For example, a very full account of Heracles is given (with a *q.v.* reference from Hercules), and summaries of the *Iliad, Odyssey, Aeneid,* etc., are given, book by book. This, like Peck's and Seyffert's works, listed below, might equally well be listed under Literature.

Oxford Classical Dictionary. 2d ed. N. G. L. Hammond and H. H. Scullard, eds. Oxford, Clarendon Press, 1970.

> The editors are Oxford's Greek and Roman history experts. Recently discovered material has been incorporated, and coverage of the late Roman Empire has been increased. The bibliographical material has been extended

to recent works. Emphasis has been placed on biography and literature. The
first edition was published in 1949.

Peck, Harry Thurston, ed. *Harper's Dictionary of Classical Literature
and Antiquities*. New York, American Book Co., 1896. Reprinted
1962 by Cooper Square Publishers (New York).

> The original work will be found in many libraries. This volume and the
> work by Seyffert, listed below, are the most inclusive, and to many the
> most interesting, compilations of general and specific information about the
> life and legends of ancient Greece and Rome.

Radice, Betty. *Who's Who in the Ancient World*. New York, Stein &
Day, 1971.

Seyffert, Oskar. *A Dictionary of Classical Antiquities*. Revised and
edited with additions by Henry Nettleship and J. E. Sandys. New
York, Meridian Books, 1956.

> Originally published in London by Sonnenschein in 1891. A wonderful
> source on such matters as artillery, armor, home design and plumbing,
> children's games, etc. Had been out of print for many years.

Sets and Series

The student will find much more detailed information in histories
of individual countries and periods, and in a number of important sets
and series. Notable among these are the Cambridge Histories, published in England at the Cambridge University Press and available in
New York from Macmillan. The original project was planned in 1896
under the direction of Lord Acton. Individual chapters in each volume
have been written by experts on the scope of the chapter. In chronological order of the periods treated, the following histories have been
published.

The Cambridge Ancient History, twelve volumes in fourteen, plus
five volumes of illustrative plates, was originally issued between 1902
and 1951. A revised edition, almost complete, was in print as of 1974.
(Volume 2, *History of the Middle East and the Aegean Region*, is to be
in two parts, of which Part 2 was "in press" in 1974.) The period covered by the set extends from prehistoric times to the Roman imperial
crisis and recovery, A.D. 143–324.

The Cambridge Medieval History, eight volumes in nine, was completed much more quickly. A two-volume condensation, *The Shorter
Cambridge Medieval History*, prepared by C. W. Previté-Orton and
published in 1952, made use of comparatively recent medieval studies.
A new edition of the *Medieval* set was begun in 1966 and is now complete.

The Cambridge Modern History, thirteen volumes and an atlas, was
completed between 1902 and 1913. This included an index volume.
The New Cambridge Modern History, 1493-1945, was compiled between 1957 and 1970, when Volume 14, *The Atlas*, was published. Vol-

ume 13, announced as *A Companion to Modern History*, had not been published as of 1974, but in 1968 *The Bibliography of Modern History*, compiled by John Roach, was issued to supplement the new edition.

Both college libraries and large public libraries are apt to purchase two sets of these very important works, one for the reference collection and one for circulation.

In 1958, the University of Michigan began to publish *The History of the Modern World*, a series on the major regions of the modern world. Each volume is written by an authority in the field. By 1974, eighteen volumes had been published, and eleven of those had already been revised and enlarged. The set includes volumes on Russia and the Soviet Union, Latin America, the Near East, Africa, the Southwest Pacific, the United States, and Great Britain.

National History—United States

The reader has no doubt observed that the first part of this chapter has been broad in scope: Atlases, whether geographic or historical, and chronologies have been worldwide in coverage. At this point, we begin to present historical reference books according to region, and though the various classification schemes place the United States well down the numerical scale, for us and our nearest neighbors north and south, the States are more important than, for instance, Austria-Hungary, which precedes us in the Library of Congress classification scheme but exists only as a part of pre-World War I history.

The books listed below alphabetically by their editors, compilers, and sometimes authors are mostly reference tools. Some, however, will be in the circulating collection, or perhaps in both reference and circulating collections. Within the group are a few books or sets dealing with Indians and black Americans, and a discussion of other historical sets dealing with periods of American history.

Adams, James Truslow, ed. *Dictionary of American History*. 2d ed. rev. New York, Scribner, 1944. 5 vols. Volume 6, Supplement 1, 1961 (J. G. E. Hopkins and Wayne Andrews, eds.). Index covering all 6 vols., 1963.

> This contains no biographical articles, as it is intended to be used with the *Dictionary of American Biography*. The articles are brief, but the coverage shows a broad interpretation of history.

——. *The Atlas of American History*. New York, Scribner, 1943.

> All maps are black-and-white outlines, many showing very small areas, as the terrain of a single battlefield, in great detail. The period covered is from Discovery to 1912.

—— and others, eds. *Album of American History*. 1970 ed. New York, Scribner, 1969. 6 vols. and index.

A companion to the preceding works. Pictures in black-and-white, illustrating American history until 1968. Many of the pictures are reproductions of old cartoons, engravings, and portraits, as well as modern photographs and cartoons. The very detailed index must be consulted, except, of course, by the browser, as the pictures are grouped roughly by period and subject.

In 1971 a republication of Volume 1, *Colonial America from the First Settlements to the Close of the American Revolution*, was issued in the belief that libraries and members of bicentennial committees would want it both as source material for costumes, floats, models, etc., for the impending celebration and as a replacement for the doubtless tattered remnants of the original volume.

Boatner, Mark Mays, III. *Encyclopedia of the American Revolution*. New York, McKay, 1966.

Carruth, Gorton and others, eds. *Encyclopedia of American Facts and Dates; with a supplement of the 70s.* 6th ed. New York, T. Y. Crowell, 1972.

Johnson, Thomas Herbert and Wish, Harvey. *The Oxford Companion to American History*. New York, Oxford University Press, 1969.

A one-volume, alphabetically arranged series of articles designed to supplement the *Oxford Companion to American Literature*. Summaries of significant times, events, and places. Thousands of cross references. Names and dates of persons who have held high offices; text of the Constitution and Amendments.

Kane, Joseph Nathan, comp. *Facts About the Presidents*. 3d ed. New York, Wilson, 1974.

A compilation of information about the presidents of the United States, by the compiler of *Famous First Facts*. Part I has a separate chapter for each president (up to Richard Nixon) and Part II draws comparisons among them from various aspects and is followed by an index. Illustrations include portraits and signatures of the presidents.

Leisy, Ernest. *The American Historical Novel*. Norman, Okla., University of Oklahoma Press, 1950.

While this is important as a source of information on novels accurately portraying various aspects of American history, it is equally important as a highly readable account of the development of the novel in America. The outstanding books on each period are commented upon in each chapter, and several useful lists are appended, with critical comments.

Lord, Clifford L. and Lord, Elizabeth H. *Historical Atlas of the United States*. rev. ed. New York, Holt, 1953.

Maps of larger areas than those in Adams's *Atlas of American History*. Particularly useful are maps showing political and economic expansion, population growth, etc., throughout our history.

Morris, Richard B., ed. *Encyclopedia of American History*. rev. and updated ed. New York, Harper, 1970.

Consists of (1) basic chronology, (2) topical chronology, (3) 400 notable Americans, with biographical sketches, (4) index. There are also maps and charts.

Stewart, George R. *American Place-Names: A Concise and Selective Dictionary for the Continental United States of America.* New York, Oxford University Press, 1970.

> An alphabetical list of about 12,000 place names (chosen from 3,500,000 names now in use). Designed for the general public, among whom will be readers of his earlier *Names on the Land* (Houghton, 1957, rev. ed.). This work includes well-known names like *Philadelphia* (of which there are about nine in the U.S.), names whose beginnings are repeated (e.g., *Black . . .* , *Lost . . .* , *Big . . .* , etc.), and unusual names like *Kokomo* or *Goodnight.* Following each name is its derivation, its state (where that information is pertinent), and historical, geographical, or folk explanations of the name. No pronunciation is given, as that varies from place to place and from time to time.

Sullivan, Mark. *Our Times: 1900-1925.* 6 vols. New York, Scribners, 1970-1972.

> The original work began publication in 1926 and has been a much-used source of illustrations, cartoons, songs, styles of dress, and general comment on the time when Mark Sullivan was a newspaper man. Those whose youth was in those times will read this new edition with delight, if their own original volumes are worn out. This reprinted edition has a new general introduction to this era of social history by Dewey W. Grantham.

Taylor, Tim. *The Book of Presidents.* New York, Arno, 1972.

> The format is similar to Kane's *Facts About the Presidents* (above) but the coverage is more detailed. Under each President entries are chronologically arranged, giving a day-to-day listing of significant events.

Webster's Guide to American History: A Chronological, Geographical, and Biographical Survey and Compendium. Charles Van Doren and Robert McHenry, eds. Springfield, Mass., Merriam, 1971.

> As the title indicates, this is (1) a chronology of events from October 12, 1492 to December 17, 1969; (2) a historical and statistical atlas; and (3) a biographical dictionary of 1,035 notable Americans. The chronology is accompanied by extracts from documents, etc., in parallel columns. Most of the chronology and many of the maps were adapted from *The Annals of America* (20 vols., 1969).

Sets and Series

At the end of the portion of this chapter which dealt with world history, some space was devoted to series of historical volumes, often under common editorship, always from a single publisher, some of which were published over several years, and some of which have been supplemented or superseded by new series. These sets have been invaluable to the student of world history. In the field of American history also, there are such series, which will be discussed briefly here.

One of the first cooperatively written series was The American Nation, edited by Albert Bushnell Hart and published by Harper (New York) between 1904 and 1918. Each of the twenty-eight volumes covered an era of American history and was written by one or more specialists in that field. Coverage ends before the beginning of the First World War, then called the European War. Each volume has its own index, and there is a general index volume.

The New American Nation series, issued by the same publisher under the editorship of Henry Steele Commager and Richard B. Morris, began publication in 1954. It is planned to be in forty volumes, each by a historian well qualified in the period covered. Each has its own index and bibliography. This too will probably have a combined index volume when the set is completed. In some ways the two sets seem to complement each other — a detail not found in the newer series is often in the older.

The Chronicles of America series, now out of print, was issued by Yale University Press (New Haven) in several editions, the one most popular with students being pocket-size, though cloth-bound. The set ended with the era of Franklin D. Roosevelt; students with short reports assigned still find it useful.

Yale University Press also published *The Pageant of America*, edited by Ralph Henry Gabriel. Its fifteen volumes, which appeared between 1925 and 1929, consist largely of pictures, and really set the stage for visual education, well before classroom use of films and filmstrips became common. In addition to the political, social, and military history of the United States, there are volumes on sports, art, literature, etc. The set is a forerunner of the *Album of American History (q.v.)*.

Finally, there is the *American Guide Series*, begun during the Great Depression of the 1930s by the Federal Writers' Project, a part of the WPA designed to give unemployed writers and hopefuls some income. A guide was developed for each state and for many large cities; some guides were very good, and a few have been reprinted and updated — the guide for Vermont was published in its 3d edition in 1968 by Houghton, Mifflin. The guides are still useful for local history. An account of the Writers' Project called *The Dream and the Deal* by Jerre Mangione was published in late 1972, and the *New Republic* for October 21, 1972, carried a long review by Malcolm Cowley, which might well suggest that a similar project would give us something better in the way of guidebooks than those published by gasoline companies.

Indians of North America

Klein, Bernard and Icolari, Daniel, eds. *Reference Encyclopedia of the American Indian*. New York, Klein, 1967.

> Lists of agencies, museums, libraries, associations, reservations, schools, periodicals, and tribal councils. Includes a bibliography (indexed by subject) and a Who's Who section with sketches of prominent Indians and others active in Indian affairs.

Hodge, Frederick Webb, ed. *Handbook of American Indians North of Mexico*. Bulletin 30 of the Bureau of American Ethnology. Washington, Government Printing Office, 1907-1910. 2 vols. Reprinted in 1968 by Scholarly Press (Grosse Pointe, Mich.).

    A standard work still in demand as a source of descriptions of tribes, biographies of notable Indians, identification of towns. Illustrated with numerous black-and-white photographs and sketches.

Blacks in America

Adams, Russell L. *Great Negroes, Past and Present*. 3d rev. ed. Chicago, Afro-Am, 1969.

    A text-reference for Black Studies.

Bergman, Peter M. *The Chronological History of the Negro in America*. New York, Harper, 1969; paperback ed., New American Library.

    A chronological account by year from 1441 to 1968. Statistics, personalities, publications, court decisions, news events. Covers blacks in all fields.

Ebony magazine. *Ebony Pictorial History of Black America*. Introduction by Lerone Bennett, Jr. Chicago, Johnson, 1971. 3 vols. Volume 1: *African Past to Civil War*; Volume 2: *Reconstruction to Supreme Court Decisions, 1954*; Volume 3: *Civil Rights Movement to Black Revolution*.

    These volumes contain more than a thousand pictures.

Fishel, Leslie H., Jr. and Quarles, Benjamin. *The Black American: A Documentary History*. rev. ed. of *The Negro American*. Glenview, Ill., Scott, 1970.

    The authors have added an index and a new chapter updating the 1967 edition to 1969, and have replaced *Negro* with *Black* in the title. Dr. Quarles is Professor of History in Morgan College.

Hughes, Langston and Meltzer, Milton. *A Pictorial History of the Negro in America*. 3d ed. Revised by C. Eric Lincoln and Milton Meltzer. New York, Crown, 1968.

    The earlier editions "tried to tell who the Negro is, where he came from, and to show what he has contributed and how he has affected, and in turn been affected by, American life, as well as to indicate where he is headed." There is a new section here on the Black Revolution, and the work continues to show the gains as well as the aims of black Americans ir the arts, education, and especially in politics and government. This book has been continuously in demand among black youth.

International Library of Negro Life and History. 10 vols. Washington Association for the Study of Negro Life and History, 1967-1968. Mary L. Fisher, comp. 2d ed. rev. and enl.

    Supplemented by a yearbook *In Black America* (1969-   ) edited by P. W. Romero. United publication available in cloth or paperback.

The Negro in American History. Mortimer J. Adler, gen. ed. Chicago, Encyclopaedia Britannica, 1969. 3 vols.

    A collection of original source materials.

National History—Canada

Dictionary of Canadian Biography. George W. Brown, gen. ed. Toronto, University of Toronto Press, 1966-   . To be in about 20 vols., chronologically arranged, so that each volume will be self-contained.

The first volume gives biographical essays and bibliographies on those connected with Canadian development from the year 1000 to 1700; the second covers 1701 to 1740. Volume 1 also contains several introductory essays on early Canada and a bibliography of manuscript and printed source materials. Volume 10, published in 1966, covers 1800 to 1880.

Encyclopedia Canadiana. John E. Robbins, ed. in chief. Toronto, Grolier, 1972. 10 vols.

Essential for the Canadian student, and most enlightening for people in other parts of the British Commonwealth and in the United States. The American Revolution, for instance, is merely mentioned because a few battles happened to take place in what is now the Province of Quebec.

Kerr, D. G. G. *A Historical Atlas of Canada.* Toronto, Nelson, 1960.

An attractive atlas, with good maps, charts, illustrations, and informative text.

Story, Norah, ed. *The Oxford Companion to Canadian History and Literature.* Toronto and New York, Oxford University Press, 1967.

Indispensable for those who want to know anything about Canada. Canadian writers, statesmen, and historical figures; Eskimo and Indian legends and tales. About 450 literary items, 1,500 historical, more than 2,300 cross references, book titles, and maps. Appendixes list administrators from New France to date of publication.

Wade, Mason. *The French Canadians, 1760-1967.* 2 vols. New York, St. Martin's, 1968. (Apparently a revised edition, but not so announced).

Explains the major grievances of the French-speaking Canadians and their attitudes toward their own government and that of "The States."

National History—Great Britain

Methuen's History of England. London, Methuen; New York, Barnes & Noble. 8 vols.

Eight volumes, each by a recognized scholar; individual volumes are frequently revised or reprinted. The dates and editions below were compiled in 1963.

England Before the Norman Conquest, by Charles Oman. 9th ed. 1949.

England Under the Normans & Angevins, by H. W. C. Davis. 13th ed. 1949.

England in the Later Middle Ages, by K. H. Vickers. 7th ed. 1950.

England Under the Tudors, by G. R. Elton. 1955.

England Under the Stuarts, by G. M. Trevelyan. 21st ed. 1957.

England Under the Hanoverians, by C. G. Robertson. 16th ed. reprinted in 1958.

England Since Waterloo, by John Marriott. 15th ed. 1954.

Modern England, 1885-1945: A History of Our Own Times, by John Marriott. 4th ed. reprinted in 1952.

Steinberg's Dictionary of British History. 2d ed. Sigfrid H. Steinberg
and others, eds. New York, St. Martin's, 1971.

Brief, signed articles on all phases of British history. Countries no longer a
part of the British Empire are treated only until their connection is ended,
e.g., the United States to 1783, Uganda to 1967.

Wiener, Joel H., ed. *Great Britain: Foreign Policy and the Span of
Empire, 1689-1971 — A Documentary History.* New York, McGraw-
Hill, 1972. 4 vols.

This makes accessible many documents which have shaped the course of
history — treaties, speeches, Commons debates, and radio broadcasts, in their
original spelling, grammar, and style. Volumes 1 and 2 deal with foreign
policy; 3 and 4 are devoted to the "span of empire." There are 1,400 pages
on Ireland.

National History—Miscellaneous

Boorman, Howard L., ed. *Biographical Dictionary of Republican
China.* New York, Columbia University Press, 1967-1971. 4 vols.

Volume 4 consists largely of a bibliography of works by the biographees
and the sources used by contributors in preparing the articles, with authors
and titles given in both Chinese characters and in transliteration.

The Far East and Australasia, 1969-   . London, Europa, 1969-   .

Annual, published each February, each volume revised extensively. Includes a Who's Who of prominent men and women.

Kish, George and others. *Economic Atlas of the Soviet Union.* 2d ed.
rev. Ann Arbor, Mich., University of Michigan Press, 1971.

Latin American Historical Dictionaries. Metuchen, N.J., Scarecrow.

Brief yet thorough coverage, with generous bibliography for these small
books.

Historical Dictionary of Guatemala, by Richard E. Moore. 1967; rev. ed.,
1973.

Historical Dictionary of Panama, by Basil C. Hedrick and Anne K.
Hedrick. 1970.

Historical Dictionary of Venezuela, by D. K. Rudolph and G. A. Rudolph.
1971.

Historical Dictionary of Bolivia, by D. B. Heath. 1972.

Historical Dictionary of El Salvador, by P. F. Flemion. 1972.

Historical Dictionary of Nicaragua, by H. K. Meyer. 1972.

Historical Dictionary of Chile, by Salvatore Bizzarro. 1972.

Learmonth, A. T. A. and Learmonth, A. M., comps. *Encyclopedia of
Australia.* London and New York, Warne, 1973.

More than 2,700 entries, including more than 50 long articles. Information
and comment blended into a source book on Australia which is both useful
and interesting. Includes maps, illustrations, and line drawings.

Patai, Raphael, ed. *Encyclopedia of Zionism and Israel.* New York,
McGraw-Hill, 1971. 2 vols.

This work has been in preparation since 1964. At that time it was to be a history of modern Israel. Since 1967, strong Zionist partisanship has changed the emphasis.

Political Africa: A Who's Who of Personalities and Parties. Ronald Segal and others, eds. New York, Praeger, 1961.

Combines a group of articles about each of the countries and colonies of Africa, in alphabetical order, with a biographical dictionary of important figures in the development of these countries. Periodic revision is planned, but no new edition has been noted to Spring 1973.

Schopflin, George, ed. *The Soviet Union & Eastern Europe: A Handbook*. New York, Praeger, 1970.

Sohn, Louis B., ed. *Basic Documents of African Regional Organizations*. Dobbs Ferry, N.Y., Oceana, 1971-1973. 4 vols. Published for the Inter-American Institute of International Legal Studies.

This series concerns the efforts of the Organization of African Unity (founded in 1963) to achieve a better life for the African peoples; to defend their territorial integrity and independence; to eradicate colonialism; and to promote international cooperation. The OAU has, so far, been ineffective politically but it has made some economic and social progress.

Includes various documents of the OAU and its precursors — some photographed from the journals or books where they first appeared, others in type; some in English, some in French.

Chapter 14

Special Reference Books
THE SOCIAL SCIENCES

HISTORY IS, of course, one of the social sciences. But, as the reader has seen, so many books have been published, revised, or updated in recent years that it seemed best to treat history separately. Similar changes have occurred in the other social sciences. Certain titles have been difficult to assign — a few which are listed under History in the preceding chapter may be repeated here in the section on politics and government.

SOCIOLOGY AND SOCIAL WORK

American Men and Women of Science: The Social and Behavioral Sciences. 12th ed. Edited by the Jaques Cattell Press. New York, Cattell/Bowker, 1973. 2 vols.

The previous edition and its supplement (1965-1968, 1970) were issued under the general title *American Men of Science*, along with earlier volumes concerning the physical and biological sciences (see Chapter 16). Psychologists and psychiatrists are included among the listings for the behavioral sciences.

Encyclopedia of Social Work. Issue 15. New York, National Association of Social Workers, 1965.

This useful (where not out of date) publication has had a varied history. Originally called the *Social Work Year Book*, it was published irregularly by the Russell Sage Foundation from 1929 to 1949, then by the American Association of Social Workers in 1951 and 1954. In 1957 the National Association of Social Workers assumed responsibility for it, and the 1965 issue announced that the *Encyclopedia* would be published at "regular" intervals of "perhaps" five or ten years. The latest issue contains a number of useful articles, notably one on the methods of treatment of drug addiction. In a college or junior college where social workers are trained, recent issues, even when irregular, will be of some use. However, for the statistical information, lists of colleges, and so forth, more regularly updated reference books must be used. See the section of this chapter dealing with education, under the subhead Directories.

Encyclopaedia of the Social Sciences. E. B. A. Seligman, ed. in chief. New York, Macmillan, 1930-35. 15 vols. (Popular edition without bibliographies, 8 vols., 1937).

Includes not only the social sciences in their narrower sense, but also the social aspects of such other fields as art and medicine. The articles are monographic in scope, many giving a history of the subject covered. Although this work is now about forty years old, it is still extremely valuable.

Gould, Julius and Kolb, W. L. *Dictionary of the Social Sciences.* New York, Free Press (Macmillan), 1964. Compiled under the auspices of UNESCO.

> This has been a very useful work, especially during the years when the *Encyclopedia of Social Work* was not published. It gives not only the definitions of terms but the history of their usage; it is still useful for this purpose.

International Encyclopedia of the Social Sciences. David L. Sills, ed. New York, Macmillan, 1968. 17 vols. (Volume 17 is an index to the entire set).

> This complements but does not entirely supersede the above. Includes anthropology, economics, geography, law, political science, psychology, sociology, and statistics.

Theodorson, George A., and Theodorson, Achilles G. *A Modern Dictionary of Sociology.* New York, Crowell, 1969.

> Concise and accurate definitions of terms used in psychology, social psychology, anthropology, and statistics. Publisher's announcement states that "more than a thousand volumes were researched . . . in the preparation of this volume."

POLITICS AND GOVERNMENT

Barone, Michael and others. *The Almanac of American Politics: The Senators, The Representatives — Their Records, States and Districts, 1972.* Boston, Gambit, 1972. Planned to be biennial, to cover each session of Congress. Cloth and paperback editions.

> The authors are three young ex-members of the staff of the Harvard *Crimson.* The material is alphabetical by state, giving for each its political coloration, census data, economic base, and state government facts; elected officials are listed by district and party, with biographical information and stands on key issues. *Business Week*'s reviewer says it is better than the "backgrounders" of *Congressional Quarterly.*

Laqueur, Walter Z. and others, eds. *A Dictionary of Politics.* New York, Free Press (Macmillan), 1971.

> About 3,000 current political terms, international in scope. No pronunciations of words, and many government agencies listed by initials only. Otherwise useful — and reasonably up to date.

Schlesinger, Arthur M., Jr. and Israel, F. L., eds. *History of American Presidential Elections, 1789-1968.* New York, McGraw-Hill in association with Chelsea House, 1971. 4 vols.

> Forty-five historians and political scientists have contributed to this. After a short article explaining the campaign issues of each election, a series of pertinent documents follows: party platforms, handbills, speeches, and newspaper articles. Especially useful to college students as a good first source.

Schlesinger, Arthur M., Jr., ed. *History of U.S. Political Parties.* New York, Chelsea House in association with Bowker, 1973. 4 vols. Volume 1, *1789-1860, From Factions to Parties;* Volume 2, *1860-1910, The Gilded Age of Politics;* Volume 3, *1910-1945, From Square*

Deal to New Deal; Volume 4, *1945-1972, The Politics of Change.*
Twenty-five historians and scholars contributed. As in the set described
above, each essay is followed by documents such as letters, debates, speeches,
etc. *The History of U.S. Political Parties* will be more useful to professors
and graduate students than to undergraduates.

Local and State Governments

Book of the States, 1935-   . Chicago, Council of State Governments,
1935-   . Biennial, with 2 supplements between issues.
> Has articles on state government in general, and tables and statistics of all
> kinds; state flowers, mottoes, laws on marriage and divorce, for example. Also
> government officials, state legislatures, etc. For more details on any one state
> it is necessary to consult its state manual.

Municipal Year Book, 1934-   . Chicago, International City Managers'
Assn., 1934-   . Annual.
> Similar in type of information to the *Book of the States,* above. Gives chief
> officials for cities of more than 10,000 population; mayors and clerks for those
> of 5,000 to 10,000.

Forty-nine of the fifty states publish a state manual or directory —
they are called by different names. Some are issued by the state, some
are authorized for publication by a commercial firm. These manuals
give the same sort of information for states that the *Statistical Abstract*
and the *United States Government Organization Manual* do for the
nation, or the *Canadian Almanac* for Canada.[1] Some state directories
have biographical sketches of officials who may not be listed in the
national Who's Who books.

Federal Government

Congressional Information Service. *Index to Publications of the United
States Congress, 1970-*   .
> Monthly, with quarterly and annual cumulations. Congressional documents
> are organized by committee. Indexes all hearings, reports, committee prints,
> and other documents produced by Congress.

Congressional Quarterly, Inc. Washington, D.C.
> Publications include the following:
> *CQ Weekly Report.* Analyzes the major issues facing Congress and records
> Congressional action. Quarterly cumulative index by name and subject.
> *CQ Almanac.* Annual. Reorganizes and cross-indexes the information in
> the *CQ Weekly Report.* Published early in the year, to cover activities of the
> previous calendar year.
> *CQ Editorial Research Reports.* Forty-eight printed reports on major issues
> published each year. Also available in two semi-annual bound and indexed
> volumes. Each report is on a single topic and may be purchased separately
> from the publisher.

---

[1] See Appendix C for an article by Jack A. Clark, describing some of these manuals.

Congress and the Nation. Volume 1, *1945-1964* (1965); Volume 2, *1965-1968* (1970). A review of politics and government after World War II. The first volume is about 2,000 pages long; the second, half the size.

Guide to the Congress of the United States: Origins, History and Procedure. 1971. Covers the relations of Congress with the executive and judicial branches.[2]

United States Government Organization Manual . . . 1935-   . Washington, Government Printing Office, 1935-   .

Originally published as a loose-leaf information service, with frequent revision by substitution of new pages. Now revised annually. Fully describes each agency of the federal government, giving the date and circumstances of its establishment, and its current chief officials. Includes a list of agencies abolished or transferred from one department to another.

United States. Congress. *Congressional Record.* March 4, 1873-   . Washington, Government Printing Office, 1874-   .

Includes complete record of all proceedings, speeches, and debates from the Forty-third Congress to the present. Any congressman or senator may request that documents from other sources, speeches made elsewhere, etc., be included in the *Record.* The complete record of congressional action includes:

Debates and Proceedings, 1st to 18th Congress.
Register of Debates, 18th to 25th Congress.
Congressional Globe, 23d to 42d Congress.

Government Officials—Biography

Friedman, Leon and Israel, Fred L., eds. *The Justices of the United States Supreme Court, 1789-1969: Their Lives and Major Opinions.* New York, Chelsea House in association with R. R. Bowker, 1969. 4 vols.

A valuable reference tool for students of American constitutional and political history. The ninety-seven justices of the Supreme Court come alive both as men and as judges. Many of these men passed into oblivion after their tenure on the Supreme Bench and were once described as "fourscore forgotten men." Very few have been the subjects of individual biographies.

Kane, Joseph Nathan. *Facts About the Presidents: A Compilation of Biographical and Historical Data.* 3d ed. New York, Wilson, 1974.

Part I gives each president a chapter; Part II gives comparative data. Useful as a quick refresher.

Sobel, Robert, ed. in chief. *Biographical Directory of the United States Executive Branch, 1774-1971.* Westport, Conn., Greenwood, 1971.

Suggested by the *Biographical Directory of the American Congress, 1724-1961* (Washington, Government Printing Office, 1961). See also Chapter 11 for comment.

Sobel's compilation gives biographies of nearly 500 persons who have served in the executive branch of the United States government. Many received short shrift in the Who's Whos of their own day.

---

[2] For complete summary, see *Reference Quarterly,* Winter 1971.

United States. Congress. *Official Congressional Directory, 1809-*
Biennial.

> See Chapter 11 for comment and for other biographical dictionaries.

Who's Who in Government, 1972/73. Chicago, Marquis, May 1972.

> This includes many of the people listed in Sobel (above), which it serves to
> update, as well as some local, state, and international figures, heads of state,
> and diplomatic representatives. The month of issue, preceding instead of
> following a national election, is noteworthy.

LAW

Most cities of any size have a body of law, which must not contro-
vert the laws of the next largest governmental unit — the town code
must comply with the county code, the county with the state, and the
state with the nation. Hence it is necessary for these codes to be available, and they will be found in the library. Some states, such as Maryland, have constitutions which need revision. Thus, every library in
Maryland must have the *Annotated Code of Maryland*, which provides
a more or less up-to-date record of the laws which in a sense amend the
state constitution, and cites examples of cases which have been decided
on the basis of these laws. Students of law must be acquainted with the
codes of their respective states in order to pass bar examinations.

At the federal level, in addition to the Constitution and its amendments, proposed amendments, and still-to-be-ratified amendments,
there is *The United States Code*, published by the House Committee
on the Judiciary (Washington, Government Printing Office). The latest
edition is that of 1970, and it includes all laws passed by Congress and
still in force on January 20, 1971, arranged in fifty *titles* or groups. Supplements are issued annually while the next edition is in preparation.
The United States Code, Annotated, nearly ten times as large and still
growing, contains records of cases showing how the laws have been
interpreted. A good reference book to help clarify this material is *The
Statutory History of the United States*, by Bernard Schwartz and others,
published in three volumes by McGraw-Hill (New York, 1969).

Librarians are frequently asked about laws relating to personal
problems — marriage, divorce, parental authority, taxes, interest rates,
wills, and partnerships. Especially in matters of marriage or divorce,
the inquirer may want to know the laws of several different states. Some
of these questions can be answered by the following books, which deal
with the rights of American citizens.

Creamer, J. Shane. *A Citizen's Guide to Legal Rights*. New York, Holt,
1971.

Dorsen, Norman, ed. *Rights of Americans: What They Are — What
They Should Be*. New York, Pantheon, 1971.

INTERNATIONAL RELATIONS

The publications of the Europa firm have already been discussed in Chapter 11, as have those of the Council on Foreign Relations and the United Nations.

Foreign Affairs, a scholarly periodical begun in 1922, has always been distinguished by its comprehensive reviews of important books on foreign relations. It is also the source of the *Foreign Affairs Bibliography*, issued every ten years. The fifth edition, covering 1962-1972, was published in 1974. Meanwhile, in 1972 the Council on Foreign Relations in conjunction with the Bowker company of New York published *The Foreign Affairs 50-Year Bibliography: New Evaluations of Significant Books on International Relations, 1920-1970*, under the editorship of Byron Dexter with a foreword by Hamilton Fish Armstrong. This gives brief appraisals of about 2,230 works, freshly looked over from the standpoint of 1970.

The following reference set is also helpful:

Worldmark Encyclopedia of the Nations. 4th rev. ed. Moshe Y. Sachs and Louis Barron, eds. New York, Harper, 1970. 5 vols.

> The first edition of this very useful work was published in one volume in 1960 and included information on 118 countries, listed alphabetically, plus a section on the UN, its subsidiaries, and related international agencies. The 4th edition includes 146 nations and has been completely revised and reset, enlarged and updated. It consists of five volumes, one devoted to international agencies and the other four dealing with the nations of the Americas, Europe, Africa, and Asia (including Australasia). Information on each country is arranged according to a numbered scheme, so that, for example, agricultural products are listed under the same number throughout the set. This consistent arrangement makes revision fairly easy, as some sections will remain unchanged indefinitely (e.g., physical features, climate, minerals). Small outline maps appear in the text, and bibliographies are included in many articles. There are, of course, other works, such as the Europa yearbooks and *The Statesman's Year-book*, which cover this material, but the numbered scheme, the large amount of information given for each country, and the bibliographies for each important entry continue to make this encyclopedia valuable. The fact that it is in five volumes makes it possible for five people to use it at the same time. If space permits, a library may well retain one previous edition for information which remains unchanged.

BUSINESS AND ECONOMICS

Barach, Arnold B. *Famous American Trademarks.* Washington, Public Affairs Press, 1972.

> A series of vignettes of trademarks, originally published in the consumer journal *Changing Times*. The stories of such trademarks as Kellogg's rooster, Prudential's Rock of Gibraltar, Hartford's stag, and so forth.

Business Periodicals Index, 1958-   . New York, Wilson, 1958-   .

> See Chapter 9.

Coman, Edwin T., Jr. *Sources of Business Information.* 2d ed. Berkeley, University of California Press, 1964.

> A revised edition of a general guide to information for businessmen, and hence for students of business and economics. Originally published by Prentice-Hall in 1949.

Daniells, Lorna M., comp. *Business Reference Sources: An Annotated Guide for Harvard Business Students.* Boston, Baker Library, Graduate School of Business Administration, 1971.

> What is good for Harvard. . . .

Editor and Publisher Market Guide. New York, Editor and Publisher Co. Annual.

> *Editor and Publisher* is a trade journal for publishers, especially of newspapers. This is a geographically arranged list of cities and towns in the United States and Canada having at least one daily newspaper. It includes a current estimate of population and lists industries, climate, character of water supply, chain stores, etc. Gives the kind of information needed by people who plan to start a business, or whose employers require them to move to a new location. Graduating college students will find it helpful in deciding where to apply for jobs or which offers to consider.

Encyclopedia of Business Information Sources. Paul Wasserman, man. ed. Detroit, Gale, 1970. 2 vols.

> This book and the two listed immediately above differ somewhat in coverage and opinion. If limited to one, libraries are most likely to choose the Harvard compilation.

Hutchinson, Lois D. *Standard Handbook for Secretaries.* 8th ed. New York, McGraw-Hill, 1969.

> There are numerous books of this type, but this is probably the most often used, as it includes business etiquette, a dictionary of business terms, and a guide to good usage.

McGraw-Hill Dictionary of Modern Economics: A Handbook of Terms and Organizations. Douglas Greenwald, ed. New York, McGraw-Hill, 1973.

> This is the second edition of a dictionary first issued in 1965. Like its predecessor, it is an essential reference for the economist and businessman, and obviously also for the student of economics. The definitions are clear and for the most part devoid of jargon. In addition to listing terms seldom found in an unabridged dictionary, this book describes private, public, and nonprofit organizations concerned with economics, and supplies bibliographic references. The terms defined include those appearing on the financial pages of newspapers, a feature useful to the private investor.

National Industrial Conference Board. *Economic Almanac*, 1940-   . Annual to 1950, biennial from 1951/1952. Occasionally irregular.

> Includes many business statistics — on prices, production, wages, etc. — as well as a glossary of terms.

Oxford Economic Atlas of the World. 4th ed. Prepared by the Cartographic Department of the Clarendon Press. D. B. Jones, advisory ed. London and New York, Oxford University Press, 1972.

Sloan, Harold S. and Zurcher, A. J. *A Dictionary of Economics*. 5th ed. New York, Barnes & Noble, 1971.

EDUCATION

American Council on Education. *American Universities and Colleges*. 11th ed. W. Todd Furniss, ed. Washington, American Council on Education, 1973.

> This directory offers detailed information on individual colleges and universities as well as comparative data. It also contains a section on the foreign student in the United States, a subject listing for professional education, and an alphabetical list of degree-conferring institutions accredited by state, regional, or national agencies. Revised approximately every four years.

College Blue Book, 1969/70. 13th ed. New York, CCM Information Corp. (Crowell, Collier & Macmillan), 1969. 10 vols.

> Lists 3,417 colleges in the United States as of July 1, 1969. A special updating service is available.

Current Index to Journals in Education, 1969-   . New York, CCM Information Corp. (Crowell, Collier & Macmillan), 1969-   . Monthly, with semiannual and annual cumulations.

> An index to more than 200 journals. The U.S. Office of Education's ERIC (Educational Resources Information Center) cooperates in the preparation of this listing.

Directory of American Scholars. 5th ed. Edited by the staff of the Jaques Cattell Press. New York, Bowker, 1969. 4 vols.

> Considered to be the most selective of the biographical dictionaries of living educators. Similar to *Who's Who in America* as to form of entry. Revised editions issued at intervals. Includes many scholars engaged in research, but the list is made up primarily of college and university *professors*. See the same editors' *American Men and Women of Science* (page 195).

Education Index, 1929-   . New York, Wilson, 1929-   . Monthly, except July and August, with annual cumulations.

> Now indexes approximately 240 publications. (See entry in Chapter 9.)

Encyclopedia of Education. Lee C. Deighton, ed. in chief. New York, Macmillan, 1971. 10 vols. (Volume 10 is the index, with *see* and *see also* references.)

> Probably replaces and certainly supplements Monroe's *Cyclopedia of Education* (1911-1913). The emphasis is on American education, but the educational systems of more than 100 countries are discussed. This is supplemented and updated by the *Education Yearbook* (New York, Macmillan and The Free Press, 1971-   ).

Encyclopedia of Educational Research. 4th ed. Robert L. Ebel, ed. New York, Macmillan, 1969.

> Like its predecessors in emphasizing research, this encyclopedia deals with testing, report cards, "learning resource centers" (they used to be called school libraries), and new methods of teaching old subjects — the New Math and the Initial Teaching Alphabet.

Encyclopedia of Modern Education. H. N. Rivlin and Herbert Schueler, eds. New York, Philosophical Library, 1943. Reissued in 1969 by Kennikat Press (Port Washington, N.Y.).

> Concise articles intended for the layman. Good material on innovators like Horace Mann, J. H. Pestalozzi, and John Dewey.

Good, Carter V., ed. *Dictionary of Education.* 3d ed. New York, McGraw-Hill, 1973.

> A reliable dictionary of terms from educational literature, and a key to some of the jargon which mars much so-called educational journalism. Earlier editions were published in 1945 and 1959. Each revision has deleted old terms and added new ones. About 8,000 new entries have been included, and there are about 33,000 cross-references. Canadian and British usages are included but foreign-language terms have been dropped. Especially useful in teacher-training institutions.

Holmes, Brian and Scanlon, D. G., eds. *World Year Book of Education,* 1971/1972-   . New York, Harcourt, 1971/1972-   .

World Guide to Universities (Internationales Universitaets-Handbuch), 1971/1972. 5 vols. Available in the U.S. from Bowker.

> Volumes I and II list the universities of Europe alphabetically by country; Volume III gives those of the United States and Canada; and Volume IV, those of Latin America, Asia, and Africa. Indexes are contained in Volume V. Each of the first four volumes has a table of contents listing universities by country and city. Subject indexes are included in Volume V. This set has some valuable features — it indicates where one may study unusual subjects such as tropical medicine or parasitology, and gives the names and specialties of faculty members and the names of librarians.

A better and less pretentious source of information than the above is *The World of Learning,* published each January by Europa and available from the International Publications Service, 114 East 32d Street, New York 10016. *The World of Learning* provides information not only on the universities of the world but also on libraries, research institutes, museums, art galleries, and learned societies. (See also Chapter 11, where this book is mentioned along with other Europa publications.)

Finally, every prospective teacher should consult the following annual; if it is not available, the state departments of education in the states where one desires to teach should be consulted.

Woellner, Robert C. and Wood, M. A. *Requirements for Certification of Teachers, Counselors, Librarians, Administrators for Elementary Schools, Secondary Schools, Junior Colleges.* Chicago, University of Chicago Press, 1935-   . Annual.

> Summarizes certification requirements for each state, including Alaska and Hawaii. Invaluable for those planning to teach, in order that they may be able to present the necessary number of "points" for the chosen state. The prospective teacher should be sure that he is consulting the latest edition. As of the 38th edition (1973/1974), Elizabeth H. Woellner has taken over the compilation of this work.

PSYCHOLOGY

English, H. B. and English, A. C. *A Comprehensive Dictionary of Psychological and Psychoanalytical Terms: A Guide to Usage.* New York, 1958.

As psychology is now considered a social science, and psychoanalysis at least partially a medical science, this might have been listed under either. Because the college student and the layman are probably more concerned with the first, in terms of definition and usage, it is listed here.

Eysenck, H. J. and others, eds. *Encyclopedia of Psychology.* New York, Herder & Herder, 1972. 3 vols.

An international work. The contributors come from various lands (many from Germany, the U.S.S.R., and Japan) and the encyclopedia itself is published in German, French, Spanish, and Portuguese, as well as in English. Its announced purpose is "to standardize terms and information. . . ." The articles range up to 4,000 words in length. There are also many short definitions, more technical than those in the dictionary by English and English, above.

Goldenson, Robert M. *The Encyclopedia of Human Behavior: Psychology, Psychiatry and Mental Health.* New York, Doubleday, 1970. 2 vols.

Definitions for the layman and student. Includes discussions of psychiatric disorders and drug abuse, case histories, illustrations, and index.

Harvard List of Books in Psychology. 4th ed. Cambridge, Mass., Harvard University Press, 1971. paperpack.

Chapter 15

Special Reference Books
LITERATURE

THE REFERENCE BOOKS listed and discussed in this chapter are, in general, concerned with English and American literature, though some of the works mentioned refer to other areas, especially to Greek and Roman literature. There is a short list of bibliographies and aids to research at the end of the chapter; a number of more scholarly bibliographies intended especially for candidates for advanced degrees will be found in Appendix A. Most listings will be alphabetical.

HISTORIES OF LITERATURE
English and American Literature

Burke, W. J. and Howe, Will D. *American Authors and Books: 1640 to the Present Day*. 3d rev. ed. Revised by Irving Weiss and A. D. Weiss. New York, Crown, 1972.

    The original work was published in 1941. Libraries will be likely to have retained early editions, as items included there have been omitted in subsequent revisions to make room for new material. This is a "dictionary catalog" of authors, publishers, magazines, book titles, poems, plays, songs, pseudonyms, plot summaries, etc. Under an author's name a representative selection of his works is listed in chronological order, pseudonyms are mentioned, and cross references made from them in their alphabetical places. If authors have been editors of books, newspapers, or magazines, these facts are noted, along with dates of birth and death, if known. Under titles of novels brief plot summaries are given, and publishers are listed, with their histories, indicating editors, changes of name, and associations with other firms. A list of best sellers, beginning with the *Bay Psalm Book* (1640), and a list of Pulitzer Prize winners are among the items of information included. The 3d edition includes brief general articles under such new headings as Black Humor, Hippie, and Underground Press.

Cambridge History of American Literature. W. P. Trent and others, eds. Cambridge, Cambridge University Press; New York, Putnam, 1917-1921. 4 vols. o.p. Reprinted without bibliographies in one volume by Macmillan in 1943.

Cambridge History of English Literature. Edited by Sir A. W. Ward and A. R. Waller. Cambridge, Cambridge University Press, 1907-1932. 15 vols. Complete set without Bibliography reprinted in 1931.

    Both this and its companion, *The Cambridge History of American Literature* (*q.v.*), are fine scholarly works but have nothing to say about contemporary literature. The biblographies, now out of date, can be supplemented by more recent publications and current indexing and bibliographic publications, a number of which are listed in Appendix B, e.g., Watson's work.

Daiches, David. *A Critical History of English Literature.* 2d ed. New York, Ronald Press, 1970. 2 vols.

First edition published in 1960. In the second edition, the author remarks that he can now present a "more expansive and balanced consideration" of twentieth century playwrights, poets, and novelists than was possible in 1960. Daiches is a critic of high standards and high standing in Britain and America.

Spiller, Robert E. and others, eds. *Literary History of the United States.* 3d ed. New York, Macmillan, 1963. 2 vols. Bibliography, with Supplements, 1948-1972.

The *Literary History* was first published in three volumes in 1948. The Bibliography, originally Volume 3 of the 1948 edition, was extended in coverage to 1958 and reissued separately in 1962. A supplement to the Bibliography, covering publications appearing between 1958 and 1970, was published in 1972.

As its title indicates, this book is not purely a history of literature, but a history of the United States in terms of its literature. This point of view is basic to the recently developed curricula in American civilization which are in some universities gradually superseding the specialization in literature, history, or politics with a combination of them, plus art, anthropology, etc., to form a synthesized study of culture.

Classical Literature

Duff, J. Wight. *A Literary History of Rome, from the Origins to the Close of the Golden Age.* 3d ed. A. M. Duff, ed. New York, Barnes & Noble; London, Benn, 1960.

———. *A Literary History of Rome in the Silver Age: From Tiberius to Hadrian.* 2d ed. A. M. Duff, ed. New York, Barnes & Noble; London, Benn, 1960.

The student of classical literature wishing to investigate its historical and mythological background should also consult the handbooks and dictionaries listed in the next section of this chapter, as well as the reference books on ancient history in Chapter 13 and on mythology in Chapter 17.

DICTIONARIES, ENCYCLOPEDIAS, AND HANDBOOKS

Allibone, S. A. *Critical Dictionary of English Literature and British and American Authors.* Supplement by J. F. Kirk. Philadelphia, Lippincott, 1858-1891. 5 vols. Volumes 1-3 listed under Allibone; Volumes 4 and 5 under Kirk. Reprinted in 1965 by Gale Research (Detroit).

These volumes give brief bio-bibliographical notes and critical comment from the standpoint of the nineteenth century. This kind of compilation is very valuable to the student of literature. Readers' tastes change during their own lifetimes; how much more change we finu when comparing our own opinions to those of more than a century ago! For further and fuller examples, see Moulton's *Library of Literary Criticism* and other titles on page 185.

Eagle, Dorothy, ed. *Concise Oxford Dictionary of English Literature.* rev. ed. New York and London, Oxford University Press, 1970.

> Authors, titles, literary terms, and fictional characters. The first edition was published in 1939; this revision contains new entries for recent authors and their works and draws upon scholarly research since 1939.

Feder, Lillian, ed. *Crowell's Handbook of Classical Literature.* New York, Crowell, 1964.

> Emphasis here is more literary than in Harvey's *Oxford Companion to Classical Literature (q.v.)*. Biographies of authors and detailed summaries of literary works, including their mythological background. Identifies characters and sometimes refers to modern novelists who write of classical times, or of mythical or quasi-mythical characters.

Fleischmann, Wolfgang B., ed. *Encyclopedia of World Literature in the 20th Century.* New York, Ungar, 1967-1971. 3 vols.

> Biographical and critical summaries of individual writers. Survey articles on literature in various countries. About 1,300 signed articles and many cross references. The editor has used, but revised and updated, Herder's *Lexikon der Weltliteratur im 20. Jahrhundert* (1960-1961). Includes Far Eastern and African writers. The American student does not often have the opportunity to read, in well-written English, the results of thorough German scholarship.

Magill, Frank N., ed. *Magill's Quotations in Context.* First series, 1965; second series, 1969. New York, Harper, 1965-

> These two volumes (there may be others to come) contain more than 3,500 quotations "drawn from more than 2,000 years of world literature." Magill gives the source, author, date, and type of work, describes the setting, and sometimes explains the meaning of each excerpt. Quotations are arranged alphabetically in each volume, with a keyword index.

> These volumes might well have been included among the books of quotations listed in Chapter 11, but are more literary in scope, going beyond the mere identification of a tantalizing fragment.

Myers, Robin, comp. and ed. *A Dictionary of Literature in the English Language: From Chaucer to 1940.* Oxford, Pergamon, 1970-1971. 2 vols.

> Volume 1 is arranged alphabetically by author and lists each author's works. Volume 2 is a title-author index — an alphabetical list of titles, 60,000 of them, giving the author's name but no page reference, as the titles in Volume 1 are alphabetical under author. An ingenious system. It may be hoped that Myers will from time to time compile new pairs of volumes for the years after 1940.

Oxford's *Companion* volumes are dependable sources of information, with brief biographies of authors, synopses (some fairly extensive) of their works, the names of literary characters, famous cases of censorship, etc. Arrangement is alphabetical. Older editions are still valuable for material left out to make way for new.

Oxford Companion to American Literature. 4th ed. James D. Hart, ed. New York and London, Oxford University Press, 1965.

This is fully revised from the 3d edition of 1956. Over 200 new authors have been added, and there are changes on nearly 90 percent of the pages.

Oxford Companion to Classical Literature. 2d ed. Sir Paul Harvey, comp. and ed. New York and London, Oxford University Press, 1937. Reprinted 1946.

Oxford Companion to English Literature. 4th ed. Sir Paul Harvey and Dorothy Eagle, eds. New York and London, Oxford University Press, 1967.

Some material in the 1939 edition has been left out to make room for new authors. This may be supplemented by Eagle's *Concise Oxford Dictionary of English Literature* (1970), above.

Oxford Companion to French Literature. Sir Paul Harvey and J. E. Heseltine, comps. and eds. New York and London, Oxford University Press, 1959.

Shaw, Harry Lee. *Dictionary of Literary Terms.* New York, McGraw-Hill, 1972.

Defines, explains, and illustrates more than 2,000 terms from the entire range of literature.

Writer's Handbook. A. S. Burack, ed. New York, The Writer, 1936-   .
Published at irregular intervals.

Includes "how to" articles on the short story, the scenario, the television script, popular verse, etc. *The Writer* is a periodical to which amateurs subscribe, hoping for hints on how to get their material published.

The Reader's Encyclopedia, edited by William Rose Benét, and *Brewer's Dictionary of Phrase and Fable* are both useful for identifying allusions, characters, and authors. These books are discussed more fully at the beginning of Chapter 11.

COLLECTIVE BIOGRAPHIES OF AUTHORS

Browning, D. C., ed. *Everyman's Dictionary of Literary Biography, English and American.* New York, Dutton, 1958.

This small volume of 752 pages gives 2,300 life histories, from Eleanor Hallowell Abbott to Israel Zangwill, ranging in time from Caedmon very nearly to the present. As the first author named demonstrates, this is for the low- and medium-brow: the reader of popular books who wants facts about their authors, and the high school student who must have them for a book report.

Contemporary Authors, 1962-   . James M. Ethridge, ed. Detroit, Gale Research, 1962-   . Frequency varies; updated cumulations published at intervals.

Only by quoting publisher's announcements is it possible to define the scope of this series. As of 1972, the series provided "full bio-bibliographical information on 28,000 writers. . . . The sketches in all . . . volumes are uniform . . . personal and career facts, a complete bibliography (if the biographee provided it — *ed.*), work in progress, sidelights, and biographical/critical sources. Over 75 percent of the listings cannot be found in any other bio-graphical reference work." Technical writers are not included, but the authors of textbooks are.

In 1974, Volumes 45 through 48 were cumulated, with an index to the entire series up to that point.

Kunitz, Stanley J. and Colby, Vineta, eds. *European Authors: 1000-1900.* New York, Wilson, 1967.

Biographies of 967 continental European authors. Lists principal works translated into English and includes 309 portraits.

Kunitz, Stanley J. and Haycraft, Howard, eds. *American Authors: 1600-1900.* New York, Wilson, 1938.

About 1,300 biographies. Sketches vary in length. Includes many states-men, religious leaders, and educators as well as professional men and women of letters. Lists principal works and includes short lists of sources and 400 portraits.

————. *British Authors Before 1800.* New York, Wilson, 1952.

Biographies of 650 authors from the earliest writers to Cowper and Burns, with 220 portraits.

————. *British Authors of the Nineteenth Century.* New York, Wilson, 1936.

More than 1,000 lives of British authors from Blake to Beardsley. Also in-cludes short summaries of the lives of eminent figures whose works, while hardly literature, have historical value. About 350 portraits.

Kunitz, S. J. and Haycraft, Howard, eds. *Twentieth Century Authors.* New York, Wilson, 1942. *First Supplement,* 1955.

Biographical and autobiographical sketches of 1,850 authors throughout the world whose works have been published in English. Includes 1,700 por-traits. Death dates added, and some textual revision in the later printings. The *First Supplement* contains about 700 sketches of authors who have be-come prominent since 1942, with 670 portraits. Supplementary material on most of the writers in *Twentieth Century Authors* has been added, with cross references to the earlier volume.

Magill, Frank N., ed. *Cyclopedia of World Authors.* New York, Harper, 1958.

This bio-bibliographical work was issued at the same time as the work by Browning listed above. The publisher's announcement stating that its 1,200 pages discuss 753 "writers of quality" immediately tells the informed reader (or at least the librarian) which of these two books will be more useful to him. The articles on fifty of the most important writers are signed.

Penguin Companions to World Literature. New York, McGraw-Hill, 1971-1972. 4 vols.

Most of us think of Penguin Books as paperback editions of English mys-teries. These are bound books, ranging from 400 to 900 pages and containing well-written biographical sketches of authors by teachers in British univer-sities. The titles are as follows:

Penguin Companion to American Literature, edited by Malcolm Bradbury and others. This complements the *Oxford Companion to American Litera-ture,* listed earlier in this chapter, by presenting writers of the later twen-tieth century and Latin American authors.

Penguin Companion to Classical, Oriental, and African Literature, edited by
D. M. Lang and D. R. Dudley. Includes Byzantine writers, while the
material on Oriental and African authors will help fill today's demands.

Penguin Companion to English Literature, edited by David Daiches. Includes authors writing in English from all the Commonwealth countries.
It is thus broader in scope than the *Oxford Companion to English Literature* (1967), above.

Penguin Companion to European Literature, edited by Anthony Thorlby.
The more than 2,500 biographies include modern authors.

Wakeman, John, ed. *World Authors*. New York, Wilson, 1975.
Biographical and autobiographical sketches of more than 950 authors, including many from Eastern Europe, Asia, Africa, and Latin America.

Burke and Howe's *American Authors and Books: 1640 to the Present Day*, listed above under English and American Literature, is another useful reference source.

CRITICISM

Allibone, S. A. *Critical Dictionary of English Literature and British and
American Authors*. Philadelphia, Lippincott, 1858-1891.
See full discussion under the heading Dictionaries, Encyclopedias, and
Handbooks, earlier in this chapter.

Curley, Dorothy Nyren and others, comps. and eds. *A Library of Literary Criticism: Modern American Literature*. 4th enl. ed. New York,
Ungar, 1969. 3 vols.
When first published in one volume in 1960, this was a not-very-successful
attempt to do for modern authors what Moulton (*q.v.*) did for English and
American authors from Beowulf through the nineteenth century. The later
edition (which is a considerable improvement and leads one to hope that
there will be more volumes and more editions to come) presents excerpts
from books, essays, reviews, and so forth, on about 300 twentieth century
American writers — poets, novelists, dramatists, and essayists. See also Temple and Tucker, below.

Gale Research Co. *Contemporary Literary Criticism*. Volume 1. Detroit,
Gale Research, May 1972.
Complements the *Contemporary Authors* series.

Moulton, C. W. *The Library of Literary Criticism of English and American Authors*. Buffalo, Moulton Publishing Co., 1901-1905. 8 vols.
Reprinted 1934 by Peter Smith (Gloucester, Mass.); new ed.
abridged and revised by Martin Tucker, with additions, published
1966 by Ungar (New York), 4 vols.
Chronological arrangement. For each author, there is a short biography,
criticism of his work in general, and criticism of individual works — all excerpted from critical writings and presented in chronological order, beginning
with the contemporaries of the author in question. A remarkable source of
information on changing literary tastes, for those we now consider the great
writers of the past were often ridiculed in their own times, while adulation
was accorded some of those whom we now scorn, or at least ignore. In the
new edition, the additions are helpful, but any abridgment is deplorable.

New York Times Book Review, 1896-   . New York, Arno. Semi-annual, with an index to each year's reviews in the July-December issue.

> These are the weekly *Book Review* sections of the Sunday *Times*, republished in permanent volumes printed on long-life paper and bound in library buckram. A five-volume cumulated index covers the years from 1896 to 1970. (Sunday issues are also included in the mirofiche cassettes of the New York *Times* which many libraries keep instead of devoting large quantities of shelf space to bound volumes. For such libraries, the cumulated book review index, which enters each review under author, title, subject, and byline, would be sufficient for access to the seventy-four years through 1970.) This series is a very valuable source of information.

Temple, Ruth Z. and Tucker, Martin, eds. *A Library of Literary Criticism: Modern British Literature*. New York, Ungar, 1966. 3 vols.

> Planned as a sequel to Moulton (*q.v.*), this quotes criticism and gives bibliographies on more than 400 British and Commonwealth authors of the twentieth century. A few historians and biographers are included. Some of the authors noted symbolize a moment or a mood (Michael Arlen, for instance, who wrote *The Green Hat*). Others are more notable for sales than for literary excellence (e.g., Hall Caine, Marie Corelli, Angela Thirkell, and P. G. Wodehouse). The selections include some American criticism of British authors.

Tucker, Martin, gen. ed. *The Critical Temper: A Survey of Modern Criticism on English and American Literature from the Beginnings to the Twentieth Century*. New York, Ungar, 1969. 3 vols.

> Unlike the work by Temple and Tucker listed above, this is intended not as a sequel but as a supplement to Moulton. The distinction is significant. The critics cited here are twentieth century critics, but the authors discussed are those in Moulton's original work.

There are several series of brief publications, each dealing with a single author and his works, which are likely to be found in both college and large public libraries among the circulating collections of biography or criticism. Any student searching for information about an author, especially a recent or little-known one, should ask a librarian about series and pamphlets.

Twayne Publishers of New York issue three series on authors: Twayne's United States Authors Series, Twayne's English Authors Series, and Twayne's World Authors Series. New titles are published frequently. Each book gives a brief biographical sketch of the author concerned and critical comment on his major works. Their subjects include both well-known writers and those who have only recently come into prominence and who, for that reason, may not be included in large historical/critical textbooks and reference tools.

The University of Minnesota Press in Minneapolis publishes excellent pamphlets on American writers, similar in purpose to the Twayne series but briefer. More than a hundred of these have been issued; they are available in Canada from Copp Clark Publishers, Toronto. The ninety-seven pieces published from 1959 to 1972 have been issued in four sturdy volumes that can be kept available for reference, while the originals circulate.

A series of useful pamphlets about English writers has been available from the British Book Centre in New York City for some years under the series title Writers and Their Work. Many of these publications, along with the University of Minnesota Press series, will be found in the pamphlet files or boxes of college libraries. In recent years the authors treated have been, in general, relatively unknown (on this side of the Atlantic, at least), but the earlier issues up to the mid-sixties often filled the gaps in the literary handbooks and biographical dictionaries then available.

POETRY—HANDBOOKS

Deutsch, Babette. *Poetry Handbook: A Dictionary of Terms.* 3d ed., rev. and enl. New York, Funk & Wagnalls, 1969. Available in cloth and paperback editions.

    A small but very useful dictionary of terms relating to verse, by an accomplished poet and critic. Many examples from poets, ancient and modern. The new edition treats briefly German contributions to poetics and cites some modern linguistic studies. Not for the beginner, who could be better served by the advice of Florence Trefethen, listed below.

Murphy, Rosalie and Vinson, James, eds. *Contemporary Poets of the English Language.* London and Chicago, St. James, 1970.

    A compilation of bio-bibliographical and critical material on approximately 1,100 modern poets. Longer critical articles on 300 poets considered outstanding by today's critics, themselves often poets as well.

Preminger, Alex, ed. *Encyclopedia of Poetry and Poetics.* Princeton, N.J., Princeton University Press, 1965.

    An alphabetical series of about 1,000 entries dealing with "the history, theory, technique and criticism of poetry from the earliest times to the present" — *Preface.* No articles on individual poets, poems, or allusions.

Spender, Stephen and Hall, Donald, eds. *Concise Encyclopedia of English and American Poets and Poetry.* New York, Hawthorn, 1963.

    Critical essays on individual poets and longer articles on genres, trends, etc. Portraits are included. Spender is, of course, a well-known poet himself.

Trefethen, Florence. *Writing a Poem.* Boston, The Writer, 1970.

    The author, herself a "working poet," is the author of a bimonthly column on poetry writing which appears in *The Writer.* Besides a glossary, there are three sections to this book: making plans, working with words, and appraising and revising. Anyone who has seen poets' original manuscripts, with the crossed-off lines, trial versions, and final version triumphant, will appreciate this practical book.

DRAMA—HISTORIES AND HANDBOOKS

Gassner, John and Quinn, Edward, eds. *The Reader's Encyclopedia of World Drama*. New York, Crowell, 1969.

The first one-volume reference source on the drama as literature; one of the publisher's Reader's Encyclopedia series. Extensive coverage, worldwide, of national drama, and articles on individual playwrights, with biographical and critical notes. Précis and criticism of the most historically significant plays, and discussion of genres. The longer articles are accompanied by bibliographies, and there are more than 300 illustrations.

Guernsey, Otis L., Jr. *Directory of the American Theater*, 1894-1971. New York, Dodd, Mead, 1971.

A cumulative index to the Best Plays series, discussed later in this chapter under Collections. Gives titles, authors, and composers for Broadway, off-Broadway, and off-off Broadway shows. Divided into sections: (1) Playwrights, Librettists, Composers, Lyricists, and Other Authors, and (2) Titles of Shows and Sources. Unfortunately, it lacks a third part: an index of directors, producers, and casts of the first productions of each play.

Hartnoll, Phyllis. *The Oxford Companion to the Theatre*. 3d ed. New York and London, Oxford University Press, 1967.

Hathorn, Richmond Y. *Crowell's Handbook of Classical Drama*. New York, Crowell, 1967.

An alphabetical list, with brief identification, of Greek and Roman dramas, giving the dramatist, title, and every proper name in the extant complete plays, and summaries of the myths on which many of the plays were based.

McGraw-Hill Encyclopedia of World Drama. New York, McGraw-Hill, 1972. 4 vols.

These large double-column volumes, well indexed and illustrated, were edited by Bernard Dukore and others — unfortunately, the editorship is not acknowledged. The coverage is not so broad as the title would suggest. As Stanley Kauffmann points out in his *New Republic* review of October 21, 1972, this is not an encyclopedia of world drama but of European and North American drama. In his article, Kauffmann comments favorably on the Gassner and Quinn *Reader's Encyclopedia of World Drama*, listed above, and suggests also Matlaw, listed below.

Matlaw, Myron. *World Drama: An Encyclopedia*. New York, Dutton, 1972.

Written entirely by Matlaw, this book covers drama from Ibsen to the present, with histories of the national dramas of eighty countries, bio-critical articles with bibliographies on hundreds of playwrights, and play synopses. It also has a character index, a general index, and illustrations.

Before we go on to the section of this chapter dealing with Shakespeare, some comment should be made on the relative scarcity of reference material on the motion picture as an art form. The last three titles listed above include considerable discussion of the film versions of plays, but there is little doubt that the best material on good motion pictures (aside from educational films) is in the reviewing media, i.e., the better magazines — *The New Republic, The New Yorker, Saturday Review/*

World — and in the Sunday editions of such newspapers as the New York *Times*. *Art Index*, given brief mention in Chapter 9, lists the following periodicals dealing with film: *Film Culture, Film Quarterly, Films in Review*, and *Sight and Sound*. Several books relating to film are listed in Chapter 12, in the section on The Performing Arts.

Shakespeare

The works of Shakespeare have been so long a source of wonder and delight that the books about him continue to multiply, and the older ones present aspects of his work which new writers and critics take for granted. It is doubtful whether any library will discard any useful book about him or his works except when it is superseded by a revised edition or becomes unusable because of its physical deterioration. The following list therefore includes the older books plus books published during the past ten years.

Asimov, Isaac. *Asimov's Guide to Shakespeare*. New York, Doubleday, 1970. 2 vols. Volume 1, *The Greek, Roman, and Italian Plays*; Volume 2, *The English Plays*.

Helpful to the teacher, indispensable to the director. Supplies religious, mythological, technical, and historical notes, and maps of the action. Asimov's range of interest and information continues to expand, and his style is readable, as always. Illustrated.

Campbell, Oscar J. and Quinn, Edward G., eds. *The Reader's Encyclopedia of Shakespeare*. New York, Crowell, 1966.

In addition to plot summaries of thirty-seven plays, this includes the characters, sources, stage history, and criticism of each. There are also references to persons, places, and subjects associated with Shakespeare, including actors, editors, and critics. Appendixes include chronologies and genealogies, and a selected bibliography.

Martin, Michael Rheta and Harrier, Richard C. *The Concise Encyclopedic Guide to Shakespeare*. New York, Horizon, 1972.

In addition to the usual plot and character information on each play, this gives definitions of Elizabethan words. Eight appendixes include a review of what is known of Shakespeare's life and theater, identification of "people of the theater," and a list of productions since 1900 in and near New York.

Muir, Kenneth and Schoenbaum, S., eds. *A New Companion to Shakespeare Studies*. Cambridge, Eng., Cambridge University Press, 1971. Also in paperback.

Supplements the 1934 *Companion to Shakespeare Studies*, edited by Harrison and Granville-Barker. Eighteen Shakespeare scholars have contributed essays on recent developments in Shakespeareana. Illustrations, notes, reading lists, a chronological table, and a subject index with cross references.

Schoenbaum, Samuel. *Shakespeare's Lives*. London, Clarendon Press (Oxford), 1970.

Sums up all the attempts (to 1970 — there have been more since) to arrive at a believable "life of Shakespeare." Includes legends, hoaxes, fables, theories. Good reading for all. Illustrated.

In Chapter 11 the reader will have been introduced to a number of books of quotations, most of which include the most commonly quoted portions of Shakespeare's plays, sonnets, and longer poems. The following works, being devoted entirely to Shakespeare, contain passages less often quoted. Like the concordances to the various translations of the Bible and to other books of quotations, these works are not only invaluable in identifying passages often quoted from Shakespeare but also indicate by omission those which "sound like Shakespeare" but are not.

Browning, D. C. *Everyman's Dictionary of Shakespeare Quotations*. New York, Dutton, 1953.

Spevack, Martin. *The Harvard Concordance to Shakespeare*. Cambridge, Mass., Harvard University Press, 1974.
> The first complete one-volume guide to every word and phrase in Shakespeare, including poems as well as plays. It has been called "indispensable," and can be used with any edition of Shakespeare's works, because the play or poem, act, scene, and line are all given.

Stevenson, Burton E. *Standard Book of Shakespeare Quotations*. New York, Funk & Wagnalls, 1965.

COLLECTIONS OF LITERARY WORKS BY FORM

Countless anthologies of poetry, plays, essays, short stories, and general literature have been published, and a later section of this chapter will discuss indexes to such collections. Poetry, especially, often suffers in anthologies because the double-column format presents the reader with an indigestible mass of type. Many textbooks for "survey courses" in English and American literature are in a sense anthologies — they contain samplings of poems, plays, and essays — but they are not indexed as such.

A useful series of collections of short stories is The Best American Short Stories, published annually by Houghton Mifflin (New York). Librarians are apt to frown upon condensed literature because, like evaporated milk, it has a "processed" flavor even when the basic substance is preserved. However, a well-known and helpful series, The Best Plays, includes abridged reading versions of current plays, in which outstanding scenes are printed as performed and much of the continuity is supplied in synopses. These volumes, issued by Dodd, Mead (New York), are compiled annually at the close of the theatrical season, which in the United States coincides roughly with the academic year. A feature of the series is a list of new plays presented during the year (in New York, principally), with the names of their authors, producers, directors, and casts. In addition, the Theatre Guild has published several volumes of its presentations with full text, and Crown

Publishers, Inc. (New York) has issued periodic volumes of complete texts in the Best American Plays series, compiled by the late John Gassner and, more recently, by Clive Barnes.

As for poetry, the sixth edition (1973) of *Granger's Index to Poetry* (see the section on indexes later in this chapter) lists and locates by title and first line more than 125,000 poems in 514 anthologies published before the end of 1970. Some anthologies are devoted to a period, as is *The Oxford Book of Modern Verse*; to a form, as is *The Oxford Book of Ballads*, which includes musical notation for the melody of each ballad; or to a subject field. There are collections of religious, patriotic, and humorous verse; poems about birds, cats, love, the sea, and even about science and mathematics.

Gale Research Company has recently reissued Carolyn Wells' *Parody Anthology* (using the 1904 edition, for some reason — perhaps because later editions, printed on wood-pulp paper during World War II, had become too fragile to reproduce), and there are other collections of parodies in both prose and verse. Sometimes the art of parody is the most subtle form of criticism. There is one more anthology which deserves special mention: *The Stuffed Owl: An Anthology of Bad Verse*, selected and arranged by D. B. Wyndham Lewis and Charles Lee and published by Coward-McCann in 1930 (paperback edition, Capricorn Books, 1962). Much of this consists of portions of poems, many from the "great and famous" such as Poe, Wordsworth, Tennyson, the Brownings, and Longfellow; the chronological range is from Cowley to Tennyson — later poets are spared. There is a hilarious nine-page subject index.

INDEXES TO COLLECTIONS OF LITERARY WORKS

The indexes listed here give in detail the contents of various sorts of collections, some originally compiled as early as 1896. The titles of these indexes indicate their contents; therefore they are given in alphabetical order under their compilers, editors, or titles. A number of the indexes are in several volumes, sometimes with changes of editor, in which cases the successive editors have been noted.

The first one is intended for specialists in the field of drama. Large universities and colleges which specialize in theater are most likely to have this work, for it is of use chiefly to drama majors and graduate students.

Breed, Paul F. and Sniderman, Florence M., comps. and eds. *Dramatic Criticism Index: A Bibliography of Commentaries on Playwrights from Ibsen to the Avant-Garde*. Detroit, Gale, 1972.

Lists articles in English on about 300 American and foreign playwrights. About 12,000 references to periodical articles and parts of books, listed under playwright, with indexes by title of play and name of critic cited.

Essay and General Literature Index: 1900-   . New York, Wilson,
1934-   .

This has already been described in Chapter 9. The seven permanent volumes issued between 1934 and 1969 analyze 9,917 collections, indexing
190,425 essays and articles. A cumulative index was published in 1973 under
the title *Essay and General Literature Index: Works Indexed 1900-1969.*

Each article is listed under editor, personal or corporate author, and title.
Publisher and publication date are given under the main entry, which is usually the author or editor. Cross references are made from title or other possible entry. While many of these books have been out of print, a large percentage have already been reprinted, and the existence of the seventy-year index
may be an incentive to publishers or reprint houses to reissue others.

Granger's Index to Poetry. 6th ed., completely rev. and enl. William
James Smith, ed. New York, Columbia University Press, 1973.

The 1st edition of *Granger's Index to Poetry* was published in 1904, and
of the ensuing five editions, the 4th, 5th and 6th have been issued at approximately ten-year intervals, with supplements published in the middle of each
decade to include anthologies published in the interim.

The 6th edition indexes 514 volumes, 121 of which have not appeared in
previous editions. There are 15 newly indexed anthologies of black poets. As
to the arrangement of the book, after the usual prefatory material (which
must be examined if one is to use the index efficiently), the reader finds the
Title and First Line Index, with more than 250,000 entries, titles and first
lines interfiled. Although in some earlier editions poems beginning with *A,
An,* or *The* were filed under *a* or *t,* here the first important word is the key,
e.g., Gilbert's "A wand'ring minstrel I" is listed under *w.* After this comes
the Author Index, listing about 12,000 poets and translators, and finally the
Subject Index, containing approximately 4,500 categories, among them
Women's Liberation and Ecology.

Presumably a supplementary volume to this edition will appear in five or
six years. Libraries are apt to keep at least the latest previous edition for
checking books still on their shelves, though the books may have gone out of
print at some earlier time.

*Play Index, 1949-   . New York, Wilson, 1953-   . 4 vols. Editors
vary.*

Indexes plays published singly or in collections. The plays — for amateurs,
radio, television, Broadway, off-Broadway, children, adults, etc. — may be in
several acts or only one. Each volume is divided into four parts. Part I is an
author, title, and subject index; the author entry includes the title, a brief
synopsis of the plot, number of acts and scenes, size of cast, number of sets
required, and bibliographic information (publisher, whether in a collection or
a separate publication, date of publication, etc.). Part II is a list of collections
indexed. Part III gives cast analyses, listing plays by the number and type of
players required. Part IV is a directory of publishers and distributors. This
type of index is especially useful to amateur and student groups, but also has
value for the student (or any individual) wishing to find one or more plays for
whatever reason.

The inclusive dates of the four volumes published to date are: 1949-1952;
1953-1960; 1961-1967; 1968-1972. The four volumes index nearly 16,000
plays.

Short Story Index. New York, Wilson, 1953-

The first volume, compiled by Dorothy E. Cook and Isabel S. Monro, indexes by author, title, and subject in one alphabet about 60,000 stories in 4,320 collections published in 1949 or earlier. Full information about each story is given, and a list of the collections indexed gives the necessary bibliographic information.

The later volumes are listed as Supplements to the parent volume. They were published in 1956, 1960, 1965, 1969, and 1974. They list 47,897 stories in 3,105 collections. Estelle A. Fidell has been editor or co-editor of all supplements listed above.

The student is advised to refer to Appendix A for research manuals, both general and in his own field, especially when faced with exhaustive research as an advanced or graduate student.

Chapter 16

Special Reference Books
THE SCIENCES

SCIENTISTS ARE careful and accurate people, systematic in their methods of work, requiring complete and exact records. For that reason, scientific literature is voluminous and has been extensively indexed and abstracted. In addition, as the sciences have expanded, especially in the twentieth century, they have begun to encroach upon each other's territory, so that where we once had neatly defined chemistry, physics, and biology, we now have, for example, biochemistry, biophysics, and physical chemistry, plus the special applications of these to the applied sciences, such as medicine, and to the social sciences, such as psychology and economics. Mathematics, which has been aptly called the handmaid of the sciences, appears both as pure science and as a necessary accompaniment to all the others, making some discoveries possible, recording and explaining others by symbolic means.

The space age in which we are now living has called for much more specialized knowledge of all the areas of science and of their interrelations and applications. Anyone who has seen on television the intricate computing machinery, the massive panels of instruments for remote control which send rockets into space, or has read of the careful preparations made to ensure the survival and comfort of the astronauts, realizes what a tremendous body of knowledge has been built up in the fields of astronomy, astronautics, and astrophysics. The physiologist has had to learn the effects of tremendous speeds and zero gravity or weightlessness not only upon the human body and the vehicles which will carry men into space, but upon the heretofore simple processes of eating and drinking. Electronics has become a major area of study, with great emphasis on increasing the power while reducing the size of instruments.

In previous editions of THE NEW LIBRARY KEY, the sciences based more upon observation than upon experimentation and extrapolation were not mentioned, i.e., botany and its practical partner agriculture, and geology, which is usually linked with geography, even though it is the basis of many of the technologies of physics and chemistry. These sciences have risen to importance with our realization that mankind is making poor use of its land and its resources. The earth's reserves of water, the very basis of life, have become polluted, and ecology has become a matter of concern. The reference sources of information about these matters are not yet abundant, but several of major importance are included in the section labeled Earth Sciences. In the newest encyclopedias, including such general encyclopedias as *Collier's* and the *Americana*, which have both strongly emphasized scientific progress, and the *World Book Encyclopedia*, which is closely allied with the curricula of the secondary schools, the earth sciences are receiving considerable attention. Finally, indexes to periodicals (see Chapter 9) are major sources of the newest information, not only from scientific journals but from the best of the general periodicals devoted to fact, opinion, and theory.

While THE NEW LIBRARY KEY has always been directed especially toward the students, faculty, and librarians of four-year, degree-granting institutions (with some material for those seeking advanced degrees), the text has been widely used in recent years at two-year community colleges, junior colleges, and technical schools. In these institutions, students are prepared for a wide variety of types of employment, especially in the technologies which form a portion of this chapter. They need, therefore, general books in the pure sciences which are the bases of their specialties; the need is all the greater if a student is planning to enroll in a regular degree program at some later date. Libraries in two-year colleges, although fully adequate in practical manuals and technical periodicals, sometimes lack up-to-date reference materials of a general theoretical nature. However, some of these works may be available from nearby public libraries.

GENERAL WORKS

Biographical Dictionaries

The people who made discoveries, developed new methods and techniques, manipulated and combined natural materials to find out what their manipulations and combinations might contribute to the life and comfort of mankind, or to its destruction — these people created science and technology. Their lives are hence the best and most exciting introduction to the study of science. None of the biographical dictionaries of scientists listed below had been published when the second edition of THE NEW LIBRARY KEY was issued, except the first, which appears here not only in a much enlarged edition but with a title expanded to fit its scope.

American Men and Women of Science: Physical and Biological Sciences. 12th ed. Edited by the staff of the Jaques Cattell Press. New York, Cattell/Bowker, 1971-1973. 6 vols. *Discipline Index*, 1973.

The first six volumes, alphabetically arranged, list about 147,000 American and Canadian scientists currently active in more than 600 areas of the physical and biological sciences. Full names, addresses, dates and places of birth, areas of specialization, current and previous industry or academic positions, education, degrees, honors, and memberships are given. The *Discipline Index* lists the scientists alphabetically within the appropriate disciplines, and those who work in more than one field are listed under as many areas of specialization as necessary. A necrology is included.

Among the sciences are agriculture, biochemistry, engineering, genetics, medicine, nucleonics, physics, and zoology, and their combinations and permutations.

Asimov, Isaac. *Asimov's Biographical Encyclopedia of Science and Technology: The Lives and Achievements of 1,195 Great Scientists from Ancient Times to the Present Chronologically Arranged*. rev. ed. New York, Doubleday, 1972.

Nearly 1,200 brief biographies, written in Asimov's informal style and arranged in chronological order according to date of birth. Each entry is numbered, and the main text is preceded by an alphabetical contents section giving each biographee's number. In a sense, this becomes an informal history of science.

Gillispie, Charles C., ed. *Dictionary of Scientific Biography*. New York, Scribner, 1970- . 8 vols. published by early 1974.

This follows the plan of the *Dictionary of National Biography*. In other words, it is a collection of articles on scientists no longer living, emphasizing their contributions to the history of science. More than half the consultants are from abroad. Individual scientists from India, China, and Japan are not covered, for lack of material, but the contributions of the schools and traditions of these areas, and of ancient Babylonian and Egyptian science, will appear in the final volume. The work is being published under the auspices of the American Council of Learned Societies. It was supposed to be in twelve volumes, but there is doubt that the coverage projected can be so compressed (Volumes 1 and 2 cover only Abailard to Buys Ballot).

World Who's Who in Science: A Biographical Dictionary of Notable Scientists from Antiquity to the Present. Allen G. Debus and others, eds. Chicago, Marquis, 1968.

This differs in two ways from Marquis's other publications in the Who's Who series. It does not include the type of personal information, such as parentage, spouse, and sons and daughters, typical of the series, but stresses the contributions to science of about 30,000 notables of all periods. Prominent living scientists are included.

Dictionaries, Encyclopedias, and Histories of Science

Asimov, Isaac. *Words of Science and the History Behind Them*. Illustrated by W. Barss. Boston, Houghton, 1959.

The title is self-explanatory. Asimov is one of the most versatile of scientific writers — his books range over many fields, and he is as well thought of by serious scientists for his factual presentations as he is by the devotee of science fiction for his well-plotted and well-written journeys into space and future times. A paperback edition of this dictionary was issued in 1969 by New American Library (New York) and a second volume, *More Words of*

Science, was published in 1972 by Houghton. Other scientific dictionaries are listed below. Each has its special value or individual point of view.

Collocott, T. C., ed. *Chambers Dictionary of Science and Technology.* New York, Barnes & Noble, 1972.

Designed to replace *Chambers Technical Dictionary* (3d edition, 1958). Revised, enlarged, and updated. Includes tables of chemical elements, metric conversion (especially useful at this time), igneous and sedimentary rocks, and charts of the plant and animal kingdoms. The spelling is generally British, but that is not an insurmountable problem.

Diderot, Denis. *A Diderot Pictorial Encyclopedia of Trades and Industry.* Edited with introduction and notes by C. C. Gillispie. New York, Dover Publications, 1959. 2 vols.

There are 485 plates showing manufacturing processes from raw materials to finished product, in trades, crafts, etc., as they were practiced two hundred years ago. Of great interest to artists as well as technicians. Plates reproduced from the original *Encyclopédie* of Diderot.

Hogben, Lancelot T. with the assistance of Maureen Cartwright. *The Vocabulary of Science.* New York, Stein & Day, 1971. Also available in paperback.

This is not a dictionary of scientific terms in alphabetical order, but in subject categories. Hogben points out that while English is basically of Germanic origin, it has borrowed, for scientific terminology, from Greek and, in many cases, from Latin. These Greek and/or Latin terms are presented in parallel columns with the English derivatives. There are also special glossaries of medical and biological Greek and Latin terms.

The advantage of such a work to the student of science is quite obvious: Instead of trying to learn and remember groups of apparently unrelated words, he learns enough about their roots to work out their meanings for himself.

McGraw-Hill Encyclopedia of Science and Technology. 3d ed. New York, McGraw-Hill, 1971. 15 vols. Annual yearbooks, 1963-   .

Any high school or college student has doubtless become intimately acquainted with this very valuable set and its yearbooks, if not in his school library, certainly in the nearest public library. As in the major general encyclopedias, the articles are consistently set up, proceeding from the general to the specific, with plenty of cross references, in addition to an index (Volume 15) and bibliographies referring the reader to other sources. The publisher claims that nearly a million words have been *added* since the second edition and two thirds of the text has been revised and updated. Eight percent of the text is on subjects not previously covered (including, as one reviewer noted, the aardvark). The 1st edition was published in 1960, and the 2d, in 1966.

Newman, James R., ed. *The Harper Encyclopedia of Science.* rev. ed. New York, Harper, 1967.

The 1st edition (1963) was in four volumes. This revision has been reduced to one volume of 1,379 pages, with many color illustrations. There are nearly 4,000 articles, many new or updated. The articles were contributed by 450 scientists, and the material is so arranged that the general reader is led from basic information to more complex developments. Includes basic bibliographies and an index.

Thorndike, Lynn. *History of Magic and Experimental Science.* New York, Macmillan, 1929; Columbia University Press, 1934-1958. 8 vols.

> Goes back to the antecedents of today's sciences: astrology, alchemy, etc. A fascinating study. The first thirteen centuries are treated in Volumes 1 and 2, while Volumes 3 to 8 deal with the fourteenth through the eighteenth centuries.

Van Nostrand's Scientific Encyclopedia. 4th ed. Princeton, N.J., Van Nostrand, 1968.

> A good general one-volume encyclopedia explaining basic concepts and defining many terms. Not for the beginner. First published-in 1938, the book is revised at (roughly) ten-year intervals. As technology is not the main concern, more frequent revision is not, perhaps, necessary.

At this point it becomes impossible to arrange the types of sciences and technologies so as to satisfy every reader. Roughly, the plan is to present mathematics first, because it is basic to the physical sciences and their offshoots and essential to the biological sciences as well; next astronomy, astronautics, and space; then chemistry, and its technical aspects; physics, electronics, and nuclear science; biology and related technologies; some general works on medicine, e.g., dictionaries, histories, and works for the layman; and finally the earth sciences.

MATHEMATICS

Grazda, Edward E. and others, eds. *Handbook of Applied Mathematics.* 4th ed. Princeton, N.J., Van Nostrand, 1966. illus.

> The 3d edition (1955) was based on the original work by M. E. Jansson and others. The use of mathematical computations in such practical operations as paper-hanging, carpentry, electric wiring, etc. Illustrated.

International Dictionary of Applied Mathematics. W. F. Freiberger, ed. in chief. Princeton, N.J., Van Nostrand, 1960.

> This was prepared by 83 specialists, and contains more than 8,000 definitions in 30 fields of science and engineering. Foreign equivalents of English terms are given, with separate indexes in German, Russian, French, and Spanish.

James, Glenn and James, R. C., eds. *Mathematics Dictionary.* 3d ed. Princeton, N.J., Van Nostrand, 1968.

> A multilingual edition of this was published in 1959. The 3d edition defines about 8,000 mathematical terms, 800 added since 1959. These later editions are principally for advanced students. In 1949 these editors compiled a small *Mathematics Dictionary* with many illustrations, which was useful for beginners.

Kramer, Edna E. *The Main Stream of Mathematics.* New York, Oxford University Press, 1951.

> A history of mathematics for the layman, beginning with a charming Hindu legend. Discusses the use of probability as "the science of the Sweepstakes," and so forth. This was reissued in paperback in 1969.

Kramer, Edna E. *The Nature and Growth of Modern Mathematics.* New York, Hawthorn, 1970.

> A cyclopedia of mathematics, from Babylonian beginnings to computers. For schools, libraries, and homes. Levels of difficulty proceed from the simplest to the most complex. (Kramer is also the author of the most intelligible textbook in educational statistics the present writer has used.)

Kurtz, Albert K. and Edgerton, H. A. *Statistical Dictionary of Terms and Symbols.* New York, Wiley; London, Chapman & Hall, 1939. Facsimile edition published 1967 by Hafner (New York).

Newman, James R., ed. *The World of Mathematics.* New York, Simon & Schuster, 1956. 4 vols. Paperback ed., 1960.

> A collection of selections from the masters and discoverers, readable and interest-provoking. The bound edition should be available in both Reference and Circulating collections. Very popular with students of mathematics at all levels.

The Universal Encyclopedia of Mathematics. Foreword by James R. Newman. New York, Simon & Schuster, 1964. Paperback ed., New American Library.

> Translated from a German handbook (*Meyer's Rechenduden*, 1960), this is an alphabetically arranged manual, covering mathematics from arithmetic through calculus. Tables and formulas.

ASTRONOMY AND SPACE TECHNOLOGY

The Atlas of the Universe. Edited by Patrick Moore, with a foreword by Sir Bernard Lovell. Chicago, Rand McNally, 1970. Produced with the support and collaboration of NASA and the U.S. Geological Survey.

> Includes 1,500 maps in color, as well as photographs and other illustrations. Partial contents: Observation and exploration of space, Atlas of the earth from space, and Atlases of the moon, the solar system, and the stars. Also glossary of terms used in astronomy and a 10,000-entry index.
>
> Yearbooks of astronomy have been published since 1970.

Moore, Patrick. *New Guide to the Planets.* New York, Norton, 1972.

> The 1st edition was published in 1954, and revised several times. The 1972 edition has been completely rewritten and has new illustrations.

Satterthwaite, Gilbert E. *Encyclopedia of Astronomy.* New York, St. Martin's, 1971.

> The compiler, formerly with the Royal Greenwich Observatory, is commended in the foreword by Patrick Moore, which emphasizes the clarity of the text and states that this will be "useful to all astronomers, and . . . will remain a standard for many years to come."
>
> Nearly 2,200 entries alphabetically arranged, with many *see also*'s. Illustrated with diagrams and photographs; for students at all levels and the layman as well.

Spencer-Jones, Harold, and others. *New Space Encyclopedia: A Guide to Astronomy and Space Exploration.* 4th rev. ed. New York, Dutton, 1974.

Stars and Stellar Systems: Compendium of Astronomy and Astrophysics. Gerald P. Kuiper and Barbara M. Middlehurst, gen. eds. Chicago, University of Chicago Press, 1960-1962. 9 vols.

> Supported in part by the National Science Foundation. The nine volumes are (1) *Telescopes*; (2) *Astronomical Techniques*; (3) *Basic Astronomical Data*; (4) *Clusters and Binaries*; (5) *Galactic Structures*; (6) *Stellar Atmosphere*; (7) *Nebular and Interstellar Matter*; (8) *Stellar Structure*; (9) *Galaxies and the Universe*. A work of major importance.

CHEMISTRY AND CHEMICAL TECHNOLOGY

The study of chemistry as "pure science," the symbols for the elements and their atomic weights, valences, etc., and the difference between organic and inorganic compounds is such a small fraction of the science's vast importance that it may appear in a single chapter of a "general science" high school textbook. It is impossible to treat individually all the aspects of chemistry, except in such fields as biological chemistry, physical chemistry, agriculture, and medicine, where some reference books may be placed. Thus in this section the reader will find more technical chemistry than theoretical. Student handbooks, dictionaries, encyclopedias, formularies, and abstracts are listed here in alphabetical order.

Brady, George S. *Materials Handbook.* 10th ed. New York, McGraw-Hill, 1971.

> An alphabetical encyclopedia listing everything that can be made into something else by chemical or physical manipulation (minerals, oils, fibers, metals) and describing both the materials and the processes by which they may be treated.

Chemical Abstracts. [Place of publication varies], American Chemical Society, 1907-   .

> At present, published weekly and arranged by subject with an author index. At the end of the year, indexes are issued listing authors (1907-   ), subjects (1907-   ), formulas (1920-   ), patent numbers (1935-   ), and to ring systems (1916-   ). In 1962, the author and numerical patent indexes, formerly cumulated annually, became semiannual, and from 1960, the subject and formula indexes have been semiannual. Cumulations of these indexes have also been published, at first every ten years, but since 1957, every five years.
>
> All of this appears very complicated, but if the indexes are consulted frequently, it is really not difficult. Every chemist or student of chemistry searches *Chemical Abstracts* before performing any experiment beyond those in textbooks, as the abstracts are derived from articles in several thousand periodicals, which could not be found in any library, no matter how large its budget. Lists of the periodicals abstracted were issued in 1946, 1951, 1956, and 1962. Since then annual supplements have appeared, under the title *Chemical Abstracts Service Source Index.*

Chemical Formulary. Harry Bennett, ed. New York, Chemical Publishing Co., 1933-   .

Issued at irregular intervals, with occasional change of publisher (Volume 15 was issued by the Tudor Publishing Company in 1970). A cumulated index to Volumes 1 through 10 was published in 1958 and replaced in 1972 by an index to Volumes 1 through 16. It is necessary to keep all volumes, as there has been no duplication of formulae, though new formulas for such useful products as soaps, paints, textiles, and pharmaceuticals appear. It is useful to manufacturers and to people who wish to make their own soap or face cream, or to experiment with pastes, glues, cleaning compounds, etc.

Hackh, I. W. D. *Chemical Dictionary, American and British Usage.* 4th ed. Revised and edited by Julius Grant. New York, McGraw-Hill, 1969.

> The emphasis is on chemistry in connection with other fields. The previous edition was published in 1944.

Hampel, Clifford A. and Hawley, Gessner G., eds. *Encyclopedia of Chemistry.* 3d ed. New York, Van Nostrand, 1973.

> A revision and updating of the 2d edition of the *Encyclopedia of Chemistry,* prepared by Clark and Hawley (1967; 1st edition, 1957). Hampel has also edited the *Encyclopedia of the Chemical Elements* (Book Centre, 1968) and the 4th edition of the *Encyclopedia of Electrochemistry* (Reinhold, 1964; reprinted 1972). Hawley, the second member of this team, is responsible for the 8th edition of the *Condensed Chemical Dictionary* (Van Nostrand, 1971), which is especially useful to the industrial chemist. It includes products and trade names, and useful facts on hazardous materials and shipping regulations.

Kirk-Othmer Encyclopedia of Chemical Technology. 2d ed., completely rev. H. F. Mark, J. J. McKetta, Jr., and D. F. Othmer, eds. New York, Interscience Publishers, 1963-1972. 27 vols., including index and supplementary material.

Few college libraries will have all the dictionaries, encyclopedias, and handbooks of technical chemistry listed above, but they may have others which are equally useful and possibly more recent. Bibliographies of technical books abound, including, for American use, the subject volume of the annual *Books in Print* (*q.v.*) and equivalent foreign annuals, such as *British Books in Print.*

One final entry is essential to the study of chemistry.

Mellor, J. W. *Comprehensive Treatise on Inorganic and Theoretical Chemistry.* London and New York, Longmans, 1922-1937. 16 vols.

> Supplementary volumes have been appearing periodically since 1956. The latest to date is Supplement 3 to Volume 8, issued in 1972.

PHYSICS, ELECTRONICS, AND NUCLEAR SCIENCE

The list of reference books in these fields is short, but current developments are reported in the scientific journals. (See Chapter 9, on indexes to periodicals, and the various indexes and guides themselves.)

Besançon, Robert Martin, ed. *The Encyclopedia of Physics*. 2d ed. New York, Van Nostrand, 1974.

> Useful to advanced high school students and to scientists needing information outside their special fields. Similar to the same publisher's *Encyclopedia of Chemistry (q.v.)*. General introductory articles and technical explanations. Cross references and a detailed index are included.

Glazebrook, Richard, ed. *Dictionary of Applied Physics*. London, Macmillan, 1922-1923. 5 vols. Reprinted by Peter Smith (Gloucester, Mass.).

Graf, Rudolf F. *Modern Dictionary of Electronics*. 4th ed. Indianapolis, Sams, 1972.

> Covers radio, television, radar, industrial and medical electronics, data processing, lasers, etc.

Gray, Dwight E., ed. *American Institute of Physics Handbook*. 3d ed. New York, McGraw-Hill, 1972.

> Intended for those using physical methods in research. New material on geoelectric and geomagnetic effects in the environment.

Hughes, L. E. C. and others. *Dictionary of Electronics and Nucleonics*. New York, Barnes & Noble, 1970.

> Alphabetical arrangement with cross references. Coverage similar to Graf, listed above. Published in England as *Chambers Dictionary of Electronics and Nucleonics*.

Isaacs, A. and Gray, H. J., eds. *New Dictionary of Physics*. 2d rev. ed. New York, Longmans, 1974.

> Announced to contain new material on nuclear physics, astrophysics, computer technology, electronics, and relativity.

Kaye, George W. and Laby, T. H. *Tables of Physical and Chemical Constants*. 14th rev. ed. Edited by A. E. Bailey and others. New York, Longmans, 1973.

Markus, John, ed. *Electronics and Nucleonics Dictionary*. 3d ed. New York, McGraw-Hill, 1966.

> The 1960 edition by Nelson M. Cooke has been revised and enlarged. The new edition was still in print in 1973, and is obviously in demand for its definitions of technological nomenclature. Includes project names, trademarks, and acronyms. Illustrated with line drawings and some photographs of equipment and processes defined.

Thewlis, James. *Concise Dictionary of Physics and Related Subjects*. Elmsford, N.Y. and Oxford, Eng., Pergamon, 1973.

Thewlis, James, ed. in chief. *Encyclopaedic Dictionary of Physics*. Elmsford, N.Y. and Oxford, Eng., Pergamon, 1961-1971. 9 vols. and 4 supplements.

> The first seven volumes were published between 1961 and 1963. Volume 8 (1963) is a subject and author index, and Volume 9 (1965) is a glossary of 13,000 English terms derived from the titles of articles in the set. Equivalents of these terms in French, German, Spanish, Russian, and Japanese are indi-

cated by code numbers referring to tables at the end of the volume. The Russian and Japanese terms are not transliterated into the familiar alphabet, but there are references from each language to all the others. Four supplements entitled *Advances in Physics* have appeared between 1966 and 1971.

This work has more than 3,600 contributors, and covers every phase of the physical sciences and related subjects, including mathematics, astronomy, crystallography, medical physics, photography, metallurgy and many phases of chemistry. The material is presented with that combination of accuracy and clarity which has come to be associated with British scientists.

In addition to the works listed above, Brady's *Materials Handbook*, described in the chemistry section, might also be useful to a physicist.

BIOLOGICAL SCIENCES

Butler, J. A. V. and Katz, B., eds. *Progress in Biophysics and Molecular Biology*. Elmsford, N.Y. and Oxford, Eng., Pergamon, 1950-

Annual review of the literature. Earlier volumes bore the title, *Progress in Biophysics and Biophysical Chemistry*.

Gray, Peter, ed. *The Dictionary of the Biological Sciences*. Princeton, N.J., Van Nostrand, 1968.

An outgrowth of the *Encyclopedia* listed below. Includes taxonomic terms and root terms from Latin and Greek. For the student rather than the research biologist.

Gray, Peter, ed. *The Encyclopedia of the Biological Sciences*. 2d ed. New York, Van Nostrand, 1970.

More than 800 articles on double-column pages. A scholarly work on the college level. All articles are signed, and bibliographic notes are included.

Gray, Peter. *Student Dictionary of Biology*. New York, Van Nostrand, 1973.

For the high school senior or college student who is not acquainted with the terminology of this science. Each word listed is followed by a simplified phonetic spelling. The roots of biological terms are given, and combining forms listed and defined.

Nordenskiöld, Erik. *The History of Biology: A Survey*. St. Clair Shores, Mich., Scholarly, 1960.

A reissue of the edition first published in 1928 by Knopf, which has been out of print for some time. Valuable to both student and teacher of biological and general sciences.

Williams, Roger J. and Landsford, E. M., Jr., eds. *The Encyclopedia of Biochemistry*. New York, Reinhold, 1967.

An alphabetically arranged treatment of broad areas. Some entries consist of introductory material for the layman; others require substantial background. Includes diagrams of the chemical composition of various kinds of cells, for example. Most articles are followed by bibliographical references, and there is a detailed index.

AGRICULTURE

Only cursory attention is given in this manual to reference sources on agriculture, as this book is directed to students at the start of their post-high-school education.

Many land-grant colleges and universities have departments or schools of agriculture, and two-year colleges in rural areas may be expected to provide courses in animal husbandry, forestry, horticulture, and so forth. But in the average liberal arts college, the major series of reference volumes will be the yearbooks of the U.S. Department of Agriculture and the *Biological and Agricultural Index* (*q.v.*), which indexes about 190 periodicals of which many deal with the numerous phases of agricultural activity.

In addition, the U.S. Department of Agriculture issues Farmers' Bulletins and other pamphlets. Many states publish useful pamphlets, which will be available in the pamphlet files of most libraries. The subject of pamphlets in general is discussed in Chapter 18, Non-Book Materials.

MEDICINE

Libraries used by the general public are cautious about making medical books available. A few medical dictionaries, anatomies, physiologies, books on first aid and elementary "what to do till the doctor comes" form the bulk of the reference collection on medicine. Books written by doctors especially for the layman on the proper home care for such common ailments as arthritis, heart disease, etc., as well as books about personal and public hygiene are most frequent in the circulating collection.

Schools of medicine, usually connected with universities and/or hospitals, of course attempt to provide in their libraries as much as they can afford of the ever-growing supply of general and special medical reference material. Training in the para-medical fields, including nursing, requires at least a small collection of medical references and textbooks, and any college library will have a basic collection.

The most nearly complete collection in the field of medicine is the National Library of Medicine, formerly the United States Army Medical Library and before 1948 known as the Library of the United States Surgeon General's Office. The printed catalogs of this collection from 1880 to date constitute a massive bibliography of medical literature, books, periodicals, and pamphlets. This catalog is the major bibliography in the field, both retrospective and current.

The books listed below, in alphabetical order, may be expected to be found in college and public libraries.

Bettmann, Otto L. *Pictorial History of Medicine*. Springfield, Ill., C. C. Thomas, 1956.

Illustrations are from the Bettmann Archive, a mammoth collection of pictures amassed by Dr. Bettmann as a labor of love and used by historians in many fields. This book is fascinating both to the layman and to the student or practitioner of medicine. Medical history is so much a part of social history and of historical fiction that this collection of illustrations is valuable to both the writer and the reader.

Clark, Randolph L. and Cumley, R. W. *The Book of Health: A Medical Encyclopedia for Everyone*. 3d ed. New York, Van Nostrand, 1973.

While this book gives valuable information on human diseases, affected organs, and treatment, it has a great many photographs in color and black-and-white of some of the more distressing results of disease, malformation, birth defects, etc., so that while very valuable for the informed reader, both as to diagnosis and treatment of common ailments, it must be used with due consideration of the emotional state of the person seeking information. For the college student studying human physiology and pathology it is useful. For a sick person or relative who has been told by an ill-advised physician to "go to the library and look up . . ." this should be the last resort.

Fisher, Richard B. and Christie, G. A. *A Dictionary of Drugs: The Medicines You Use*. New York, Schocken, 1972. Also in paperback.

Descriptions of about 300 drugs most used for common diseases. Listed in alphabetical order by generic name, with indexes by trade name and simplified chemical name. Entries give pertinent information on use and side effects, but dosages are omitted. Narcotics commonly abused are listed, for better understanding of possible chemical reactions. Both British and American trade names are listed.

Stedman, Thomas L. *Stedman's Medical Dictionary*. 22d ed. rev. Baltimore, Williams & Wilkins, 1972. (Previous editions, 1961 and 1966.)

The most recently and most frequently revised American medical dictionary. Definitions are exceedingly brief, and the layman may have to resort to an unabridged dictionary for clarification. The *Random House Dictionary of the English Language* is especially good for medical and other scientific terms.

Stein and Day International Medical Encyclopedia. rev. ed. J. A. C. Brown, ed. New York, Stein & Day, 1972.

Every phase of medicine, including acupuncture and an ancient chart used in its practice. Readable and well illustrated with transparencies and other color and black-and-white items. Includes population control, drug addiction, heredity, etc.

Thomson, William A. R., ed. *Black's Medical Dictionary*. 29th ed. New York, Barnes & Noble, 1971.

British in origin; first published in 1906 and widely used. The present editor's preface exhorts the reader to remember that "the human body, like human nature, has scarcely changed over the ages, except in certain quite superficial aspects." A pertinent philosophical reminder.

EARTH SCIENCES

This comparatively new branch of science is, of course, not new at all. But the human race is, at long last, learning that the resources of the earth are not inexhaustible. The greater part of this chapter has been, in a sense, a preparation for this small section, which contains few books so far, but *ecology*, a comparatively new word in our vocabularies, and all its synonyms, subdivisions, and relationships with plant, animal, and human life on earth are treated voluminously in the press — daily, weekly, and monthly. The few new reference works which specialize in ecology are listed below, but a re-reading of this chapter will impress the reader with the ecological implications in every section.

Elsevier's Dictionary of Hydrogeology in Three Languages: English, French, German. Compiled and arranged by Hans-Olaf Pfann-kuch. New York, American Elsevier, 1969.

There are 3,040 entries, in the three languages, each defined in its own language, with cross references to similar terms in the other two.

According to the *Random House Dictionary*, the definition of *hydrogeology* is the study of "the occurrence and distribution of underground water." *Webster's Third* defines it as "a branch of geology concerned with the occurrence and utilization of surface and ground water and with the functions of water in modifying the earth, especially by erosion and deposition." Between them, the two definitions make clear the importance of water above and below ground and the necessity of conserving it, using it wisely, cleaning up its sources and surroundings — a very important part of what is now termed ecology.

Encyclopedia of Earth Sciences. New York, Reinhold, 1966-

The following volumes, edited by Rhodes Whitmore Fairbridge, have been issued:

Volume 1, *The Encyclopedia of Oceanography* (1966). Useful to everyone from high-school students to specialists. Includes diagrams, subsurface maps, charts of currents, etc.

Volume 2, *The Encyclopedia of Atmospheric Sciences and Astrogeology* (1967).

Volume 3, *The Encyclopedia of Geomorphology* (1968).

Todd, David Keith, ed. *The Water Encyclopedia: A Compendium of Useful Information on Water Resources.* Port Washington, N.Y., Water Information Center, 1970.

Among the chapter headings are "Climate and Precipitation," "Water Use," and "Water Quality and Pollution Control." Consists largely of tabulated information with commentary; there is a section, for example, on industrial wastes.

Chapter 17

Special Reference Books

MYTHOLOGY, RELIGION, AND PHILOSOPHY

IN THE SECOND edition of THE NEW LIBRARY KEY, there were thirty-seven titles listed in this section. This edition contains almost twice as many: some old, some new, some reprints of valuable books which have been out of print, some revised editions. It has seemed logical to treat mythology first and then the major religions of the world before proceeding to specific Western faiths. Obviously, there can be no point where one set of beliefs ends and a new one begins.

The books about the history of Christianity include the Orthodox Eastern Church, the Roman Catholic Church, and all branches of Protestantism. The Roman Catholic Church alone has been responsible for a large body of historical, biographical, and general encyclopedic material, and the Protestant denominations have been treated as a group in a number of semi-encyclopedic works. Versions of the Judaeo-Christian Bible and reference books which pertain to it — concordances, dictionaries, etc. — follow. Finally we come full circle to philosophy, branches of which may or may not have religious antecedents or descendants.

The last five years have seen a resurgence of interest in religion and philosophy among young people. When the television program "College Bowl" was at its peak, the number of contestants who were majoring in philosophy, with the intention of going on for graduate study and then teaching "on the college level," was astonishing. Certainly many college students are no longer content with traditional religion but are joining groups where Yoga, meditation, and oriental practices and costumes seem to give them more satisfaction. Libraries are better equipped with books on these subjects than they were ten years ago.

MYTHOLOGY

Funk & Wagnalls Standard Dictionary of Folklore, Mythology, and Legend. Maria Leach, ed. New York, Funk & Wagnalls, 1949-1950. 2 vols. Revised ed. in 1 vol., 1972.

The articles in this work are alphabetically arranged, and many bear the contributor's initials. They are useful for details on mythological characters (Heracles, for example) and on holidays and festivals in various countries at different times. Some revisions and deletions have been made in the one-volume edition, and coverage of twelve major world religions has been added. The index is termed, "Key to countries, regions, cultures, culture areas, peoples, tribes, and ethnic groups."

Larousse Encyclopedia of Mythology. With an introduction by Robert
Graves. New York, Prometheus Press, 1959.

> "Translated by Richard Aldington and Delano Ames and revised by a panel
> of editorial advisers from the Larousse Mythologie Générale [1935], edited
> by Felix Guirand." Contains many illustrations. Discusses folklore, religious
> customs, and legends. Not strictly an encyclopedia, but a highly readable and
> attractive volume. Distributed by Putnam.

MacCulloch, John A. and others, eds. *The Mythology of All Races.* 12
vols. plus index. Boston, Marshall Jones, 1916-1932. Reprinted in
1972 by Cooper Square Publishers (New York).

> Each volume discusses the mythology of a different race or ethnic (i.e., lan-
> guage) group. The index by subject and mythological personage leads to
> comparative study of such universal myths as those concerned with floods,
> eclipses, and other natural phenomena. The great number of flood stories in
> the Middle East, for instance, tends to validate Noah's experience. Illustrated.

Robinson, H. S. and Wilson, K. *Encyclopaedia of Myths and Legends
of All Nations.* Edited by B. L. Picard. London, Kaye & Ward,
1967.

> Available in the United States and Canada from the British Book Centre
> (New York).

Tripp, Edward. *Crowell's Handbook of Classical Mythology.* New York,
Crowell, 1970.

> Intended for the layman reading the classics. Most entries are personal or
> place names, alphabetically arranged. Each major myth is told in full. Cita-
> tions are usually to the Loeb Classical Library.

RELIGION
World Religions

The books listed in this section deal with the major religions of the
world. Judaism and Christianity are included in most of these volumes,
but will also be treated in later sections of this chapter.

Brandon, Samuel George Frederick, ed. *A Dictionary of Comparative
Religion.* London, Weidenfeld & Nicolson; New York, Scribner,
1970.

> Contributions of twenty-eight British scholars cover all aspects of world
> religion, prehistoric to present, and, according to the Preface, "treat . . . reli-
> gions proportionately to their significance in the history of human culture." It
> attempts to update Hastings (see next entry). Alphabetical arrangement of
> articles, some only one or two sentences, others five or more pages. The syn-
> optic index arranges entries under specific religions.

Hastings, James, ed. *Encyclopaedia of Religion and Ethics.* New York,
Scribner, 1908-1927. 12 vols. plus index. Reissued in 1951 in 7 vols.
and in 1973 in 13 vols.

> See the last section of this chapter for other material about philosophy,
> and also the work edited by Brandon, above.

Landis, B. Y. *World Religions: A Brief Guide to the Principal Beliefs and Teachings of the Religions of the World and to the Statistics of Organized Religion.* New York, Dutton, 1957.

> A small book, valuable especially for the statistics, which are difficult to find elsewhere. For statistics of membership in various denominations in the United States and Canada, see the *Yearbook of American and Canadian Churches,* the *Catholic Almanac,* and other statistical yearbooks, such as *World Almanac* and *Information Please Almanac.* The publications of the United Nations may also be helpful.

Life (magazine). *The World's Great Religions.* New York, Time, Inc., 1957.

> Based on feature articles in six issues of *Life,* the volume has the same superb color illustrations and the large page size of the original articles. Since the discontinuance of the magazine, a new abridged printing of *The World's Great Religions* has been published as a Deluxe Golden Book, for grade 9 up.

Parrinder, Geoffrey. *A Dictionary of Non-Christian Religions.* Philadelphia, Westminster, 1973. American ed.

> Brief treatment of the same sort of material to be found in Brandon (*q.v.*).

Schaff, Philip and Herzog, Johann. *New Schaff-Herzog Encyclopedia of Religious Knowledge.* New York, Funk & Wagnalls, 1908-1912. 12 vols. plus index. Reprinted in 1950 by Baker Book House (Grand Rapids, Mich.). Supplemented by: *Twentieth Century Encyclopedia of Religious Knowledge.* L. A. Loetscher, ed. in chief. Baker, 1955. 2 vols.

> An important reference set. It is based on an earlier German work, and the sections on Christianity are thus somewhat Protestant in tone. Other religions are covered as well.
>
> The two supplementary volumes are listed in the 1973 *Books in Print* merely as "2 Supplements." No further supplements have been added to date.

Judaism

There are several encyclopedias of Judaism either recently published, recently revised and updated, or valuable for their less recent point of view. The first two listed here were published in 1972.

Encyclopaedia Judaica. New York, Macmillan, 1972. 16 vols. Yearbook, 1973- .

> Unlike many multi-volume works, this was completely compiled and published within five years. Thus the analytical index (over 500 pages) could be presented in the first volume, along with critical comment on earlier Jewish encyclopedias. Volume 1 also identifies contributors, lists synagogues and Hebrew newspapers and periodicals, and provides the Jewish calendar to 2020 (A.D.). Like most encyclopedias, this one has many biographical and geographical entries, the latter recounting the history of the Jewish people in various places. It includes an extended treatment of the liturgy and describes the contributions of Jews to science, medicine, and the performing arts. About 25,000 entries and 8,000 illustrations, many in color. No doubt readers of Harry Kemelmann's series of mystery novels, in which crimes are solved by recourse to the Torah and the Talmud, will find interesting material here.

Shulman, Albert M. *Gateway to Judaism: Encyclopedia Home Reference*. London, Yoseloff, 1972. 2 vols.
> Distributed in the United States by A. S. Barnes (Cranberry, N.J.).
> Useful and interesting to the layman. Concise introduction to doctrines, customs, and ceremonies. Nothing on modern Israeli literature. Comprehensive index.

A number of older Jewish encyclopedias are still useful. Some which were out of print have been reissued, usually with a change of publisher or editor.

The Jewish Encyclopedia. Isidor Singer, ed. New York, Funk & Wagnalls, 1901-1906. 12 vols. Reprinted in 1964 by Ktav (New York).
> Next in importance to the *Encyclopedia Judaica*. This may be supplemented, but is not superseded, by the *Universal Jewish Encyclopedia*.

Universal Jewish Encyclopedia. New York, Universal Jewish Encyclopedia, 1939-1943. 10 vols. *Reading Guide and Index*, edited by Isaac Landman, 1944. Reprinted in 1973 by Ktav (New York).

There are two recent one-volume Jewish encyclopedias. *The New Jewish Encyclopedia*, edited by David Bridger with Samuel Wolk, was published by Behrman House (New York) in 1962. It contains many biographies and illustrations, is extremely readable, and has an American emphasis. *The Standard Jewish Encyclopedia*, edited by Cecil Roth, was printed in Jerusalem by the Massadah Publishing Company in 1958-1959 and in New York by Doubleday, under the direction of an American advisory board. A 4th edition entitled *The New Standard Jewish Encyclopedia* was issued by Doubleday in 1970. These one-volume works are useful when the multi-volume sets are not available.

The following work emphasizes Israel and Zionism rather than the traditional religious aspects of Judaism.

Patai, Raphael, ed. *Encyclopedia of Zionism and Israel*. New York, McGraw-Hill, 1971. 2 vols.
> This work describes the immigration to Israel by refugees from European countries who were escaping from oppression and by other Jews, not necessarily endangered, who were dissatisfied with their position as second-class citizens. The settlement of Palestine during the latter half of the nineteenth century became a cause later taken up by members of the Zionist movement in the United States and elsewhere. There are about 3,000 signed articles in this encyclopedia, some reflecting strong partisanship, and numerous illustrations. Covers the relations of modern Israel with other nations, especially the United States and the Arab countries; the culture and economics of Israel; and the exploration of Biblical sites. Anyone who has read, even partially, *The Source*, by James Michener, which uses an archaeological expedition as the link between modern kibbutz life and the ancient past, will appreciate the variety of material here.

Christianity

Most of the reference material on Christianity in general is to be found in the encyclopedias and dictionaries described at the beginning of this chapter, under World Religions. In these volumes and in the general encyclopedias listed in Chapter 7, the reader will find material on the Orthodox Eastern Church, medieval Christianity, and the development of the Reformation in Western Europe and Great Britain. By judicious use of library catalogs and bibliographies and with help from librarians, the reader can also obtain biographical and historical information on the various steps in the development of Protestantism.

Books described here as *ecumenical* contain information and statistics on Roman Catholic and Protestant churches, and in some cases (or in some parts of the country) on the Greek and Russian Orthodox faiths as well. Material on the Bible will follow.

Attwater, Donald, ed. *A Catholic Dictionary*. 3d ed. New York, Macmillan, 1958. Paperback ed., 1961.

> More than 5,000 entries explaining terminology used in the Roman Catholic Church, the sections of the Mass, the names and origins of religious orders, etc.

Catholic Almanac, 1904-   . Publisher varies. Annual.

> Formerly the *National Catholic Almanac*, this was, for many years, designed to be *the* home reference book for Catholic readers, and included such general information as winners in various sports, first aid instructions, and the Constitution of the United States. More recent editions, published in New York by Doubleday, have left out the non-Catholic information. The 1974 edition was published by Our Sunday Visitor (Huntingdon, Ind.) and is available in both cloth and paper covers. It includes lists of American bishops and cardinals and of patron saints, as well as articles on the taxation of church property and the ethical aspects of medical procedures such as heart transplants. It also provides biographical information on missionaries, the texts of papal speeches, and statistics.

Encyclopedic Dictionary of the Western Churches. T. C. O'Brien, ed. New York, Corpus Books, 1971.

> More than a hundred contributors have produced 2,300 original articles on Western Christianity. Ecumenical.

Gaustad, Edwin Scott. *Historical Atlas of Religion in America*. New York, Harper, 1962.

> Readable text giving the history of the various denominations in America, with maps of different dates showing the changes in distribution of each sect. This is not, of course, so statistically up to date as the *Yearbook of American and Canadian Churches*, below, but the maps are helpful. Ecumenical.

Maryknoll Catholic Dictionary. Albert J. Nevins, comp. and ed. Wilkes-Barre, Pa., Dimension Books, 1965.

> Defines standard Catholic words and terms, and explains changes in the liturgy and in Catholic thinking since the second Vatican Council. Includes

contemporary theories and terminologies as they apply to Catholic life — useful to non-Catholics. This dictionary is intended for the United States and Canada and includes biographical information on deceased Catholics (to 1965) of both nations. Abbreviations, forms of address, and lists of patron saints and popes.

Mead, Frank S. *Handbook of Denominations in the United States.* 5th rev. ed. Nashville, Tenn., Abingdon, 1970.

Brief historical sketches give the doctrines of more than 200 denominations and the latest information on mergers: e.g., Unitarian with Universalist, Evangelical and Reformed with Congregational, etc.

New Catholic Encyclopedia: An International Work of Reference on the Teachings, History, Organization, and Activities of the Catholic Church, and on All Institutions, Religions, Philosophies, and Scientific and Cultural Developments Affecting the Catholic Church from Its Beginning to the Present. Imprimatur. Prepared by an editorial staff at The Catholic University of America (Washington, D.C.). New York, McGraw-Hill, 1967. 15 vols. including index.

Emphasis is on the Roman Catholic Church in the United States and other English-speaking countries, but the encyclopedia is international in scope. For example, there are seventeen pages on Africa, with reference to sixty-two separate countries or regions. The articles are all signed, and uniformly excellent in content and readability. Each has a bibliography, some with brief annotations. The culture of basically Catholic nations is treated in articles entitled "Hungarian Art," "Hungarian Literature," etc. Illustrated.

Yearbook of American and Canadian Churches, 1916-   . Publisher varies; issued under the auspices of the National Council of the Churches of Christ in the U.S.A., New York, 1916-   . Annual.

This yearbook includes statistics on the numbers of churches and their membership, and information on theological seminaries, denominational colleges and universities, religious periodicals, etc. The 1973 edition was edited by Constant H. Jacquet, Jr., and published by Abingdon (Nashville and New York).

Saints

Information about saints is in great demand for a number of reasons. A person may wish to know what saint is connected with the day of his birth, what saint's name to take at confirmation, or who is the patron saint of a particular occupation or condition. The lives of saints are examples for those who need inspiration, much as Abraham Lincoln, or more recently Martin Luther King, may inspire others.

A number of biographical compilations have been in use for many years. No one of these books can answer all the questions, hence libraries usually have as many as they can afford. A list of those which have proved the most useful follows, in alphabetical order.

Attwater, Donald. *Dictionary of Saints.* New York, Kenedy, 1958.

See note under Butler's *Lives of the Saints.*

The Book of Saints. 5th rev. ed. Compiled by the Benedictine monks of
St. Augustine's Abbey, Ramsgate, England. New York, Crowell,
1966.

> Corrected and enlarged from the 4th edition (1941). Gives brief biogra-
> phies and adds persons beatified or canonized during the interval between
> editions.

Butler, Alban. *Lives of the Saints.* Complete ed., rev. and supplemented
by Herbert Thurston and Donald Attwater. New York, Kenedy,
1956. 4 vols.

> A revised and modernized edition of a major work, which will be found in
> most libraries. The saints are arranged chronologically, according to the days
> of the year with which they are associated. This work is supplemented and
> indexed by Donald Attwater's *Dictionary of Saints,* above, which is alpha-
> betically arranged and gives the month and day for each saint.

Delaney, John J. and Tobin, J. E. *Dictionary of Catholic Biography.*
New York, Doubleday, 1961.

> Includes about 13,000 churchmen and laymen, medieval and modern. Ap-
> pendixes give the patron saints of vocations and places, the symbols used to
> represent the saints in art, and a chronological chart of popes and world
> rulers.

Drake, Maurice and Drake, Wilfred. *Saints and Their Emblems.* Philadelphia, Lippincott, 1916. Reprinted in 1972 by Gale (Detroit).

> Lists names and dates (where possible) and the emblems relating to each
> saint. Illustrated.

Englebert, Omer. *The Lives of the Saints.* Translated by Christopher
and Anne Fremantle. New York, McKay, 1951. Paperback ed.,
Collier-Macmillan, 1964.

> Arranged chronologically by the days of the year. One or more saints men-
> tioned for each day, the more important treated in articles of one or two
> pages. Alphabetical index. Fuller accounts will be found in Butler, described
> above, and in any of the Catholic encyclopedias already discussed.

The Bible

In the last nineteen or twenty years, there have been many changes
in our knowledge of ancient times and ancient books. The Dead Sea
Scrolls and other manuscripts have shed new light on the authenticity
of several Biblical narratives. This section will list handbooks, atlases,
and historical studies of the beliefs and archaeology of what are called
"the Bible lands."

Any student of the Judaeo-Christian Bible knows that whatever
edition is currently in use is based on ancient manuscripts in Hebrew,
Greek, and Latin, and on early translations into the Latin Vulgate and
the vernacular tongues — French, German, and English. These early
translations have in turn been retranslated, revised, and sometimes converted into amazingly modern and colloquial English, which may be
distasteful to those who have been brought up with the Douay (Roman

Catholic) or King James (Church of England) versions, the latter having been used by all Protestant churches until the early years of the twentieth century. The following book provides an excellent, highly readable introduction to the history of the major translations into English.

Bruce, F. F. *The English Bible: A History of Translations from the Earliest English Versions to the "New English Bible."* New rev. ed. New York, Oxford University Press, 1970.

> The first edition (1961) followed the publication of the New Testament portion of the *New English Bible*, and the revised edition followed the publication of the complete Bible, including the Apochrypha, in 1970.
>
> This is an extremely interesting book, not as exhaustive as the commentaries which will be listed later, but a good introduction both for the college student taking a course in "Bible" and for the graduate student, seminarian, or member of the clergy. Among versions described here are Wycliffe's Bible, the Elizabethan Bible, and Moffatt's translation (1926), considered by some to be a rendering into Scots. A portion of the version in Old English is reproduced, for which a translation is thoughtfully provided. Catholic versions discussed here include the Confraternity Version, now called the New American Bible, and the Westminster Version, as well as the translations by Msgr. Ronald Knox from the Latin Vulgate. An interesting development is a translation into Basic English, a simplified form of the language sometimes used as an international auxiliary language.

Reference books about the Bible are grouped into four categories: Bible dictionaries and cyclopedias; dictionary-type books dealing chiefly with daily life during the period in which Biblical events are considered to have occurred and including some accounts of archaeological discoveries which have bearing on these matters; atlases showing the locales mentioned in the Bible; and concordances and dictionaries of quotations. For advanced students, especially the clergy, there are in the reference collection such series as *The Interpreter's Bible*, which will be listed in Appendix B, but which the beginning student will probably not have occasion to use.

Dictionaries and Cyclopedias

A number of these refer to specific versions of the Bible.

The Bible Companion: A Complete Pictorial and Reference Guide to the People, Places, Events, Background and Faith of the Bible. William Neil, ed. New York, McGraw-Hill, 1960.

> "Designed to provide the kind of knowledge of the contents and background of the Bible which will enable an ordinary reader who is unfamiliar with the jargon of the theologians . . . to read the Bible with deeper understanding and greater profit" — *Introduction.* This is keyed to the King James Version. For archaeological discoveries since 1960, it might be wise to supplement this and Hasting's *Dictionary* (below) with the most recent Jewish, Catholic and non-sectarian encyclopedias, current books and periodical articles on "the fertile crescent."

Encyclopedic Dictionary of the Bible. Translated from the Dutch by Louis F. Hartman. New York, McGraw-Hill, 1963.

> This reflects the official Roman Catholic point of view after the second Vatican Council.

Hasting, James. *Dictionary of the Bible.* Revised ed. by Frederick C. Grant and H. H. Rowley. New York, Scribner, 1963.

> Revised edition of a work originally based on Hasting's earlier five-volume *Dictionary* (1898-1904) but completely rewritten for the layman. Hebrew and Greek words are transliterated, whereas in the original work there were many in the Greek and Hebrew alphabets.
>
> The editors' preface states that "the old edition was based on the Revised Version of the Bible. . . . The present edition is based on the Revised Standard Version . . . with cross references from both the Authorized Version and the Revised Version forms." The new edition reflects recent archaeological discoveries, greater knowledge of Biblical languages, and such new sources as the Dead Sea Scrolls.

Neil, William. *Harper's Bible Commentary.* New York, Harper, 1963.

> References in this commentary are to the Revised Standard Version and the King James Version. According to the publisher, it may be used from grade 9 up.

Woods, Ralph, ed. *Catholic Companion to the Bible.* Philadelphia, Lippincott, 1956.

Life in Biblical Times

Archaeological Encyclopedia of the Holy Land. Avraham Negev, ed. New York, Putnam, 1972.

> Describes archaeological findings which pertain to the life and culture of the area from prehistory to the Byzantine era. Includes glossary and chronological table.

Brownrigg, Robert. *Who's Who in the New Testament.* New York, Holt, 1971.

Comay, Joan. *Who's Who in the Old Testament, Together With the Apocrypha.* New York, Holt, 1971.

> This volume and Brownrigg's (above) recount what is known or assumed about all the people mentioned in various Jewish and Christian scriptures — individuals and groups, such as the Sanhedrin. Illustrations include maps and reproductions of works of art.

Heaton, E. W. *Everyday Life in Old Testament Times.* New York, Scribner, 1956.

> Illustrations include floor plans of homes and temples, implements, costume, etc.

Miller, M. S. and Miller, J. L. *Encyclopedia of Bible Life.* Rev. ed. New York, Harper, 1955.

> An attempt to give a well-rounded picture of life in Bible times. Classified arrangement. Each chapter has many references to scriptural chapter and verse, and a bibliography listing modern sources.

——. *Harper's Bible Dictionary.* 8th ed. New York, Harper, 1973.

> Illustrated by photographs, maps, line drawings, and many tables. Excellent on costume, food, plants, etc., of Biblical times.

Pfeiffer, Charles F., ed. *The Biblical World: A Dictionary of Biblical Archaeology*. Grand Rapids, Mich., Baker Book House, 1964.

> Discusses only those aspects of Biblical history which have been clarified by archaeology. Black-and-white illustrations.

Atlases and Geography

Baly, Denis and Tushingham, A. D. *Atlas of the Biblical World*. New York, World, 1970.

Baly, Denis. *The Geography of the Bible: A Study in Historical Geography*. New rev. ed. New York, Harper, 1974.

Grollenberg, L. H. *Atlas of the Bible*. Translated and edited by J. M. H. Reid and H. H. Rowley. New York, Nelson, 1956.

> Has 37 eight-color maps, 408 photographs of places mentioned in the Bible, much history and the latest archaeological discoveries (up to publication date, of course). Based on the King James Version, but there are index references to the Douay, Knox, and Revised Standard versions.

The Oxford Bible Atlas. 2d ed. Herbert G. May and others, eds. New York, Oxford University Press, 1974.

> Twenty-six maps illustrating Bible history, plus extensive historical matter connected with each.

Van der Meer, Frederic and Mohrmann, C. *Atlas of the Early Christian World*. Translated and edited by M. F. Hedlund and H. H. Rowley. New York, Nelson, 1958.

> Includes 42 maps in color and 620 photographs.

Wright, G. E. and Filson, F. V. *The Westminster Historical Atlas to the Bible*. Rev. ed. Philadelphia, Westminster Press, 1956.

> Considerable text discussing Biblical history and eighteen large color maps. Table of dates placing events in chronological order.

Concordances

A definition of the word concordance is given in Chapter 3. Of late, concordances to the works of prolific prose writers, especially of the nineteenth century, have been compiled, but the word is still connected in most people's minds with the Bible or the works of Shakespeare. As new translations of the Bible are published, concordances to them must be compiled, as the new versions use more modern vocabularies; no concordance to the *New English Bible* (1961-1970) has yet been prepared.

Interfiled here among the concordances the reader will find two books of Bible quotations and a concordance to the American *Book of Common Prayer*, which is so widely used in Protestant churches that the churchgoer is likely to be as familiar with its phraseology as with that of the Bible.

Cruden, Alexander. *Concordance*.

> A concordance to the King James Version, this was first published in 1737, is still in use, and various versions of it are still in print, issued by a number

of publishers. Just as the name Webster is closely associated with dictionaries and Roget with thesauruses, the name Cruden is still connected with concordances to the Bible. Probably neither Cruden, Strong, nor Young would recognize the modern editions of the concordances which bear their names.

Ellison, John W., comp. *Nelson's Complete Concordance of the Revised Standard Bible.* New York, Nelson, 1957.

Huggett, Milton and Pye, J. M., eds. *A Concordance to the American "Book of Common Prayer."* New York, Church Hymnal Corp., 1970.

> Computer-produced and exhaustive. *The Book of Common Prayer* is one of the great literary, as well as religious, works in English. This concordance is based on the 1928 revision and includes words used as early as 1549. *The Book of Common Prayer* is presently being revised, but this concordance will have value as an aid to the historical usage of literary and theological terms.

Stevenson, Burton Egbert, ed. *The Home Book of Bible Quotations.* New York, Harper, 1949.

> Unlike most books of quotations, this includes a table of contents, which is an alphabetical list of the subjects under which quotations are listed, with *see also* references to related subjects. Under each subject in the text itself, the quotations are arranged in the order of their appearance in the Bible — Old Testament first, then New Testament. Some quotations are long, and may appear more than once in the index, which gives page and item number.

Strong, James. *The Exhaustive Concordance of the Bible.* New York, Hunt, 1894.

> One of the most complete indexes to the King James Version.

Thompson, Newton and Stock, Raymond. *Complete Concordance to the Bible (Douay Version).* 4th rev. and enl. ed. St. Louis, Mo., Herder, 1945.

> Since the version used by the Roman Catholic Church contains more books than the King James Version, and the translation of many passages differs also, separate concordances are necessary.

Young's Analytical Concordance to the Bible. 22d American ed. Revised by W. B. Stevenson. New York, Funk & Wagnalls, 1955.

> This includes words in Hebrew and Greek, names of people and places, and an article, "Recent Discoveries in Bible Lands," by W. F. Albright.

PHILOSOPHY

Encyclopedia of Philosophy. Paul Edwards, ed. in chief. London, Collier-Macmillan; New York, Macmillan/Free Press, 1967. 8 vols. incl. index.

> Professor Edwards was assisted by an international editorial board of 153 scholars. Contributors number about 500, from 24 countries. Articles (1,450 of them) are arranged alphabetically and vary in length from half a column to more than 50 pages. Each has its own bibliography, and references to other pertinent articles are placed *before* the major articles. Readable and authoritative.
>
> The only previous general work is J. M. Baldwin's *Dictionary of Philosophy and Psychology* (New York, Macmillan, 1901-1907), published in three volumes of which the last is a bibliography compiled by Benjamin Rand.

Klibansky, Raymond, ed. *Contemporary Philosophy: A Survey.* Florence, Italy, La Nuova Italia Editrice in cooperation with l'Institut International de Philosophie (Paris), 1968-1971.

Distributed in the United States and Canada by Mario Casalini, Ltd., Montreal. The French edition is entitled *La Philosophie Contemporaine: Chroniques.*

Each volume is devoted to a special area, as follows:

Volume I, *Logic and Foundations of Mathematics.* 1968.

Volume II, *Philosophy of Science.* 1968.

Volume III, *Metaphysics, Phenomenology, Language and Structure.* 1969.

Volume IV, *Ethics, Aesthetics, Law, Religion, Politics, Historical and Dialectical Materialism, Philosophy in Eastern Europe, Asia, and Latin America.* 1971.

Urmson, J. O., ed. *Concise Encyclopedia of Western Philosophy and Philosophers.* New York, Hawthorn, 1960.

Chapter 18

NON-BOOK MATERIALS

THE READER WHO BEGAN by thinking of encyclopedias as the first and best source of information has already been disillusioned many times. He has learned that multi-volume reference books, having required a long period of preparation, may fail to give the latest information, and, being selective, may omit mention of the subject he wishes to learn about. He may be interested in a topic too specific or too new to warrant a book about it. The possibility that recent periodical articles will fill this information gap leads the reader to the periodical indexes, only to find that his topic is treated only in journals for the specialist, which are not in his library. Ignoring, for the time being, the possibility of going to another library, or arranging for interlibrary loan, which is never instantaneous, the student follows the obvious path and asks a librarian.

PAMPHLETS

Libraries which cannot afford subscriptions to expensive journals which are not likely to receive frequent use fill these gaps with free or inexpensive pamphlets, which are often as valuable and as accurate as articles in journals. The term *pamphlet* is used to signify a publication of fewer than one hundred pages (some consider fifty pages a size more easily handled), not bound in hard covers like a book, but not a periodical or a "paperback." To complicate matters, pamphlets frequently appear in series, issued at regular intervals, and are sometimes received by subscription, or because of membership in an organization.

A pamphlet deals with a single topic and is complete in itself. No one ever has any trouble differentiating between pamphlets and periodicals, so there is no need to dwell upon points of difference. The most prolific sources of pamphlets are government agencies, whether local, state, national, or international. These government publications are usually accurate and dependable, though they sometimes show political bias. Among the best known and most widely distributed are the Farmers' Bulletins of the United States Department of Agriculture, the bulletins and leaflets of the Office of Education, and the publications of the Children's Bureau. The United Nations and its divisions are responsible for many pamphlets, and there are a number of useful publications of the British government, issued by Her Majesty's Stationery Office, as ours are by the Government Printing Office. State and city boards of education publish courses of study for the subjects taught in their schools, and other divisions of state and local governments issue reports, historical papers, and guides to (or advertisements for) local attractions such as fairs, festivals, and concerts.

The reader will come upon pamphlets sponsored by associations such as the Foreign Policy Association, the educational departments of labor unions, the Boy Scouts of America, the League of Women Voters, professional and occupational groups like the National Education Association, and such foundations as the Twentieth Century Fund and the Carnegie Foundation for the Advancement of Teaching.

State and local chambers of commerce and publicity offices distribute illustrated brochures singing their own praises as scenic vacation spots, or potential locations for business and industry. And industry itself publishes countless pamphlets, usually free, giving descriptive and historical information about its own products. While these are naturally intended to advertise the products, they are accurate, up to date, and usually excellently written and illustrated.

The reader wishing to know how to secure pamphlets for himself will find information on catalogs and indexes later in this chapter. For the average library patron, the most important question is, "How do I find these useful pamphlets in this library?" The best advice is, "Ask a librarian," for pamphlets are handled in a number of ways and arranged according to various schemes. The most frequently used methods are described below.

Vertical Files

Many pamphlets, especially those of only a few pages, are filed alphabetically by subject in deep-drawer filing cabinets known as *information files* or *vertical files* (because the materials are filed standing on edge). Subject headings are assigned to all pamphlets and clippings which are then placed in folders marked with the same headings, just as a businessman's secretary files his correspondence. The subject headings are similar to those used in the catalog; many libraries make cross references in the catalog to the headings used in the vertical files.

Libraries make frequent use of clippings, especially on matters of local interest, such as a series of newspaper articles on the origins of street names, or local industries, or some problem of local importance such as crime, juvenile delinquency, or substandard housing. Many of the weekly news magazines have one or two feature articles worth preserving, though much of the magazine's contents is out of date as soon as printed. Others publish fine color plates of works of art, scientific subjects, etc., which are more useful and can be better preserved in a clipping file or picture file than if they remained stored in back files of periodicals. Pamphlets and clippings should be dated.

A library's policy about access to the pamphlet files is likely to be similar to its policy about closed versus open stacks, which in turn depends to a great extent upon the size of the collection. If a reader should replace a pamphlet in the wrong folder, it will be as good as lost for months, until someone chances upon it, whereas a book in the wrong place may be found at once, or in a day or two. Therefore even a library with open shelves may restrict reader use of the pamphlet files, or request readers not to put anything back, though they may be permitted to take things out.

The scarcity of cross references in a vertical file adds to the need for professional assistance in using it. The smaller the file, the less relationship there may be between the headings used there and those used in the catalog. Where the catalog will show an entry for every person whose biography is on the shelves, the pamphlet file may have only a dozen folders under BIOGRAPHY, divided by alphabetical groups, or have a folder labeled PRESIDENTS, another EXPLORERS, and another SCIENTISTS, for example.

In fact, the arrangement of a pamphlet file, though it is alphabetical by subject, is nevertheless more like a classification scheme than like a catalog. Some libraries use the same class numbers in the file as they do on the books, and eliminate the need for alphabetical headings. This method is especially useful in a collection of pictures, where a classed grouping of artists by medium, country, and period is more logical than alphabetical arrangement.

Classified Pamphlets

Because filing cabinets are costly and also require a great deal of floor space, the library whose space and funds are limited may shelve pamphlets with the books on the same subjects, assigning classification numbers, but grouping the pamphlets at the end of each class, in heavy boxes. Some libraries have special compartmented shelves for pamphlets, and place them all together, sometimes using a system of colored bands to signify the class numbers. But even when the larger pamphlets are on shelves, some file space is needed for those too thin or too tall to stand. Finally, of course, the subject matter and the authority of many pamphlets is so important that they are cataloged like books, and often bound in permanent covers. At this point, of course, they become books, and are found through the catalog.

Government Documents

Publications of the United States Government Printing Office are sometimes shelved according to document number, which, in practice, means that they are arranged chronologically, in series, by issuing department, very much as periodicals are arranged. This method is frequently followed by the depository libraries which automatically receive all goverment publications issued for public use. (Many publications, including those "classified" as confidential or secret are available only to a limited number of people, and much mimeographed material, not printed at the Government Printing Office, does not go to depository libraries.) The libraries which are depositories for UN publications (and previously for those of the League of Nations) shelve these the same way, i.e., in series.

But there are comparatively few depository libraries. In others, government publications are selected from lists and catalogs just as books and other pamphlets are, and treated in the same ways; books like the *Statistical Abstracts*, *Census Reports*, and *Agriculture Yearbooks* are classified, cataloged, and shelved like other books; government publications that take the form of pamphlets are treated like other pamphlets.

Indexes and Catalogs of Pamphlets and Government Documents

Among the sources of information about pamphlets are the catalogs and checklists of government publications. United Nations publications are listed in checklists published by United Nations Publications, Room LX-2300, New York 10017. *A Guide to the Use of United Nations Documents*, by Brenda Brimmer and others, was issued in 1962 by Oceana Publications (New York). It includes references to the specialized agencies and special bodies of the UN, which have issued close to a million documents in English since 1953. Her Majesty's Stationery Office issues a monthly list of British government publications of general interest; the list and the publications may be secured from the British Information Services, 845 Third Avenue, New York 10022. *The Catalogue of Government Publications*, issued annually by H. M. Stationery Office since 1922, gives a fuller list of British official publications. A consolidated index is published every five years. Representatives of other governments also issue material about their countries to which the reader may be directed by his library.

The United States Superintendent of Documents issues the *United States Government Publications: Monthly Catalog*, which lists publications arranged by department, with a full index, cumulated annually. *A Cumulative Subject Index to the Monthly Catalog of U.S. Government Publications, 1900-1971* in 14 volumes is currently (1974) being issued by the Carrollton Press, Inc., 1647 Wisconsin Avenue, Washington, D.C. 20007. Subject entries, much more exact than those in the original catalogs and indexes, are given in a single alphabet, thus eliminating search through twenty-one biennial *Document Catalogs* (1900-1940), two *Decennial Indexes* (1941-1950, 1951-1960), and eleven *Annual Indexes* (1961-1971). In addition, the publisher is making available, in combination with the index volumes, the full text of the *Monthly Catalog* in several kinds of microform. A semimonthly folder, *Selected United States Government Publications*, may be received free by any library or individual wishing to be on the mailing list, and a series of more than seventy Price Lists, also free, and periodically brought up to date, gives the titles of publications on related subjects which are available. Many of the federal departments also publish catalogs of their own publications. The *Monthly Checklist of State Publications* issued by the Library of Congress lists all the publications which the individual states send to the Library of Congress.

Other sources of information on non-book printed materials are given below. Some of them have already been listed in earlier chapters, to which reference is made here.

Andriot, John L. *U.S. Government Serials and Periodicals*. McLean, Va., Documents Index, 1971. 3 vols.

> Volume 1 lists government agencies alphabetically by their official names; Volume 2 is a list of both current and no longer published serial publications of federal agencies as of January 1, 1971. Many entries have descriptive annotations. Volume 3 gives publications of abolished agencies, and provides an index to Volumes 2 and 3.

Biological and Agricultural Index. New York, Wilson, 1964-   .

> Includes pamphlets. See Chapter 9 for descriptive annotation.

Boyd, Anne Morris and Rips, R. C. *United States Government Publications*. 3d ed. New York, Wilson, 1950.

> Gives a brief history of public printing and describes the major publications and series of each government department. Though not recently revised, will take the place of Andriot, above, for student use.

Leidy, W. P. *Popular Guide to Government Publications*. 3d ed. New York, Columbia University Press, 1968.

Mechanic, Sylvia. *Annotated List of Selected United States Government Publications Available in Depository Libraries*. New York, Wilson, 1971.

Public Affairs Information Service Bulletin. New York, Public Affairs Information Service, 1915-   .

> Includes pamphlets. See Chapter 9 for descriptive annotation.

Schmeckebier, L. F. *The Government Printing Office: Its History, Activities, and Organization*. Baltimore, Johns Hopkins Press, 1925. Reprinted by AMS Press (New York).

Vertical File Index. New York, Wilson, 1932-   .

> Originally entitled *Vertical File Service Catalog*, this is a subject and title index to pamphlets considered to be of interest to general libraries. It does not pretend to be a complete list of all pamphlets issued, and inclusion does not necessarily constitute recommendation. The *Index* is issued monthly, except August, and contains a list of current available pamphlets, booklets,

leaflets, and mimeographed materials. The contents are arranged alphabetically by subject, giving titles, number of pages, publishers, publication dates,
descriptive notes, and price, if any. A title index follows, giving the subject
under which full description may be found.

In earlier years, an annual cumulation was published, but as the *Index* includes many free and inexpensive pamphlets which go out of print rapidly,
the annual was discontinued in 1965, because cumulations would be likely
to include items no longer available and would add to the subscription price
without adding to the value of the *Index*.

AUDIO-VISUAL MATERIALS

Various types of non-book materials were listed in Chapter 1, and
have been mentioned incidentally in subsequent chapters. Not all libraries collect all kinds, but each has its usefulness, and if the library one
uses has all these extra resources, so much the better.

Pictures and Maps

It would be hard to imagine a library without pictures and maps.
We are not referring to those bound in books as illustrations, nor to
atlases, but to separate items. The library's vertical file contains many:
pictures clipped from magazines and from discarded books, maps from
National Geographic Magazine, maps provided by gasoline distributors
or state tourist agencies. As demand grows, reproductions of paintings
are purchased and mounted on heavy cards, maps mounted on cloth
and attached to rollers are hung from map cases similar to those in
history and geography classrooms. As collections grow, pictures and
maps are separated from the miscellaneous vertical file. The reader will
find that the largest public and university libraries have separate departments for maps and for pictures. Individual libraries have developed
their own schemes for arrangement. Again, the reader must ask the
librarian.

Slides, Films, and Recordings

Today many teachers use 35mm slides, filmstrips, and motion pictures to illustrate and clarify their subjects. In some schools and colleges
each department owns a collection; in others there is an audio-visual
center, sometimes separate, sometimes connected with and adminis-
tered as a department of the library. Large public libraries also have
such departments, with films, slides, and records available for loan. The
student should find out about such collections; they may be as varied
as the book stock in subject coverage. For the artist there will be color
slides of paintings, photographs of buildings, sculpture; for the physician, motion pictures of operations, or of organisms multiplying beneath
the microscope; for the mathematician, slides or filmstrips demonstrating theorems in geometry, or explaining the uses of trigonometry; for
the biologist, motion pictures taken with a reduced-speed camera,

showing actual growth of a plant, a dragonfly issuing from its chrysalis stage, or, thanks to Disney, the birth of a buffalo calf; for the sociologist, the rehabilitation of a slum, or a neglected child.

On the whole, library film collections are likely to be "educational," though not always obviously so. Some of the most entertaining cartoons convey a serious message, and documentary films like *Man of Aran* are as exciting as many features designed for entertainment.

The magnificent series of color films on art, narrated by Kenneth Clark, and the still more recent series on the history of America, narrated by Alistair Cooke, each narrator revealing his own particular favorites, have been purchased by libraries and shown repeatedly, especially in public libraries and branches equipped with projection booths. Public television presents not only these series but also other British productions, such as *The Forsyte Saga*. These dramatizations and others like them are apt to be parts of the collections in college and university film libraries. Any television viewer who has seen these in black-and-white will welcome the opportunity to see, perhaps repeatedly, the color originals.

In the field of recordings it has become as common to collect records of poetry readings, speeches, and radio broadcasts, as of singers and orchestras. The following indexes list plays and poems which have been recorded on discs or tape.

Chicorel, Marietta, ed. *Chicorel Theater Index to Plays in Anthologies, Periodicals, Discs, and Tapes.* New York, Chicorel Library Publishing, 1970-   .

    The first two volumes are limited to printed sources, but all later volumes include discs and tapes. The index is international in scope, and includes plays from antiquity to the present.

————. *Chicorel Index to Poetry on Discs and Tapes: Poetry-on-Media.* New York, Chicorel Library Publishing, 1973.

    Poems on 500 recordings are indexed by title, first line, poet, reader, and director.

————. *Chicorel Index to the Spoken Arts on Discs, Tapes, and Cassettes.* New York, Chicorel Library Publishing, 1974.

    Includes recordings of poems, plays, short stories, essays, speeches, and documents. About 60,000 entries.

Colleges may make tape recordings of lectures or of performances by student musical organizations. Also, it has become a common practice for colleges to make color sound films of a variety of undergraduate activities for the use of alumni groups, to attract new students, while the department of athletics makes extensive use of motion pictures to show good and bad performance.

A type of recording of great importance to many Americans is the Talking Book, an album of records for use by the blind, containing the text of a whole book, read aloud by one of an army of volunteers, many of them professional actors. These albums, made under the auspices of the Library of Congress Division for the Blind, are distributed through regional centers (libraries) designated by the Library of Congress. On request of any blind person, the albums are mailed, postage free, to and from the regional center nearest him. A list of the centers may be obtained from one's own library or from the Division for the Blind and Physically Handicapped, Library of Congress, Washington, D.C. An informative pamphlet, *Books for the Blind and Physically Handicapped: A Postscript and an Appreciation*, by Howard Haycraft, who was for several months a "legal user" of Talking Books, is available from the Division.

Another source of recordings for the blind is Recording for the Blind, Inc., established in 1951 to provide recordings of educational material for students anywhere in the country, free of charge. The books are recorded on tape, by volunteers who must be familiar with the subject matter being read, and transferred to 16⅔ rpm discs. A full description of this service to students is in the *Saturday Review*, vol. 45, p. 53-54, August 18, 1962. New information may be secured from the Division for the Blind and Physically Handicapped, Library of Congress, if there is no regional center nearby, and from most college libraries.

These talking books, as well as books and magazines in Braille, have made it possible for the blind not only to endure their affliction better but also to secure an education which might otherwise be denied them. It has been a personal satisfaction to learn that the previous edition of THE NEW LIBRARY KEY was recorded by a woman for use by a blind student.

Microforms

Microforms are greatly reduced photographs of book, magazine, pamphlet, or newspaper pages — reduced so that they can be stored economically. They can be read by use of a "reader" which enlarges the image to its original size (or larger, when, for instance, a single column of a newspaper page is to be examined minutely, or when the user requires enlargement because of defective eyesight).

Microfilm

The first microform in general use, in the late 1930s, reproduced newspapers on 35-millimeter film. Not only did this process reduce the storage space required for back issues, but it also preserved the contents, because the paper used for the average daily newspaper (known as *newsprint*) is usually poor grade which deteriorates rapidly, as anyone who has a treasured clipping or has used newspapers to store household goods knows from experience. As far as libraries are concerned, those which had bound files of, for instance, the New York *Times* needed to subscribe to the costly rag-paper edition and then pay for binding a volume sixteen by twenty-four inches, weighing perhaps twelve pounds and (considering the present size of the *Times*) consisting of only two month's issues. On 35-mm film, the same amount of reading matter could be stored on one reel of film about the size of a sandwich, in a metal box (35-mm is the same width as commercial theater film).

A number of companies are now in the business of providing microfilm copies of out-of-print books, provided that there is no copyright in force, which libraries may purchase or borrow from one another for the use of scholars. Some universities accept from Ph.D. candidates one negative and two positive copies of their theses, instead of the printed and bound copies previously required. (The printed copies were distributed in three ways: The university would hold a number available for loan, set aside a larger number for exchange with other universities, and offer the remainder for sale to libraries and individuals.) Theses and ordinary-size books are usually reproduced on 16-mm film, twice the width of "home movies," and may be stored in cartridges or cassettes. (This is the size which is used to record music, and any modern young person between the ages of eight and twenty-eight is familiar with the cartridges and cassettes.)

Microcards

The next development in microreproduction was microprint, technically referred to as micro-opaque. By this method, the text of a book or magazine was reduced so that an entire issue of a magazine could be printed on six-by-nine-inch cards. The original *Saturday Review of Literature* was one of the first magazines to appear in this form, in about 1951. Microcards, of course, require a different type of reading machine from microfilm. The cards are available in various sizes: three-by-five, four-by-six, five-by-eight, and six-by-nine.

Microfiche

A microfiche (or fiche) is a card-size sheet of film, which, again, may carry many images. Again, an entire issue of a periodical may be reproduced on a single three-by-five- or four-by-six-inch sheet. This is naturally a better reproduction method for an illustrated magazine or book. The large size (ultrafiche) permits thousands of images per fiche, reduced more than ninety times.

By taking advantage of these types of reduced copies of books and documents, many libraries are able to secure important research tools which it would be quite impossible for them to purchase in book form, and to store them in a fraction of the space which the originals would occupy.

Sources of Information About Audio-Visual Materials

For the benefit of librarians beginning to establish collections of non-book materials and on the assumption that some of the readers of THE NEW LIBRARY KEY are teachers, teachers in training, or are planning to specialize in machine-readable materials, a brief list of bibliographies and catalogs of sources of such items follows. A word of caution, however, is necessary. At the time of this writing, not only machine-readable materials but even subscriptions to the catalogs of free materials are very costly in comparison to books. The decision to purchase such items, or even acquire them free of charge, depends upon the budget and the availability of storage space. As has already been stated, the space needed to store, for example, the full run of an important newspaper on microform is not great, but the cost of machines by which to read it may be prohibitive, especially if the machines are complex, or if several different types of machine are needed, or if duplicate machines must be ordered so that several people can use the material at one time.

Sources of information concerning non-book printed materials and government documents have already been mentioned in the text. A brief list of sources of information on audio-visual materials will be given here.

Educators Progress Service, Inc., Box 497, Randolph, Wis. 53956.
> *Educators Guide to Free Films,* 1941-   . Annual.
> *Educators Guide to Free Filmstrips,* 1949-   . Annual.
> *Educators Guide to Free Tapes, Scripts, and Transcriptions,* 1955-   . Annual.
> *Educators Guide to Free Guidance Materials: A Multi-Media Guide,* 1962-   . Annual.
> This includes not only films, filmstrips, slides, and tapes, but also scripts, transcriptions, and other printed materials.
> *Educators Guide to Free Social Studies Materials,* 1961-   . Annual.

NCR/Microcard Editions, 5500 So. Valentine Way, Englewood, Colo. 80110.
> *Guide to Microforms in Print,* 1961-   . Annual.
> Includes books, newspapers, and journals, whether or not the originals are in print or out of print. Microforms are available in various languages, including Russian, German, French, and Chinese.

> *Subject Guide to Microforms in Print,* 1962-   . Biennial.
> Most titles listed in this guide are microform editions of printed material, but some are marked "orig.," meaning that microform is the only means of publication.

NICEM (National Information Center for Educational Media), University of Southern California, University Park, Los Angeles, Calif. 90007.

> This organization has been producing special lists of non-book media since about 1969. NICEM offers a number of indexes in subjects at present in great demand: Health and Safety Education, Vocational and Technical Education, Black History and Studies, and Ecology — all multimedia. A full list of this material, as well as an index to producers and distributors, may be secured by writing to NICEM as well as to the other two firms listed above.
>
> NICEM is a non-profit organization, and their "update subscription" to 14 indexes in 10 volumes "costs but $256" for the year 1973-1974, according to the brochure. This should reinforce the warning above, about the necessity for carefully weighing the potential use of a multimedia service, even an inexpensive one.

Two books by Louis Shores, one of the most respected teachers of librarianship, should be added here.

Audiovisual Librarianship. Littleton, Colo., Libraries Unlimited, 1973. *Instructional Materials: An Introduction for Teachers.* New York, Ronald Press, 1960.

> A most detailed and inclusive work describing everything from encyclopedias to flannel board, globes to sandboxes, with suggestions for their use. Especially valuable to teachers (and librarians) in elementary schools.

GLOBES, MODELS, AND SPECIMENS

Almost every library of any size has one or more globes, showing the political divisions of the earth's surface and its physical features, for not even the most accurate map displays the true relationships between places on the earth as well as a globe.

Models and specimens are not so frequently parts of a library's collection. Some libraries have museums connected with them, where models of ships, planes, simple mechanical devices, geologic formations, etc., may be seen. If a college has a visual aids department, such things are properly part of its resources. The same is true of specimens, whether of rocks and minerals, or of the life stages of a boll weevil, or of the steps in converting crude petroleum into gasoline, or in changing a piece of cedar into a pencil.

It is especially true of a college or university library that anything which may be termed a tool of learning may be properly considered library material. Only limitations of space and of funds make some kinds of things impractical. But the greater the diversity and extent of a library's collection, the more effective it is in its educational function, and the greater the challenge to the student to take advantage of its diversity.

APPENDIXES

FOR THE USE of librarians, instructors, and graduate students as well as undergraduates, who are the major targets of this barrage of bibliographic information, three appendixes are added here, partly to make the text of each chapter less overwhelming, partly to bring together three different types of information. In Appendix A, there are suggestions for the undergraduate, to whom the book is addressed, on gathering and using data for research papers in specific fields. Appendix B contains detailed bibliographies and sources of information for a more advanced group — students in honors courses, graduate students, members of the faculty, and librarians seeking to build the college library collection to meet the needs of their clientele. In both appendixes, items will be grouped according to the chapters in the text to which they apply.

Appendix C is for the librarian-instructors who will, it is hoped, be the mentors to whom students and faculty alike go for informed assistance in solving their problems. It is the writer's experience that a series of formal or informal discussions (ideally both) will dispel the all too common illusion that librarians are always too busy to answer questions. That is their reason for being in libraries. The first part of Appendix C is an alphabetical list, with comments, of the sources used by the writer in preparing the three editions of THE NEW LIBRARY KEY. Some of the titles have been searched for, others are old friends, and a few have been come upon by chance — newspaper articles, book reviews in unlikely places, etc. Everything in Appendix C is useful; much is good reading besides.

Appendix A

Research Handbooks and Bibliographic Manuals

GENERAL

Barzun, Jacques and Graff, H. F. *The Modern Researcher*. rev. and enl. ed. New York, Harcourt, 1970.

> The authors' preface states that this will be of use to any researcher, though it has been most widely used for guidance in historical research. Jacques Barzun is a writer of great skill and charm. His other books do not fall within the scope of THE NEW LIBRARY KEY but are a delight to read.

Hackman, Martha L. *The Practical Bibliographer*. Englewood Cliffs, N.J., Prentice-Hall, 1970.

> F. N. Cheney, in her review of this book in the *Wilson Library Bulletin*, December 1970, describes it as "useful for the beginning graduate student," but it is possible that she may underestimate the members of the junior and senior classes.

A Manual of Style. 12th ed. rev. Chicago, University of Chicago Press, 1969.

> A complicated and meticulous manual, generally used as a reference by advanced degree candidates. Mentioned, with brief comment, in Chapter 6 (see Index for page reference).

Williams, Cecil B. and Stevenson, A. H. *Research Manual for College Studies and Papers*. 3d ed. New York, Harper, 1963.

> This book is referred to in Chapter 6, with reference to bibliographic form.

GEOGRAPHY AND HISTORY (Chapter 13)

Coan, Otis W. and Lillard, R. G. *America in Fiction: An Annotated List of Novels That Interpret Aspects of Life in the United States*, 4th ed. Stanford, Calif., Stanford University Press, 1956.

> It is unfortunate that this has apparently not been brought up to date, as it lists novels by such divisions as pioneer life and levels of economic or social condition (e.g., minorities, immigrants, old families, etc.). Some of the books listed later in this chapter will supplement it to some extent, and the student may find much newer material in such compilations as the *Fiction Catalog* and in the subject index to recent volumes of *Book Review Digest* and *Book Review Index* (see Chapter 10).

Lock, Muriel. *Geography: A Reference Handbook*. 2d rev. and enl. ed. Hamden, Conn., Shoe String Press, 1972.

Minto, C. S. *How to Find Out in Geography*. Oxford, Eng., Pergamon, 1967.

> A beginner's guide to about 650 books, periodicals, and atlases. Arranged by the Dewey system, showing how broad the interests of geographers are.

For research in history, Barzun and Graff's *The Modern Researcher*, listed above, will be particularly helpful.

THE SOCIAL SCIENCES (Chapter 14)

White, Carl M. and others. *Sources of Information in the Social Sciences: A Guide to the Literature*. 2d ed. Chicago, American Library Association, 1973.

> Lists reference sources in individual subjects; useful critical annotations. Includes publications through 1972. The 1st edition was published in 1964.

Politics and Government

Brock, Clifton. *The Literature of Political Science*. New York, Bowker, 1969.

> A well-written guide to the literature of the field — abstracts, book reviews, government publications, public opinion, etc.

Winton, Harry N. M., ed. *Publications of the United Nations Systems: A Reference Guide.* New York, Bowker, 1973.

> This consists of: an outline of the UN and its related agencies, listing the major publications of each; a list of selected reference publications of all units; a list of periodical publications; and, finally, a subject index.

Economics and Business

Fletcher, John, ed. *The Use of Economics Literature.* Hamden, Conn., Archon, 1971.

> Similar in purpose to Barzun's *The Modern Researcher*, discussed earlier in this Appendix.

Manley, Marian C. *Business Information: How to Find and Use it.* Newark, N.J., Newark Public Library; New York, Harper, 1955.

> According to a letter from Bernard Schein, the librarian at the Newark Public Library, still in print as of 1973.

Wasserman, Paul and others, comps. *Encyclopedia of Business Informamation Sources.* 2d ed. Detroit, Gale, 1970. 2 vols.

Education

Burke, Arvid J. and Burke, Mary A. *Documentation in Education.* New York, Teachers College, Columbia University, 1967.

> A revision of *How to Locate Educational Information and Data*, 4th ed., revised in 1958 by Carter Alexander and A. J. Burke. Burke's preface states that "the book always . . . has provided guidance for more sophisticated documentary or bibliographic work in education."

LITERATURE (Chapter 15)

Altick, Richard D. *The Art of Literary Research.* Text ed. New York, Norton, 1964.

> Altick has a delightful style, has written a number of studies based on thoughtful research and selection, and has an unusually good chapter on libraries.

Bateson, F. W. *The Scholar Critic: An Introduction to Literary Research.* Boston, Routledge & Kegan Paul, 1972.

——. *A Guide to English Literature.* 2d ed. New York, Anchor (Doubleday), 1968.

> Brief commentary on various periods of English literature. Introductions to literary criticism in English and to literary scholarship, useful to students, form the last two chapters.

Bell, Inglis. *A Reference Guide to English, American, and Canadian Literature.* Vancouver, Canada, University of British Columbia Press, 1971.

> Helpful to the undergraduate as a preliminary list of sources; usability and availability are stressed, as well as quality.

Bond, Donald F., comp. *A Reference Guide to English Studies.* 2d ed. Chicago, University of Chicago Press, 1971.

> Available in hard cover and paperback.

SCIENCE AND TECHNOLOGY (Chapter 16)

Bottle, R. T., ed. *The Use of Chemical Literature*. 2d ed. Hamden, Conn., Archon, 1969.

>One of a new series of literature guides entitled Information Sources for Research and Development. Except for the chapters on Beilstein and on patents, the contents of the first edition have been largely rewritten. New chapters have been added on polymer science and on "less conventional sources of information."

Bottle, R. T. and Wyatt, H. V., eds. *The Use of Biological Literature*. 2d ed. Hamden, Conn., Archon, 1969.

>Another volume in the series Information Sources for Research and Development.

Technical Book Review Index, 1917-   . New York, Special Libraries Association (235 Park Avenue S., New York 10003), 1917- Monthly except July and August.

>Annual index, no cumulation. Similar to *Book Review Digest* (*q.v.*). Beginning in January 1973, the coverage quotes reviews from periodicals in all scientific, technical, and medical (except clinical) subjects. Coverage is planned to include the life sciences and mathematics, management and the behavioral sciences. Includes textbooks, dictionaries, encyclopedias, and occasional fiction.

Tuma, Jan J. *Engineering Mathematics Handbook*. New York, McGraw-Hill, 1970.

>Planned like a cookbook, with topics completed on one page or on a two-page spread. Comparable to Grazda (*q.v.*) but with more advanced material for engineers.

Appendix B

Detailed Bibliographies – Sources of Information for Librarians, Members of the Faculty, and Graduate Students

THESES AND DISSERTATIONS

Listings of theses completed or in progress must be searched by the candidate for a doctoral degree before he makes a final decision as to his thesis topic, to be sure that his topic has not already been treated as he plans to treat it and that no previous study has refuted his theory. Some colleges of education (Columbia Teachers College, for instance) give an Ed.D. instead of a Ph.D. and permit the candidate to choose a topic which will advance his efficiency in his present or prospective position. Even in such cases, he must make sure that his topic does not resemble too closely one already written or announced.

Listed below are a number of indexes to doctoral dissertations, monographs, and other research. Similar listings are available for theses accepted in countries other than the United States and the British Isles.

Doctoral Dissertations Accepted by American Universities, 1933/34-1954/55. New York, Wilson, 1934-1956. 22 vols.

This publication was superseded by *Index to American Doctoral Dissertations*, listed below.

Index to American Doctoral Dissertations, 1955/56-1959/60. Ann Arbor, Mich., University Microfilms, 1956-1960. Annual to 1960.

Alphabetical listings by institution, subject, and author.

Index to Theses Accepted for Higher Degrees in the Universities of Great Britain and Ireland, 1950/51-   . London, ASLIB (Association of Special Libraries and Information Bureaux), 1953- Annual.

Arranged by subject classification. A cumulated issue covering the previous decade was published in 1961.

Microfilm Abstracts. Ann Arbor, Mich., University Microfilms, 1938-1951. 11 vols. Semiannual.

A guide to dissertations and monographs available on microfilm. Superseded by *Dissertation Abstracts*, below.

Dissertation Abstracts. Ann Arbor, Mich., University Microfilms, 1952-   . 6 issues per year.

THE ARTS (Chapter 12)

A few of the following titles have only recently been announced for publication. Where a review has been available, it will be noted.

The British Film Catalog, 1895-1970: A Reference Guide. Denis Gifford, ed. New York, McGraw-Hill, 1973. 2 vols. Volume 1, *Silent Films*; Volume 2, *Sound Films*.

According to the publisher's announcement, this set contains a guide to every British feature film ever made (15,000 films). All traceable information for each film is included: studio, running time, director, cast, and plot. Interviews with most of the remaining pioneers of the British film industry.

Duckles, Vincent, comp. *Music Reference and Research Materials: An Annotated Bibliography.* 3d ed. New York, Free Press, 1974.

Replaces earlier editions of this useful work. Includes a new section on Music History in Pictures and treatment of individual composers.

Eagon, Angelo. *Catalog of Published Concert Music by American Composers.* 2d ed. Metuchen, N. J., Scarecrow Press, 1969.

Lists works in broad groupings — jazz, vocal, instrumental. Gives publishers of scores.

International Index to Film Periodicals, 1972-   . Karen Jones, ed. New York, Bowker, 1973-   .

Indexes 60 periodicals; multiple listing by subject, title, and film personality. The editor is associated with the International Federation of Film Archives in Brussels, Belgium.

Lucas, E. Louise, comp. *Art Books: A Basic Bibliography on the Fine Arts.* Greenwich, Conn., New York Graphic Society, 1968.

> This is a revision and enlargement of the *Harvard List of Books on Art* (1952). It includes monographs on individual artists, which do not fall into the category of General Reference Books.

Nicoll, Allardyce. *English Drama, 1900-1930.* Cambridge, Eng., Cambridge University Press, 1973.

> Supplements Nicoll's six-volume *History of English Drama, 1660-1900.* Of the 1,083 pages of this latest volume, about 450 are devoted to a historical survey of "The Beginnings of the Modern Period," pages 452 to 1053 present a "Handlist of Plays," and there is an index.

Schoolcraft, Ralph Newman, ed. *Performing Arts Books in Print to 1971: An Annotated Bibliography.* New York, Drama Book Specialists, 1973. Quarterly supplement, 1971-   .

> This title and the preceding one are reviewed at length in *College & Research Libraries,* January 1974.

HISTORY (Chapter 13)

American Historical Association. *Guide to Historical Literature.* George F. Howe and others, eds. New York, Macmillan, 1961.

> A revision of the 1931 edition of the *Guide* (edited by G. M. Dutcher and others). While its coverage of publications between 1931 and 1957 is extensive, that between 1957 and 1960 is less complete. Late completion of some sections made them more nearly up to date. This is a valuable aid to the student of history, specifically because of its emphasis on the relation of literature to history, politics, economics, law, art, and philosophy. It is amply supplemented by Poulton's 1972 bibliography, listed below.

Hamer, Philip M., ed. *Guide to Archives and Manuscripts in the United States.* New Haven, Conn., Yale University Press, 1961.

> Compiled for the United States National Historical Publications Commission.

Harvard Guide to American History. Oscar Handlin and others, eds. Cambridge, Mass., Harvard University Press, 1954.

> According to the preface, covers publications through 1950, but some published as late as 1954 are listed.

Miller, Elizabeth W. *The Negro in America: A Bibliography.* Cambridge, Mass., Harvard University Press, 1970. Compiled for the American Academy of Arts and Sciences.

Poulton, Helen J. with the assistance of Marguerite S. Howland. *The Historian's Handbook: A Descriptive Guide to Reference Works.* Norman, Okla., University of Oklahoma Press, 1972.

> This is a more than adequate supplementary guide to update the American Historical Association's *Guide to Historical Literature* (q.v.). It deals with the problems of the researcher, whether student or scholar, and discusses more than 900 books as well as the use of archives, serials, and newspapers. Includes a general index and a special title index for quick reference.

Thompson, Lawrence S., comp. *The Southern Black, Slave and Free: A Bibliography of Anti- and Pro-Slavery Books and Pamphlets and of Social and Economic Conditions in the Southern States from the Beginnings to 1950.* Troy, N.Y., Whitston, 1970.

> The works listed here are available in microform.

THE SOCIAL SCIENCES (Chapter 14)

White, Carl M. and others. *Sources of Information in the Social Sciences: A Guide to the Literature.* 2d ed. rev. Chicago, American Library Association, 1973.

> The 1st edition was published in 1964 — "a guide for reference librarians, scholars, and students." The 2nd edition includes books published through 1972. The scope of the social sciences is broadened to include history, geography, economics, business administration, sociology, anthropology, psychology, education, and political science. Many cross references.

Government

Bogdanor, V. B. *A Bibliography for Students of Politics.* New York, Oxford University Press, 1971.

> British viewpoint.

Congressional Quarterly. *Guide to the Congress of the United States: Origins, History and Procedure.* Washington, D.C., Congressional Quarterly, 1971.

Freund, Paul A., gen. ed. *The Oliver Wendell Holmes Devise History of the Supreme Court of the United States.* New York, Collier-Macmillan, 1971-   . To be in 11 vols.

> Several volumes have been published, each written by a distinguished legal scholar. This work was made possible by a legacy of $263,000 bequeathed to the United States by Associate Justice Holmes.

Lester, Daniel and Lester, Marilyn, comps. *Bibliography of U.S. Government Serial Publications, 1789-1970.* Washington, D.C., United States Historical Documents Institute, 1971.

The United States Historical Documents Institute is also producing a *Checklist of U.S. Public Documents, 1789-1970* on 118 microfilm cartridges with four hard-cover computer-based indexes, and it has announced, as of 1971, a semiannual cumulative updating service on microfilm, indexes to be in paperback. The indexes will be compiled by Daniel and Marilyn Lester, who prepared the bibliography above.

International Relations

Dimitrov, T. D., comp. and ed. *Documents of International Organisations: A Bibliographic Handbook.* London, International University Publications; Chicago, American Library Association, 1973.

Includes documents of the UN and its specialized agencies, also EEC, OECD, and the Council of Europe. A directory of international organizations tells how and where to obtain their documents.

Foreign Affairs 50-Year Bibliography: New Evaluations of Significant Books on International Relations, 1920-1970. Edited by Byron Dexter; foreword by H. F. Armstrong. New York, Bowker, for the Council on Foreign Relations, 1972.

See entry in Chapter 14, under International Relations.

Psychology

Buros, Oscar K., ed. *Mental Measurements Yearbook*, 1938, 1940, 1949, 1953, 1959, 1965, 1972 (2 vols.). Imprint varies.

Since 1953, published by Gryphon Press (Highland Park, N.J.).

Classified listing of standardized tests of all kinds; general intelligence, aptitude, performance, personality. Each test is fully described and reviews of it which appeared in journals are reprinted, usually in full. Each volume contains new material, therefore does not supersede previous volumes. The editor's plan, in spite of the title *Yearbook*, was to issue a supplementary volume biennially. Obviously circumstances (perhaps World War II) intervened. For information on available tests, even the latest volume is probably already partly out of date. But for the student of the history of testing, even the earliest has its uses. For a list of tests in print in 1961 see Buros' *Tests in Print* (Gryphon, 1961).

The seventh (1972) *Yearbook* lists 1,157 tests, including 640 not previously issued and 453 tests revised or supplemented since last listed; 798 original reviews of 546 tests by 439 specialists; 181 reviews of 115 tests excerpted from 41 journals; a bibliography of 664 books on testing, plus 554 book reviews excerpted from 89 journals; an up-to-date directory of 243 test publishers, etc., ending with a classified index to tests and reviews.

——. *Personality Tests and Reviews*. Highland Park, N.J., Gryphon Press, 1970.

More than a third of all the references in this volume refer to the Rorschach and Minnesota Multiphasic Personality Inventory tests. This volume includes an index to the first six volumes of Buros' *Mental Measurements Yearbook*, described above.

Harvard List of Books in Psychology. 4th ed. Cambridge, Mass., Harvard University Press, 1971. Paperback.

Useful also to undergraduates.

Psychological Abstracts, 1927-   Lancaster, Pa., American Psychological Association, 1927-

Formerly monthly, now bimonthly; has annual subject and author indexes. A cumulated subject index was published in Boston by G. K. Hall, covering 1927 to 1960, and two supplements, the latest dated 1971, have been issued, along with cumulated author indexes.

LITERATURE (Chapter 15)

Blanck, Jacob N., comp. *Bibliography of American Literature*. New Haven, Conn., Yale University Press, 1955-   .

> A bibliography of the works of American writers who died before 1930.

Gohdes, Clarence. *Bibliographical Guide to the Study of the Literature of the U.S.A.* 3d ed., rev. and enl. Durham, N.C., Duke University Press, 1970.

> The author claims that every page of the 1st edition (1953) has been changed, and that all obsolete titles in the 2d edition (1963) have been eliminated. This is no small claim. A bibliography of bibliographies of the authors included, which was a feature of the 2d edition, has also been dropped from the current volume.

Hirschfelder, Arlene B., comp. *American Indian Authors: A Representative Bibliography*. New York, Association on American Indian Affairs, 1970.

> There are brief annotations, a list of authors by tribe, and a list of Indian periodicals. Much has been published by American Indians in recent years. The Association can doubtless furnish current information.

Nilon, Charles H., comp. *Bibliography of Bibliographies in American Literature*. New York, Bowker, 1970.

> Lists approximately 6,500 bibliographies, arranged by author, genre, literary period, and special category. Detailed subject index with numerous cross references.

Lang, David M., ed. *Guide to Eastern Literatures*. New York, Praeger, 1971.

> Middle Eastern and Far Eastern literatures, including Arabic, Jewish, Indian, Chinese, Japanese, and Korean. Each chapter is by a specialist and includes historical background and brief treatment of individual authors and their work. Bibliographies and index. No doubt current interest in other cultures than our own, which has already brought about broader interest in their languages, is leading to the study of their literature as well.

Parks, George B. and Temple, R. Z. eds. *The Literatures of the World in English Translation: A Bibliography*. New York, Ungar, 1967-   . Volume 1, *The Greek and Latin Literatures*; Volume 2, *The Slavic Literatures*, edited by R. C. Lewanski; Volume 3, *The Romance Literatures*.

> This series is jointly sponsored by the American Library Association and the National Council of Teachers. Volume 1 includes sections on the history and theory of translation. For the specialist, the Ph.D. candidate, etc.

Watson, George, ed. *The New Cambridge Bibliography of English Literature*. New York and London, Cambridge University Press, 1969-   . To be in 5 vols.

> Volume 1, *600-1600* (1974); Volume 2, *1660-1800* (1971); Volume 3, *1800-1900* (1969); Volume 4, *1900-1950* (1972). Volume 5 is to be a cumulative index to the set. Each volume, however, contains an index to primary authors and some subjects.

In all volumes only literary authors writing in English and native to or mainly resident in the British Isles are listed. The general arrangement is by genre — poetry, the novel, drama, etc. The first three volumes are based on the 1940 edition of the *Cambridge Bibliography of English Literature* and its 1957 supplement. Volume 4 is entirely new.

THE SCIENCES (Chapter 16)

Chemical Abstracts, 1907-   . Easton, Pa., American Chemical Society, 1907-   .

   The most up-to-date source of information on research in the fields of chemistry and chemic technology. For a brief description, see entry under Chemistry in Chapter 16, above. Only examination and use, as pointed out there, can give the student familiarity with it.

Grogan, Denis. *Science and Technology: An Introduction to the Literature.* new rev. ed. Hamden, Conn., Shoe String Press, 1973.

Herner, Saul. *A Brief Guide to Sources of Scientific and Technical Information.* Washington, D.C., Information and Resources Press, 1970. Paperback.

   Originally developed as a guide to train scientists and engineers seeking work-related scientific and technical information. Uses the "problem-solving" approach. The reviewer in *Library Journal* (P. R. Penland) recommends this for all libraries, including high school collections. However, many people reject the "problem-solving" technique as tedious and unproductive.

International Bibliographies of Dictionaries. 5th ed. New York, Bowker, 1972.

   Over 700 dictionaries in more than 100 languages are grouped under some 50 subject headings in the fields of science, technology, and economics. Listed in *Library Journal*'s annual list of the "Best Reference Books."

Jenkins, Frances B. *Science Reference Sources.* 5th ed. Cambridge, Mass., MIT Press, 1969. Cloth and paperback eds.

Medical Books in Print. New York, Bowker, 1972-   . Annual.

   Books listed by author and by title, with a subject index. As with most of the Bowker Books in Print series, the annual usually appears in the spring.

*Scientific and Technical Books in Print, 1972-   * . New York, Bowker, 1972-   . Annual.

   Indexed by author, title, and subject. Computerized arrangement and index.

Winton, Harry N. M., comp. and ed. *Man and the Environment: A Bibliography of Selected Publications of the United Nations System, 1946-1971.* New York, Bowker, 1972.

   The only source, to date, which appears to deal extensively with all the areas comprised in the science we now term *ecology.* The encyclopedias are still sending the reader from volume to volume, while periodical literature, although every month more concerned about the state of the earth and its atmosphere, must give us our information piecemeal.

   Harry Winton is the former chief of the Documents Reference Section, Dag Hammarskjold Library, United Nations. More than 1,200 publications of the UN and related agencies dealing with the problems of the world's environment are listed here. Fifty-nine subject areas are covered, with publications listed chronologically by date of publication, giving title, author and/ or editor, bibliographic description, and description of contents. A sampling from the list of subjects covered includes environmental pollution, population growth, animal, plant, and water resources, food additives, and soil science.

RELIGION (Chapter 17)
Bible Texts—Annotated

The Anchor Bible. New York, Doubleday, 1964. 51 vols.

A new translation in fifty-one volumes, each with an introduction and notes. Each volume deals with one book of the Bible and gives examples of early and late translations from Hebrew, Greek, and Latin into and from French, German, English, and other languages, and points out possible interpretations and misinterpretations of various texts. The volumes vary in size depending upon the length of the original and the translators' problems. Much of the commentary in the short volume examined for this annotation was highly colloquial and often humorous. This set has great value for those dealing with devotees of *Godspell; Jesus Christ, Superstar*; and other popular presentations.

The Interpreter's Bible. New York and Nashville, Tenn.; Abingdon, 1951-1957. 12 vols.

Detailed treatment of both the King James and the Revised Standard versions of the Bible. Volume 12 includes an article on the Dead Sea Scrolls, a literary chronology of the Bible, an index of scripture cited out of context, and an index of subjects.

Bible Dictionaries and Commentaries

The Cambridge History of the Bible. Cambridge, Eng., Cambridge University Press. 3 vols.

Volume 1, *From the Beginnings to Jerome.* P. R. Ackroyd and C. F. Evans, eds. 1970.

Volume 2, *The West from the Fathers to the Reformation.* G. W. H. Lampe, ed. 1969.

Volume 3, *The West from the Reformation to the Present Day.* S. S. Greenslade, ed. 1963.

Articles are contributed by prominent scholars and represent current biblical scholarship. The title of Volume 2 may be misleading, as the book traces the influence of the scriptures on European culture up to the time of Erasmus; most of the material on the Reformation proper is in Volume 3.

The Interpreter's Dictionary of the Bible. New York and Nashville, Tenn.; Abingdon, 1962. 4 vols.

An authoritative work designed to accompany the multi-volume *Interpreter's Bible.* Contains bibliographies. The longer articles are signed.

The Interpreter's One-Volume Commentary on the Bible. Charles M. Laymon, ed. New York and Nashville, Tenn.; Abingdon, 1971.

This book does not, of course, give the text but includes contributions by Protestant, Roman Catholic, and Jewish scholars. It is not aimed at the theologian, but at the layman wishing explanation of puzzling passages, etc.

The New Westminster Dictionary of the Bible. Henry S. Gehman, ed.
Philadelphia, Westminster, 1970.
 Includes biographies, summaries of the various books of the Bible, pronunciation of proper names, descriptions of things and places, and sixteen full-
 color maps taken from the *Westminster Historical Atlas of the Bible.* References are usually to the Revised Standard Version. This work replaces the
 smaller 1944 edition.

Appendix C

Books and Articles About
Reference Books

THE BOOKS AND PERIODICALS listed here will provide the librarian-
instructor with background material which will enrich and enliven the
teaching of "library lessons" with anecdotes about such people as Melvil
Dewey, William Frederick Poole, Benjamin Perley Poore, and Halsey
W. Wilson — people whose solutions of their own problems have solved
many recurring problems of library users to this day. Some of these
books are historical and descriptive studies of famous publications, such
as the Marquis Who's Who series, and the Oxford, Webster, and other
dictionaries. Several newspaper articles are included, which offer vivid
accounts of the dictionary-making process.

 After the annotated list of books, periodicals, and articles which
follows, there is a list of sources used in preparing this edition of THE
NEW LIBRARY KEY.

Barton, Mary Neill and Bell, Marion V., comps. *Reference Books: A
 Brief Guide.* 7th ed. Baltimore, Md., Enoch Pratt Free Library,
 1970.
 Though based on the collection of the Enoch Pratt Free Library, this is
 useful anywhere as a guide to important books. Many titles are annotated at
 length, with frequent references to similar or related books. A pocket-size
 book with a thirty-page index — authors, titles, and subjects interfiled.

Cheney, Frances Neel. *Fundamental Reference Sources.* Chicago, American Library Association, 1971.
 A textbook for beginning library school students, covering sources which
 would probably be used in the first term or semester of a course in reference
 work: bibliographies, current and retrospective; biographical collections;
 dictionaries; encyclopedias; statistical data; and atlases and gazetteers.
 Cheney has a well-deserved reputation as a teacher of reference work, and
 her reviews of reference books, which appeared for many years in the *Wilson
 Library Bulletin*, are masterpieces of succinct, informative, and frequently

impish comment. However, the average reference librarian is likely to suspect that this text covers its subject matter much more fully than the author herself would in the classroom. The publisher's announcement places this between the Scylla and Charybdis of Shores' *Basic Reference Sources* (o.p.) and Winchell's *Guide to Reference Books*, the first being a readable survey of information sources and the second an all-encompassing bibliography, with short annotations, of books in many languages.

Clark, Jack A. "State Manuals: A Potpourri of Information." *Reference Quarterly*, Winter 1972, pp. 186-88.

Clark quotes a librarian as saying that the writers of these annuals "put in all the things teachers tell the kids to look up" — a good deal of very valuable, up-to-date information.

Cole, Dorothy E. "Britannica 3 as a Reference Tool: A Review." *Wilson Library Bulletin*, June 1974, pp. 821-25.

An experienced reference librarian and professor at the SUNY (Albany) School of Library and Information Science reviews the 1974 edition of the *Encyclopaedia Britannica*. Those who may have heard that it would be easy for any high school student to use the new encyclopedia will be interested in this reviewer's conclusion: "Don't discard your old edition."

Collison, Robert. *Encyclopedias: Their History Throughout the Ages . . . from 350 B.C. . . . .* 2d ed. New York, Hafner, 1966.

Collison has written a number of excellent textbooks for library schools in Britain. Like most of his erudite compatriots, he writes books that are a pleasure to read, no matter how weighty their subject matter.

Courtney, Winifred F., ed. *The Reader's Adviser.* 11th ed. rev. and enl. New York, Bowker, 1969.

Volume 1 is entitled *World Literature*; Volume 2 has no general title but covers everything in print from religion to the "lively arts." Earlier editions were designed mainly for booksellers. It appears that this, being more selective, will be even more useful to the librarian and the general reader than its predecessors.

Kogan, Herman. *The Great EB: The Story of the Encyclopaedia Britannica*. Chicago, University of Chicago Press, 1958.

An entertaining as well as informative history of a publishing venture which began about two hundred years ago. For a picture of the almost insurmountable difficulties encountered by the publishers of any encyclopedia, not the least of which are the foibles and shortcomings of editors and writers, this is invaluable, and, in spots, very funny. The author's enthusiasm for his subject may be tempered for the reader by such articles as the *Library Journal* evaluation listed below and various reviews of the 1974 *EB*, listed in *Book Review Digest* and *Book Review Index* for 1974 and 1975.

Larson, Cedric A. *WHO; Sixty Years of American Eminence: The Story of Who's Who in America.* New York, McDowell, Obolensky, 1958.

Like Kogan's book, listed above, this is both informative and entertaining. Among other bits of curious information is the ingenious method of dealing with would-be imitators. These two books, with Lawler's, which follows, will supply much human interest material to enliven lectures and assignments on reference books.

Lawler, John. *The H. W. Wilson Company: Half a Century of Bibliographic Publishing*. Minneapolis, University of Minnesota Press, 1950.

A life of the founder, Halsey W. Wilson, who was so often frustrated by the lack of an index to publishers' catalogs when he tried to find books for his customers that he began publication of the *Cumulative Book Index* and *The United States Catalog* while working his way through the University of Minnesota as a bookseller. He went on to develop the many Wilson indexes, such as *Readers' Guide to Periodical Literature*, which make the search for books and magazine articles so easy for library users. This gives excellent detail on the publication methods, as well as much human interest material.

Library Journal, April 15, 1961 (The 1961 Reference Book Issue).

This issue contains two detailed evaluations of multi-volume reference works: On pages 1549-1551 is a report, by Julius R. Chitwood, on an examination and evaluation of the 1961 printing of the *Encyclopaedia Britannica* by a committee of nineteen librarians from the staff of the Indianapolis Public Library. On pages 1552-1557 is a detailed review of the first edition of the *McGraw-Hill Encyclopedia of Science and Technology*. The various fields included in the set are evaluated by specialists, most of them professors, three of them librarians in special libraries.

Martin, Richard (staff reporter). "The Word Watchers." *Wall Street Journal*, November 28, 1973.

This article, covering five half-columns of the November 28, 1973, issue of the *Wall Street Journal*, describes in detail the people who are collecting material for a new 4th edition of the Merriam-Webster international dictionary (the title of the new edition is not available as yet) and for companion volumes, e.g., the collegiate, shorter, and pocket editions. It also describes some of the methods of finding new words and defining them, choosing which shall be added, etc.

Murray, Sir James Augustus Henry. *New English Dictionary*. Oxford, Eng., Clarendon Press, 1888-1933. 10 vols. and supplements.

The Preface, in Volume 1, describes the plan of work for this monumental compilation, and a discussion of the vocabulary gives further background. See also article by Israel Shenker, *infra*.

Poole, William Frederick. *Poole's Index to Periodical Literature*. 3d ed. Boston, Osgood, 1882. Reprinted in 1958 by Peter Smith (Gloucester, Mass.).

Preface, pp. iii-xii, tells the origin of the index, the plan under which it was compiled, and the difficulties encountered in trying to bring together the work of fifty volunteer indexers. More human interest material. See Chapter 9 for a description of the *Index*.

Poore, Benjamin Perley, comp. *A Descriptive Catalogue of the Government Publications of the United States, September 5, 1774-March 4, 1881*. Washington, D.C., Government Printing Office, 1885.

The Preface describes the troubles endured by the compiler — from incompetent assistants assigned to the job by grateful congressmen to the erratic numbering of documents by the public printers. Poore accepted these tribulations with good grace, and describes them with humor.

In libraries where Poore's catalog is not available, this preface may be found quoted in its entirety in Schmeckebier and Eastin, listed below.

Roberts, Arthur D. *Introduction to Reference Books.* 3d ed. rev. London, Library Association, 1956.

While not, of course, up to date, this quasi-textbook for British library students has much general information on reference work, including treatment of the special problems of special libraries, and on the history of reference books, especially of encyclopedias. Highly readable.

Salamanca, Lucy N. *Fortress of Freedom: The Story of the Library of Congress.* Philadelphia, Lippincott, 1942.

Schmeckebier, L. F. and Eastin, R. B. *Government Publications and Their Use.* 2d rev. ed. Washington, D.C., Brookings Institution, 1969.

Poore's preface is reprinted here.

Shenker, Israel. "Oxford Dictionary To Get an Updating, Its First in 39 Years." *New York Times,* July 12, 1972.

A remarkable "special" datelined Oxford, England, July 11. Brief comment on the history of the *OED* and an interview with Robert W. Burchfield, editor of *A Supplement to the Oxford English Dictionary*, of which Volume I (A-G) was published in 1972. Volume II (H-P) is scheduled for 1975 and Q-Z for 1977. Shenker concludes with the prediction that the third volume will end with *zzz.* "Anyone who gets that far will deserve his rest."

Sonnenschein, William Swan. *Best Books.* 3d ed rev. London, Routledge, 1910-1935. 6 vols. Reissued in 1969 by Gale Research (Detroit) with a preface by Francesco Cordasco.

Mary N. Barton says of this: "The greatest books on all subjects, of every period, and in several tongues, are gathered together and classified in this tremendous work, the standard long general bibliography. Each volume covers one or more subjects; Volume 6 is a detailed index. Notes are only occasional and very brief, the mere fact of inclusion is in itself indication that the compiler considered the book one of enduring value."

Tebbel, John. "A Century of *The World Almanac.*" *Saturday Review,* December 9, 1967, pp. 62-63.

A history of almanacs in general (since 1638) and *The World Almanac* in particular. A highly informative, entertaining, and provocative article. The *Almanac's* latest publisher, Newspaper Enterprises Association, republished the first edition in 1967, and announced plans to put on film all editions, from first to last, whenever that may be.

Times (London). "Choosing a Dictionary." *Times Literary Supplement,* October 13, 1972, pp. 1211-14.

Includes a list of the twenty-three dictionaries discussed: British, American, Scottish, and Canadian. Prices are given in British currency. This issue of the *TLS* contains several articles on dictionaries, including one by R. W. Burchfield, editor of the *Supplement to the OED.*

Webster's Dictionary of Synonyms. Springfield, Mass., Merriam, 1942-   . Frequently revised.

Included in the prefatory material is History of Synonymy, which describes earlier works of the same type and the development of the theory of synonymy.

Wilson, Louis Round and others. *The Library in College Instruction: A Syllabus on the Improvement of College Instruction Through Library Use.* New York, Wilson, 1951. Reprinted in 1973 by Greenwood Press (Westport, Conn.).

   Intended for the prospective college teacher or teacher in service. Includes long lists of books and teaching materials by which the college teacher can improve his teaching. Includes such units as The Selection of Materials for Effective College Instruction and The College Library as a Teaching Instrument.

Sources Used to Enrich and Update This Edition of THE NEW LIBRARY KEY

For the sample copies of library rules and regulations and the guide to the arrangement of books in a medium-sized college library (Figures 1 and 2), I am indebted to Dorothy O'Connor, Circulation Librarian of the Harry A. Sprague Library of the New Jersey State College at Montclair.

Chapter 4, Library Catalogs, is based almost entirely on my own experience as a cataloger in school, public, and college libraries. The sample cards are partly from previous editions of this book, with the most recent ones provided by the Catalog Department of the Enoch Pratt Free Library. Marian Sanner, Chief of the Processing Division there and editor of the revision of Esther Piercy's *Commonsense Cataloging* (New York, Wilson, 1974), warned me to study the 18th edition of the Dewey Decimal Classification. John Phillip Immroth's *Guide to the Library of Congress Classification* (Rochester, N.Y., Libraries Unlimited, 1968) contributed a great deal to understanding of the LC system, which I used from 1965 to 1969, when the Enoch Pratt Library was beginning its program of reclassification. Immroth's book, plus the suggested comparison devised by Howard McGaw, Professor of Learning Resources at Western Washington State College in Bellingham, were helpful in writing Chapter 5, Library Classification Systems.

From Chapter 7 on, the following sources have been used to verify editions of books listed in previous editions of the KEY and to find new titles of reference books which have appeared since 1963:

American Library Association. Annual list of "Best Reference Books," most of which have been reviewed and noted elsewhere. This list appears in *Library Journal.*

College & Research Libraries, 1963-

Library Journal, 1960-   . Reviews, especially those listed under "Reference."

New Republic, 1970-   . This magazine sometimes carries reviews of reference books.

Publishers' Trade List Annual, 1974.

Reference Quarterly, 1960-   . *RQ* is the organ of the Reference Divi-
    sion (now the Reference and Adult Services Division) of the ALA.
Sheehy, Eugene P. *Guide to Reference Books*. 8th ed. Supplements.
        See entry under Winchell, Constance M.
Wilson Library Bulletin, 1963-   . Especially useful during the years
    when Frances N. Cheney was choosing the reference books to be
    reviewed. Currently the reviews are directed in the main to school
    and small public libraries.
Winchell, Constance M. *Guide to Reference Books*. 8th ed. Chicago,
    American Library Association, 1967.
        Supplemented biennially under the editorship of Eugene P. Sheehy, as
    well as by semi-annual lists of reference books published in the January and
    July issues of *College and Research Libraries*, the organ of the Association of
    College and Research Libraries, a division of the American Library Associa-
    tion. Sheehy's supplements are also referred to as "Winchell."
        With its supplements, this is the most complete and most nearly up-to-date
    bibliography of reference books. Includes works in many languages and for
    many specialties, but is particularly strong in bibliography, the humanities,
    and the social sciences.

Many of the books included in THE NEW LIBRARY KEY are sources
long used — from library school both as a student and later as Associate
Professor; from the experience of building a college library collection
at Montclair; from work with inquirers at the public libraries in Springfield (Ohio) and Baltimore; and from weekly visits to the Book Selection
Room at the Enoch Pratt Library during my time there as a Branch
Librarian. Since my retirement, I have had generous cooperation from
Department Heads and other staff members at the Central Library and
several branches.

Some of the annotations on dictionaries — English, bilingual, and
multilingual — are dependent upon the expertise of Professor B. Hunter
Smeaton, whose reviews appear in *Library Journal*. I have acknowledged my debt to him in a letter, and was pleased to see a special "pro-
file" of him in the book review section of a recent issue of *LJ*. Whenever
the books have been available for examination, I have verified my impressions, but in recent years this has not often been possible, since
library funds have been curtailed.

The discussions of encyclopedias both in English and in foreign
languages reflect long experience in using them, as well as available
reviews of those in English in *RQ* and, for a time, in the ALA *Booklist
& Subscription Books Bulletin*. The latter, even when incorporated in
Booklist some years ago, was usually not available until long after the
books were on our library shelves. Fortunately, weekly book review
sections of the New York *Times* and the late lamented *Herald Tribune*
helped. A year's experience in cataloging books in languages I did not
know was helpful in using encyclopedias in those same languages.

INDEX

Books written by two or more authors are indexed under one name only.

A.L.A. Annual list of best reference books, 245

A.L.A. Booklist and Subscription Books Bulletin, 246

Abbreviations: bibliographic, 8; dictionaries of, 99-101; in footnotes, 73; foreign language, 73, 85

Abridged Readers' Guide, 115-16

Acquisition department. See Order department

Acronyms, dictionaries of, 99-101

Acting. See Theater

Adams, A. K. Home Book of Humorous Quotations, 132

Adams, J. T. ed. Album of American History, 162-63; Atlas of American History, 162; Dictionary of American History, 162

Adams, R. L. Great Negroes, Past and Present, 166

Africa South of the Sahara, 139

Agricultural Index, 116

Agriculture, 204

Album of American History, 162, 165

Alexander, C. How to Locate Educational Information and Data, 232

Allibone, S. A. Critical Dictionary of English Literature, 181, 185

Allusions, literary, handbooks of, 128-31

Almanac of American Politics, 171

Almanacs, 138-41

Altick, R. D. The Art of Literary Research, 232

America in Fiction, 231

American Art Directory, 151

American Association of Museums. Official Museum Directory, 151

American Authors and Books, 180, 185

American Authors: 1600-1900, 184

American Book of Days, 129

American College Dictionary, 89-90

American Council on Education. American Universities and Colleges, 177

American Guide series, 165

American Heritage Dictionary, 90

American Heritage Guide to Archaeology, 156

American Historical Association. Guide to Historical Literature, 235

American Historical Novel, 163

American history, 162-66

American Indian Authors: A Representative Bibliography, 238

American Indians, 165-66

American Institute of Physics Handbook, 202

American Language, 97

American Men and Women of Science: The Physical and Biological Sciences, 195-96

American Men and Women of Science: The Social and Behavioral Sciences, 170

American Nation series, 164

American Nicknames, 131

American Place-Names, 164

American Universities and Colleges, 177

American Usage: The Consensus, 96

Anchor Bible, 240

Andriot, J. L. U.S. Government Serials and Periodicals, 223

Annotated List of Selected United States Government Publications Available to Depository Libraries, 223

Annual Magazine Subject Index, 1907-1949, 107

Annual Register of World Events, 138

Antonyms, dictionaries of, 93-94

Apel, W. ed. Harvard Dictionary of Music, 143

Apollo: An Illustrated Manual of the History of Art, 151

Appendixes, 33

Appleton's Cyclopaedia of American Biography, 134

Applied Science & Technology Index, 116

Archaeological Encyclopedia of the Holy Land, 215

Archaeology, 156-57

Architecture, 152

Arrangement of books on shelves, 61-63

Art, 148-52; bibliographies, 234-35

Art Index, 116, 152

Art of Literary Research, 232

Artists, biographies of, 150-51

Arts, 142-52

Ash, L. Subject Collections, 114

Asimov, I. Asimov's Biographical Encyclopedia of Science and Technology, 196; Asimov's Guide to Shakespeare; 189; Words of Science and the History Behind Them, 196-97

Astronomy, 199-200

Athletics, motion pictures for, 225
Atlas Antiquus, 158
Atlas of American History, 162
Atlas of the Bible, 216
Atlas of the Biblical World, 216
Atlas of the Classical World, 157
Atlas of the Early Christian World, 216
Atlas of the Universe, 199
Atlas of Western Civilization, 158
Atlases, 153-55; Biblical, 216; historical, 157-58
Attwater, D. ed. Catholic Dictionary, 211; Dictionary of Saints, 212
Audio-visual materials, 11, 224-29
Australian Books in Print, 124
Author entries, 39-47
Authors, biographies of, 183-85
Ayer Directory of Newspapers, Magazines and Trade Publications, 118

B.B.C. See British Broadcasting Corporation
Baker, T. ed. Biographical Dictionary of Musicians, 143
Baldwin, J. M. Dictionary of Philosophy and Psychology, 217
Baly, D. Atlas of the Biblical World, 216; The Geography of the Bible, 216
Barach, A. B. Famous American Trademarks, 175
Barnes, Clive, comp. Best American Plays series, 191
Barnhart, C. L. ed. American College Dictionary, 89-90; Barnhart Dictionary of New English Since 1963, 90; New Century Cyclopedia of Names, 128
Barone, M. Almanac of American Politics, 171
Bartlett, J. Familiar Quotations, 132
Barton, M. N. Reference Books: A Brief Guide, 241
Barzun, J. The Modern Researcher, 230
Basic Documents of African Regional Organizations, 169
Bateson, F. W. The Scholar Critic: An Introduction to Literary Research, 232
Bell, I. Reference Guide to English, American, and Canadian Literature, 232
Benét, W. R. Reader's Encyclopedia, 128-29
Bennett, H. ed. Chemical Formulary, 200-201
Bergman, P. M. Chronological History of the Negro in America, 166; comp. Concise Dictionary of 26 Languages, 105
Bernier, G. ed. Illustrated History of Music, 144
Bernstein, T. M. Miss Thistlebottom's Hobgoblins, 96
Berrey, L. V. American Thesaurus of Slang, 97

Besançon, R. M. Encyclopedia of Physics, 202
Best American Short Stories, 190
Best Books, 244
Best Plays, 190
Besterman, T. World Bibliography of Bibliographies, 120
Bettmann, O. L. Pictorial History of Medicine, 205
Bible, 214-17, 240-41
Bible Companion, 214
Biblical World: A Dictionary of Biblical Archaeology, 216
Bibliographic abbreviations, 8
Bibliographic detail, 64-67, 71-72
Bibliographic Index, 116, 120
Bibliographic manuals, 230-41
Bibliographical Guide to the Study of the Literature of the U.S.A., 238
Bibliographies, 120-27; for term papers, 64-67, 71-72, 109, 113-14; specialized, 233-41
Bibliography of American Literature, 238
Bibliography of Bibliographies in American Literature, 238
Bibliography of Modern History, 162
Bibliography of U.S. Government Serial Publications, 236
Bibliothèque Nationale (Paris): catalog, 38
Bilzer, B. Paintings of the World's Great Galleries, 151
Biographical dictionaries, 134-38
Biographical Dictionary of Republican China, 168
Biographical Encyclopaedia and Who's Who of the American Theatre, 147
Biographies: of actors and playwrights, 146-47; of artists, 150-51; of authors, 183-85; of blacks, 166; Canadian, 167; classification of, 63; dictionaries of, 134-38; of government officials, 173-74; of Indians, 166; of musicians, 143-44; of saints, 212-13; of scientists, 170, 195-96
Biography Index, 116
Biological & Agricultural Index, 116, 223
Biological sciences, 203
Bjørklund, O. Historical Atlas of the World, 157
Black American: A Documentary History, 166
Blacks in America, 166; bibliography, 235-36
Black's Medical Dictionary, 205
Blanck, J. N. comp. Bibliography of American Literature, 238
Blind, library materials for the, 226
Bliss, A. J. Dictionary of Foreign Words and Phrases in Current English, 98
Blurb, 29-30
Boatner, M. M. Encyclopedia of the American Revolution, 163

Bogdanor, V. B. *A Bibliography for Students of Politics*, 236
Bond, D. F. comp. *Reference Guide to English Studies*, 232
Book jacket, 29-30
Book of Days, 129
Book of Festivals and Holidays, 130
Book of Health, 205
Book of Presidents, 164
Book of Saints, 213
Book of the States, 172
Book of World-Famous Music, 145
Book Review Digest, 115, 126
Book Review Index, 126-27
Book selection aids, 125
Booklists, 120-26
Books, 29-36; arrangement in libraries, 15-16, 20, 61-63; on microfilm, 227; talking, 226
Books Abroad, 127
Books in Print, 122
The Bookseller, 124
Boorman, H. L. ed. *Biographical Dictionary of Republican China*, 168
Borrowers, 16, 18, 21, 25
Bottle, R. T. ed. *The Use of Chemical Literature*, 233; *The Use of Biological Literature*, 233
Bowker Company, R.R., 123
Boyd, A. M. *United States Government Publications*, 223
Bradshaw, A. *World Costumes*, 147
Brady, G. S. *Materials Handbook*, 200, 203
Brandon, S. G. F. ed. *Dictionary of Comparative Religion*, 208
Bray, W. *American Heritage Guide to Archaeology*, 156
Breed, P. F. comp. *Dramatic Criticism Index*, 191
Brewer, E. C. *Brewer's Dictionary of Phrase and Fable*, 129, 183; *Reader's Handbook of Famous Names in Fiction*, 129
Brewer's Dictionary of Phrase and Fable, 129, 183
Bridger, D. ed. *New Jewish Encyclopedia*, 210
Briggs, M. S. *Everyman's Concise Encyclopedia of Architecture*, 152
Brimmer, Brenda. *Guide to the Use of United Nations Documents*, 222
Brinson, P. *International Book of Ballet*, 148
Britain: An Official Handbook, 139
Britannica Junior, 84
"Britannica 3," 83-84, 242
British Authors Before 1800, 184
British Authors of the Nineteenth Century, 184
British Books in Print, 124
British Broadcasting Corporation. *BBC Pronouncing Dictionary of British Names*, 98

British Film Catalog, 1895-1970, 234
British Museum: catalog, 38; copyright office, 124
British National Bibliography, 124
Brock, C. *Literature of Political Science*, 231
Brockhaus Enzyklopaedie, 86
Brockhaus' Konversations-Lexikon, 86
Browning, D. C. ed. *Everyman's Dictionary of Literary Biography*, 183; *Everyman's Dictionary of Shakespeare Quotations*, 190
Brownrigg, R. *Who's Who in the New Testament*, 215
Browsing room, 28
Bruce, F. F. *The English Bible: A History of Translations*, 214
Bruncken, H. *Subject Index to Poetry*, 114
Bryant, M. M. *Current American Usage*, 96
Burack, A. S. ed. *Writer's Handbook*, 183
Burke, A. J. *Documentation in Education*, 232
Burke, W. J. *American Authors and Books*, 180, 185
Buros, O. K. ed. *Mental Measurements Yearbooks*, 237; *Personality Tests and Reviews*, 237
Business, 175-77
Business Information: How to Find and Use It, 232
Business Periodicals Index, 116, 175
Butler, Alban. *Lives of the Saints*, 213
Butler, Audrey, comp. *Everyman's Dictionary of Dates*, 129
Butler, J. A. V. ed. *Progress in Biophysics and Molecular Biology*, 203

CBI. 120-21, 123
Call numbers, 26, 46
Cambridge Ancient History, 156, 161
Cambridge History of American Literature, 180
Cambridge History of English Literature, 180-81
Cambridge History of the Bible, 240
Cambridge Italian Dictionary, 104
Cambridge Medieval History, 161
Cambridge Modern History, 161-62
Campbell, G. *The Book of Flags*, 157
Campbell, O. J. ed. *Reader's Encyclopedia of Shakespeare*, 189
Canada: history, 167
Canada (yearbook), 139
Canaday, J. E. *Lives of the Painters*, 150
Canadian Almanac and Directory, 138
Canadian Books in Print, 125
Carroll, D. *Dictionary of Foreign Terms in the English Language*, 98
Carruth, G. *Encyclopedia of American Facts and Dates*, 163
Cartography. *See* Atlases; Maps

Catalog cards, 39-54
Catalog of Published Concert Music by American Composers, 234
Cataloging department, 26
Catalogs, library, 37-54; arrangement, 50-52; author entries, 39-47; book form, 38-39; classed, 38; classification systems, 55-63; cross references, 52-54; subject entries, 47; subject headings, 13, 50-52; title entries, 48-49, 54; use, 50
Catholic Almanac, 211
Catholic Companion to the Bible, 215
Catholic Dictionary, 211
Catholic Periodical and Literature Index, 116
Catholic University of America. New Catholic Encyclopedia, 212
Chambers, R. The Book of Days, 129
Chambers Dictionary of Science and Technology, 197
Chambers Technical Dictionary, 197
Chambers's Biographical Dictionary, 134
Chambers's Encyclopaedia, 83
Chambers's Twentieth Century Dictionary, 88
Champlin, J. D. Cyclopedia of Painters and Paintings, 150
Checklist of U.S. Public Documents, 1789-1970 (microfilm), 236
Chemical Abstracts, 200, 239
Chemical Abstracts Service Source Index, 200
Chemical Dictionary, 201
Chemical Formulary, 200-201
Chemistry, 200-201
Cheney, F. N. Fundamental Reference Sources, 241-42
Cheney, S. W. The Theater: Three Thousand Years of Drama, Acting and Stagecraft, 146
Chicago University Press. Manual of Style, 66, 231
Children's Catalog, 125
Choice, 126
"Choosing a Dictionary," 244
Christensen, E. O. Guide to Art Museums in the United States, 152
Christianity, 211-13. See also Bible; World religions
Chronicles of America series, 165
Chronological History of the Negro in America, 166
Chronologies, 158-60
Cinema, 148
Circulation, 20, 25
Citizen's Guide to Legal Rights, 174
Clark, J. A. "State Manuals: A Potpourri of Information," 242
Clark, R. L. The Book of Health, 205
Classification systems, 15-16, 55-63
Coan, O. America in Fiction, 231

Cole, D. E. "Britannica 3 as a Reference Tool: A Review," 242
Collation, 46
College & Research Libraries, 245
College Blue Book, 177
College libraries, 22-28
Collier's Encyclopedia, 83
Collison, R. Encyclopedias: Their History, 242
Collocott, T. C. Chambers Dictionary of Science and Technology, 197
Columbia Encyclopedia, 82
Columbia Lippincott Gazetteer of the World, 155
Coman, E. T. Sources of Business Information, 176
Comay, J. Who's Who in the Old Testament, 215
Commager, H. S. ed. New American Nation series, 165
Companion to Modern History, 162
Complete Concordance to the Bible (Douay Version), 217
Composers of Tomorrow's Music, 144
Composers Since 1900, 144
Comprehensive Dictionary of Psychological and Psychoanalytical Terms, 179
Comprehensive Treatise on Inorganic and Theoretical Chemistry, 201
Compton's Encyclopedia and Fact-Index, 84
Concise Encyclopedia of English and American Poets and Poetry, 187
Concise Encyclopedia of Western Philosophy and Philosophers, 218
Concise Oxford Dictionary of English Literature, 182
Concordance to the American "Book of Common Prayer," 217
Concordances, 35; Bible, 216-17; Shakespeare, 190
Congressional Directory, 174
Congressional Information Service. Index to Publications of the U.S. Congress, 172
Congressional Quarterly: publications, 172-73; 236
Contemporary Authors, 183-84
Contemporary Literary Criticism, 185
Contemporary Philosophy, 218
Contemporary Poets of the English Language, 187
Contents, table of, 32
Continuous cumulation, 107-8
Continuous revision, 81
Copperud, R. H. American Usage: The Consensus, 96
Copyright, 31
Costume, 147
Cottrell, L. ed. Concise Encyclopedia of Archaeology, 156
Council on Foreign Relations: publications, 139, 175, 237

Courtney, W. F. ed. *Reader's Adviser*, 242

Craigie, W. A. *Dictionary of American English on Historical Principles*, 94

Crawford, M. D. C. *One World of Fashion*, 147

Creamer, J. S. *Citizen's Guide to Legal Rights*, 174

Critical Dictionary of English Literature and British and American Authors, 181, 185

Critical History of English Literature, 181

The Critical Temper: A Survey of Modern Criticism, 186

Criticism, literary, 185-87

Cross references, 34, 52-54

Crowell's Handbook of Classical Drama, 188

Crowell's Handbook of Classical Literature, 182

Crowley, E. T. *Acronyms and Initialisms Dictionary*, 100; *Reverse Acronyms and Initialisms Dictionary*, 100

Cruden, A. *Concordance* (Bible), 216-17

Cummings, P. *Dictionary of Contemporary American Artists*, 150

Cumulation, continuous, 107-8

Cumulative Book Index, 120-21, 123

Cumulative Subject Index to Monthly Catalog of U.S. Government Publications, 222

Curiosities of Popular Customs, 131

Curley, D. N. comp. & ed. *Library of Literary Criticism: Modern American Literature*, 185

Current American Usage, 96

Current Biography, 135

Current Index to Journals in Education, 177

Cutter numbers, 63

Cyclopedia of Painters and Paintings, 150

Cyclopedia of World Authors, 184

Cyclopedias. *See* Encyclopedias

DC, 56-58

Daiches, D. *Critical History of English Literature*, 181; ed. *Penguin Companion to English Literature*, 185

Dance, 148

Dance Through the Ages, 148

Daniells, L. M. *Business Reference Sources*, 176

Davenport, M. *The Book of Costume*, 147

De Ford, M. A. *Who Was When?* 158

Departmental libraries, 24

Desk-Book of Idioms and Idiomatic Phrases, 97

De Sola, R. *Abbreviations Dictionary*, 101

Deutsch, B. *Poetry Handbook*, 187

Devambez, P. *Praeger Encyclopedia of Ancient Greek Civilization*, 159

Dewey, M., 241

Dewey Decimal Classification system, 56-58, 245

Dictionaries, 76-77, 87-105; abridged, 89-91; of abbreviations, 99-101; of acronyms, 99-101; biographical, 134-38; etymological, 94-95; foreign language, 101-5; of pronunciation, 98-99; rhyming, 99; of slang, 97-98; of synonyms, 93-94; of symbols, 105; of usage, 95-97

Dictionary catalogs, 37-38

Dictionary of American Artists, 150

Dictionary of American Biography, 135

Dictionary of American English on Historical Principles, 94

Dictionary of American-English Usage, 97

Dictionary of American History, 162

Dictionary of American Painters, Sculptors and Engravers, 150

Dictionary of Americanisms on Historical Principles, 95

Dictionary of Applied Physics, 202

Dictionary of Art Terms, 149

Dictionary of Artists in America, 150

Dictionary of Battles (Eggenberger), 159

Dictionary of Battles (Harbottle), 159

Dictionary of Biblical Archaeology, 216

Dictionary of British History, 168

Dictionary of Canadian Biography, 135, 167

Dictionary of Canadianisms on Historical Principles, 96

Dictionary of Catholic Biography, 213

Dictionary of Classical Antiquities, 161

Dictionary of Comparative Religion, 208

Dictionary of Contemporary American Usage, 96

Dictionary of Dates, 158

Dictionary of Drugs, 205

Dictionary of Economics, 177

Dictionary of Education, 178

Dictionary of Electronics and Nucleonics, 202

Dictionary of Foreign Terms in the English Language, 98

Dictionary of Hydrogeology, 206

Dictionary of Literary Terms, 183

Dictionary of Modern English Usage, 96

Dictionary of National Biography, 135-36

Dictionary of Non-Christian Religions, 209

Dictionary of Politics, 171

Dictionary of Scientific Biography, 196

Dictionary of the Social Sciences, 171

Dictionnaire de l'Académie Française, 92

Dictionnaire du Français Contemporain, 102

Diderot, D. *Encyclopédie*, 85

Diderot Pictorial Encyclopedia of Trades and Industry, 197

Dimitrov, T. D. *Documents of International Organizations: A Bibliographic Handbook*, 236-37

Directory of American Scholars, 177

Directory of the American Theater, 188

Dissertation Abstracts, 234

Dissertations, 233-34

Doctoral Dissertations Accepted by American Universities, 234
Documents of International Organizations, 236-37
Documents of Western Civilization, 159
Documents on American Foreign Relations, 139
Dorsen, N. ed. Rights of Americans, 174
Douglas, G. W. The American Book of Days, 129
Downs, R. B. American Library Resources, 114; Resources of New York City Libraries, 114; Resources of Southern Libraries, 114
Drake, M. Saints and Their Emblems, 213
Drama, 188-190; bibliography, 235; as literature, 180-93
Dramatic Criticism Index, 191
The Dream and the Deal, 165
Dreyfuss, H. Symbol Sourcebook, 105
Duckles, V. comp. Music Reference and Research Materials: An Annotated Bibliography, 234
Duff, J. W. Literary History of Rome, 181
Dupuy, R. E. Encyclopedia of Military History, 159
Dust jacket, 29-30

Eagle, D. ed. Concise Oxford Dictionary of English Literature, 182
Eagle, S. ed. Library Resources in London and South East England, 115
Eagon, A. Catalog of Published Concert Music by American Composers, 234
Earth sciences, 206
Ebony Pictorial History of Black America, 166
Ecology, 206; bibliography, 239-40
Economic Almanac, 176
Economic Atlas of the Soviet Union, 168
Economics, 175-77
Editor and Publisher Market Guide, 176
Education, 177-78; bibliography, 232
Education Index, 117, 177
Educators Guide series, 228
Edwards, E. Words, Facts and Phrases, 130
Edwards, I. E. S. Cambridge Ancient History: Prolegomena and Prehistory, 156
Edwards, P. ed. Encyclopedia of Philosophy, 217
Eggenberger, D. Dictionary of Battles, 159; Flags of the U.S.A., 130
Eichelberger, C. L. comp. A Guide to Critical Reviews of United States Fiction, 1870-1910, 127
Electronics, 201-3
Electronics and Nucleonics Dictionary, 202
El-Hi Textbooks in Print, 126
Ellison, J. W. comp. Nelson's Complete Concordance of the Revised Standard Bible, 217

Elsevier's Dictionary of Hydrogeology, 206
Enoch Pratt Free Library (Baltimore), 39
Enciclopedia Italiana, 86
Enciclopedia Universal Ilustrada Europeo-Americana, 86
Encyclopaedia Britannica, 83-84, 242-43
Encyclopaedia Britannica World Atlas, 154
Encyclopaedia Judaica, 209
Encyclopaedia of Myths and Legends of All Nations, 208
Encyclopaedia of Religion and Ethics, 208
Encyclopedia Americana, 83
Encyclopedia Canadiana, 167
Encyclopedia of American Facts and Dates, 163
Encyclopedia of American History, 163
Encyclopedia of Ancient Greek Civilization, 159
Encyclopedia of Atmospheric Sciences and Astrogeology, 206
Encyclopedia of Australia, 168
Encyclopedia of Bible Life, 215
Encyclopedia of Biochemistry, 203
Encyclopedia of Chemistry, 201
Encyclopedia of Business Information Sources, 176, 232
Encyclopedia of Concert Music, 145
Encyclopedia of Earth Sciences, 206
Encyclopedia of Education, 177
Encyclopedia of Educational Research, 177
Encyclopedia of Geomorphology, 206
Encyclopedia of Human Behavior, 179
Encyclopedia of Jazz, 145
Encyclopedia of Jazz in the Sixties, 145
Encyclopedia of Military History, 159
Encyclopedia of Modern Education, 178
Encyclopedia of Oceanography, 206
Encyclopedia of Physics, 202
Encyclopedia of Poetry and Poetics, 187
Encyclopedia of Psychology, 179
Encyclopedia of Social Work, 170
Encyclopedia of the American Revolution, 163
Encyclopedia of the Social Sciences, 170
Encyclopedia of World Art, 149
Encyclopedia of World History, 160
Encyclopedia of World Literature in the Twentieth Century, 182
Encyclopedia of Zionism and Israel, 168, 210
Encyclopedias, 24-26, 76-85; children's, 80, 84; foreign language, 85-86
Encyclopedic Dictionary of the Bible, 215
Encyclopedic Dictionary of the Western Churches, 211
Encyclopédie Française, 85
Endpapers, 30
Engineering Index, 117
Engineering Mathematics Handbook, 233
Englebert, O. Lives of the Saints, 213

English, H. B. *Comprehensive Dictionary of Psychological and Psychoanalytical Terms,* 179
English Drama, 1900-1930, 235
ERIC, 177
"Espasa," 86
Essay and General Literature Index, 115, 192
Etiquette, 130
Etymology, dictionaries of, 94-95
Europa Publications, 139
Europa: The Encyclopaedia of Europe, 139
Europa Yearbook, 139
European Authors, 1000-1900, 184
Evans, B. "But What's a Dictionary For?" 89; *Dictionary of Contemporary American Usage,* 96; *Dictionary of Quotations,* 133
Everyday Life in Old Testament Times, 215
Everyman's Dictionary of Dates, 129
Everyman's Dictionary of Literary Biography, 183
Everyman's Dictionary of Music, 142
Evolution of Fashion, 147
Ewen, D. Composers series, 144-45
Eysenck, H. J. *Encyclopedia of Psychology,* 179

"Fact finders," 128
Facts About the Presidents, 163
Facts on File, 117
Famous American Trademarks, 175
Famous First Facts, 130
The Far East and Australasia, 139, 168
Farmers' Bulletins, 219
Feather, L. G. *Encyclopedia of Jazz,* 145; *Encyclopedia of Jazz in the Sixties,* 145
Feder, L. ed. *Crowell's Handbook of Classical Literature,* 182
Federal government, 172-73
Federal Writers' Project. *American Guide Series,* 165
Fernald, J. C. ed. *Funk & Wagnall's Standard Handbook of Synonyms, Antonyms and Prepositions,* 93
Festivals of Western Europe, 131
Fiction, 11-12
Fiction Catalog, 115, 125
Fielding, M. *Dictionary of American Painters, Sculptors and Engravers,* 150
Fifty Centuries of Art, 151
Film, 148, 224-25; catalogs and indexes, 234
Filmgoer's Companion, 148
Fines, J. *Who's Who in the Middle Ages,* 159
Fines and rental charges, 17, 21, 25
"Firsts" (*Famous First Facts*), 130
Fishel, L. H. *The Black American: A Documentary History,* 166

Fisher, M. L. comp. *International Library of Negro Life and History,* 166
Fisher, R. B. *Dictionary of Drugs,* 205
Flags, 129-30, 157
Flags of the U.S.A., 130
Flags of the World, 129
Fleischmann, W. B. ed. *Encyclopedia of World Literature in the Twentieth Century,* 182
Fletcher, B. F. *History of Architecture on the Comparative Method,* 152
Fletcher, J. ed. *The Use of Economics Literature,* 232
Flyleaf, 31
Focal Encyclopedia of Film and Television Techniques, 148
Folksingers and Folksongs in America, 145
Follett, W. *Modern American Usage,* 96; "Sabotage in Springfield," 89
Footnotes, 5, 36, 70-73
Foreign Affairs Bibliography, 175
Foreign Affairs 50-Year Bibliography, 175, 237
Foreign language dictionaries, 101-5
Foreword, 32
Fortress of Freedom, 244
Fowler, H. W. *Dictionary of Modern English Usage,* 96
Franklin classification scheme, 15-16
Franklyn, J. *Which Witch?* 99
Freedley, G. *A History of the Theatre,* 146
French Canadians, 1760-1967, 167
Freund, P. A. *Oliver Wendell Holmes Devise History of the Supreme Court,* 236
Friedman, L. *Justices of the United States Supreme Court,* 173
Frontispiece, 31
Fuld, J. J. *Book of World-Famous Music: Classical, Popular and Folk,* 145
Funk & Wagnall's Modern Guide to Synonyms and Related Words, 93
Funk & Wagnalls New Standard Dictionary, 88
Funk & Wagnalls Standard Dictionary of Folklore, Mythology, and Legend, 130, 207
Funk & Wagnall's Standard Handbook of Synonyms, Antonyms, and Prepositions, 93

Gabriel, R. H. ed. *The Pageant of America,* 165
Gassner, J. comp. *Best American Plays,* 191; *Reader's Encyclopedia of World Drama,* 188
Gateway to Judaism, 210
Gaustad, E. S. *Historical Atlas of Religion in America,* 211
Gazetteers, 155
Geddie, W. ed. *Chambers's Twentieth Century Dictionary,* 88

Gehman, H. S. ed. *New Westminster Dictionary of the Bible*, 241

Geisinger, M. *Plays, Players & Playwrights*, 146

General reference books, 128-41

Geography, 153-56; research manuals, 231

Geography: A Reference Handbook, 231

Geography of the Bible, 216

German Books in Print, 125

Gilbert, M. *Recent History Atlas*, 157

Gillispie, C. C. *Dictionary of Scientific Biography*, 196

Glazebrook, R. *Dictionary of Applied Physics*, 202

Globes, 229

Glossary, 33-34

Gohdes, C. *Bibliographical Guide to the Study of the Literature of the U.S.A.*, 238

Gohm, D. *Antique Maps of Europe*, 157

Goldenson, R. M. *Encyclopedia of Human Behavior*, 179

Gombrich, E. H. *The Story of Art*, 151

Good, C. V. ed. *Dictionary of Education*, 178

Gould, J. *Dictionary of the Social Sciences*, 171

Government, 171-74; bibliographies in, 231-32, 236

Graf, R. F. *Modern Dictionary of Electronics*, 202

Grand Larousse de la Langue Française, 102

Grand Larousse Encyclopédique, 85

Grande Encyclopédie, 86

Granger's Index to Poetry, 192

Gray, D. E. ed. *American Institute of Physics Handbook*, 202

Gray, P. *Dictionary of the Biological Sciences*, 203; *Encyclopedia of the Biological Sciences*, 203; *Student Dictionary of Biology*, 203

Grazda, E. E. *Handbook of Applied Mathematics*, 198

Great Britain. Central Office of Information. *Britain: An Official Handbook*, 139

Great Britain. Central Statistical Office. *Annual Abstract of Statistics*, 139

Great Britain: biography, 135-36; history, 167-68

Great Britain. H.M. Stationery Office, 139, 219; monthly list of British government publications, 222

Great Composers, 1300-1900, 144

Great Documents of Western Civilization, 159

Great EB: The Story of the Encyclopaedia Britannica, 242

Great Negroes, Past and Present, 166

Great Photographers, 150

Greek-English Lexicon, 102

Green, S. *World of Musical Comedy*, 146

Grogan, D. *Science and Technology: An Introduction to the Literature*, 239

Grollenberg, L. H. *Atlas of the Bible*, 216

Grosse Bertelsmann Weltatlas, 154

Grosse Brockhaus, 86

Grove's Dictionary of Music and Musicians, 142-43

Guernsey, O. L. *Directory of the American Theater, 1894-1971*, 188

Guide to Archives and Manuscripts in the United States, 235

Guide to Eastern Literatures, 238

Guide to Historical Literature, 235

Guide to Microforms in Print, 228

Guide to the Use of United Nations Documents, 222

Guinagh, K. *Dictionary of Foreign Phrases and Abbreviations*, 98

The H. W. Wilson Company, 243

Hackh, I. W. D. *Chemical Dictionary, American and British Usage*, 201

Hackman, M. L. *The Practical Bibliographer*, 231

Haggar, R. G. *Dictionary of Art Terms*, 149

Haggin, B. H. *New Listener's Companion and Record Guide*, 145

Half title, 31

Halliwell, L. *The Filmgoer's Companion*, 148

Hamer, P. M. *Guide to Archives and Manuscripts in the United States*, 235

Hammond, Inc. (Maplewood, N.J.), 153-54

Hammond, N. G. L. ed. *Oxford Classical Dictionary*, 160-61

Hampel, C. A. *Encyclopedia of Chemistry*, 201

Handbook of American Indians, 166

Handbook of Applied Mathematics, 198

Handbook of Classical Mythology, 208

Handbook of Pseudonyms and Personal Nicknames, 131

Handicapped, materials for, 226

Handlin, O. ed. *Harvard Guide to American History*, 235

Harbottle, T. B. *The Dictionary of Battles*, 159

Harper Encyclopedia of Science, 197

Harper's Bible Commentary, 215

Harper's Bible Dictionary, 215

Harper's Dictionary of Classical Literature and Antiquities, 161

Harper's Dictionary of Music, 143

Harper's Latin Dictionary, 102

Hart, A. B. ed. *American Nation series*, 164

Hart, J. D. ed. *Oxford Companion to American Literature*, 182-83

Hartman, L. F. tr. *Encyclopedic Dictionary of the Bible*, 215

Hartnoll, P. *Oxford Companion to the Theatre*, 188
Harvard Dictionary of Music, 143
Harvard Guide to American History, 235
Harvard List of Books in Psychology, 179, 237
Harvey, P. comp. & ed. *Oxford Companion to Classical Literature*, 183; *Oxford Companion to English Literature*, 183; *Oxford Companion to French Literature*, 183
Hastings, J. *Dictionary of the Bible*, 215; *Encyclopaedia of Religion and Ethics*, 208
Hathorn, R. Y. *Crowell's Handbook of Classical Drama*, 188
Hayakawa, S. I. *Funk & Wagnall's Modern Guide to Synonyms and Related Words*, 93
Haycraft, H. *Books for the Blind and Physically Handicapped*, 226
Heaton, E. W. *Everyday Life in Old Testament Times*, 215
Hedrick, B. C. *Historical Dictionary of Panama*, 168
Herner, S. *A Brief Guide to Sources of Scientific and Technical Information*, 239
Heyden, A. A. M. van der. *Atlas of the Classical World*, 157
Hill, M. H. *The Evolution of Fashion*, 147
Hirschfelder, A. B. *American Indian Authors: A Representative Bibliography*, 238
Historian's Handbook, 235
Historical Atlas of Canada, 167
Historical Atlas of Religion in America, 211
Historical Atlas of the United States, 163
Historical Chart of the Humanities, 158
Historical Dictionary of Bolivia, 168
Historical Dictionary of Chile, 168
Historical Dictionary of El Salvador, 168
Historical Dictionary of Guatemala, 168
Historical Dictionary of Panama, 168
Historical Dictionary of Venezuela, 168
Historical Statistics of the United States, 131
History, 156-69; of art, 151; bibliographies in, 235-36; of literature, 180-81; of music, 144-45; national, 162-69; research manuals for, 231; of science, 196-98; sets and series in, 161-62, 164-65; of theater, 146
History of American Presidential Elections, 171
History of Magic and Experimental Science, 198
History of Photography, 151
History of U.S. Political Parties, 171-72
Hodge, F. W. *Handbook of American Indians*, 166
Hogben, L. T. *Vocabulary of Science*, 197
Holmes, B. ed. *World Year Book of Education*, 178
Holofcener, L. *Practical Dictionary of Rhymes*, 99

Home Book of Bible Quotations, 217
Home Book of Humorous Quotations, 132
Home Book of Proverbs, Maxims, and Familiar Phrases, 133
Homonyms, 98-99
Hotton, J. C. *Slang Dictionary*, 97
Hoyt, J. K. *New Cyclopedia of Practical Quotations*, 133
Huggett, M. ed. *Concordance to the American "Book of Common Prayer,"* 217
Hughes, L. *Pictorial History of the Negro in America*, 166
Hughes, L. E. C. *Dictionary of Electronics and Nucleonics*, 202
Humanities Index, 117
Hutchinson, L. D. *Standard Handbook for Secretaries*, 176

Ickis, M. *Book of Festivals and Holidays the World Over*, 130
Illiteracy, functional, 9
Illustrated Dictionary of Ceramics, 150
Illustrated History of Music, 144
Illustrations, list of, 32
Immroth, J. P. *Guide to the Library of Congress Classification*, 15n, 245
Imprint, 46
In Black America, 166
Index of a book, 34-36
Index to American Doctoral Dissertations, 1955/56-1959/60, 234
Index to Legal Periodicals, 117
Index to Publications of the United States Congress, 172
Index to Reproductions of American Paintings, 152
Index to Reproductions of European Paintings, 152
Index to Theses Accepted for Higher Degrees in the Universities of Great Britain and Ireland, 234
Indexes, 106-18; 120-25; basic periodical, 106-8; book, 120-25; general, 114-15; of pamphlets, 222-24; specialized, 115-18
Indians of North America, 165
Industrial Arts Index, 117
Information files, 220-21
Information Please Almanac, 140
Initialisms, dictionaries of, 99-101
Inter-library loan, 18
International Bibliographies of Dictionaries (science, technology, and economics), 239
International Book of Ballet, 148
International Cyclopedia of Music and Musicians, 143
International Dictionary of Applied Mathematics, 198
International Encyclopedia of Film, 148
International Encyclopedia of the Social Sciences, 171

International Index, 117
International Index to Film Periodicals, 234
International Library of Negro Life and
History, 166
International Medical Encyclopedia, 205
International relations, 175; bibliographies
in, 236-37. See also Chapter 11
International Who's Who, 136
International Yearbook and Statesman's
Who's Who, 136
Interpreter's Bible, 240
Interpreter's Dictionary of the Bible, 240
Interpreter's One-Volume Commentary on
the Bible, 240
Introduction, 32-33
Introduction to American Archaeology, 156
Introduction to the Dance, 148
Ireland, N. O. comp. Index to Women
of the World, 136
Ireland, 168
Irregular Serials and Annuals, 118
Isaacs, A. ed. New Dictionary of Physics,
202
'Isms, 98

James, E. T. ed. Notable American Women,
1607-1950, 136
James, G. Mathematics Dictionary, 198
Jenkins, F. B. Science Reference Sources,
239
Jewish Encyclopedia, 210
Johnson, B. New Rhyming Dictionary and
Poet's Handbook, 99
Johnson, T. H. Oxford Companion to Amer-
ican History, 163
Jones, T. Harrap's Standard German and
English Dictionary, 103
Jordan, R. F. The World of Great Archi-
tecture: From the Greeks to the Nine-
teenth Century, 152
Joys of Yiddish, 98
Judaism, 209-10
Junior High School Library Catalog, 125
Justices of the United States Supreme
Court, 173

Kane, J. N. Facts About the Presidents, 163,
173; Famous First Facts, 130; Nicknames
and Sobriquets of U.S. Cities and States,
130
Kaye, G. W. Tables of Physical and Chem-
ical Constants, 202
Keller, H. R. Dictionary of Dates, 158
Kerr, D. G. G. Historical Atlas of Canada,
167
Kiepert, H. Atlas Antiquus, 158
Kirk-Othmer Encyclopedia of Chemical
Technology, 201
Kirkus Reviews, 126

Kish, G. Economic Atlas of the Soviet
Union, 168
Klein, B. Reference Encyclopedia of the
American Indian, 165
Klein, E. Comprehensive Etymological Dic-
tionary of the English Language, 95
Kleiner, R. Index of Initials and Acronyms,
101
Klibansky, R. ed. Contemporary Philosophy:
A Survey, 218
Kogan, H. The Great EB: The Story of the
Encyclopaedia Britannica, 242
Koltay, E. I. Irregular Serials and Annuals,
118
Kramer, E. E. Main Stream of Mathematics,
198; Nature and Growth of Modern
Mathematics, 199
Kuiper, G. P. Stars and Stellar Systems:
Compendium of Astronomy and Astro-
physics, 200
Kunitz, S. J. American Authors: 1600-1900,
184; British Authors Before 1800, 184;
British Authors of the Nineteenth Cen-
tury, 184; European Authors: 1000-1900,
184; Twentieth Century Authors, 184
Kurtz, A. K. Statistical Dictionary of Terms
and Symbols, 199

LC, 56, 59-63
Landis, B. Y. World Religions: A Brief
Guide, 208-9
Landman, I. ed. Universal Jewish Ency-
clopedia, 210
Lang, D. M. ed. Guide to Eastern Litera-
tures, 238
Langenscheidt's New Muret-Sanders Ency-
clopedic Dictionary of English and Ger-
man, 104
Langer, W. L. Encyclopedia of World His-
tory, 160
Laqueur, W. Z. ed. Dictionary of Politics,
171
Larned, J. N. New Larned History for
Ready Reference, Reading, and Research,
160
Larousse, Librairie, 85
Larousse du XXe Siècle, 85
Larousse Encyclopedia of Ancient and Me-
dieval History, 160
Larousse Encyclopedia of Archaeology, 156
Larousse Encyclopedia of Mythology, 208
Larousse Modern French-English, English-
French Dictionary, 102
Larson, C. A. Who, 137n, 242
Latin American Historical Dictionaries
series, 168
Latin literature, 181, 238
Law, 174; index to periodicals in, 117
Lawler, J. The H. W. Wilson Company:
Half a Century of Bibliographic Publish-
ing, 243

Lawless, R. M. *Folksingers and Folksongs in America,* 145

Laymon, C. M. ed. *Interpreter's One-Volume Commentary on the Bible,* 240

Leach, M. ed. *Funk & Wagnalls Standard Dictionary of Folklore, Mythology and Legend,* 207

Learmonth, A. T. A. *Encyclopedia of Australia,* 168

Learning resource centers, 9

Ledésert, R. P. L. ed. *Harrap's New Standard French and English Dictionary,* 103

Leidy, W. P. *Popular Guide to Government Publications,* 223

Leisy, E. *American Historical Novel,* 163

Leitner, M. J. *Dictionary of French and American Slang,* 103

Lester, D. comp. *Bibliography of United States Government Serial Publications,* 236; *Checklist of United States Public Documents* (microfilm), 236

Lewenski, R. C. comp. *Subject Collections in European Libraries,* 115

Lewis, N. *New Roget's Thesaurus of the English Language in Dictionary Form,* 94

Lexicography, 91-93, 243-44

Librarians, functions of, 28, 76

Library classification systems, 55-63

Library in College Instruction, 245

Library Journal, 126, 243, 245

Library of Congress, 15-16; classification system, 56, 59-63; Division for the Blind and Physically Handicapped, 226; *New Serial Titles,* 119

Library resources: American, 40; British, 40; European, 114-15

Library rules, 16, 19-21, 25

Libros en Venta, 125

Liddell, H. G. *Greek-English Lexicon,* 102

Literary History of Rome, 181

Literary History of the United States, 181

Literature, 180-93; bibliographies in, 238-39; drama as, 188-90; research manuals, 232

Literature of Political Science, 231

Literatures of the World in English Translation, 238

Lives of the Painters, 150

Lock, M. *Geography: A Reference Handbook,* 231

London Times History of Our Times, 160

Lord, C. L. *Historical Atlas of the United States,* 163

Lucas, E. L. *Art Books: A Basic Bibliography,* 235

Macchi, V. ed. *Dictionary of the Italian and English Languages,* 104

MacCulloch, J. A. ed. *Mythology of All Races,* 208

MacDonald, D. "The String Untuned," 89n

McGaw, H. F., 61, 62, 245

McGraw-Hill Dictionary of Art, 149

McGraw-Hill Dictionary of Economics, 176

McGraw-Hill Encyclopedia of Science and Technology, 197, 243

McGraw-Hill Encyclopedia of World Drama, 188

McSpadden, J. W. *Operas and Musical Comedies,* 145

Magazines. See Periodicals

Magill, F. N. ed. *Cyclopedia of World Authors,* 184; *Magill's Quotations in Context,* 182

Magill's Quotations in Context, 182

Main Stream of Mathematics, 198

Mallett, D. T. *Mallett's Index of Artists,* 150

Mallett's Index of Artists, 150

Man and the Environment, 239-40

Mangione, J. *The Dream and the Deal,* 165

Manley, M. C. *Business Information: How to Find and Use It,* 232

Mansion, J. E. *Harrap's New Standard French and English Dictionary,* 103; *Harrap's Shorter French and English Dictionary,* 103; *Harrap's Standard French and English Dictionary,* 103

Manvell, R. *International Encyclopedia of Film,* 148

Maps, 224. See also Atlases

March of Civilization, 158

March's Thesaurus-Dictionary, 94

Marks, J. *New French-English Dictionary of Slang and Colloquialisms,* 103

Markus, J. ed. *Electronics and Nucleonics Dictionary,* 202

Martin, J. *Introduction to the Dance,* 148

Martin, M. R. *Concise Encyclopedic Guide to Shakespeare,* 189

Martin, R. "The Word Watchers," 243

Maryknoll Catholic Dictionary, 211-12

Materials Handbook, 200

Mathematics, 198-99

Mathematics Dictionary, 198

Matlaw, M. *World Drama: An Encyclopedia,* 188

Mattfield, J. *Variety Music Cavalcade, 1620-1969,* 145

Matthews, M. M. *Dictionary of Americanisms,* 94-95

May, H. G. *Oxford Bible Atlas,* 216

Mead, F. S. *Handbook of Denominations in the United States,* 212

Mechanic, S. *Annotated List of Selected United States Government Publications Available to Depository Libraries,* 223

Media, 148, 224-25

Medical Books in Print, 239

Medicine, 204-5; bibliography, 239

Meer, F. van der. *Atlas of Western Civilization,* 158

Mellor, J. W. *Comprehensive Treatise on Inorganic and Theoretical Chemistry*, 201

Mencken, H. L. *The American Language*, 97

Mental Measurements Yearbooks, 237

Methuen's History of England, 167-68

Metropolitan Opera Annals, 146

Meyers Enzyklopaedisches Lexikon, 86

Microcards, 227

Microfiche, 227

Microfilm, 226-27

Microfilm Abstracts (dissertations), 234

Microforms, 226-28

The Middle East, 139

Milestones of History, 160

Miller, E. W. *The Negro in America: A Bibliography*, 235

Miller, M. S. *Encyclopedia of Bible Life*, 215; *Harper's Bible Dictionary*, 215

Minto, C. S. *How to Find Out in Geography*, 231

Mirkin, S. M. *What Happened When?* 158

Miss Thistlebottom's Hobgoblins, 96

Mitchell, A. *Historical Chart of the Humanities*, 158

Models, 229

Modern American Library of Literary Criticism, 185

Modern American Usage, 96

Modern Dictionary of Electronics, 202

Modern Dictionary of Sociology, 171

Modern Researcher, 230

Monro, I. S. *Index to Reproductions of American Paintings*, 152; *Index to Reproductions of European Paintings*, 152

Moore, P. *Atlas of the Universe*, 199; *New Guide to the Planets*, 199

Moore, W. G. *A Dictionary of Geography*, 155

Morris, R. B. ed. *Encyclopedia of American History*, 163

Motion pictures, 148; bibliographies of, 234

Moulton, C. W. *Library of Literary Criticism*, 181, 185

Muir, K. *New Companion to Shakespeare Studies*, 189

Multi-media. *See* Audio-visual materials

Municipal Yearbook, 172

Murphy, R. ed. *Contemporary Poets of the English Language*, 187

Murray, J. A. H. *New English Dictionary on Historical Principles*, 95, 243

Museums, 151-52

Museums of the World, 152

Music, 142-46; bibliographies in, 234-35; recordings of, in libraries, 224-25

Music Reference and Research Materials, 234

Music Since 1900, 144-45

Myers, B. S. *McGraw-Hill Dictionary of Art*, 149

Myers, R. *Dictionary of Literature in the English Language from Chaucer to 1940*, 182

Mythology, 207-8

Mythology of All Races, 208

NCR/Microcard Editions. *Guide to Microforms in Print*, 228; *Subject Guide to Microforms in Print*, 228

N.E.D., 95

National Atlas of the United States of America, 155

National Geographic Atlas of the World, 154

National Industrial Conference Board. *Economic Almanac*, 176

National Library of Medicine, 120

Nature and Growth of Modern Mathematics, 199

Negev, A. ed. *Archaeological Encyclopedia of the Holy Land*, 215

Negro Almanac, 130

The Negro in American History, 166

Negroes in the United States, 166; bibliographies, 235-36

Neil, W. *Harper's Bible Commentary*, 215; ed. *Bible Companion*, 214

Nelson's Complete Concordance of the Revised Standard Bible, 217

New American Nation series, 165

New Cambridge Bibliography of English Literature, 238-39

New Cambridge Modern History, 161-62

New Catholic Encyclopedia, 212

New Century Classical Handbook, 160

New Century Cyclopedia of Names, 128

New Century Italian Renaissance Encyclopedia, 159

New Dictionary of Physics, 202

New Encyclopedia of the Opera, 145

New English Dictionary on Historical Principles, 95

New Guide to Planets, 199

New Jersey State College at Montclair. Harry A. Sprague Library, 245

New Listener's Companion and Record Guide, 145

New Oxford History of Music, 144

New Republic, 245

New Serial Titles, 119

New Westminster Dictionary of the Bible, 241

New-York Historical Society. *Dictionary of Artists in America, 1564-1860*, 150

New York Times Biographical Edition, 136

New York Times Book Review, 126, 186

New York Times Encyclopedic Almanac, 140

New York Times Everyday Reader's Dictionary of Misunderstood, Misused, Mispronounced Words, 97

New York Times Film Reviews, 1913-1968, 148

New York Times Index, 117

New York Times Obituaries Index, 1858-1968, 136

Newhall, B. *History of Photography from 1839 to the Present Day,* 151

Newman, J. R. ed. *Harper Encyclopedia of Science,* 197; *World of Mathematics,* 199

Newspapers, 12; directory of, 118; on microfilm, 227-28

NICEM (National Information Center for Educational Media), 229

Nicholson, M. *Dictionary of American-English Usage,* 97

Nicoll, A. *English Drama, 1900-1930,* 235

Nilon, C. H. comp. *Bibliography of Bibliographies in American Literature,* 238

Nineteenth Century Readers' Guide, 107

Nonfiction, 11-12

Noory, S. *Dictionary of Pronunciation,* 99

Nordenskiöld, E. *History of Biology,* 203

Notes (term paper), 65-70; footnotes and bibliography, 70-75

Nouveau Petit Larousse, 103

Nuclear science, 201-3

O.E.D., 95

Obituaries, 135-37

O'Brien, T. C. ed. *Encyclopedic Dictionary of the Western Churches,* 211

O'Connor, D., 245

O'Dwyer, J. *Glossary of Art Terms,* 149

Official Associated Press Almanac, 140

Oliver Wendell Holmes Devise History of the Supreme Court, 236

One World of Fashion, 147

Onions, C. T. *Oxford Dictionary of English Etymology,* 95; *Shorter Oxford Dictionary,* 95

Opera, 145-46

Operas and Musical Comedies, 145

Orbis: Encyclopaedia of Extra-European Countries, 139

Order department, 25-26

Origins, 95

Orkin, M. M. *Speaking Canadian English,* 97

Osborne, H. ed. *Oxford Companion to Art,* 149

Our Times: 1900-1925, 164

Out-of-print books, 227

Overdue books, 25

Oxford Book of Ballads, 191

Oxford Book of Modern Verse, 191

Oxford Classical Dictionary, 160-61

Oxford Companion to American History, 163

Oxford Companion to American Literature, 182-83

Oxford Companion to Art, 149

Oxford Companion to Canadian History and Literature, 167

Oxford Companion to Classical Literature, 183

Oxford Companion to English Literature, 183

Oxford Companion to French Literature, 183

Oxford Companion to Music, 143

Oxford Companion to the Theatre, 188

Oxford Dictionary of English Proverbs, 133

Oxford Dictionary of Quotations, 133

Oxford Economic Atlas of the World, 176

Oxford English Dictionary, 95, 244

Oxford History of Music, 144

Oxford Latin Dictionary, 102

P.A.I.S., 118

PTLA, 121-23, 245

Pageant of America, 165

Paintings of the World's Great Galleries, 151

Palmer, R. R. *Historical Atlas of the World,* 158

Pamphlets, 11, 219-24

Parks, G. B. ed. *The Literatures of the World in English Translation: A Bibliography,* 238

Parliamentary procedure, 131

Parodies, 191

Parrinder, G. *Dictionary of Non-Christian Religions,* 209

Partridge, E. *Origins: A Short Etymological Dictionary of Modern English,* 95; *Slang Today and Yesterday,* 98; *Usage and Abusage,* 97

Patai, R. ed. *Encyclopedia of Zionism and Israel,* 168, 210

Payne, B. *History of Costume,* 147

Peck, H. T. ed. *Harper's Dictionary of Classical Literature and Antiquities,* 161

Penguin Companion to African Literature, 185

Penguin Companion to American Literature, 184

Penguin Companion to Classical, Oriental and African Literature, 185

Penguin Companion to English Literature, 185

Penguin Companions to World Literature, 184-85

Penguin Dictionary of Quotations, 132

Performing arts, 142-48

Periodicals, 12-14, 16; directories of, 118-19; indexes to, 106-119

Personal names, filing, 52

Personality Tests and Reviews, 237

Pfeiffer, C. F. ed. *The Biblical World: A Dictionary of Biblical Archaeology,* 216

Phaidon Dictionary of Twentieth Century Art, 149

Philosophy, 217-18

Physics, 201-3; bibliographies in, 239

Pictorial History of Medicine, 205

Pictorial History of the Negro in America, 166

Picture collections, 224

Pincherle, M. *Illustrated History of Music,* 144

Play Index, 1949-1972, 192

Plays, Players and Playwrights, 146

Ploski, H. A. ed. *Negro Almanac,* 130

Poetry, 36, 187, 191-92; recordings of, 225. See also Rhyming dictionaries

Political Africa: A Who's Who of Personalities and Parties, 169

Political Handbook and Atlas of the World, 139

Politics, 171-74; bibliographies in, 231-32, 236

Polyglot dictionaries, 105

Poole, W. F., 106, 241; *Cumulative Author Index, 1802-1906,* 107; *Poole's Index to Periodical Literature,* 106-7, 243

Poore, B. P., 241; comp. *Descriptive Catalogue of the Government Publications of the United States (1774-1881),* 243-44

Popular American Composers, 144

Popular Guide to Government Publications, 223

Post, E. *Etiquette,* 130

Poulton, H. J. *Historian's Handbook,* 235

The Practical Bibliographer, 231

Praeger Encyclopedia of Art, 149

Preface, 32

Preliminary pages, 30-33

Preminger, A. ed. *Encyclopedia of Poetry and Poetics,* 187

Preparation department, 26-27

Printed catalogs, book form, 37, 38

Progress in Biophysics and Molecular Biology, 203

Pronunciation, dictionaries of, 98-99

Proverbs, dictionaries of, 132-34

Pseudonyms as catalog entries, 53-54

Psychological Abstracts, 237

Psychology, 179; bibliographies in, 237

Public Affairs Information Service Bulletin, 118, 223

Public Library Catalog, 125

Publications of the United Nations Systems, 232

Publishers' Trade List Annual, 121-23, 245

Publishers Weekly, 124

Pugh, E. *Dictionary of Acronyms and Abbreviations,* 101

Quotations, 132-34

Radice, B. *Who's Who in the Ancient World,* 161

Ragazzini, G. comp. *Follett/Zanichelli Italian Dictionary,* 104

Ramondino, S. ed. *New World Spanish-English and English-Spanish Dictionary,* 104

Random House Dictionary (unabridged), 88

Random House Dictionary, College Edition, 90

Reader services, 23-24

Reader's Adviser, 242

Reader's Encyclopedia, 183

Reader's Encyclopedia of Shakespeare, 189

Reader's Encyclopedia of World Drama, 188

Readers' Guide to Periodical Literature, 107-8, 110-12; *Abridged . . . ,* 115-16

Readers' Guide Supplement, 117

Reading machines, microform, 226

Recording for the Blind, Inc., 226

Recordings, 225-26

Recto, 30

Reference books, 10, 11, 14, 128; books and articles about, 241-45; general, 128-41

Reference department, 10, 23

Reference Encyclopedia of the American Indian, 165

Reference Guide to English, American and Canadian Literature, 232

Reference Guide to English Studies, 232

Reference Quarterly (RQ), 246

Reinach, S. *Apollo: An Illustrated Manual of the History of Art,* 151

Religion, 208-17; bible texts and commentaries, 240-41

Repertoire des Livres Disponibles, 125

Requirements for Certification of Teachers, 178

Research handbooks, 230-33

Research Manual for College Studies, 231

Research papers, 64-75

Reserve books, 23

Reverse Acronyms and Initialisms Dictionary, 100

Reynolds, B. ed. *Cambridge Italian Dictionary,* 105

Rhyming dictionaries, 99

Rigdon, W. ed. *Biographical Encyclopaedia and Who's Who of the American Theatre,* 147

Rivlin, H. N. ed. *Encyclopedia of Modern Education,* 178

Robert, H. M. *Robert's Rules of Order,* 131

Roberts, A. D. *Introduction to Reference Books,* 244

Robertson, S. *Development of Modern English,* 92n

Robinson, H. S. *Encyclopaedia of Myths and Legends of All Nations,* 208

Roget's International Thesaurus, 3d ed, 94
Roget's Thesaurus of the English Language, 94
Rosten, L. *The Joys of Yiddish*, 98
Roth, C. ed. *Standard Jewish Encyclopedia*, 210
Rybicki, S. *Abbreviations: A Reverse Guide*, 101

Sabin, R. ed. *International Cyclopedia of Music and Musicians*, 143
Saints, 212-13
Salamanca, L. N. *Fortress of Freedom: The Story of the Library of Congress*, 244
Sanner, M., 245
"Sansoni," 104
Satterthwaite, G. E. *Encyclopedia of Astronomy*, 199
Savage, G. *Illustrated Dictionary of Ceramics*, 150
Schaff, P. *New Schaff-Herzog Encyclopedia of Religious Knowledge*, 209
Schlesinger, A. M. ed. *History of American Presidential Elections*, 171; *History of U.S. Political Parties*, 171-72
Schmeckebier, L. F. *Government Printing Office: Its History, Activities and Organization*, 223
Schoenbaum, S. *Shakespeare's Lives*, 189
Scholar Critic: An Introduction to Literary Research, 232
Scholes, P. A. *Oxford Companion to Music*, 143
School libraries, 9
Schoolcraft, R. N. ed. *Performing Arts Books in Print to 1971*, 235
Schopflin, G. ed. *The Soviet Union and Eastern Europe: A Handbook*, 169
Schwartz, B. ed. *Statutory History of the United States*, 174
Science, 194-296; bibliographies, 239-40; research manuals, 233
Science and Technology, 239
Sciences, Social. *See* Social sciences
Scientific and Technical Books in Print, 239
Sculpture, 148-51
Sears, M. E. *Song Index*, 146
"See" and "see also" references, 52-54
Segal, R. ed. *Political Africa: A Who's Who of Personalities and Parties*, 169
Seligman, E. B. A. ed. *Encyclopedia of the Social Sciences*, 170
Seltzer, L. E. *Columbia Lippincott Gazetteer*, 155
Senior High School Library Catalog, 125
Serials, 14, 118-19
Series title, 31
Seyffert, O. *Dictionary of Classical Antiquities*, 161
Shakespeare, 189-90
Shankle, G. E. *American Nicknames*, 131

Sharp, H. S. *Handbook of Pseudonyms and Personal Nicknames*, 131
Shaw, H. L. *Dictionary of Literary Terms*, 183
Sheehy, E. P. *Guide to Reference Books* (supplements), 246
Shenker, I. "Oxford Dictionary to Get an Updating," 244
Shepherd, W. R. *Historical Atlas*, 158
Shores, L. *Audiovisual Librarianship*, 229; *Instructional Materials: An Introduction for Teachers*, 229
Short Story Index, 193
Shorter Cambridge Medieval History, 161
Shorter Oxford Dictionary, 91, 95
Shulman, A. M. *Gateway to Judaism*, 210
Sills, D. L. ed. *International Encyclopedia of the Social Sciences*, 171
Slang: dictionaries of, 97-98; foreign, 101-5
Slides, 224-26
Sloan, H. S. *Dictionary of Economics*, 177
Slonimsky, N. *Music Since 1900*, 144
Smeaton, B. H., 246
Smith, C. ed. *Collins Spanish/English, English/Spanish Dictionary*, 104
Smith, W. G. ed. *Oxford Dictionary of English Proverbs*, 133
Smith, W. J. ed. *Granger's Index to Poetry*, 192
Sobel, R. ed. *Biographical Directory of the U.S. Executive Branch*, 173
Social sciences, 170-79; bibliographies in, 231-32, 236-37
Social Sciences Index, 118
Sohn, L. B. ed. *Basic Documents of African Regional Organizations*, 169
Song Index, 146
Sonnenschein, W. S. *Best Books*, 244
Sorell, W. *Dance Through the Ages*, 148
Sources, list of, 33, 74-75, 113-14
Sources of Business Information, 176
South American Handbook, 140
Soviet Encyclopedia, 86
Soviet Union and Eastern Europe: A Handbook, 169
Space Encyclopedia: Guide to Astronomy and Space Exploration, 199
Space technology, 199-200
Specimens, 229
Spencer-Jones, H. *New Space Encyclopedia*, 199
Spender, S. ed. *Concise Encyclopedia of English and American Poets and Poetry*, 187
Spevack, M. *Harvard Concordance to Shakespeare*, 190
Spicer, D. G. *Festivals of Western Europe*, 131; *Yearbook of English Festivals*, 131
Spiller, R. E. ed. *Literary History of the United States*, 181

Stagecraft, 146-47
Stamp, L. D. *Dictionary of Geography*, 155
Standard Catalog series, 125-26
Standard Handbook for Secretaries, 176
Stars and Stellar Systems, 200
State manuals, 172
"State Manuals: A Potpourri of Information," 242
Statesman's Yearbook, 140
Statistical Abstract of the United States, 140
Statistical Terms and Symbols, 199
Statistics. *See* Yearbooks
Statutory History of the United States, 174
Stedman's Medical Dictionary, 205
Stein and Day International Medical Encyclopedia, 205
Steinberg, S. H. ed. *Dictionary of British History*, 168; *Historical Tables, 58 B.C.–A.D. 1965*, 159
Stephen, L. ed. *Dictionary of National Biography*, 135-36
Stevenson, B. E. ed. *Home Book of Bible Quotations*, 217; *Home Book of Proverbs*, 133; *Home Book of Quotations*, 133; *Standard Book of Shakespeare Quotations*, 190
Stevenson, W. B. *Young's Analytical Concordance to the Bible*, 217
Stewart, G. R. *American Place-Names*, 164
Stieler's Atlas of Modern Geography, 154
Stillman, F. *Poet's Manual and Rhyming Dictionary*, 99
Story of Art, 151
Strong, J. *Exhaustive Concordance of the Bible*, 217
Student assistants, 25
Stuffed Owl: An Anthology of Bad Verse, 191
Style manuals, 66, 72, 230-31
Subject catalog, 38
Subject Collections in European Libraries, 115
Subject departments, 24
Subject entries, 47
Subject Guide to Books in Print, 123
Subject Guide to Forthcoming Books, 124
Subject Guide to Microforms in Print, 228
Subject Index to Poetry, 114
Sullivan, M. *Our Times: 1900-1925*, 164
Symbol Sourcebook, 105
Synonyms: dictionaries of, 93-94, 244

Tables of contents, 32
Tables of Physical and Chemical Constants, 202
Talking books, 225-26
Taylor, F. H. *Fifty Centuries of Art*, 151
Taylor, T. *The Book of Presidents*, 164
Tebbel, J. "A Century of the World Almanac," 244

Technical Book Review Index, 233
Technology, 194-206; bibliographies in, 239; research guides in, 233
Television, 148
Temple, R. Z. ed. *Library of Literary Criticism: Modern British Literature*, 186
Terry, W. *The Dance in America*, 148
Textbooks in Print, 126
Theatre Guild plays, 190
Theodorson, G. A. *Modern Dictionary of Sociology*, 171
Thesaurus, 93-94
Theses: bibliographies of, 233-34; doctoral, microfilm editions, 227
Thewlis, J. *Concise Dictionary of Physics and Related Subjects*, 202; *Encyclopaedic Dictionary of Physics*, 202-3
Thompson, L. S. comp. *The Southern Black, Slave and Free: A Bibliography*, 236
Thompson, N. *Complete Concordance to the Bible (Douay Version)*, 217
Thomson, W. A. R. *Black's Medical Dictionary*, 205
Thorndike, L. *History of Magic and Experimental Science*, 198
Thorne, J. O. ed. *Chambers's Biographical Dictionary*, 134
Times (London). *Times Atlas of the World*, 154-55
Title entries, 48-49, 54
Title page, 31
Todd, D. K. *The Water Encyclopedia*, 206
Trade lists, 123
Trefethen, F. *Writing a Poem*, 187
Treharne, R. F. *Muir's Historical Atlas, Ancient, Medieval, and Modern*, 158
Trent, W. P. ed. *Cambridge History of American Literature*, 180
Tripp, E. *Crowell's Handbook of Classical Mythology*, 208
Tripp, R. T. comp. *International Thesaurus of Quotations*, 133-34
Tucker, M. ed. *The Critical Temper: A Survey*, 186
Tuma, J. J. *Engineering Mathematics Handbook*, 233
Twayne's authors series, 186
Twentieth Century Authors, 184

Ulrich's International Periodicals Directory, 13, 14, 118
Ultrafiche, 227
Undergraduate library, 24
Union List of Serials in the United States and Canada, 14, 119
United Nations: publications, 222; *Statistical Yearbook*, 140; *Yearbook of the United Nations*, 140
U.S. Bureau of American Ethnology. *Handbook of American Indians*, 166

U.S. Bureau of the Census. *Historical Statistics of the United States*, 131; *Statistical Abstract of the United States*, 140

U.S. Congress. *Biographical Directory, 1774-1961*, 137; *Congressional Record*, 173; *Official Congressional Directory*, 137

U.S. Department of Agriculture. *Farmers' Bulletins*, 204, 219; yearbooks, 204

U.S. Geological Survey. *National Atlas of the United States of America*, 155

United States Catalog, 1899-1928, 121-23

United States Code, 174

United States Code, Annotated, 174

United States government, 172-74; bibliographies in, 236; publications of, 222, 243-44; research manuals for, 231

United States Government Organizational Manual, 173

U.S. Government Printing Office, 221-22

United States Government Publications: Monthly Catalog, 222

U.S. Government Serials and Periodicals, 223

United States history, 162-66; bibliographies in, 235-36; research manuals for, 231

United States in World Affairs, 139

U.S. Library of Congress, 15, 244; Division for the Blind and Physically Handicapped, 226

U.S. National Library of Medicine, 204

U.S. Office of Education: bulletins and leaflets, 218; Educational Resources Information Center (ERIC), 177

Universal Encyclopedia of Mathematics, 199

Universal Jewish Encyclopedia, 210

University of Michigan. *History of the Modern World*, 162

University of Minnesota Press. Pamphlets on American writers, 186-87

Urdang, L. *The New York Times Everyday Reader's Dictionary of Misunderstood, Misused, Mispronounced Words*, 97; ed. *Random House Dictionary, College Edition*, 90

Urmson, J. O. ed. *Concise Encyclopedia of Western Philosophy and Philosophers*, 218

Usage: dictionaries of, 95-96; foreign words in English, 98

Usage and Abusage, 97

Use of Biological Literature, 233

Use of Chemical Literature, 233

Use of Economics Literature, 232

Vanderbilt, A. *Etiquette*, 131

Van der Meer, F. *Atlas of the Early Christian World*, 216

Van Nostrand's Scientific Encyclopedia, 198

Variety Music Cavalcade, 145

Verso, 30

Vertical File Index, 223-24

Vertical File Service Catalog, 223-24

Vertical files, 220-22

Viorst, M. *Great Documents of Western Civilization*, 159

Vizetelli, F. H. *Desk-Book of Idioms and Idiomatic Phrases*, 97

Vocabulary of Science, 197

Vox Modern College Spanish and English Dictionary, 105

Wade, M. *The French Canadians, 1760-1967*, 167

Wahrig, G. *Das Grosse Deutsche Wörterbuch*, 103

Wakeman, J. ed. *World Authors*, 185

Walsh, W. S. *Curiosities of Popular Customs*, 131; *Handybook of Curious Information*, 131

Walton, M. *'Isms*, 98

Ward, A. W. *Cambridge History of English Literature*, 180-81

Ward, J. O. ed. *Oxford Companion to Music*, 143

Wasserman, P. *Encyclopedia of Business Information Sources*, 232

Water Encyclopedia, 206

Watson, G. ed. *New Cambridge Bibliography of English Literature*, 238-39

Webster's Biographical Dictionary, 137

Webster's Guide to American History, 164

Webster's New Collegiate Dictionary, 91

Webster's New Dictionary of Synonyms, 94

Webster's New Geographical Dictionary, 156

Webster's New International Dictionary, 2d ed., 89, 92

Webster's New World Dictionary of the American Language, 91; college ed., 91

Webster's Third New International Dictionary, 89

Weekly Record, 124

Weiss, I. ed. *American Authors and Books: 1640 to the Present Day*, 180

Wells, C. *Parody Anthology*, 191

Wentworth, H. *Dictionary of American Slang*, 98

Wer Ist Wer? das Deutsche Who's Who, 137

Westminster Historical Atlas to the Bible, 216

What Happened When? 158

Which Witch? 99

Whitaker, J. *Whitaker's Almanack*, 124

White, C. M. *Sources of Information in the Social Sciences*, 231, 236

Whitfield, J. S. *Improved Rhyming Dictionary*, 99

Whiting, B. J. comp. *Proverbs, Sentences, and Proverbial Phrases: From English Writings Mainly Before 1500*, 134
Who Was When? 158
Who Was Who, 137
Who Was Who in America, 138
Who's Who, 137
Who's Who in America, 137, 242
Who's Who in American Arts, 150
Who's Who in Government, 174
Who's Who in the Ancient World, 161
Who's Who in the Middle Ages, 159
Who's Who in the New Testament, 215
Who's Who in the Old Testament, 215
Who's Who in the Theatre, 147
Who's Who of American Women, 137
Wiener, J. H. ed. *Great Britain: Foreign Policy and the Span of Empire, 1689-1971*, 168
Wilcox, R. T. *The Dictionary of Costume*, 147
Willey, G. R. *Introduction to American Archaeology*, 156
Williams, C. B. *Research Manual for College Studies and Papers*, 231
Williams, R. J. *Encyclopedia of Biochemistry*, 203
Wilson, H. W. 120-21
Wilson, J. G. *Appleton's Cyclopaedia of American Biography*, 134
Wilson, L. R. *The Library in College Instruction*, 245
Wilson Library Bulletin, 246
Winchell, C. M. *Guide to Reference Books*, 246
Winton, H. N. M. comp. & ed. *Man and the Environment: A Bibliography*, 239-40; ed. *Publications of the United Nations Systems*, 232
Woellner, R. C. *Requirements for Certification of Teachers*, 178
Women, biographical dictionaries, 136-37
Wood, C. *Unabridged Rhyming Dictionary*, 99

Woods, R. *Catholic Companion to the Bible*, 215
"Word Watchers," 243
Words, Facts and Phrases, 130
Words of Science, 196-97
World affairs, 138-41, 175
World Almanac and Book of Facts, 140, 244
World Authors, 184
World Bibliography of Bibliographies, 120
World Book Encyclopedia, 84
World Costumes, 147
World Guide to Universities, 178
World history, 157-58
World of Learning, 178
World of Mathematics, 199
World of Musical Comedy, 146
World of Twentieth Century Music, 144
World religions, 208-9
World Religions: A Brief Guide, 208-9
World Who's Who in Science, 196
World Year Book of Education, 178
Worldmark Encyclopedia of the Nations, 175
World's Great Religions, 209
Wright, G. E. *Westminster Historical Atlas to the Bible*, 216
Writers and Their Work, 187
Writer's Handbook, 183
Writing a Poem, 187
Wyndham Lewis, D. B. comp. *The Stuffed Owl: An Anthology of Bad Verse*, 191

Yale Chronicles of America series, 166
Yearbook and Guide to East Africa, 141
Yearbook and Guide to Southern Africa, 141
Yearbook of American and Canadian Churches, 212
Yearbook of English Festivals, 131
Yearbooks, 138-41
Young's Analytical Concordance to the Bible, 217